Human Resource
Problem Solving

Human Resource Problem Solving

ROBERT BRUCE BOWIN

Professor of Management
California State College, Bakersfield

PRENTICE-HALL, INC., ENGLEWOOD CLIFFS, NEW JERSEY 07632

Library of Congress Cataloging-in-Publication Data

BOWIN, ROBERT BRUCE. (date)
  Human resource problem solving.

  Includes bibliographies.
  1. Personnel management. I. Title.
HF5549.B774 1987   658.3   86-9335
ISBN 0-13-446345-5

Editorial/production supervision and
  interior design: *Nancy Savio-Marcello*
Cover design: *Diane Saxe*
Manufacturing buyer: *Harry Baisley*

Printed in the United States of America

10 9 8 7 6 5 4 3 2 1

ISBN 0-13-446345-5 01

PRENTICE-HALL INTERNATIONAL (UK) LIMITED, *London*
PRENTICE-HALL OF AUSTRALIA PTY. LIMITED, *Sydney*
PRENTICE-HALL CANADA INC., *Toronto*
PRENTICE-HALL HISPANOAMERICANA, S.A., *Mexico*
PRENTICE-HALL OF INDIA PRIVATE LIMITED, *New Delhi*
PRENTICE-HALL OF JAPAN, INC., *Tokyo*
PRENTICE-HALL OF SOUTHEAST ASIA PTE. LTD., *Singapore*
EDITORA PRENTICE-HALL DO BRASIL, LTDA., *Rio de Janeiro*

Dedicated to my parents,
Mildred and Robert Bowin, Sr.

CONTENTS

PREFACE

As you progress through this book, you will encounter empirical research studies that may be extremely complex in methodology and statistical techniques. Such studies are presented to acquaint you with the breadth of the research and its thoroughness, as well as possible applications to the real-life work of human resource management. In an attempt to make these empirical studies more readable, I have rewritten them in an abridged, paraphrased style to simplify some of the technical terminology and structure. I have attempted to reduce the scholarly language in which the studies were originally written to a style more readily understood by the average human resource professional and college student. This is not a criticism of the original authors, who are writing for their own scholarly peer group, nor of the average human resource professional or college student, who cannot be expected to have developed comprehension of very stylized reporting and sophisticated research techniques. The non-empirical studies are more easily read, but I have also paraphrased them for purposes of emphasis.

It should be noted that in attempting to reduce complexity to simplicity, some of the subtle inferences may be lost. If this has occurred, or if there are misinterpretations, the error is mine. As in any scientific process, verification of the original study is the final assurance. Fortunately, such a task is made easier, since most of the research journals cited will be found in college or local libraries. Please address any problems of interpretation, and so on, to me at the School of Business and Public Administration, California State College, Bakersfield, 9001 Stockdale Highway, Bakersfield, CA 93311.

Although some readers may be encouraged to pursue their own endeavors in empirical research, many are more interested in understanding these findings and the possible applications in the real world of human resource management. If you are among the latter, do not despair. There is a simple yet effective method to obtain this goal. Most of the more involved empirical research studies that follow are presented in a similar format. Usually, a brief description is given of what the study was attempting to investigate, followed by a description of the sample and the test instruments used to obtain data. Then follows a description of the methodological and statistical techniques, presented more for the benefit of those with empirical research interests than of the general student interested in human resource management. For the latter, a general scrutiny of the methodological and statistical techniques via a fast reading may be more appropriate. After the methodological and statistical techniques, the study results or findings are presented. Again, in some of the empirical studies, these findings can be rather complex and numerous, often following one after another. For the more generally oriented student, a fast reading of this section may again be more appropriate, since the final summary review section summarizes the most important research findings, and a careful reading there will provide an effective knowledge base.

I hope that these suggested approaches to the material in this book will make it an enjoyable learning experience for those concerned with human resource management and for those who are interested in the contributions of empirical research techniques.

CHAPTER ONE

THE RESEARCH-INCIDENT METHOD

BACKGROUND

Within a relatively short period, the world of work for today's human resource manager has undergone fundamental changes, both in job complexity and in professional status. This has been largely the result of recent federal legislation, the full effect of which is still evolving, and the threat of foreign competition in local and international markets.

The continuing scenario of complexity and rapid changes shows no sign of abating in the near term. Human resource practitioners face the problem of maintaining credibility and professional achievement in an environment increasingly dominated by computer printouts and computational procedures. The past reliance upon only intuition and people skills is no longer effective. For the sake of personal employment viability, they must be replaced by a skill in conducting research and utilizing research findings. Further, this skill will place the profession of human resource management upon a more scientific foundation. This is the perceived intent of the material that follows.

The case approach to solving business problems has gained wide acceptance in our system of higher education. However, one problem in this approach is its dependence upon recall of past learning. Even though computers have total recall (and this is debatable at times), people too often do not. Unfortunately, when we are unable to recall established procedures or techniques that apply to particular situations, the temptation is to rationalize or improvise. The result is confusion or error that may lead to ineffective reasoning and performance deficiency. That is, a person forgets the natural explanation for the situation and resorts to unreal causes—a situation that becomes particularly misleading when it results in conjecture. Any process that is nurtured from rumors, unsupported statements, so-called personal experiences, or "expert" sources whose own research may be lacking does not meet the test of analytical thought. Often we use as a fact a quotation from someone who, in essence, is merely quoting someone else. The point of accountability thus becomes blurred, and any substantiation for the original statement becomes lost.

If we are willing to accept the substance of the comments above, a large portion of "knowledge" from sundry sources is thereby eliminated, or at least put in doubt. Where do the human resource professional and college student then turn in the search for validity? Fortunately, the answer is simple: the empirical research journals that are available at public and college libraries.

Most of us will agree that management is part an art and part a science. At any one point on a time continuum, management may be more art than science and, at another point, more science than art. A portion of this scientific management base will be found in the empirical research journals.

We should be aware that there are differences between journals. In this book, we will tend to emphasize journal articles that are empirically based and have been subjected to statistical analysis. This bias will downplay articles that deal only with people's experiences or casual thinking. Why do we do this? Simply because these casual-thinking articles do not allow us to duplicate (replicate) the particular situation presented. In many cases, we do not know the types of subjects involved, their personalities and environments, or the data-collection techniques. Further, we do not know whether their results are *statistically significant.* (Note: Most of the italicized terms will appear in the Glossary.)

Why is it so important that the results of a journal article be statistically significant? To start with, a journal article may present one or several hypotheses. These hypotheses are what the author wishes to test to determine what is to be accepted and what is to be rejected. Will a certain variable cause a certain reaction? For instance, does cigarette smoking cause a certain type of cancer? To establish statistical significance, we decide upon a *level of significance* and then conduct an appropriate statistical test. The significance level tells us the probability of our rejecting the hypothesis when, in fact, it is true. A level of significance at the .05 level means that there are five chances in 100 of our being wrong in rejecting a true hypothesis; a .01 level of significance means there is only one chance in 100 of wrongful rejection; and .001 means there is only one chance in 1,000. If our statistical test tells us to accept the hypothesis, depending upon the previously chosen level of significance, we are correct 95 percent of the time, or 99 percent, or 99.9 percent.

But some words of caution. There may be a problem of causality, in that the result of the study may not be caused by the variables used. For instance, is the quality of handwriting "caused" by the size of one's hands? one's age? Also, the statistical tests predict group behavior, not individual behavior. However, even with this limitation on attempting to apply the journal-article findings, it would appear that this approach is still a more scholarly and disciplined endeavor than reliance upon what one person assumes is intuitively plausible observations. Such intuitively plausible experiences may be no more than individualized behavior caused by gastric distress or an overactive headache. Of course, what, in the final analysis, is ever really proven? In theory, nothing. If we were to prove as a "fact" that the sun rises in the east and sets in the west, it would be necessary to observe every sunrise and sunset ad infinitum.

If empirical journal articles are to be approached with such a limitation, why include them as an input for our "knowledge base"? We all remember the old proverb, "A little knowledge is a dangerous thing." But on the other hand, a little knowledge is better than no knowledge at all. The real danger lies in our not knowing how little our knowledge is. The ancient Romans had a word for this type of learning experience—*gravitas*. It means patience, stamina, and weight of judgment.

FORMAT OF THIS BOOK

Regardless of the preceding statements in favor of relying on the empirical research journals, this text will not ignore the non-empirical journals. The rationale for this position is direct and simple. Despite the lack of research rigor in the non-empirical journals, they do represent the thinking of a significant group of human resource professionals, and therefore they indicate current problems and trends of thought in the field. Although many such articles only report on how problems are resolved at a particular organization, and thus their results cannot be generalized, they do provide empirical researchers with ideas for testing. So in keeping with a systems concept of providing a unified whole or completeness to our quest, these non-empirical journals are considered a part of our research schema.

The format of this book is set up to maximize your learning experience. The chapters represent functional work areas in which the human resource manager is expected to demonstrate a professional approach to people problems. They contain real-life incidents that have demanded attention from the human resource office. Each incident narrative is followed by a section containing observations obtained from empirical research journals, and each chapter ends with abstracts of two non-empirical research articles.

The observations in the research studies are not intended to be the last word on a subject. They are provided to stimulate thought and act as a new source of input into your knowledge base. After you read the section, it is hoped that you will have gained new insight into the problem areas, developed an awareness of the subtle complexities surrounding the behavior, and found a possible approach that will contribute to resolving the situation.

Each incident section concludes with a list of references for the observations presented. This provides you the opportunity to review each author's research. (The superscript number after the author's name refers to the "References" number.) Since most articles have several hypotheses, a review of the references will provide additional knowledge input. Perhaps your own intellectual curiosity will cause you to search out other journal articles and thus gain a broader insight into the causes of human behavior. In essence, what you will be discovering in the empirical research and non-empirical journals is information that will be published in standard course textbooks only after many years.

RESEARCH DESIGN:
AN OVERVIEW

This section offers the human resource professional and college student a brief review of research design and research methods. The following information provides sufficient background for completion and interpretation of most empirical research. Those desiring a higher level of competence should consult the statistical texts available through the college or local library.

In attempting to do empirical research, we must utilize a framework that will provide accurate, valid, and objective results. This we do through a research design that answers the questions the research sets out to explore and also controls variance or differences. The research design is like a set of instructions given to the researcher to gather and analyze the data in certain ways. In effect, the research design functions as a blueprint.

One type of variance or difference that is important for the researcher to control is the maximizing of experimental variance. That is, the research design should allow for the experimental conditions—such as fear and money—called *independent variables* to be as different as possible. Generally, variables are observations of fact, such as freight-car loadings, that can be classified into value categories. Knowing the value of the independent variable assists us in determining the value or direction of the *dependent variable*. This permits distinguishing the variation resulting from the effect of, say, the independent variables of fear and money upon a person's risk-taking behavior (a dependent variable) from other factors that may be affecting that behavior. The value of money (an independent variable) permits predicting the value associated with taking a chance (a dependent variable). This allows the individual variances or differences of fear and money to be separated from the total variance of other factors affecting the behavior of taking a chance. However, a danger here is deducing that when one variable is considered independent and the other dependent, a cause-and-effect phenomenon may take place. There may be other factors causing the reaction, or the roles of the two variables may be reversed.

Another type of variance or difference that needs to be controlled is the *extraneous variable* that is not considered important to the study and needs to be eliminated or minimized. Thus, in the example above, regarding the behavior of taking a chance, it may be decided to control the extraneous variable of a certain age group in determining the effect of fear and money upon behavior. This can be accomplished simply by eliminating the particular age group from the data, thereby making the study age grouping as homogeneous as desired. Another approach would be to select the participants in the experiment randomly, to ensure that each member of the population age group (of which our experiment sample is part) has an equal chance of being selected. Still another approach would be to include the variable in the research design. This would be done by matching people by age groups, such as five- or ten-year categories.

The final variance that needs to be controlled is called *error variance*. In most research, some fluctuations in the data occur that are unpredictable, perhaps not identified, sometimes caused by guessing or fatigue, or possibly by unreliable measurements. The control of error variance requires that the conditions of the research—such as unplanned noise, interruptions, or distraction—are controlled by the researchers. Error variance can be further decreased through appropriate tests, accurate test scoring, and correct statistical analysis. But despite our efforts to control error variance, it will always exist in some measurable degree.

For effective research design, it is critical to know the *validity* of the test instrument being used to measure the variables. An effective approach is to consult the *Mental Measurement Yearbook,* formerly edited by the deceased Oscar Krisen Buros but now edited by James B. Mitchell, Jr., available at college and public libraries. The yearbook is published yearly and, since the death of Buros, is now being published by the University of Nebraska at Lincoln. It contains descriptions of most test instruments, a critique of their appropriate strengths and weaknesses, and where the instruments may be obtained. One source for test instruments is private organizations such as the Institute for Personality and Ability Testing, Inc., 1801 Woodfield Drive, Savoy, Illinois 61874, which supplies professionals in the human resource field. As to determining statistical test selection and techniques, anyone with access to computer facilities will find extremely helpful the *Statistical Package for the Social Sciences,* by Nie et al., McGraw-Hill, 1975.

In research design, the question of validity, of actually measuring the concept in question, is always present and of vital concern. To evaluate the appropriateness of an experimental design, one considers the *construct validity.* It is important that the variables being researched (fear, money) are actually associated with the behavior (taking a chance) under investigation. For example, if the observed behavior is tying a string, would the variables of fear and money be pertinent? Probably not.

Another research-design validity problem to be considered is *statistical validity.* Perhaps the data are wrong. For example, in a study of married couples (assuming that the federal polygamy laws are observed), if the number of females exceeds the number of males, one might question the accuracy of the data.

There is also the problem of research-design *internal validity.* Do the changes in the dependent variable (behavior of taking a chance) actually occur because of changes in the independent variables (fear, money)? For example, if there were a bias (white, college graduates, males) in selecting the participants for researching voter behavior, the results would be extremely questionable.

A final research-design validity consideration is that of *external validity.* Do the findings of the research relate to the general outside world, or merely to a tightly controlled experimental situation? Is it an artificial event? This problem is usually traceable to a situation in which the sample group is not representative of the real-world population. In such a case, applying the research results to real-world events produces unanticipated psychological behavior. An example would be the *Hawthorne effect,* in which the psychological effects of motivation are emphasized over the physical environment.

A problem occurs in research design when two or more variables work together in influencing a result. This is known as *interaction.* In controlling for interactions, it is necessary that the experimental and control groups all have equal proportions representative of those variables affecting the experiment. However, the attainment of such representation usually occurs only under the most ideal of conditions. In real life, it would be difficult for a research design to control for a large number of variables and their interactions. One problem in attempting to resolve this issue is that although the benefits of randomization increase with the sample size, the reverse occurs as smaller and smaller categories are designated in an effort to minimize interaction. The true experimental design is randomized to, it is hoped, control other variables threatening the experiment's internal validity (any change in the experiment is due to the treatment and other variables). For a more comprehensive treatment of research design, see the reference librarian of your college or local library.

RESEARCH METHODS

Several techniques or methods are utilized by authors of empirical journal articles. The selection of a particular method is usually determined by the situation in which the study is to be conducted. For instance, a television anchorperson would probably prefer to interview a newsworthy personality within the more controllable environment of the television studio but, if that were not possible, would accept a brief curbside exchange. The same is true in the world of empirical research.

The ultimate experimentation method is the *true experiment*. However, it is not the most commonly used method, because it requires the random assignment of research subjects. It is usually restricted to laboratory experiments in which the variables can be tightly controlled, as opposed to field experiments taking place in the real world.

Perhaps the "best" method is the quasi-experimental design of the experimentation method in which the independent variable (for example, fear) is studied as to its effect on the dependent variable (for example, the behavior of taking a chance). When this design format is conducted in a real-life setting such as a factory, it is called a field experiment. The design for such a study usually follows this format:

	FIRST STEP	SECOND STEP	THIRD STEP
Control group (no fear treatment)	Pretest	No fear treatment	Posttest
Experimental group (receives fear treatment)	Pretest	Receives fear treatment	Posttest

For both the control and experimental groups, a pretest is administered to measure the level of the dependent variable (the behavior of taking a chance) that is present before the experiment begins. This information is generally obtained through a questionnaire that meets the requirements of validity: actually measuring the dependent variable and not some other variable. It also meets requirements of reliability by measuring the exact amount of the dependent variable present at any one time. However, a problem here is to ensure that members of the control and experimental groups are similar in characteristics such as age, sex, education, and so on. Another requirement would be that all the subjects or participants had been randomly selected. That is, everyone within the total population from which the sample was selected had an equal opportunity to be selected. Since these requirements are often difficult to achieve, the control group should, as a minimum, possess the most pertinent characteristics of the experimental group.

The second step in the method is to introduce the independent variable (fear) to those in the experimental group while withholding it from the control group.

The third step is to administer at the posttest the same questionnaire used at the pretest. If the questionnaire scores are not statistically significant for the control group, then any change occurring in the experimental group is assumed to be caused not by events in the general environment, but by the specific treatment (fear). If the questionnaire scores are statistically significantly different between the control and experimental groups, it can be stated that in this sample there was a difference in the behavior of those taking a chance (dependent variable) when they were exposed to fear (independent variable) from that of those not exposed to fear. However, the acceptance of such a finding would depend upon the selection and assignment of the sample group, and also whether other independent variables (Democrat or Republican, and so forth) were not introduced to the study and did not affect the dependent variable (taking a chance).

Even the simple example used above suggests that the experimentation method is a rigorous and exacting procedure. It can be used either in a laboratory setting where independent variables are more precisely controlled or in a field location (office, shopping mall, or the like) where the control of independent variables becomes less exact.

A second research method, which incorporates some of the rationale of the experimentation method but lacks the formal methodology, is the *correlation method*. As in the experimentation method, the correlation method observes variables to determine whether changes in one variable are consistently associated with changes in the other. However, whereas the experimentation method varies the independent variable, thereby providing the opportunity to observe its effect upon the dependent variable, the correlation method does not attempt to vary the independent variables. As a result, the degree of certainty as to the cause-and-effect relationship found in the correlation method cannot be accepted with the same confidence as relationships found with the experimentation method. Additional problems with the correlation method include the question of randomness and the control of independent variables so that the observed effect results from one variable and not a combination of variables.

A third research method to be presented is the *questionnaire* or *survey method*. This approach is related more to the correlation method than to the experimental method. The questionnaire or survey method provides a quick approach to gathering substantial data but suffers from the fact that it is largely self-reporting and permits little flexibility to introduce new independent variables into the study format.

The majority of the empirical research studies utilize the experimentation and correlation methods. Although these techniques contribute to the authenticity of the research findings, they may suggest to the first-time observer some problems in validating those findings. If you are weak in research-design methods or statistical research techniques, you are probably overconcerned with this problem. First of all, the empirical research studies referenced in this book have all been published in *referred journals*. This means that each article has been reviewed by recognized scholars in the subject area for correct research methodology to ensure reliability and validity. In essence, these reviewers serve as "gatekeepers" to prevent poor-quality research from being published. Even though experts do occasionally err, it is reassuring to know that these empirical journal articles have survived a rigorous examination.

Since the experimentation and correlation methods involve statistical techniques, a brief review of statistical framework would be helpful. First, statistics is an academic discipline that is applied to numerical data to assist in making decisions under situations of uncertainty. Two commonly made distinctions in the discipline of statistics are *descriptive* and *inferential*. *Descriptive statistics* summarizes or describes a sample, whereas *inferential statistics* generalizes from a sample to make estimates and inferences about a larger population. Now, a population consists of all possible observations about a specific event; the sample consists of only some of these observations. Since the sample is only a small part of the larger population, extreme care must be exercised to collect sample data that are representative.

For instance, a simple random sample requires that every element in the population has an equal chance of being selected for the sample. This is very time-consuming, and it is very difficult, if not impossible, to list every element for large or diverse populations. A less complicated sampling approach that usually achieves the randomness of the simple random sample is a systematic sample system. This involves using a random number table, usually found in statistics texts, selecting one number as a start, then selecting the other data at some equal interval—say, every fifth, tenth, or twentieth entry in the random number tables. Of course, a problem here is that if your data go from a low to a high in some type of cycle, then the equal interval selected to sample the data may not be representative of the population.

Of importance to sampling and statistical techniques is the *normal distribution*. However, before proceeding, one must understand that the sample mean represents data from a population of observations and is calculated like any arithmetic average. With this sample mean, one can use the normal distribution to find the probability or frequency of a particular event's occurring over a number of times. The *normal curve* permits making inferences or deductions about the value of the population mean when only the sample mean can be directly calculated.

The logic of the preceding statement is evident when one considers the characteristics of the normal distribution. The normal distribution is shaped like a bell, with a rounded top that is symmetrical about its center, with the sides or tails sloping off indefinitely in both directions. That is, "cutting" the bell down the middle would produce two equal halves that would be symmetrical, each half containing 50 percent of the observations. The result of this symmetry is that the *mean* (average), the *mode* (most frequently occurring value or observation), and the *median* (the central value or midpoint of a number of observations) all occur at the center of the bell, and all have the same value.

These characteristics result in a relationship between the mean of the normal distribution and its standard deviation. A *standard deviation* is the square root of the mean of the squared deviations or differences obtained by subtracting the mean from a series of observations. The shape of the normal distribution permits us to state the proportion of the population that will lie between so many standard deviations from the mean. In effect, the standard deviation allows us to "cut up" the bell-shaped normal distribution into standardized slices that contain a known percentage of the total observations. Thus, we can say that 68 percent of all observations lie within 2 standard deviations, one on each side, of the mean; or 95 percent of the observations lie within 1.96 standard deviations on both sides of the mean. The importance to empirical research is that if a sample of two groups from the same population, resulting in two differing sample means, lie within 1.96 standard deviations of each other, they are considered "equal," and it is assumed that any difference in their means was the result of random, chance variations in sampling. Thus, the resulting difference in the two means is likely to occur but does not signify a real difference in the population means of the two different samples.

We can further state as a result of the sample means being within the 1.96 standard deviations that 95 percent of our data or observations lie within these standard deviations, and only 5 percent lie without. That is, we can expect this situation to occur in 95 out of 100 samplings. So there appears to be no significant difference between the two differing sample means or the populations they represent. Thus, if our two differing sample means represented two different secret ingredients that cured a headache, the difference between them would not be large enough to warrant that one was significantly better or worse than the other. Only when the difference between the two sample means becomes too large to be dismissed as chance variation between random samples can the means be classified as not being equal.

One statistical method in empirical research is *hypothesis testing*. This inferential method is used to reject or accept a specific approach or "solution" to a particular area of concern. It is used to test a proposal and reach a decision beyond reasonable doubt while ensuring that the result did not occur by pure chance.

The procedure is to set forth a *null hypothesis* and an *alternate hypothesis*. The null hypothesis is not to be rejected unless the contrary evidence is overwhelming, because of the possibility of error. One error, *Type I error*, is rejection of the null hypothesis when it is true. The null hypothesis is favored when in doubt, since a Type I error is considered the more serious error. The *Type II error* is accepting the null hypothesis when it is false.

In designing a test for the null hypothesis, the researcher can control the probability of a Type I error. In testing the null hypothesis, the other choice is the alternate hypothesis. Since the null hypothesis is given the benefit of the doubt because we do not want to reject it if it is true, the alternate hypothesis assumes the burden of testing beyond a reasonable doubt.

One way to reduce both Type I and Type II errors is to increase the sample size. However, this is not always a practical consideration, owing to availability, time, and cost. So the question arises of the extent to which the probability of a Type I error is allowable. This is determined by the number of standard deviations selected. If 1.96 standard deviations is chosen as the level of significance we wish to maintain, any finding within 1.96 standard deviations will occur 95 percent of the time, with any differences resulting from chance fluctuations in sampling. In the empirical research literature, this is referred to as a *P value*, the probability that a Type I error has occurred. You will find various probabilities expressed: .05, .01, .001. Usually they are expressed in the text of the research article or as notations to diagrams. $P<$ means the probability is less than, $P>$ means the probability is more than, and $P=$ means the probability is equal to the percentage following. These *P* levels are the levels of significance and provide the basis for accepting or rejecting the null hypothesis. However, be aware that there is no guarantee, since the sample data may not be an accurate representation of the population from which they came.

To test hypotheses, one first formulates a *hypothesis* and then chooses a *decision rule*. The decision rule indicates how one plans to use the sample result. For instance, it may be decided that to be marketable, a new gasoline additive must increase mileage by 20 miles in a 100-mile test run. The decision rule would then be to market the product if the sample mean of the test run exceeds 20 miles and not market it if the mean is less than 20 miles. In formulation of the hypothesis, the null and alternate hypotheses are opposite, and when one is true, the other is false. The null hypothesis is so worded as to be the one the decision maker desires to disapprove. Thus, the null hypothesis would be not to market the additive if the sample mean is less than or equal to (≤) 20 miles. The alternate hypothesis would be to reject the null hypothesis and accept the alternate hypothesis if the sample mean exceeds (>) 20 miles. Now, owing to chance sampling error, an incorrect decision may be made—that is, a Type I error to market an ineffective additive, which would be to reject the null hypothesis when it is true, or a Type II error not to market an effective additive, which would be to accept the null hypothesis when it is false.

A statistical formula is available in most basic statistical textbooks by which we may compute the chances that these various errors will occur. The formula requires data input from the decision maker based upon personal evaluation of the risks involved and their acceptability in case one of the error types becomes a reality. Generally, the chance of one error type's occurring can be reduced only by increasing the probability or likelihood of the other error type's occurring. In empirical research, the willingness of the researcher to commit a Type I error is usually established at .05, although it may be lower. That is, only 5 percent of the time will the researcher be willing to reject the null hypothesis when it is true. This is referred to as the *level of significance*.

Once the sample mean has been determined, the decision rule is implemented. The result is statistically significant if the null hypothesis is rejected, any difference is attributed to chance, and the sample mean falls into the critical or acceptance region of the normal distribution. This decision can be facilitated by the standard normal variable Z, for use with large samples—usually more than 30 subjects or observations. The formula for the Z statistic and a conversion table, generally called "Areas under the Standard Normal Curve," are found in statistics textbooks. Thus, the decision is made to accept or reject the null hypothesis at a level of significance that indicates acceptance of the probability of a Type I error. However, the wording of the alternate hypothesis will determine whether a *one-tail* or *two-tail test* is used. This refers to the two tails or "ends" of the normal distribution curve. The one-tail test of the alternate hypothesis is specific, in that it asserts that any significant difference lies in a particular specified direction. With a two-tail test, we are merely looking for a difference in either direction. Since the two-tail test is in two directions, less is assumed. Thus, the alternate hypothesis for a two-tail test would be, "Is the variable *different?*" whereas for a one-tail test it would be written, "Is the variable *less* (or *more*) than 10 (or some other standard)?"

Another statistical test in hypothesis testing is the *t statistic*. It is used where the distribution of data resembles a normal distribution, the population standard deviation is known or assumed, and the sample size is not over 30 observations. This is based on the Central Limit Theorem, which states that regardless of the sampling distribution of data as the sample size becomes larger, the sampling distribution of means tends toward the bell shape of a normal distribution. The formula for t is very similar to Z (again, refer to a college textbook). Once the sample size is larger than 30, the distribution of t becomes practically identical with that of the standard normal variable Z, at which point Z can then be used to approximate t. The procedure to reach a decision on whether to accept or reject the null hypothesis is the same for the Z statistic except that one consults a table generally called "Critical Values of Student t Distribution," which features a column called "Degrees of Freedom." The degrees of freedom in a t test for a mean is $n - 1$, or the sample size decreased by 1. Generally, the more degrees of freedom you have, the more information is available to test the hypothesis.

The *Chi-Square statistic* is used in hypothesis testing most commonly to test whether or not two variables are independent, to compare several population proportions, and to summate the frequency deviation between actual data and their expected frequencies.

Statistical independence is obtained if two events take place and the occurrence of either event does not affect the probability of the other. In use of the Chi-Square statistic, the actual and expected frequencies of an event are compared so the null hypothesis of independence can be accepted or rejected. For instance, customers' responses (frequencies) are obtained as to their preference for a product. The test helps determine whether the responses given actually matter in selecting the product or if the reasons given (variables) are independent and therefore not related to the choice of the product.

With more than two populations that would require comparing several proportions, a different approach is used. For instance, three distinct personality types are tested to determine whether they should be hired or not hired for a particular job category. The null hypothesis would be that there are no differences in the three types available for hiring, and the alternate hypothesis that at least two of the proportions would be different. A table of six cells would be constructed, with the three personality types listed horizontally and the two job classifications, hired or not hired, listed vertically, forming a 3-by-2 matrix. Then the matrix is coded with the observed frequencies in one row and the expected frequencies in another row. These are calculated per the Chi-Square formula, resulting in a test statistic that is compared in the Chi-Square Distribution table to determine whether the null hypothesis is accepted or rejected and at what level of significance.

Another common use of the Chi-Square statistic is testing for *goodness of fit*. This statistic supplies a number that characterizes the amount of deviation or differences resulting from measurements of an event and the expected frequencies of obtaining those measurements. The resulting number is compared to the Chi-Square Distribution table to determine whether the measurements of the event do indeed measure a normal distribution and the level of significance.

The *analysis of variance* is another statistical test used in empirical research to test hypotheses. Although the analysis of variance compares the means of two populations and may thus appear to be misnamed, the technique accomplishes this through comparing sample variances. This requires using the probability distribution called the *F distribution.* Sample data are collected that have been exposed to several treatments to see if these treatments have had different results. For instance, different amounts of pay-incentive "treatments" may be applied to a sample group to determine any different results in productivity. The sample data are collected, then converted into a test statistic to determine whether the null hypothesis is rejected or accepted. In obtaining the test statistic, the total variation between the treatments and the sample groups is computed.

The *treatments sum of squares, SST,* summarizes the variability between the same results and indicates the explained variations. The *error sum of squares, SSE,* summarizes within-sample variability and indicates the unexplained variations. The problem is to decide whether the variation that is explained is of significant size, sufficient to justify rejecting the null hypothesis. In the example above, the null hypothesis would probably be that the treatment populations have similar means. To compare the explained and unexplained variations requires determining their ratio through computation of the treatments mean square (MST) and the error mean square (MSE). The resulting computations are summarized in the ANOVA table, the letters obtained from ANalysis Of VAriance. The ratio of these variances, MST and $MSE,$ equal the F statistic. Once the F statistic is obtained, the F Distribution Table is consulted for the appropriate level of significance and the decision is made. The theoretical conditions for using the F distribution are that each sample population must be normally distributed with identical mean and standard deviation and that all sample observations are independent.

Sometimes studies in the empirical research journals need to predict the values of unknown variables. *Regression analysis* takes the known value of a variable and uses it to estimate the unknown value of the other variable. It indicates the relationship of one variable to another. For example, we might use intelligence (a known variable) to predict behavior (an unknown variable). When several variables, such as ability, length of schooling, and references, are used to make such a prediction, the statistical technique is called *multiple regression.*

Regression analysis may also be used to test hypotheses. It obtains predictions of one variable by using the known values of another variable. Because of statistical variability, such predictions are only estimates of actual values, so they are subject to error. The analysis starts with data on pairs of observed happenings, one number for each variable. These values are then plotted on a graph or scatter diagram, with the horizontal axis for the independent variable and the vertical axis for the dependent variable. Although the dependent variable is a function of the independent variable, this does not mean that the dependent variable is caused by the independent variable. A straight line, or linear relationship, appears to be a meaningful summary of the sample information and "fits" the data points on the graph. The straight line used to describe the relationship between the dependent and independent variables is called the *estimated regression line.* The line of "fit" need not be a straight line—it could be curvilinear or U-shaped—but straight lines describe most data and are among the most common regression relationships.

Regression analysis considers the relation between the variables in only one direction, the effect of the independent variable on the dependent variable. When the slope of the regression line is positive, the value of the dependent variable will increase as values for the independent variable increase, indicating a direct relationship of the dependent to the independent variable. However, when the slope of the regression line is negative (the dependent variable becomes smaller for larger values of the independent variable), the dependent variable is inversely related to the independent variable. An example of such an inverse relationship would be a decrease in physical stamina (dependent variable) as the distance being run (independent variable) increases. In other situations, we might have a perfect correlation, where the variables are directly related, or an uncorrelated condition. In this last condition, the regression line would be horizontal, so that the value of the dependent variable is itself independent of the independent variable. This means that the independent variable is valueless as a predictor of the dependent variable.

The statistical technique of fitting the straight line to the data on the graph is the method of *least squares,* which minimizes the squares of the vertical data deviations separating these data points from the line. The *least-squares regression line* goes through the point that corresponds to the means of the independent variables and the dependent variables. Also, the sum of the deviations of the dependent variables from the regression line is zero. Once the regression equation has been completed, predictions of the dependent variable can be made. Part of this statistical technique is the computation of the *standard error of estimate,* which expresses the degree of data scatter in our graph, indicating the extent to which predictions may be subject to sampling error. Also, the technique provides a formula to determine a confidence prediction limit, using the value for t found in the Student t Distribution Table. When the sample size is 30 or more, the normal distribution curve applies, with Z replacing the t statistic.

When the statistical technique requires a measurement of the degree to which two variables are related, the formula for estimating the value of one variable from another is provided by *correlation analysis*. This statistical technique is also useful in hypothesis testing. By calculation of a single number from the data, it can be shown how closely two variables can move together. Although correlation analysis is used in regression analysis to indicate how adequately the regression line illustrates the dependent variable's fluctuation in value, it is generally used only to indicate the strength of the relationship between the two variables. Correlation analysis by itself seeks to find a suitable index that indicates how strongly related the two variables are. In regression analysis, one variable is treated as dependent and the other as independent. But in correlation analysis, we investigate the interdependence of the variables.

There are three kinds of correlations: positive, negative, and zero. A positive correlation exists when changes occur in one direction for one variable and a similar change occurs for another variable; that is, as one variable becomes larger, so does the other. A negative correlation occurs when the variables move apart in opposite directions. One variable becomes larger while the other becomes smaller. However, although the case is rather unlikely, a variable may not move either up or down relative to the movement of another variable. So even though there is a directional movement in correlations, there is also a strength in the relationship. This occurs as the data observations cluster closer to the straight line referred to earlier in our discussion about regression analysis. Generally, the closer data observations are to the straight line, the higher the degree of correlation and the stronger the relation. The numerical index that measures this relationship is called the *correlation coefficient*. Using a statistical formula to obtain this statistic allows us to indicate the magnitude or strength of the association between the variables. Yet the correlation coefficient does not measure causation, and high correlations may not necessarily indicate a cause-and-effect relationship. To obtain the level of significance for the finding, another statistical formula allows us to compute the *t* distribution statistic. However, it is important to understand that although the correlation coefficient may be high (.6 or .7), it may not be statistically significant from zero, so there is no correlation. Conversely, a low correlation coefficient (.2) may be statistically significant from zero, so there is a correlation. This is the result of sample size; a low correlation coefficient may be statistically significant because of a large sample size, whereas a high correlation coefficient may not be statistically significant owing to a small sample size.

This brief and simplistic review of the statistical methodology used in the empirical journals will be adequate for an understanding of what the researchers are attempting to accomplish. A more detailed knowledge of statistical techniques will be required of those who aspire to do their own empirical research.

CHAPTER TWO

SELECTION: RECRUITING

INTRODUCTION

Recruiting is pivotal to the successful operations of the human resource department and to achieving the organization's strategic plans. All the human resource functional areas are important, but the recruiting function is significant in that so much is dependent upon its effectiveness. Failure to recruit talented young people may mean a delay in implementing new plans, may prevent the company from maintaining its competitive position, and may disrupt the wage structure and employee morale, since the alternative is to hire older, more experienced, more costly people.

For large companies, recruiting is a continuous process, whereas for the small company, it is an occasional activity. Between these two circumstances are a gamut of activities dictated by demographic factors, present and future economic activity, and the composition of the organizational workforce as to age, sex, skill, and race.

The signal to begin the recruitment process may be a human resource planning study in a larger firm, an untimely departure in a smaller firm, a promotion that creates a vacancy, an early retirement, the introduction of a new product line, or a rise in the economy resulting in a surge of orders.

Human resource planning can become a complex specialized activity that places the human resource manager at the administrative heart of the organization. In this type of situation, the human resource manager becomes a key person in the formulation and implementation of business strategy, since this requires the availability, both present and future, of skilled personnel necessary to ensure success. In fact, in such an organizational structure, practically all business decisions relative to marketing, production, finance, and management would require the input of the human resource manager, since the availability and cost of personnel would be a critical factor.

Recruiting, then, is the critical process that must be able to supply the required personnel at the required time, within the required cost limits. Some organizations develop five- and ten-year plans in which human resource planning is part of the total process, providing evaluative input as to present skill levels and projected skill requirements, and evaluating projected sources of recruitment such as the labor market, in-house training programs, and the external educational system. In reality, most organizations do not utilize human resource planning at the highest organizational level even though there it would be most effective. Most planning usually occurs at the operational level, and it is relatively short-term. But such planning should be future-oriented and anticipative rather than now-oriented and merely reacting.

In any event, the company needs to have a recruiting strategy that reflects its philosophy, anticipates manpower requirements, and takes into account labor-market conditions. When new employees are needed, many companies follow a policy of promoting from within. However, as people within the company move up the promotion ladder, there is always a need to fill the vacancy of the last person promoted. Such an in-house policy promotes employee morale and provides the company with a person whose past work record is well known, reducing the chance of any unpleasant surprises that might result from a new hire. Although promoting from within is relatively easy for the management ranks, at the lower levels there may be union seniority lists that indicate those who are eligible. Most companies promoting from within post the vacancies to provide an equal opportunity for all employees to indicate their interest.

Also included in the company's recruiting strategy is the hiring of outside personnel. This may involve the use of temporary and part-time employees. Such a situation develops when regular employees take vacations, or a short-term illness occurs, or a large, one-time order is placed, or the work being performed is seasonal. Whether the work is permanent or temporary, many outside sources are available to the company. These include walk-in applicants looking for employment; unions that maintain hiring halls or lists of available members looking for work; advertising in the media, such as newspapers; private employment agencies; the U.S. Employment Service; and training schools or colleges. Regardless of whether the employment search is inside or outside the organization, one of the initial steps is to provide those involved with a job description detailing the required tasks and duties, required behaviors, and necessary personal qualifications. This simple step reduces the number of inquiries resulting from the recruitment search and provides a more qualified group from which selection can be made, an advantage to both the company and the applicants.

The U.S. Employment Service (USES) is a major recruiting source, operating more than 2,400 offices nationwide that are staffed by state employees although funded by the federal government. These state agencies usually maintain local public employment offices even in small communities. Unemployed persons register with these offices as being ready to accept suitable employment and are thus able to receive weekly unemployment benefits. This provides a group of experienced workers with a wide range of skills who are available for immediate employment. However, employers tend to list only lower-skilled jobs with the USES rather than higher-skilled jobs. The USES offices offer services other than just matching applicants with job openings. These services include assisting employers with testing, job analysis, evaluation programs, and local wage surveys. Those seeking employment are offered vocational counseling, training on how to apply for a job, and interview techniques. Another service is a computerized job bank that daily lists all job openings in the local area.

The private employment agencies, both local and national, charge a fee to the unemployed person seeking work or charge the company for whom they are seeking applicants. Some of these private agencies have become very specialized (such as dealing only in restaurant and hotel workers); others recruit for a variety of positions. Generally, those agencies do recruiting and a preliminary screening of applicants that may include testing, interview and résumé skills, and career counseling. A company using a private employment agency needs to supply accurate information about its organization, up-to-date job descriptions, and honest salary information. Included among the private employment agencies are executive search firms, which work for a client firm to seek out people with certain qualifications. They do not accept fees from the person being placed in a job but are paid by the company for their services.

College campus recruiting has become the prime source for both large and medium-sized companies seeking managerial and professional personnel. These companies usually prepare brochures for distribution by the college recruitment office prior to their arrival on campus. The campus interview is generally an initial screening taking 30 to 60 minutes, with acceptable applicants then given closer scrutiny in additional interviews at some off-campus company facility. Some companies offer part-time summer work programs so as to learn more about the applicants. Most companies recruiting on campus maintain statistical reports to determine how many are first interviewed and then invited for further interviews, how many are interviewed further, and the number of job offers. These statistics and others serve to suggest the campuses where the company does the best recruiting and any problem areas that may be developing with its recruiting program.

A problem peculiar to college recruiting is that since it is usually done by larger firms, those students who prefer smaller firms may have no other choice but to join the larger ones and later become dissatisfied, thus contributing to a high turnover rate. Related to this problem is the number of applicants who accept employment but do not show up for work. In some companies, this figure may reach 15 percent or more. It appears that the recruitment process needs to be directed toward applicants possessing the abilities and motivation required by the company, and also needs a stay-in-touch program until the applicant begins work.

Since the recruitment process is the preliminary step in the selection process, it must be properly planned or it will have a negative effect on the company's efforts to comply with equal employment laws. Such planning consists of two steps: The job opening should be announced in an area where the job market is likely to respond, and those applicants who are qualified must be made aware of the announcement in order to respond. The recruitment sources mentioned earlier (newspaper ads, employee referrals or word of mouth, colleges, walk-ins, USES, private agencies) have been attacked by various equal employment enforcement agencies as having an adverse effect on a protected group or as not attracting a large enough number of applications. A limited number of applicants is usually the result of using a limited number of recruitment sources. Any recruitment notice must be careful not to discourage or to limit opportunities of employment to protected groups. While the wording of the recruitment notice is important, the phrasing must not limit the non-job-related characteristics of those applying—for example, by specifying a male when a female could do the job as well, requiring a higher level of education than is really necessary, and specifying a good credit rating when that has no relationship to job performance. Most of the problem is with the word selection; for instance, *well-groomed* or *presentable* would cover both male and female groups. However, only if there is imbalance in the workforce and evidence of a negative effect on protected groups would the recruitment process be questioned by the regulatory agencies.

Some employers regard word of mouth to be an excellent source of applicants. However, this source of recruitment receives close scrutiny by the regulatory agencies, since experience indicates that a worker will rarely refer a member of another race. This, then, effectively limits the hiring of minorities unless there is a demonstrable affirmative action package being implemented by the company to encourage minorities and women to apply. Such a package would be active recruitment from many sources, such as the Urban League, women's groups, Hispanic groups, minority media, minority churches, and minority schools. When only traditional recruitment sources are used, an adverse effect is likely, but by using many sources, including local minority community groups, the company should experience no problems with the equal employment regulations.

RESEARCH INCIDENTS

Research Incident 2-1:
Recruiter Milton Sparks Remembers the Old Days

- What is the overall effect of equal employment quotas for protected groups upon the organizational environment?
- How does the trait of authoritarianism affect the evaluator in the evaluating process as it relates to female applicants?
- Do male and female role stereotypes influence the final decision a recruiter makes?

Milt Sparks knew that the last day at the home office before his upstate college recruiting trip was always hectic. But this year, it was the last *three* days. They were filled with meetings, all of them concerned with recruiting. Milt attributed this sudden change to the new vice-president of human resources, who had come to the company last year after being with a *Fortune* 500 company for five years. The man had a Ph.D. degree from a prestigious eastern university, and the top brass had rolled out the red carpet for him. Milt, on the other hand, had never finished college; his 39 years of human resource experience were his degree. Of course, back then it was called personnel management.

Over the years, Milt Sparks had become quite a legend to his peers. His authoritarian style was unique, ranging from a kind of Spanish Inquisition to the role of a humanistic priest counseling his flock. The results were outstanding; many highly regarded people, both at the home office and scattered around the globe, had all been originally recruited by Milt. So Milt's comments during several of the meetings were listened to by his fellow recruiters with more than the usual attention. However, the results were always the same: Milt was treated with respect by whoever was conducting the meeting, but the new procedures remained unchanged. Each recruiter was given an ideal profile for each particular opening; a standardized, structured question procedure that varied for different positions; a checklist evaluation form to be completed after each interview; and suggested quotas for minority groups, based on available college demographics. The three days of meetings included topics such as College Attitudes Today, The Ideal Candidate, Follow-Up Questions, Body Language, Company Past and Future, Halo and Other Problems, Hello and Goodbye, Industry Starting Salaries and Benefits, Minority Consideration and Placement, and Company Opportunities for Women.

Milt dozed through most of the meetings; they were just too technical and far-out for him. That first look in the eye and a firm handshake were the old reliables.

At the conclusion of the meeting on the third day, the college recruiting assignments for the next month were passed out. Milton Sparks noticed that some of the larger universities that he usually recruited had been replaced on his list with smaller, rural colleges. On top of that, a younger female recruiter had been assigned to the larger universities.

RELEVANT EMPIRICAL RESEARCH STUDIES

Research Study 2-1-A

What effect do the attitudes and characteristics of a recruiter have in determining the suitability of the applicants selected?

Simas and McCarrey[1] studied the role of recruiter authoritarianism in the evaluation of candidates in a recruitment situation. The subjects were volunteers responding to a request by the Public Service Commission of the Canadian federal government. These volunteers completed the Revised F Scale, which measured, among other qualities, an uncritical attitude toward authority, a preoccupation with issues of dominance and power, and a tendency toward rigidity and stereotyping. They were then selected at random and placed in three groups—high authoritarians, moderate authoritarians, and low authoritarians—until each group had 14 males and 14 females. The subjects then watched four videotaped simulated cases in which job applicants, two males and two females, were recruited for an entry-level management position requiring minimal technical knowledge but a familiarity with government. The videotapes were constructed with the help of two full-time recruitment specialists. The subjects were provided with a job description; an evaluative instrument with which to measure dimensions of evaluation (good-bad, valuable-worthless, fair-unfair), potency (strong-weak, hard-soft, rugged-delicate), and activity (active-passive, sharp-dull, fast-slow); and a ranking form to indicate the order of hiring preference for the four people.

The results of the study indicated no significant difference between the ratings for the two male applicants or between those for the two female applicants on the evaluation, potency, and activity dimensions. Further analysis found that high authoritarians, both male and female, rated the male applicants significantly more positively than they did the female applicants. However, the high, moderate, and low authoritarians all demonstrated a significant difference from one another in their ratings when evaluating the male applicants. It was found that male and female high authoritarians evaluated the male applicants significantly more positively than did the low but not the moderate authoritarians of both sexes.

Also, the more authoritarian the subjects, male or female, the higher they rated male job applicants on the evaluative dimension (good-bad, valuable-worthless, fair-unfair). However, there was no such relationship between authoritarianism and female job applicants' ratings on the evaluative dimension. An analysis of the data on the potency dimension (strong-weak, hard-soft, rugged-delicate) reveals that regardless of the authoritarianism levels of the males and females, they rated male applicants as being more potent than female applicants. Also, the moderate-authoritarian males rated both the male and female job applicants significantly higher on the potency dimension than did the moderate-authoritarian females. It appears that the higher one's score on the authoritarianism measure, the higher both males and females rated male job applicants on the potency dimension.

In regard to the activity dimension (active-passive, sharp-dull, fast-slow), only the high authoritarians demonstrated significant differences in their ratings of the job applicants. The high authoritarians of both sexes rated the male job applicants as significantly more active than female applicants. Further, the high-authoritarian females rated all the job applicants as being significantly more active than did the high-authoritarian males. Once again, the more authoritarian the males and females, the higher the male job applicants were rated on the activity dimension.

Summary Review of Research Study 2-1-A   In a majority of the rankings of the applicants, the high-authoritarian subjects of both sexes demonstrated a preference for hiring the male applicant. They differed from the low authoritarians in terms of overevaluating the male applicants rather than underevaluating the female applicants. What appears to be expressed is not necessarily a poor view of the females but more of an extremely high opinion of the males.

The potency ranking appears to be an item in which the males and females were consistently stereotypically differentiated. Generally, the activity ranking did not differentiate between male and female applicants; only the high authoritarians found male applicants more active than female applicants. As to the evaluative ranking, the suggestion is that although high authoritarians overestimated the male applicants, they did not view the female applicants as any less active than do the moderate and low authoritarians. There appears to be a relationship between the degree of authoritarianism and evaluations of male and female persons. Further, this relationship appears to demonstrate itself in discriminating against females by a preference for hiring males.

The authors suggest caution in interpreting the study results, since the interviews were videotaped and not face to face, the volunteer subjects might not have been typical, and not all the possible subtle interview differences, including nonverbal behavior, might have been equal in all the interviews.

Research Study 2-1-B

What is the effect of male/female role stereotypes in the decision mix of a recruiter's conclusion to hire or not to hire?

Cohen and Bunker[2] studied a sample obtained from two large southern universities of 150 male job recruiters whose prime responsibility was to interview students at college placement offices. These recruiters were told that each would evaluate only one applicant, and they were supplied packets of materials from their placement-office directors, who requested their cooperation in a study designed to investigate the decision process in a placement interview.

Each packet contained a one-page job description for one of two jobs, either an editorial assistant or a personnel technician. These two positions were selected to indicate sex-role orientations but were not so obvious as to sensitize the recruiters as to the study's real purpose. The recruiters indicated that they perceived both jobs as being equal in status and responsibility. Each packet also contained an application blank, completed by either a male or a female, that was identical to the others except for name and physical characteristics. Another item was an interview transcript that was generally an extension of material in the application blank, with the information being the same for both sexes. Also included were a six-item performance evaluation form to determine the applicant's abilities, and a 29-item semantic differential scale to determine suitability for the job by selecting a bipolar adjective (efficient-inefficient). The final packet item concerned biographical data to be obtained from the recruiter, such as age, experience, company size, and so on.

The results of the study indicated that a disproportionately larger number of females were acceptable for the editorial-assistant position than were acceptable for personnel technician. The opposite was true for the males. The recruiter samples from the two universities did not demonstrate significant differences in finding the applicants either acceptable or unacceptable for hiring. Also, there were no differences among the recruiters as to biographical data. In regard to the six questions contained in the performance evaluation form, there appeared to be little effect upon the recruiters' decision to hire or not hire. However, for both positions, applicants' responses to the experience and training questions were significant in hiring. Only for the male editorial assistant was the question concerning desire to work for the company significant. None of the six questions for the female editorial assistant was significant. However, for the female personnel-technician applicants, the question of being well informed in that occupational area was significant for being hired. For the female applicants, only five items of the 29-item semantic differential scale were found to be significantly discriminating. Thus, females were seen as being more consistent, more friendly, more interesting, more confident, and wiser. Those applicants, both male and female, who applied for positions where the sex role was not consistent with the position (male editorial assistants and female personnel technicians) were regarded as considerably more competitive than those applying for sex-role-consistent positions (male personnel technicians and female editorial assistants).

It appears from the results that people whose sex is not considered appropriate for the job they apply for must be considered more task-qualified for the job than those applying for jobs where their sex is considered appropriate.

Summary Review of Research Study 2-1-B   Apparently, sex discrimination begins at the early stages of the selection process—namely, the recruitment interview. The study suggests that such discrimination occurs as a result of applicants' applying for a position that is traditionally occupied by a member of the opposite sex. This type of discrimination takes place for males as well as females. Unfortunately, the present study was unable to determine which attitudes combined to form a decision pattern. There was little agreement between replies to the performance evaluation questionnaire and the decision to hire. The only consistent result had to do with the relationship of the "appropriate" sex to a particular job. Thus, the editorial assistant was considered the proper job for a female, and the personnel technician was considered appropriate for a male. If a male were to be considered acceptable as an editorial assistant, he must have the appropriate experience and training, and also be desirous of working in that capacity. Interestingly, the female applicant for editorial assistant was not required to have any specific qualifications. On the other hand, the hiring decision for the female personnel technician related to how knowledgeable she was about the job. For the semantic differences, sex was responsible for differences on only five of the 29 items, and then it was the females who were rated as more favorable than the males. Otherwise, there was relatively little perceived difference between the male and female applicants relative to their sex or their job.

Research Study 2-1-C

Even today, many companies find that the composition of their workforce does not begin to approach the composition of the local population. Sometimes, in an effort to overcome years of unintended discrimination, subtle (and sometimes, not too subtle) quotas are "suggested." What may happen when a company enters the quota chase?

Kroeck and others[3] used a computer simulation to predict recruitment and performance outcomes under different quota goals. The authors developed a set of logarithms to find commonality in data resulting from repetitious operations. The computer simulation program required several assumptions, notably these: Some type of selection test would be used for all applicants; a limited number of positions were to be filled, based upon the target-group proportions and specified by a fixed quota; all applicants who were offered a job would accept and then be evaluated by some measurable aspect of performance; and the relationship between the selection test and the performance measure would apply equally to the groups.

A study of this type requires the use of symbols and terms that may be confusing to some, and perhaps most. Simply put, the computer simulation investigates two alternative recruitment policies, open and closed, and two alternative selection approaches, minimum cutoff and ranking. Both the open and closed recruitment policies use a score of predictor variables to establish a minimum cutoff point from which to select applicants. Once the desired number of applicants is obtained, there is no longer a need to recruit. Under the closed recruitment policy, there is a fixed pool of applicants, so employment is not open to all who may wish to apply. Generally, the open policy has more stringent standards, and the closed policy is more lenient.

The computer simulation program combined these options into four different recruitment and selection strategies. The International Mathematical and Statistical Library (1979) Subroutine GGNSM randomly generated populations of applicant scores. A population of 50,000 sizes was generated. The variable mix of the minority proportion of the population was varied from 10 to 50 percent in increases of 10 percent. Other variables were minimum qualifications, imposed quotas, the various minority groups' mean difference, and the correlations of the selection tests and performance. There were 750 populations generated for evaluation of these variables in every possible combination. However, the authors report that the study's results regarding selection without replacement from a fixed applicant pool were similar to those of an earlier study by another author, whose reported data were for the open recruitment case. The current study found that if the cutoff on evaluation data such as a test score was set at the eightieth percentile and a quota was established at twice the population minority representation, ten times more applicants would be required than the number hired. To locate 200 qualified applicants would require the processing of 2,000 applicants. However, if the quota were equal to the minority representation in the population, only 1,000 applicants would be recruited. When a quota is double the minority representation, that doubles the required recruitment. The same is true for a triple quota, and so on.

Another finding was that there was no "adverse impact" on the majority group when a minority quota of about 25 percent exists and the minority group is 20 percent of the population. (There is no adverse impact if the ratio of the selection ratios of two groups is not ⅘ or larger.) However, with a minority quota greater than 25 percent, there is an increasingly greater adverse impact on the majority group. The result is that increases in minority quotas will result in the rejection of larger proportions of majority applicants. In selecting from a fixed applicant pool, 25 percent of the acceptable majority would not be hired if the quota was twice that of a 20 percent minority representation. Also, if there was a .5 standard deviation mean difference between the majority and minority groups, the average effect would be to triple the rejection of the qualified majority. A 10 percent minority quota with only 5 percent of the overall population being in that minority is likely to have an effect of a 40 percent minority quota when the minority group is 20 percent of the overall population. The rejection of qualified majority members may be extensive under such circumstances.

Summary Review of Research Study 2-1-C   When a minority-group quota is established that slightly exceeds that group's representation in the general population, the result can have considerable effect upon recruitment, the number of qualified nonminority-group members rejected, and a performance differential. The result may be consequences that had not been anticipated or intended when the quotas were first proposed. The necessary recruitment and the resulting rejection of qualified majority-group members may be very high under certain quota situations, creating reverse discrimination.

Further, certain quota systems could result in the selection of only a few top-scoring majority applicants, with many of the marginally qualified minority applicants being accepted. Although the overall result may not greatly reduce the average qualification level, it is likely that the differences between the majority and minority would increase, creating potential job-performance and promotion problems.

Although the computer model in the study offered several advantages of prediction, it was limited by the assumptions that all applicants offered a position would accept, that minority members would apply for jobs in proportion to their representation in the general population, and that the linear relationships of the model were valid.

REFERENCES

[1]Simas, K., and M. McCarrey, "Impact of Recruiter Authoritarianism and Applicant Sex on Evaluation and Selection Decisions in a Recruitment Interview Analogue Study," *Journal of Applied Psychology*, 64 (1979), 483–91.

[2]Cohen, S.L., and K.A. Bunker, "Subtle Effects of Sex Role Stereotypes on Recruiters' Hiring Decisions," *Journal of Applied Psychology*, 60 (1975), 566–72.

[3]Kroeck, K.G., G.V. Barrett, and R.A. Alexander, "Imposed Quotas and Personnel Selection: A Computer Simulation Study," *Journal of Applied Psychology*, 68 (1983), 123–36.

QUESTIONS

1. How should the human resource office approach the issue of quotas? Are there any unusual problems to consider? Explain.
2. There are two personalities in a first-time recruitment situation, those of the recruiter and the recruitee. What effect, if any, do the attitudes and characteristics of the recruiter have upon the process?
3. Have you ever applied for a position where there was a definite stereotype role involved? What takes place in such a situation?

Research Incident 2-2:
Shirley Igol Ends a Busy Day Recruiting

- Does the personality of the recruiter have an effect on the applicant's decision to join or not join that company?
- What becomes more important in the applicant's decision process—the information provided in the interview, or the actions of the recruiter?
- Will employees' employment tenure differ depending upon their source of recruitment, such as newspaper advertisements or employment agencies?
- What is the effect of the source of recruitment upon employee performance?

Shirley Igol checked her watch; it was 5:30 P.M. A long day, and a very long last interview. Shirley rubbed her eyes and wondered why that had taken an additional 15 minutes. A good thing it hadn't happened in an earlier interview, or the whole day's recruiting schedule would have been out of whack.

Shirley began to fill out the forms on this last candidate. The first one required her judgment of predicted performance if the person were hired. She quickly checked a 10, the highest possible score. Now Shirley knew why the interview ran over—she had been trying to present the company in the best possible light to the highly desirable applicant. Yet the vibes just weren't there. The applicant had an ideal profile, very well qualified in all respects, yet the chemistry between the two never caught on. A female M.B.A. with an undergraduate degree in petroleum engineering—what a catch she would be!

Shirley stared at the next line on the form: candidate's interest in the company. The lowest score was a 1, and that should have been circled, but instead Shirley slowly checked a 5, feeling it looked more consistent with the 10 predicted performance rating.

After completing a few more forms, Shirley started to her car, still thinking about her interview with the female M.B.A. with a B.S. degree in petroleum engineering. Certainly the way Shirley was dressed hadn't caused the problem; her attire was strictly woman executive on the way up. And no one knew more about the company's proud history and its generous salary and benefit plans. What else had taken place? The training program and dual promotion ladders were right up her alley. Thinking back, that was probably the best part of her recruitment effort. The candidate had seemed genuinely interested then and asked several appropriate questions. But after that, the discussion had turned to the company's efforts in pollution control, energy conservation, and employee safety, and suddenly, Shirley had realized that her knowledge of those areas was lacking and that her answers were not as crisp and to the point as they had been earlier in the session. However, overall there had to be more than that; the interview had never got going.

It was about three weeks later at the home office that fellow recruiter George Sharply stuck his head into Shirley's office and said in a loud voice, "Hey, that female M.B.A. engineer of yours has declined our offer to visit. How did you scare her off?"

RELEVANT EMPIRICAL RESEARCH STUDIES

Research Study 2-2-A

To the person being interviewed, the interviewer is the company. Accurate knowledge of the company, the position being offered, training programs, and promotional opportunities are part of the recruiter's lore, but sometimes not all.

What is the effect of the recruiter upon the job applicant? Can the personal characteristics of the recruiter influence the applicant to make a decision either positively or negatively?

Schmitt and Coyle[1] say that college recruiting on campuses serves to attract a pool of managerial and technical talent. They point out that the recruiter must obtain information about the interviewee and evaluate it, while presenting the company in a most favorable light.

The present study investigated the effect of the recruiter in the selection process. Subjects were 237 Michigan State University undergraduates who interviewed for jobs at the University Placement Center. These students—51 percent either business or management majors, 28 percent engineering majors, and 68 percent male—completed a questionnaire that consisted of three parts. In the first part, students responded to 74 items indicating their perception of the interview. The second part contained nine questions relative to any decisions or impressions that may have occurred as a result of the interview. The questions included an estimate of whether a job offer would be received, an estimate of whether a job offer would be accepted, how the interviewee performed, whether after the interview there was a more or less favorable view of the company, the perception of the interviewer's competence, perception of the interviewer's pleasantness, and whether the interviewee would pursue further job interest in that company if there was no further word from it. These items were the dependent variables. In the third part, the questionnaire investigated demographic variables, such as parents' occupational status and income, sex, expected income, college major, and previous work experience.

The statistical analysis of the 74 items in the first part of the questionnaire indicated six items of importance. The most important item was empathic in direction and related to the interviewer's warmth and thoughtfulness. The next item of importance was how the interview was conducted—that is, whether the questions being asked were redundant, if they were clear, and when the interviewer was asked questions by the interviewee, whether the answers were specific. The third item reflected the forcefulness and self-confidence of the interviewer. The next related to the interviewer's correctness, the manner in which thoughts were presented, and the pattern of speech. The fifth factor centered on the extent to which job information was presented, such as salary, promotion opportunities, and the characteristics of the position in question. The final factor related to how the interviewer expressed personal opinions and attempted to determine the interviewee's opinions.

Overall, the study suggests that the recruiter's personality was important to the interviewee in regard to acceptance of employment, the perception of the company, and the perception of the interviewer. It appears that the interviewees formed an impression of the interviewer's perceived personality characteristics as to goodness or badness, and this impression was an important factor in their employment decisions. The goodness or badness appeared to be affected by the recruiter's manner of delivery and willingness or ability to provide job information. Interestingly, the interviewer's perceived aggressiveness and self-confidence appeared to have little effect upon the person being interviewed. If the interviewees believed the interviewer was warm interpersonally and also demonstrated a businesslike manner while presenting job information, this was interpreted as an interest in employing them. Although the interview can be generally considered an interpersonal situation between the recruiter and the applicant, one factor mentioned previously that is not interpersonal but still proved important was the amount of information given on the nature of the job being sought.

Summary Review of Research Study 2-2-A It appears that when employment becomes a real possibility, the job itself is more completely discussed, and this is an important consideration. Even though applicants can and do obtain information about the company, what is unique about the interview is the personality of the interviewer. So the good recruiter causes applicants to consider the company as a possible employer through interpersonal mannerisms and the way the job is presented. The interview, then, is important to the act of accepting a job, in relation to one's perception of the company and the interviewer. Perception of the interviewer centers on impressions of goodness or badness. Other interviewer perceptions include manner of delivery and ability to supply job information. Interestingly, the applicant's view of the aggressiveness and self-confidence of the interviewer did little to affect the applicant's decision.

The authors caution that there are some limitations on the study's results, including the facts that all information resulted from mailed questionnaires; that although the students were instructed to react to their last interview, there was no way of determining whether they referred to a more global experience; and that there is the possibility that the applicant's attitudes might change depending upon later acceptance or rejection.

Research Study 2-2-B

Does it make a difference whether recruitment is from one source or another? What is the influence of the recruiter upon the job applicant's perception of the desirability of the job being applied for? Do applicants' preferences for certain recruiters actually influence their job choices?

Rynes and Miller[2] conducted two experimental investigations using simulated videotaped recruitment interviews to research the effects of recruiter characteristics on applicants' job choices. In the first experiment, four videotaped sessions of a simulated campus interview for an entry-level sales position were produced to demonstrate two levels of recruiter affect with two levels of recruiter knowledge. The recruiter behavior that represented a positive effect included steady eye contact, frequent smiling, nods of encouragement, verbal approval of applicant responses, and positive response to the applicant's humor. The recruiter behavior that represented a negative effect included rarely smiling, fidgeting with items on the desk rather than eye contact, ignoring the applicant's humor, and appearing to want to terminate the interview quickly.

With respect to the level of recruiter knowledge in the high condition, the company's average salary offer was revealed as $15,000; in the low condition, salaries were simply described as competitive. Other high/low-condition examples were specific job titles versus no specific job titles, definite geographical assignment versus vague statements, and specifics about fringe-benefit packages as opposed to nonspecifics. Further, in the high condition, the recruiter responded promptly; in the low condition, hesitatingly.

The subjects were 137 undergraduate students who viewed the tapes as part of a lecture on organizational recruitment and job choice. Ninety-four percent were business majors, average age 23, and 61 percent males. Before viewing one of the four tapes, students received an oral presentation about the organization, a written fact sheet regarding characteristics of entry-level sales offers in the last recruiting session, and advice to be prepared to answer questions after seeing the tape. Each subject saw only one of the four tapes.

The study found that the positive-affect recruiter was perceived to better represent his organization, and to be more likely to extend second-interview invitations and endorse job offers to the applicant. Also, the positive-affect recruiter resulted in more favorable perceptions of how the company treated its employees, although this did not result in feelings of overall job attractiveness or of how well the company rewarded employees. Further, the positive-affect recruiter motivated students to be more willing to attend a second interview, but did not motivate them enough to follow up the interview by phone or to accept a job offer.

The study also found that the amount of information the recruiter offered was significant, in that students expressed how well he represented the company, felt that they would receive further consideration by the company, and perceived greater attractiveness in the job and the company. The more extensive the recruiter information, the more willing the students were to place a follow-up phone call.

In the second experiment, both the job characteristics and the recruiter affect were manipulated to determine how job attractiveness and recruiter behavior influenced students' reactions. The recruiter affect was controlled as in the first experiment. In regard to job attractiveness, two levels were created. One was highly attractive, with excellent starting salary, excellent benefits and working conditions, and a 50 percent chance of obtaining one's preferred location, or at least one of the top three preferences. The less attractive job offered less starting salary, fewer benefits, and no choice of geographical location.

The 178 students were drawn from a second lecture class of the same undergraduate class. These students were 90 percent business majors, 55 percent males, with an average age of 23. Experimental procedures were similar to those in experiment 1. The positive-affect recruiter once again received more favorable evaluations of his performance as a company representative. Also, the students had increased expectancies that he would recommend a second interview or agree with a decision to offer a job. However, unlike the case with experiment 1, recruiter affect did not influence job attractiveness, company attractiveness, or students' willingness to pursue the job offer—a failure to replicate. The manipulation of job attractiveness was strongly related to overall evaluation of job attractiveness, as in such factors as perceptions of how well the company was likely to treat its employees, and willingness to accept second-interview invitations and job offers. No differences were found in willingness to follow up with the recruiter if no contacts were initiated by the company. Finally, with respect to the attractiveness manipulation, students perceived a lower chance of receiving a job offer for the highly attractive job than for the less attractive job.

Summary Review of Research Study 2-2-B   Applicants appear to regard the behavior of the interviewer as signals determining the possibility of receiving job offers. This seems appropriate, since the applicants are the ones selecting those companies they are interested in for interviewing. A problem occurs in regard to the characteristics of the interviewer as they affect the applicant's view of the climate of the company. Only in the first experiment were the interviewer's characteristics found to be associated with how well the organization treated its employees and the acceptance of a second interview. This did not occur in the second experiment. Both experiments found willingness to accept a job offer or attend a second interview to be heavily influenced by job information rather than by the eye contact or smiles of the recruiter. Thus, in this instance, features of the interview appeared more important than interviewer characteristics. The applicants seemed to regard recruiter failure to provide specific job information as a reflection of low recruiter interest in the applicant and/or an attempt to avoid mentioning unattractive job characteristics.

The authors suggest that differences between the two experiments may result from the fact that in experiment 1, the job was presented as if average favorability, whereas in experiment 2, it was presented as above or below average favorability. Perhaps recruiter behaviors have the most influence in jobs that are neither attractive nor unattractive.

Research Study 2-2-C

Do employees who were selected from different recruiting sources demonstrate varying employment tenure?

Decker and Cornelius[3] conducted an extensive study of the personnel records of 2,466 employees from an insurance company, a bank, and a professional abstracting service. The bank sample consisted of all personnel hired; the professional abstracting service sample was of "exempt" personnel; and the insurance company sample was of sales agents. The bank sample contained 514 employees, the professional abstract sample 199 employees, and the insurance company 1,753 employees. The recruitment source of the employee was coded into one of five categories: newspaper advertisements, employment agencies, employee referrals, walk-ins, and "other." Each employee was traced for twelve months. At the end of that time, the employee either had left the company or was still on the payroll. The authors made no distinction between voluntary and involuntary terminations.

It was found, in analyzing the employee quit rate of the three companies by the source of referral, that a consistently good recruiting source was employee referrals and a consistently poor recruiting source was employment agencies. It was also found that the source of referral was significantly related to job tenure in the bank and insurance company samples. The authors report on two other studies, in which employee referrals were the best source of applicants, with newspaper ads and employment agencies generally the worst sources. It is suggested that the reason employee referrals are the best source may be that employees have more accurate information available to them regarding the job, resulting in a more realistic picture of the work and the organization.

Summary Review of Research Study 2-2-C   The study suggests that applicants referred to a company through informal methods, such as employee recommendation, remain with the organization longer than those recruited through more formal methods, such as employment agencies.

Research Study 2-2-D

What effect, if any, does the source by which a person was recruited have upon employee performance, absenteeism, and work attitudes?

Breaugh[4] studied a sample of 112 research scientists, 70 males and 42 females, doing applied research, with college degrees in either biology or chemistry. The data were gathered from the employees through a self-report questionnaire concerning biographical information and work attitudes, plus their personnel files. Four recruiting sources were identified: newspaper ($n = 30$); college placement ($n = 24$); journal/convention advertisement ($n = 26$); and self-initiated ($n = 32$). The absenteeism data were obtained from personnel records, as were the supervisory ratings of the research scientists' performance. A statistical analysis of the demographic variables of the four recruiting sources revealed no significant differences with respect to employee age, sex, years of education, years with the company, years in present position, or years under present supervisor.

The results of the study indicate that the source of recruitment is strongly related to subsequent job performance, absenteeism, and work attitudes. Those employees who were recruited through college placement offices and, to a lesser degree, through newspapers were inferior in performance (quality and dependability) to those establishing company contact on their own initiative or through a professional-journal/convention advertisement.

In regard to absenteeism, employees obtained through newspaper ads missed almost twice as many days as those referred by the other sources. The college-placement-office recruits responded with significantly lower levels of job involvement and satisfaction with their supervisor than did those from the other recruiting sources. The study suggests that college placement offices and newspaper advertisements recruit a poorer type of employee than do journal/convention advertising and self-initiated contacts.

Summary Review of Research Study 2-2-D   The study indicates that the source by which employees are recruited can have significant effect. Recruiting sources appear to affect the quality of employee performance, absenteeism, and work attitudes. The author says that new employees who have complete and accurate knowledge about the new job will be more productive and more satisfied than those with less complete and less accurate information. Since this study is based on a single sample obtained from a single company, any generalizing of results should be done with caution.

REFERENCES

[1]Schmitt, N., and B.W. Coyle, "Applicant Decisions in the Employment Interview," *Journal of Applied Psychology*, 61 (1976), 184–92.

[2]Rynes, S.L., and H.E. Miller, "Recruiter and Job Influences on Candidates for Employment," *Journal of Applied Psychology*, 68 (1983), 147–54.

[3]Decker, P.J., and E.T. Cornelius III, "A Note on Recruiting Sources and Job Survival Rates," *Journal of Applied Psychology*, 64 (1979), 463–64.

[4]Breaugh, J.A., "Relationship between Recruiting Sources and Employee Performances, Absenteeism, and Work Attitudes," *Academy of Management Journal*, 24 (1981), 142–47.

QUESTIONS

1. As the human resource manager, what do you look for in your recruiters? Explain.
2. You are responsible for training a new group of recruiters. What is your program?
3. What appeals to prospective employees in a recruitment session that causes them to become positive about the job and the organization? to become negative? Explain.
4. Job performance, absenteeism, and work attitudes—how are these factors affected by recruiting source? Or are they? Discuss.

Research Incident 2-3:
Mary Moran Hears a Rumor

- How sensitive should a recruiter be to the interpersonal needs of the applicant, and what is the effect of this sensitivity?
- Sometimes the newly hired applicant fails to report to work. What can be done to prevent this from happening?

• What are some techniques to prepare the newly hired applicant for the world of work? How effective are they?

"I'm always the last to know," mused Mary Moran. Here she was, elbow-deep into next year's budget request for her recruiting group, and a rumor kept disrupting her train of thought: "No more outside recruiting." True, she had only overheard the rumor from the next table during a break, but in this company, with its informed, chatty communication style, yesterday's rumor usually became today's accomplished fact.

The company had a long history in the manufacture of machinery for the shoe industry, but in the past ten years, it had phased into the copy machine business and was now progressing into the office communication business. Ten years before, when Mary Moran was put in charge of the new recruiting function, the company had been virtually unknown outside of the shoe business and generated practically no name recognition on college campuses, let alone any enthusiasm to join a shoe company. Yet somehow, Mary and her group had recruited an outstanding pool of talent that now made up nearly all of the present senior-management group. Also, the company now enjoyed an international reputation as one of the top 50 of the *Fortune* 500 group. Of course, with the firm now well regarded as a prosperous and future-oriented organization, unsolicited résumés flooded the human resource office, requiring a special group just to evaluate them and schedule initial interviews. So, unlike the old days, applications far outran the vacancies.

With the annual budget review a fact of life, it was probably time for the recruitment function to come under scrutiny, since management considered its operation a lean machine. Mary broke another point on her pencil and decided to mull over the situation and devise a strategic counter to the rumor, which by now she regarded as fact. A recent personnel article had pointed out that some companies were even considering dropping college recruiting. Mary knew that some of her company's present superstars had been directly recruited from campuses. Would these types approach the company today uncalled, or would some competitor catch them with a red-carpet treatment? On the other hand, Mary thought, there are some problems in the recruiting process, but are they severe enough to cancel it?

RELEVANT EMPIRICAL RESEARCH STUDIES

Research Study 2-3-A

What problems are caused by the recruiter in the recruitment interview? Is there a great difference between the best and the worst interviewer? What problems stem from the recruitee's interpersonal needs as they influence the interview?

Alderfer and McCord[1] studied the problems of the reactions of the recruitee to the recruitment interview. The authors believe that the total needs the recruitee brings to the recruitment interview may represent a part of that person's personality. It would appear that fulfillment of the applicant's interpersonal needs would have an effect upon satisfaction with the recruitment interview, and that this satisfaction would be most likely expressed by acceptance of a job offer. The interpersonal need that may be most relevant would be a mutually trusting and respectful relationship with significant other people. If so, those with high needs would evaluate more positively those recruitment interviews satisfying their interpersonal needs than would those low on such needs.

The study sample was 112 male first- and second-year master's-degree business students, 65 of whom were looking for permanent jobs and 47 of whom were first-year students looking for summer jobs. The 112 represented approximately 50 percent of those master's students looking for a job. They responded to a questionnaire distributed in their mailboxes.

The questionnaire contained two parts relevant for this study. In the first section were two lists of job attributes on different pages. The lists included items such as high salary, predictable future, and advancement opportunities. Each list contained eleven items; the students first ranked them to form the ideal job, then distributed 100 points among the items, with the highest points to those items they preferred and the lowest to those least preferred. They completed the first list before proceeding to the second. Several items were repeated on both lists, although the order differed. Two items were of particular relevance to this study: helpful and cooperative associates, and a boss who provided autonomy, help when needed, and recognition when deserved. These two items served to provide the operational definitions for interpersonal-need strength.

The second part of the questionnaire asked the students to give their impressions of three recruitment interviews they had experienced: the best, the worst, and one considered average. The first two questions asked the students to estimate the probability that they would receive a job offer and the probability that they would accept it. Following were 17 six-point Likert Scale items dealing with the student's observations about the interview; they were developed from a group interview with some second-year students engaged in a job search.

The results of the study for the second part of the questionnaire demonstrated several ways the best interviews can be distinguished from the worst. There was a significant mean estimate of .73 for receiving a job offer from the best interviews, .23 for the worst interviews, and .54 for the average interviews. Regardless of the estimate of the interview, the likelihood of accepting a job offer was always less than the likelihood of receiving an offer. The data also indicated a significant relationship between a recruitee's expectation of receiving a job offer and of accepting it. Of the 17 items on the second part of the questionnaire, 15 significantly discriminated between the best and worst recruitment interviews.

The recruitee evaluated certain perceived behaviors of the recruiter to determine whether the interview was evaluated highly. The desired recruiter behaviors included the recruiter's being able and willing to answer questions, telling about other M.B.A.'s careers, asking the candidate to discuss his strengths and weaknesses, asking a technical question, indicating the distinct possibility of a high salary, and being familiar with the recruitee's background.

The perceived recruiter attitudes made a difference in evaluating the interview more positively. The interview was considered more positive if the recruiter seemed interested in the recruitee's particular contribution, and if the recruiter appeared to be a successful younger person.

From the recruitee's point of view, a positive evaluation of the recruitment interview resulted from the recruitee's being very interested in getting an offer, feeling that he could handle anything the recruiter asked, and liking and trusting the recruiter. However, if the recruitee became uncomfortable during the interview, this tended to lead to a negative evaluation.

The perceived interview characteristics that were significantly related to expecting to receive a job offer were the recruiter's being willing and able to answer questions, appearing interested in the recruitee, understanding the M.B.A. point of view, being trustworthy and likeable, being interested in the recruitee's contribution and familiar with his background, seeming to be a successful younger person, and not causing the recruitee to be uncomfortable. Of this group, the highest correlation was with showing an interest in the recruitee's contribution.

The interaction between the need strengths as measured by the first part of the questionnaire and the perceived interpersonal-need satisfaction scale characteristics was analyzed, with unexpected results. The interpersonal-need satisfaction scale represented those 17 questionnaire items that seemed to indicate that the recruitee would feel more respected and valued if these characteristics were found in the interview. The analysis was made by correlating the two and testing the difference between the best and worst interviews. The significant correlation between the need for respect from associates and interpersonal-need satisfaction was .357 in the worst interviews and $-.012$ in the best. The significant correlation between need for respect from superiors and interpersonal-need satisfaction was .336 in the worst interviews and $-.227$ in the best. It appears that the recruitees with higher interpersonal-needs experienced less satisfaction in the best interviews than did those with lower interpersonal needs. Further, those recruitees with higher interpersonal needs tended to experience more need satisfaction in the worst interviews than did those with lower interpersonal needs. This suggests that those with high interpersonal needs will not find even the best recruiting interviews as interpersonally satisfying as will those with lower needs. There appears to be an absolute level of the interpersonal climate that is reached in the recruitment interview.

Summary Review of Research Study 2-3-A   The perceived satisfaction of the interpersonal needs of applicants is related to their positive evaluation of the recruitment interview. Supportive, interested recruiter behavior may result in positive applicant reaction. Positive applicant reaction may also result from the interview itself if questions are asked that are technically relevant to the applicant's field and require evaluation of his or her strengths and weaknesses. Although the questions may appear confronting rather than supportive, they do allow the applicant to demonstrate competence and may result in a positive reaction. The perceptions of the applicants that the recruiter was interested and supportive of them was related to their evaluation of the interview, to their expectation of receiving a job offer, and to their expectation of accepting the job offer. However, the perception of the recruiter's asking the applicants to confront their strengths and limitations was related only to the evaluation of the interview, not to the expectation of either receiving or accepting a job offer. The recruiter's discussion of other M.B.A. careers was significantly related to expecting to accept a job offer but not to expecting to receive a job offer. The applicant's interest in receiving a job offer was related to expecting to accept a job offer rather than to expecting to receive one. The positive correlation of expecting to receive and expecting to accept the job offer was significant within the best, worst, and average types of recruitment interviews.

Certain recruiter traits and behaviors are related to the stated likelihood of an applicant's accepting a job offer. So if the recruiter states that a high salary is possible, tells of other M.B.A.s' careers, and appears successful and young, the probability is higher that the applicant will accept a job offer.

The unexpected finding was the relationship between the needs of the applicant and the satisfactions resulting from the recruitment interviews. Those for whom interpersonal needs are quite important were not as likely to see even the best interviews as interpersonally satisfying as were those with lower interpersonal needs. This suggests that there may be an absolute level of the interpersonal climate in a recruiting interview.

The authors suggest some limitations of the present study, in that the students' retrospective accounts of their interviews may be distorted from memory losses and peer discussions with others who had seen the same recruiter.

Research Study 2-3-B

One of the problems that arises in the recruiting process is the result of the recruiter's success. The applicant is made an offer by the company and accepts, but never shows up on the agreed date to begin employment. What can the company do to ensure that those they hire will actually go to work?

Ivancevich and Donnelly[2] conducted a study of the effects of a positive reinforcement program on college seniors who rescind a job-offer acceptance previously made. A survey was made of 19 large industrial corporations to determine the number of college graduates who, after accepting a position, either later rejected it or never showed up. All 19 companies reported a back-out rate; some indicated that it was over 16 percent.

Of the original 19, two companies agreed to participate in the study. One, located in New York, in the preceding year had hired, through the main corporate office, 131 college seniors in business administration and liberal arts for nontechnical positions. The other company, located in Chicago, in the preceding year had hired 140 college graduates in engineering and physical science for technical positions. The New York company had had a back-out rate of 10.9 percent.

The study lasted for 18 months, during which time the New York company received 186 formal job-offer acceptances from college seniors and the Chicago company received 206. As the acceptances were received, the applicants were assigned alternately to a control group and an experimental group, resulting in 196 in each group.

These college seniors had had other possible job alternatives before accepting the offers by these companies. A random sample of 20 percent of those who accepted the job offer and then backed out showed that each had had at least one other job offer. For those who accepted and reported for work, the average was 3.6 job offers; those who backed out averaged 3.3.

The control-group seniors were sent some company literature and a confirmation that their letters of acceptance had been received by the personnel department. Those in the experimental group were sent the same literature and confirmation, but they also received three randomly spaced personal telephone calls from the personnel office, pointing out positive factors about the company and the correctness of the college senior's choice. The first call was made as soon as the formal acceptance of the job offer was received in the personnel office. Those in the personnel office who did the telephoning (six persons in New York and seven in Chicago) emphasized opportunities for advancement, the challenge in the work, the positive aspects of the community, and other, similar advantages.

The results of the study show that the New York company experienced a 2.15 percent back-out rate for the experimental group versus a 10.75 percent back-out rate for the control group. This difference was significant at less than a .02 level of significance. For the Chicago company, the back-out rate was 2.91 percent for the experimental group versus 10.68 percent for the control group. This was a significant difference at less than a .05 level of significance. The positive reinforcement programs used in both companies appear to have had a significant effect on lowering the back-out rate.

Summary Review of Research Study 2-3-B The study investigated the effects of a positive reinforcement program on the back-out rate of college seniors who officially accepted a company job offer. The experimental sample was 196 college seniors who had accepted offers in technical and nontechnical positions in two firms, one in New York and the other in Chicago. The positive reinforcement program consisted of three random phone calls from the personnel office stressing the benefits of company employment and the wise choice of the recruitee. The result of the program was a significant reduction in the number of college seniors who backed out of their earlier formal acceptance of the job offer.

Research Study 2-3-C

Most information of a realistic nature that is presented to the recruitee is given prior to the decision of whether or not to join the organization. What would be the effect of giving the recruitee realistic information about the job after the decision to join has been made but prior to his or her reporting for work? Will such information aid the recruitee in coping with the new environment? Will this reduce turnover?

A different approach to the problem of recruitee resignations was presented by Ilgen and Seely[3] in a study of new cadets entering the U.S. Military Academy. New cadets report to the academy two months prior to the start of the school year to undergo an intensive familiarization program to help them avoid what could be a physically and psychologically stressful adjustment to their new environment. A booklet had been developed to candidly describe the two-month summer training and the daily routine of the school year. It contained interviews and critical incidents obtained from the regular cadets and officers. Included were the mundane and stressful activities that are not usually included in promotional material. Booklet drafts had been circulated among regular cadets and officers to obtain feedback on the accuracy and relevance of the material.

The booklet was distributed to the new cadets the first week of June, with the two-month familiarization program beginning July 1. A random sample of 234 new cadets received the booklet, and a control group of 234 were randomly selected to not receive the booklet.

The results of the study were based on voluntary resignations over the two-month summer familiarization period for the experimental and control groups. During this period, 27 from the control group resigned and 14 from the experimental group who received the booklet. This difference was significant at less than a .05 level of significance. It appears that the candid information presented after the decision to join had been made but before entering the organization reduced the number of cadets who chose to voluntarily resign.

Summary Review of Research Study 2-3-C   This study examined the effects on turnover of giving realistic information about the organization to new recruitees who are about to join. The information was based on interviews and critical incidents to be encountered in a psychologically and physically stressful two-month training period. After the recruitees had decided to join the U.S. Military Academy but prior to their reporting, a random experimental sample was sent this realistic information in a booklet, and a random control sample was not. At the end of the two months' training, the turnover rate of the experimental sample was significantly lower than that of the control sample. The authors attribute the lower turnover to the effects of the realistic information contained in the booklet.

REFERENCES

[1]Alderfer, C.P., and C.G. McCord, "Personal and Situational Factors in the Recruitment Interview," *Journal of Applied Psychology*, 54 (1970), 377–85.

[2]Ivancevich, J.M., and J.H. Donnelly, "Job Offer Acceptance Behavior and Reinforcement," *Journal of Applied Psychology*, 55 (1971), 119–22.

[3]Ilgen, D.R., and W. Seely, "Realistic Expectations as an Aid in Reducing Voluntary Resignation," *Journal of Applied Psychology*, 59 (1974), 452–55.

QUESTIONS

1. What types of questions affect the recruitee's evaluation of the recruitment interview? of the recruiter? Discuss implications.
2. What was the "unexpected result" of the Alderfer and McCord study? Discuss relative to structuring the recruitment interview.
3. How can the human resource department overcome the problem of successful recruiting in which the recruitee formally accepts the company job offer but never shows up for employment? Does the solution require a complex procedure? Are there any possible negative effects? Explain.
4. What effect can realistic information about the stressful environment of an organization have upon the turnover of new organizational members? Explain.

NON-EMPIRICAL RESEARCH ARTICLE ABSTRACTS

Abstract 2-1

- Should recruitment be a permanent position or a stepping stone to "richer" personnel functions, such as compensation and benefits administration, or training and development?
- Why does the nature of corporate recruiting work against its success?
- How does the climate within the organization affect successful recruitment qualities?

Donn L. Dennis,[1] Director of Professional Staffing, Allied Bancshares, Inc., Houston, Texas, answers these questions in a 1984 article.

The author points out that although the recruitment function is considered a definite part of the personnel department, line management considers it to be inefficient and a necessary evil, candidates view recruiters as unimaginative junior-level bureaucrats, and personnel professionals regard recruiting positions as merely an entry into more demanding human resource administration positions.

Contributing to this low regard for the recruiting function is the fact that it has a process rather than a project orientation. That is, other personnel functions can culminate in completed projects and studies, but recruiters are engaged in a never-ending process of searching for many applicants for a variety of jobs at one time, constantly dividing their attention rather than concentrating it. This process of searching never ends; it is always in progress.

Another contributing factor is that the position of recruiter is not recognized as requiring a specialist. A national search firm even advertised it as requiring no previous experience. All one needs to be a recruiter is people skills; and since anyone in a supervisory position believes he or she has people skills, every supervisor is a recruiter. These supervisors may not understand wage and salary analysis, labor relations, or training and development programs, but they still believe they can do recruiting. The author says that this attitude results in "back-seat drivers" who believe as supervisors that they could easily do the recruiter's work if only they had more time.

These problems stem from a lack of direction, a lack of understanding, and a lack of support. To overcome the lack of direction requires a linkage to management development as part of corporate strategic planning. This would require the corporate recruitment effort to have one paramount purpose: to assist the organization in filling open positions with qualified people who produce career path patterns that are acceptable to the organization. By the tying of qualifications and career development to corporate planning, a measure of direction is applied to the recruitment process.

The author cites a lack of understanding by management of the nature and function of the corporate recruitment effort. Several misconceptions about recruiting by line managers are listed: the belief that the function of the recruiter is to hire, whereas actually, most recruiters only screen; the belief that employment agencies should never, or should always, be used, overlooking these agencies' value in certain circumstances and the cost of overuse; the belief that advertising for a position is adequate for the placement task; the belief that professional-level positions can be and should be filled quickly, without recognizing that the recruiter may be attempting to fill 15 positions at once; and the belief that the cost of recruitment is not high, which fails to recognize the 30 percent agency fees, the cost of a vacant slot, and the costs of relocation.

The problem of lack of support includes management's cavalier attitude toward interviewing procedures, such as often canceling interviews on short notice. Lack of support is also indicated by having no methods to measure recruitment effectiveness and not providing rewards for the successful recruiter. When the corporation believes that recruiters are unskilled and replaceable, the result is a high turnover rate. Such lack of support is indicated by management's frequently working directly with the candidates and agencies, effectively bypassing the recruiter.

The author believes that successful recruitment depends on the organization. It requires that for recruitment selection, the organization recognize that it takes a special breed to succeed as a recruiter and that success will vary in different organizations. The successful recruiter requires intelligence, enthusiasm, communication skills, self-confidence, persistence, a mind for detail, and ability to represent the company. Further, recruiters must be trained in what the organization is attempting to accomplish through its recruitment effort—its organizational philosophy and objectives. It is important that recruiters be knowledgeable about the positions they are attempting to fill and understand the relationship of those positions to the organization. They need to know current legal requirements affecting the recruitment process, as well as the organization's compensation, training, and communications programs.

Once this training has been accomplished, the effective recruitment effort requires effective procedures. Flexible standards need to be established for avoiding slow turnaround for hiring decisions and reimbursement of expenses; nonprepayment of major interviewing expenses; inconsistent candidate evaluations owing to lack of standards and formalized procedures; poor use of employment advertising and employment agencies; problems of identifying, storing, and retrieving candidate information; and inability to measure the recruiting workload and recruiting success.

The author concludes that recruitment is a staff service function. Its effectiveness requires senior management's concern and the involvement of the managers doing the hiring in the recruitment process. This means that managers must possess some knowledge of recruitment costs, interviewing techniques, and the legal requirements of equal opportunity/ affirmative action. Given this attention, corporate recruitment can better serve the objectives of the organization.

REFERENCE

[1] "Are Recruitment Efforts Designed to Fail?" by Donn L. Dennis, copyright September 1984. Reprinted with the permission of *Personnel Journal,* Costa Mesta, California; all rights reserved.

QUESTIONS

1. According to this article, how is the recruiting function viewed by the organization and its managers?
2. How do recruiters regard their position in the human resource hierarchy? What contributes to this perception? What is the result?
3. Suggest specific changes that may be needed in an organization to help provide the recruiting function with a more professional status. How would you implement these changes?

Abstract 2-2

- How does a direct-mailing recruitment program fit into a company's overall advertising budget?
- What are the mechanics of a direct-mailing recruitment program, and what is the availability of support sources?
- To whom is the direct-mailing recruitment program directed, and how can their interest in the company be stimulated?

Richard Siedlecki, a principal of Market-Direct Advertising, Mission Viejo, California, has written an article that answers these questions.[1]

The author points out that a direct-mailing program not only reinforces the company's current advertising campaign but also helps to locate the hard-to-find prospects. The result could be an advantage over other companies that are competing for the same job candidates. Direct mailing usually has a higher cost per reader and respondent than do other media;

yet it may be the most effective medium when the cost is compared to the quality of the new hires.

Several suggestions are offered for planning a direct-mail recruitment plan. The author says that it is necessary to determine the objective the company is trying to achieve within budgetary constraints. This requires developing a profile of the prospective recruits as to who they are and whether the budget permits a local, statewide, regional, national, or international search. Also, a decision must be made as to sources used to obtain the prospects' names, such as associations, trade organizations, and current employees.

The next suggestion is the type of corporate image to develop. The company could project images of being big, loaded with benefits, and fast growing, or of encouraging management team participation. Such an image should project company position that would distinguish the firm from other companies in the same industry. The author suggests that results from the direct mailing may be more contingent upon how the company is positioned than how the mailing itself is written.

So it is important to select the best people-oriented benefit relative to that job opening—that is, a distinctive and competitive idea that will directly benefit the prospect. This becomes the company's promise to that person.

Another suggestion is to outline the major points to be emphasized in the mailing. This will enable the copywriter to highlight the company's philosophy, its leadership position in the industry, and how the particular job opening is part of the overall company plan for success.

Finally, obtain three to five different mailing lists from various list directories to test their effectiveness. These can be obtained from Standard Rate and Data Service, Inc., 5201 Old Orchard Road, Skokie, IL 60077. Other list sources include magazine subscriber lists, professional associations, trade groups, credit organizations, business directories, and special-interest groups. There are also list brokers, list managers, list compilers, and direct-mail specialists whose names can be obtained from Direct Mail/Marketing Association, 6 East 43rd Street, New York, NY 10017.

The mechanics of the mailing (folding, stuffing, sealing, mailing) can be handled by the company if the number involved is small. In this case, the *Mailer's Guide,* which can be obtained from the local U.S. Postal Service, will be valuable. For a large mailing, a mailing house or lettershop may be preferred. Contact the Mail Advertising Service Association, 7315 Wisconsin Avenue, Station 818-E, Bethesda, MD 20814, for a list of members.

A timetable should be established showing copywriting deadlines, mailing dates, and expected response dates. Also, track the costs of the mailing, including a cost per inquiry and a cost-to-hire analysis. The mailing should be coded to indicate type of career person mailed to, date of mailing, and type of job opening, to further analyze the effectiveness of the mailing.

The author indicates that in any direct-mail recruitment campaign, half the battle is to get the recipient to open the envelope. Teasers on the outside of the envelope may help, such as, "To the engineer who's looking to make $50,000 this year," or, "Personal and confidential."

The letter enclosed in the mailing should be of sufficient length to get the message across, perhaps two to four pages. However, length limits are arbitrary, since the prospect will read longer letters if they are readable, interesting, benefit-oriented, and personal.

The letter should be warm and human, stressing the employment opportunities and the benefits. The job qualifications should be outlined in the letter. The sign-off portion of the letter should request a response such as mailing the enclosed card or telephoning during certain hours. A postscript, which is usually read, presents the opportunity to state a final short, strong message.

Including a well-designed flyer or brochure is helpful, showing pictures of people involved in their work, not pictures of company executives or of buildings. A simple one-color piece is adequate.

Included in the mailing is a postpaid response card designed to make it easy for the person to respond. The offer contained in the letter should be summed up on the card so that the sender will know what to expect by return mail. Included on the card is space for the sender to note names and addresses of other prospects. These names represent one of the lowest-cost referrals. Also, include space to indicate "not interested" but where recipients can write in a job title they *would* be interested in.

The author concludes that direct-mail recruitment is developing into an important medium for all sizes of companies. It is a personal, flexible, and testable medium that works well with existing company recruitment advertising programs.

REFERENCE

[1]"Creating a Direct Mail Recruitment Program," by Richard Siedlecki, copyright April 1983. Reprinted with the permission of *Personnel Journal*, Costa Mesta, California; all rights reserved.

QUESTIONS

1. What is meant by the positioning strategy of the company's direct-mail recruitment program? Is this the same as corporate image?
2. Since half the battle of any direct mailing is to get the recipient to open the envelope, what can be done to ensure this?
3. The letter enclosed in the direct-mail recruitment program should be two to four pages in length. However, it may be longer. What is the reasoning offered by the author?

CHAPTER THREE

SELECTION: APPLICATION BLANK

INTRODUCTION

When a well-designed application blank is completed by the applicant, it becomes an important source of information to the human resource specialist. At the professional white-collar level, the application blank and the résumé are probably the two most important documents in supplying the employer with information about the applicant at this early stage of the employment process. Of the two, the application blank offers the easiest method by which to substantiate applicant information, since résumés are increasingly written by professional employment consultants whose writing skills may exceed the employment skills of their clients. At both the white- and blue-collar levels, a well-designed application blank requires the applicant to organize past data in a format that helps to eliminate generalities and fuzzy details. That the information on the application blank must be true and accurate becomes clear to applicants when they are requested to sign their names attesting to its truth and accuracy, with inaccuracies cause for dismissal.

Perhaps this is why so many companies, for all positions, with the possible exception of the highest level, insist that applicants complete and sign application blanks. Application blanks vary from company to company, and they may also vary within a company for different levels of positions. Thus, the level at which the applicant applies may determine the type of application blank to be used. For top-level management, a résumé or a letter using a similar style format is all that is required. At other levels, standard application blanks are more likely to be used to obtain the routine administrative detail such as name, address, phone, Social Security number, education, training, and work experience. The result is an organized approach that quickly and efficiently obtains a variety of information about the applicant. The completed application blank becomes an important link between recruitment and selection, since it provides another avenue of applicant data to evaluate and, if necessary, to explore.

The value of the application blank to the human resource specialist is demonstrated by its tendency to grow as new items are added. Care must be taken to include only those items that are actually used in the selection process and that meet federal and state fair-employment interpretations. It should be pointed out that federal law, guidelines, and court decisions do not prohibit any questions on the application blank other than those concerning arrests. However, other inquiries must be job-related and cannot be used to discriminate, with the burden of proof upon the employer.

Unfortunately, many employers, in an effort to avoid discrimination charges, have eliminated many past standard information items on the application blank. Although individual state laws may be more stringent than federal legislation, employers may ask for an applicant's race on the application blank. This in itself is not illegal. However, such an item must be job-related and not used to discriminate. For instance, if the race question is asked but no members of a certain racial group are being hired, the company can be successfully challenged. Even a simple question asking the salary expected in the next five years can be an indication of discriminatory intent if the company is unable to demonstrate a business purpose for that question. An item asking an applicant's age is not illegal if the company can demonstrate a job-related reason for including it. A more difficult item to ask would be height and weight, since that appears to rule out protected groups such as women and certain ethnic groups. Yet as specific job requirements, such as for police and prison guards, such questions are legal. Even marital status may be asked on the application blank as long as it is asked of both sexes, unless the state law prohibits it (as in California). Since federal law allows companies to have a no-spouse hiring rule, depending upon the state, this question can be asked, but it must be asked of both sexes.

Other questions that, on the surface, may create problems for the employer but are legal if job-related include the husband's or wife's occupation and the length of time at present address. It may be difficult for the employer to prove that such questions do not discriminate against women in regard to pay (for example, that if the husband earns good money, the woman may be paid less) and against certain ethnic groups who tend to change addresses frequently.

The area of physical characteristics is one that requires careful consideration. For instance, the employer would find it extremely difficult to defend having similar positions with different physical-characteristics requirements. The question of physical characteristics is further complicated by the fact that several state laws are more stringent than federal laws. One procedure that companies use is to first ask the applicant to complete a preemployment medical history. The assumption here is that the applicant is more apt to be honest in written statements than in oral ones. Again, the questions should be tailored for individual jobs, since a history of rheumatic fever may not be job-related to ineffectiveness at a particular position. However, consideration should be given to health questions that would be important in a situation requiring emergency treatment on the company premises. Perhaps the safest approach in developing physical-characteristics items for the application blank is to consult with a physician. This does create special problems, since the physician needs to be familiar with the jobs in question before deciding upon any restrictions. Also, when job descriptions change, the physician will need to be consulted again.

References have been a standard item on application blanks, although their use appears to be decreasing. Research has demonstrated their rather low correlation with success on the job. Correlation has increased somewhat in the case of unstructured letters of recommendation requested from employers as opposed to use of the standardized questionnaire. However, the unstructured letters require interpretation by the prospective employer that may not be accurate. In addition, the equal opportunity laws have caused many employers to reconsider the reference application-blank item because of the legal interpretations regarding invasion of privacy. Without detailing the legal niceties, an employer may be sued for releasing detrimental employee information when such information is revealed to the public. Usually, the public is considered a small group of people; when such detrimental information is revealed to only one person, the employer is usually safe from a judgment. The defense offered by the employer is the qualified-privilege doctrine holding that the employer acted in his own interests or those of the public. Generally, courts have held that the public good is best served by the free exchange of information between the prospective employer and the former employer.

The accuracy or validity of information provided by the applicant on the application blank may vary considerably on certain items. Some distortion of the facts occurs quite regularly, but there are occasions when the information presented is completely false. Some of the most common violations are in time spent in previous employment, overstatement of rate of pay, and reasons for leaving the previous employment.

Thus, wording becomes a delicate matter, since state and federal laws examine every aspect of the application blank. It would be impossible to have a separate application blank for every job, so the best compromise (other than eliminating all suspicious items) is to design one that is flexible and designates the questions that apply only to certain jobs. Applicants would need to answer only those questions that are job-related, so the specter of intent to discriminate diminishes.

An approach to scoring the application blank in an objective manner is the weighted application. This method helps to overcome the problem of selection and wording of questions on the application blank, since these questions are now related to some measure of job success. More common usage of the weighted application blank has been for salary increases, absenteeism, job turnover, and success predictions. An advantage of this system is the ready availability of application blanks over a period of time, since they are continually being filled out, thus allowing a study to begin immediately. The requirements are quite simple: a specified time period, a specific job or personnel category, and the variable (turnover, absenteeism) to be investigated.

The weighting of the application-blank items is relatively straightforward. There are more complex (and perhaps confusing) techniques that do not add much more validity. The secret here, as in other statistical applications, is to obtain a large enough sample size to receive the benefits of the normal distribution. One such simple method is to take a large sample and divide it at the median into high and low groups based on the variable to be investigated (turnover, absenteeism, and so on). The application blanks completed during the designated period are then checked to determine how many in the low and in the high groups answered the particular question or item. Then a total is determined and converted into a percentage of those responding in the same way, which, when rounded off, becomes the weight. An analysis is then made to determine what answers to the questions or items appear to identify particular people with the variable being investigated. First, merely "eyeballing" the scores between the low group and the high group would indicate how responses from such categories as marital status, education, work experience, military service, and the like, distinguish the two groups. In fact, by use of the weights, three or four response categories may score high enough to be used only as a predictor of the variable being investigated. An interesting aspect of the weighted application blank is that there appear to be no responses that are universally predictive. Some of the responses and combinations of responses are difficult to explain in any logical context. For some, the weighted application may appear to be less science and more chance.

Similar to the weighted application blank is the biographical inventory, which has even less general support. The biographical inventory usually contains a large number of items in a multiple-choice format that are not covered in the standard application blank. These include values, opinions, interests, attitudes, hobbies, social relations, health, and so forth. For instance, one question might ask how creative the applicant is, with a choice to be selected from several descriptions, ranging from "less creative than most" to "more highly creative than most." The items selected are viewed as predictors. They are weighted by the same process used in the weighted application blank. However, a cross-validation process deletes from the final form those items failing to distinguish between the low and high job occupants. A requirement for both techniques is a continual updating of response categories, since change does occur over time.

Even the best-designed application blank, thoroughly and honestly completed by the applicant, can become an ineffective instrument in the employment process when subjected to the individual value systems of decision makers. Human resource professionals look to training as the method to solve such organizational problems, but although effective, it is an expensive, time-consuming, continuing activity that has to be allocated on a priority basis. With that in mind, a quick "Band-Aid" approach to overcoming decision makers' occasional irrational preferences is to have them preview the application prior to meeting the applicant. This appears to be an effective method, with advantages and disadvantages as indicated in this chapter by two empirical journal articles.

In the past, the employment application blank has always been an important instrument, a source of applicant information that helped determine whether the selection process would continue and also indicated further areas of required investigation. Then, with the advent of equal opportunity laws, employees became wary of the application blank as a predictive and investigative instrument. Today, the application blank is being reevaluated as a powerful and valid instrument in the employment process.

RESEARCH INCIDENTS

Research Incident 3-1:
The Employment Application and Betty Brown

- How accurate are handicapped persons in an interview session when providing information about their disability and employment history?
- How many discrepancies are revealed when the information provided by applicants on their application blanks is verified with previous employers?
- Do employees exhibit prejudice toward disabled applicants? Is more prejudice exhibited toward certain disabilities?
- What value can be placed on references? Is there a better method?

Betty Brown had been hired two months previously as a food handler in the company cafeteria. Her employment application showed that she was 48 years old, was married with three children (none of whom now lived at home), and that for the past ten years, her husband had been employed as a janitor. Betty's past work history included four previous jobs with other companies in food service. The unemployed intervals between these jobs were explained as the result of either the closing down of cafeterias, sickness in the family, or the need to be home caring for growing children. The company had administered a battery of tests, including the Otis Intelligence Scale and the Wonderlic Personality Inventory. Betty's scores were slightly below average but at an adequate level for work as a food handler. A company physician had examined Betty and found her health satisfactory. References from past employers indicated that she was a satisfactory employee.

Since the company was doing work for the Department of Defense, a routine security check was initiated for this nonsensitive position. Now, two months later, the security check was forwarded to the personnel office. The report disclosed that Betty Brown was an epileptic and that she had listed on her employment application only those positions she had voluntarily quit, not those from which she had been fired because of her condition. This explained the satisfactory references from past employers. Her condition was controllable with medication, so it was not detected during the company physical. Since the company already employed several handicapped people, Betty's physical condition was not of immediate concern, but her deliberate concealment of information on the employment application raised the question of whether she should be retained as an employee.

RELEVANT EMPIRICAL
RESEARCH STUDIES

Research Study 3-1-A

How accurate is the information provided by the applicant on the employment application?

Weiss and Davis[1] investigated the employment problems of the physically handicapped. By use of an interview approach, 91 physically handicapped people and their relatives were asked a series of questions. Only the interviewer and the person being interviewed were present during the session. Since the interview was part of a process by which the handicapped person would receive financial assistance, one would expect the interview to be taken seriously. Of the 91 interviews, 39 were with the handicapped person and 52 were with an adult relative of the handicapped person. The interviews were designed to gather factual material relating to the handicapped person's disability and employment history. The personal information that was collected relative to the disability was validated from agency records. It included age, sex, marital status, education, veteran status, nature of disability, age at disablement, and whether the person had received assistance from the agency. The other source of validation was employers, who were sent a questionnaire asking employee information as to job title, job duties, hours, pay, and length of employment.

The results of the study indicated no significant difference in the accuracy of the information obtained from the handicapped persons and that from the adult relatives. The least invalid item was the sex of the handicapped person. A low of 10 percent invalidity was found on the nature of the disability. The highest invalidity, 50 percent, resulted from the question of having received agency assistance. Relatively high percentages of invalidity occurred on length of employment, age at disablement, education, pay, and job titles. On items pertinent to employment, there was a median invalidity of 22 percent, and on items of personal history, a median invalidity of 12.5 percent but with a range of 0 to 55 percent.

Summary Review of Research Study 3-1-A   It appears that information from secondary sources can be as trustworthy as that from primary sources, since information obtained from relatives of the handicapped was as valid as information obtained from the handicapped themselves. The validity of answers varied with the type of information. It ranged from 100 percent for the sex of the person to 50 percent for whether any agency assistance had been received.

This suggests the need to validate each interview question. Further, it questions the research value of interview data whose validity depends upon the rapport between interviewer and interviewee. The largest amount of invalidity was in the question of agency assistance, although relatively large amounts of invalidity were found in length of employment, job title, and pay. These responses may be occasioned by considerations of ego and social responsibility. The authors find the assumption that interview data are valid to be indefensible based upon the present study and other related studies.

Research Study 3-1-B

In another study of accuracy, Goldstein[2] examined the data provided on an application blank for a sample of 111 job applicants. This information was matched with that of previous employers. The applications were for the position of nursing aide in a group of nursing homes located in a large eastern city and owned by one corporation. The data were collected over a nine-month period. Information collected from the application blanks and sent to previous employers for verification included marital status, position held, dates of employment, salary of employee, and why the employee left. The 111 employers' responses to the survey said that 15 percent of the applicants had never worked for them. Married females who might have been employed under their maiden names were excluded from .his count. On a positive note, the largest amount of agreement between applicant and past employer was on the previous position held. However, the highest percentage of disagreement was on the reason for leaving the employer. These disagreements were 25 percent of the total and were clear-cut; for example, the applicant reported leaving because of low pay but was actually dismissed for violation of company rules. Discrepancies were largest for duration of previous service and salary earned. There was 57 percent disagreement on the length of employment service. Most of the applicants overestimated rather than underestimated their employment time, with the average overestimation being 16 months.

Summary Review of Research Study 3-1-B   A substantial number of discrepancies occurred between the responses on the application blanks and information provided by the previous employer. However, this was not true of all employees; of the 94 that were verified as being past employees, the employers found 31 sets of data accurate. The remaining 63 employers found inaccuracies in two of the following four categories that were examined: previous position held, duration of employment, previous salary earned, and reason for leaving.

The author finds that inaccurate information is as likely to surface on the application blank as in an interview, since the pressure to obtain a job is equal in both situations. Interview studies find the most inaccurate information in duration of previous employment and previous salary earned. These were also the two most inaccurate categories in this present study of application blanks.

Research Study 3-1-C

How perceptive was Betty Brown as to the negative effect her condition would have upon the interviewer's evaluation?

Rickard and others[3] conducted a study of prejudice toward various disabilities, using an instrument of 56 stimulus items to measure social distance. The instrument, a questionnaire modified by the author, attempts to describe a person on a number of characteristics rather than just one. For the present study, the instrument was developed to include disability (deaf, confined to a wheelchair, epileptic, discharged from a mental institution, discharged from a prison, discharged from a tuberculosis sanatorium, and with no physical defect), sex (male or female), competence (barely competent, highly competent), and sociability (sociable, unsociable). Using all possible combinations, 56 items were constructed; for example, a deaf male, highly competent, unsociable; or a deaf female, highly competent, unsociable; and so on. These 56 items were randomly tested in the instrument, with instructions to indicate feelings about hiring such a person by circling a response on a seven-point scale ranging from "strongly recommend" to "strongly oppose."

The instrument may be scored in different ways, but since the present study was concerned with employer prejudice, scoring was relevant to that purpose. Thus, two scores were obtained: a prejudice score of individual employers toward each disability, and a prejudice score for a group of employers. These are called the Index of Individual Employer Prejudice and the Index of Group Employer Prejudice. Two potential types of employers hiring disabled persons were surveyed with the questionnaire: 25 personnel directors, and 87 school administrators and potential administrators enrolled in a college class in school administration. The questionnaire was completed by the personnel directors for only an accountant position; the school administrators filled it out for both the positions of accountant and third-grade teacher.

The results of the study show that both groups displayed significantly higher prejudice scores for each disability group than for the nondisabled group. The only exception to this was that the personnel directors were not prejudiced between the tuberculosis group and the nondisabled group. The school administrators' scores were significantly more prejudiced for both the accountant and teacher positions when considering the deaf, the epileptic, and the wheelchair groups; however, there was more prejudice when the disabled person was being considered for the teacher position.

The personnel directors, when asked to consider applicants with each disability as candidates for an accountant position, indicated that the epileptic would be the disability most opposed, with a prison record a poor second. The school administrators said the same about candidates for third-grade teacher—the epileptic was most opposed, with a prison record a poor second. However, when the administrators were asked about hiring an accountant, a reversal took place; the prison record became the most opposed, the epileptic a poor second, and a mental-hospital record third. Since the Rickard instrument also measures factors influencing the employment ratings—namely, sex, competence, and sociability—an analysis was made of the personnel directors' decisions. For all the six disabilities, the personnel directors indicated that competence would exert the greatest influence in the (positive) hiring decision. However, of the six disabilities, the competence influence would be highest for tuberculosis and lowest for the epileptic.

Summary Review of Research Study 3-1-C   The employers were prejudiced toward disabled applicants, who were rejected more significantly than were nondisabled applicants. Although the prejudice strength varied among the disabilities, it was stronger toward the epileptic and those discharged from prison than toward those discharged from a tuberculosis sanitarium.

The personnel directors and school administrators displayed similar prejudices. However, the school administrators were more prejudiced toward the prison-discharged person than toward the epileptic, and were generally less prejudiced than the personnel directors, except for the tuberculosis type. Also, the school administrators demonstrated more prejudice in the third-grade teacher position than in the accountant position.

Sex appeared not to be important in qualifying for the accountant position for people who were ex-tuberculars, in wheelchairs, deaf, or epileptic. However, the female sex was a significant negative factor in rating prison parolees or ex-mental patients. The sociability factor was significant in all cases, being almost as important as the disability. Yet competence exerted the greatest influence in hiring the disabled. The authors suggest that increased competence for the disabled, attained through overtraining, may compensate for prejudice toward disabled applicants.

Research Study 3-1-D

With the possibility of so much unreliable information appearing on the application blank, what value can be placed on the references?

A study by Carroll and Nash[4] indicated that the conventional reference check was of little practical value. Instead, the authors suggest that references complete a forced-choice reference check on the applicant. They designed a forced-choice reference check instrument that was validated on a sample of 111 clerical employees at the University of Maryland. The instrument contained a series of pairs of positive-sounding statements from which the reference would choose one. An example would be, "has many worthwhile ideas" or "completes all assignments." Another example: "always works fast" or "requires little supervision."

Summary Review of Research Study 3-1-D　Carroll and Nash concluded that the negative conclusions in the literature about the validity of the reference check would be reversed if a forced-choice approach were used. In determining the predictive validity of the forced-choice reference check, the authors found some interesting exceptions. The forced choice was not predictive if the previous job held by the applicant was substantially different from the current job. Also, there was no predictive validity if the reference had had less than two months to observe the applicant in the position.

REFERENCES

[1]Weiss, D.J., and R.V. Davis, "An Objective Validation of Factual Interview Data," *Journal of Applied Psychology,* 44 (1960), 381–85.

[2]Goldstein, I.L., "The Application Blank: How Honest Are the Responses?" *Journal of Applied Psychology,* 55 (1971), 491–92.

[3]Rickard, T.E., H.C. Triands, and C.H. Patterson, "Indices of Employer Prejudice toward Disabled Applicants," *Journal of Applied Psychology,* 47 (1963), 52–55.

[4]Carroll, S.J., and A.N. Nash, "Effectiveness of a Forced-Choice Reference Check," *Personnel Administration,* 35 (1972), 42–46.

QUESTIONS

1. With reference to the research incident, how would you improve the format of the application blank to eliminate the Betty Brown problem?
2. Discuss reference checks as a method to discover irregularities. To what extent, costwise, would you recommend them?
3. Why did Betty Brown conceal information on the application blank? Was she justified?
4. What are your reasons to consider the employment application as an effective selection device? Are there other alternatives?

Research Incident 3-2:
Joe Wonder and the Weighted Application Blank

- Will a weighted application blank that is designed for a particular organization be suitable to use in other organizations?
- Can a weighted application blank be designed to identify theft-oriented people? What consideration should be given to race and sex groups?
- Is there a need for periodic cross-validation of the distinguishing characteristics of weighted application blanks? What factors should be considered?

Joe Wonder was recruited by the Gigantic Tool Company to work in its personnel department. Joe was a recent graduate of State University, having majored in human resource management. Fortunately for Joe, State University offered a specialized major in human resource rather than the usual college offering of one or two human resource courses. It was for this very reason that Gigantic Tool hired Joe. Top management felt that the personnel department needed some new ideas.

It was at the first personnel staff meeting that Joe had a chance to demonstrate his wares. Management had done a review of departments with high turnover and the suspicion of theft, and now the question arose of the need to improve the quality of new hirees. The use of lie detectors was brought up and debated to death; then Joe Wonder proposed reviewing the company's application blanks as a device to solve the problems. After a round of comments provoking laughter, such as proposals to ask on the application blank, "Do you steal?" and, "When do you plan to leave?" Joe was allowed to present his idea.

His suggestion was a weighted application blank. There was plenty of evidence that it worked. Joe's approach was simple and direct: "Let's use a sample group to determine those who have quit early and those who stayed. Divide them into high and low groups, then check out the previously filled-out application blanks to see if the two groups differ in their answers to items. Ditto for the theft problem." This suggestion by the new member of the department received a great deal of debate. Finally, the personnel manager, somewhat suspicious of top management's insistence on hiring someone for his department, agreed to let Joe Wonder give it a try. What was there to lose?

RELEVANT EMPIRICAL
RESEARCH STUDIES

Research Study 3-2-A

In what areas have weighted application blanks been used successfully? What are some of the items selected to be used?

Robinson[1] conducted a study of female clerical turnover in a bank. His review of past empirical studies validating the use of weighted application blanks included studies done on office turnover, credit risks, and tenure of factory workers. The Robinson study attempted to develop a weighted application blank that would identify those female applicants who are most likely to be long-term versus short-term employees. It was determined that the direct costs to the bank per new employee were $400 and that it took 15 months to amortize these costs. A study of employment records showed that 80 percent of those who quit the bank did so by the end of 15 months, and that became the study cutoff point.

The application blanks of 100 short-term and 100 long-term employees were randomly selected. Items were selected and assigned weights (−3 to +3) depending upon the difference in the proportion of short-term versus long-term employees responding to the item. Then a cross-validation sample of 50 short-term and 50 long-term application blanks was randomly drawn and scored. The result was correct identification of 80 percent of the short-term employees, although there was a 30 percent rejection of the long-term employees. Some of the 27 items that differentiated the typical short-term employee showed her to be between the ages of 20 and 25, single, her mother probably worked, she did not have the obligations of a home and family, she lived with her parents, and she had attended college. In other words, the short-term female was at an age of maximal freedom along with minimal responsibility, or at the age when she marries and raises a family.

On the other hand, the long-term employee was older than 30 years, married, with her youngest child in school, owned a home, and appeared to have established organizational roots. She usually had not attended college and did not have the skills to move past bookkeeping or the simple clerical level. If such a person was first employed as a bookkeeper, she was as likely to quit as if she had been hired as a clerk.

Summary Review of Research Study 3-2-A   The items that differentiated between the short-term and the long-term employees were generally the same as in other weighted-application-blank studies. However, the items in the present study were different enough to suggest the need of custom-designing such an instrument to a particular organization.

Research Study 3-2-B

Can a weighted application blank be developed that can predict applicants who might steal?

Rosenbaum[2] reports several tests designed specifically to predict employee theft. These include the Stanton Pre-employment Survey, the Personnel Security Preview, and the FACT Test. Although all claim high validity, Rosenbaum questions the appropriateness of administering a lengthy test for low-level, temporary jobs, because of the risk that threatening questions may alienate applicants. To overcome these objections, he suggests a weighted application blank as an inoffensive technique to identify potentially high-risk employees.

In a pilot study, Rosenbaum was provided with 250 applications from a Detroit mass merchandiser: 125 from people who admitted cashier theft and 125 from former cashiers not caught stealing who had voluntarily terminated with a recommendation for rehire. Various responses were identified and assigned weights. Of 35 items tested, eleven were identified as potentially useful. Eliminating overlapping items, Rosenbaum classified five primary predictors each with a weight of 2: weight 150 pounds or more, Detroit address, two or more previous jobs, does not wear eyeglasses, and application carelessly prepared. Two lesser predictors with a weight of 1 were these: at present address less than 13 years, and weight less than 130 pounds. When the weights for the seven predictors were applied to a group of 50 applicants and another 100-applicant group, the significance level was well beyond .001 in identifying high-risk people.

Rosenbaum used the same procedure to select items in a supermarket study, resulting in a new group of weighted responses. As in the mass-merchandising study, there was one sample of 100 to determine the weights and two validation samples of 50 and 100 each. In this study, ten responses were identified as being statistically useful for the weighted application: full-time work sought, in case of emergency no relative is to be contacted, number of dependents other than none, not in school, not living with parents, application is of substandard appearance, does not indicate a middle initial, does not own an automobile, recently consulted a physician, and new employee is black. For the responses above, all were assigned weights of 2 except for number of dependents and not living with parents, which were assigned a weight of 1. If the ten predictor weights had been applied to the sample of 50, and if a cutting score of 5 was used to identify the high-risk employees, the result would have been that 31, or 62 percent of the 50, were properly placed. The correlation for the group of 50 was .30, and the correlation for the group of 100 was .27. The author also notes that when a skeptical corporation security official used the unit weights in a different sample of 20 applicants, 75 percent were properly placed, or 15 out of the 20.

Summary Review of Research Study 3-2-B The author recommends that weighted application blanks designed to determine theft-oriented people be used only to identify high-risk employees for security observation and not as a screening device for applicants. This study indicates that weighted application blanks are more valid when they are designed for specific jobs. Also, weighted blanks should be specific as to race, job, time, place, age, and sex. Further, separate scoring keys should be developed for each race–sex group, such as black females or white males.

Research Study 3-2-C

How accurate are weighted application blanks over a period of time?

Roach[3] performed a second cross-validation of a weighted application blank for predicting tenure of female clerical workers working for an insurance company. The first sample group was of lower-salary employees hired during 1952–53; Roach's cross-validation sample consisted of employees hired during 1954–55. The termination group included only voluntary quits and excluded discharges or resignations owing to pregnancy. The original group was tested with the Life Office Management Association Test, and the Roach group was tested with the Wonderlic personnel test. Although the two tests appear very similar, one cannot be certain that they are equivalent, so part of the Roach study data must be approached with caution.

The application-blank items were weighted and selected, as in the original study, to differentiate between the long-term and short-term tenure groups. Roach found that the scores of the short-tenure and long-tenure groups overlapped in the low-score range; 7.7 percent of the long-tenure group had scores below 12, compared to 14.3 percent for the short-tenure group. This would appear to make the test instrument not useful as a rejection device for eliminating those applicants who would be poor tenure risks.

However, there was less overlap in the top-score range; 22 percent of the long-tenure group but only 4.8 percent of the short-tenure group scored above 20. The study also found that the correlation between the scores and criteria in the first cross-validation was .46 and in the second cross-validation was .29, a substantial difference. Testing for differences in responses indicated that four of the eleven weighted items demonstrated significant discrimination between the long- and short-tenure groups, but two items provide a reversal of direction. An analysis of the item–criterion correlations in the second cross-validation show almost all less than those in the first cross-validation.

An examination of the individual test items for validity showed that some performed quite well in the second Roach study. These items included age at time of application, length of time married at time of application, source of reference to the company, and reason for leaving the last job. However, items that discriminated in the first cross-validation but failed to discriminate or reversed direction in the second test were difference between salary expected and salary received, average tenure on last three jobs, father's occupation, is related to or knows company employees, and the Wonderlic test score.

Summary Review of Research Study 3-2-C   Roach suggests some reasons that the second cross-validation study failed to support the first validation. In the area of labor-market conditions, the company hired many additional clerical workers during a "tight" labor market, resulting in a less-selective hiring policy. This in turn may have resulted in a rather unselected population compared with the usual employee population. In the area of personnel policies, a policy change took place allowing the hiring of relatives, which would affect the item "is related to or knows company employees." Another policy change was a major alteration in the salary schedule, with an increase in beginning salaries. This may have affected the item "difference between salary expected and salary received." An unknown factor of influence would be the use of the Wonderlic personnel test instead of the Life Office Management Association test.

The Roach study does suggest the need of periodic cross-validation of weighted application blanks to ensure continuing validity of the items selected for distinguishing characteristics.

REFERENCES

[1]Robinson, D.D., "Prediction of Clerical Turnover in Banks by Means of a Weighted Application Blank," *Journal of Applied Psychology*, 56 (1972), 282.

[2]Rosenbaum, R.W., "Predictability of Employee Theft Using Weighted Application Blanks," *Journal of Applied Psychology*, 61 (1976), 94–98.

[3]Roach, D.E., "Double Cross-Validation of a Weighted Application Blank over Time," *Journal of Applied Psychology*, 55 (1971), 157–60.

QUESTIONS

1. The weighted application blank attempts to eliminate people with undesirable characteristics from being hired. From a human resource management viewpoint, is this attainable? Discuss.

2. Recognizing the direction of equal employment opportunity legislation, do you anticipate any problems in implementing a weighted application blank? Explain.

3. As a human resource specialist for Gigantic Tool, you are in charge of a group chosen to design a weighted application blank. What problems, if any, do you anticipate, and what is their resolution?

Research Incident 3-3:
Marilynn Leonard Plants a Seed

- Does previewing the application blank before meeting the applicant for the first time prejudice the interviewer?
- What is the effect of previewing on the total accuracy and stereotype accuracy of the interviewer?
- How does previewing affect the role of the interviewer as an information gatherer and as a judge?

Marilynn Leonard had strong ties to the application blank. Her dissertation at State University was on the validity of application-blank information. In fact, it was her work in revising the company's old application blank and then applying the new information that had caught the eye of the senior vice-president of personnel. That fortunate incident, plus six years of hard work in the personnel office (last year it had been changed to human resource), plus this year's early retirement of the human resource manager, resulted in Marilynn's having a new job and a new title.

So with just a few months as the human resource manager, Marilynn Leonard carefully pondered the memo before her. It was from the recently hired trainee, Harry Newcomb, who was suggesting scrapping the application blank and replacing it with a 3"-by-6" card containing little more than name and address. His rationale was that application-blank information prejudiced anyone reading it, setting in motion stereotyped images that either inflated or deflated the applicant's worth. Since Harry had a master's degree from the private More Prestigious University, it had been generally felt that he would bring to the company the latest human resource evolutionary (some believed revolutionary) thought.

The next day, Marilynn met with Harry. First she complimented him on his thorough and interesting suggestion. However, in the interests of looking at both sides of the issue, she "suggested" that he proceed further and determine the direction of research in the empirical journals. Handing him a reference from the *Journal of Applied Psychology* as a "seed," Marilynn asked Harry to contact her the following week and report on his findings.

*RELEVANT EMPIRICAL
RESEARCH STUDIES*

Research Study 3-3-A

What is the effect upon employment decisions of previewing the information contained in employment applications prior to meeting the applicant? Does it have any effect on the quality of employment decisions?

Tucker and Rowe[1] investigated the effect of the application blank on the decision quality of employment interviewers. The sample was 28 experienced employment interviewers representing eleven different organizations: four manufacturing companies, four employment agencies, two insurance companies, and one educational institution. Twelve of the employment interviewers were females and 16 were males. These experienced recruiters interviewed a third-year undergraduate student in psychology who was role-playing as an applicant for a hypothetical position. Half the interviewers were provided with an application blank prior to the interview and the other half were not. The role-playing student was provided with a thorough biographical history that attempted to cover every type of question that might be asked during the interview. He was free to improvise answers to questions not covered in the biographical history, but he was instructed to give the same answer if that question came up again in another interview. The student was asked to act as a dispassionate disseminator of information, so as to control extraneous variables. Pilot interviews were conducted with the student, and the authors believed he was convincing in the role.

The application blank resembled a standard form, and its content was derived from the biographical history data given to the student.

A job description written for the job was entitled, "Supervisor of Animal Care Attendants." This job was chosen because it was unlikely that any of the 28 interviewers would be familiar with it, thus eliminating any preconceptions or stereotypes. The job was basic enough so that the interviewer needed only the information contained in the job description to be effective.

A 20-item questionnaire was developed to measure the interviewer's knowledge of the applicant at the initial decision point. The 20 items were obtained by providing two experienced interviewers with the application blank and the biographical history, then asking them to rate 50 information categories as to their relevance or irrelevance in a decision to hire or not hire. Only items on which there was consensus were selected, and the judges rank-ordered them as to relevant or irrelevant information. The first ten relevant and the first ten irrelevant items became the questionnaire.

The design of the application blank provided that ten items could be answered from the blank alone and ten items could not. The final form of the questionnaire consisted of five relevant application-blank items, five irrelevant application-blank items, five relevant non-application-blank items, and five irrelevant non-application items. The purpose was to provide both a quantitative and a qualitative analysis of information at the initial decision point. When that decision point was reached, the interviewers were required to indicate on a seven-point scale their degree of confidence in the initial decision. Two manipulation check items were used to determine whether the interviewer suspected that the interview would be terminated and also whether the interviewer was behaving normally.

The study's success depended upon the ability to stop the experiment without alerting the interviewer. This was achieved by providing the interviewer with a seven-point reject–accept scale that recorded the decision at the very moment it was made. Thus, the applicant could see when the interviewer had made the employment decision, and then the applicant would terminate the interview.

The procedure was to have the interviews conducted at the interviewer's place of work. The experimenter accompanied the applicant to the interviewer's company and introduced himself while the applicant remained in the background. The interviewer was told that this was an experiment to improve selection interviews and that he or she would be expected to make a final hiring decision. The interviewer was then given a job description, the application form if that was the condition, and the reject–accept scale, with instructions to record the initial decision at the moment it was reached. The experimenter left the interviewer's office and started a stopwatch, which was stopped when the applicant left the office after terminating the interview.

The results of the study indicated that for the manipulation checks, none of the interviewers suspected the interview would be terminated, and all interviewers believed they acted normally.

There was no significant difference in the mean times to reach a decision between interviewers with an application blank and those without one, and both groups were equally confident in their initial decision to hire or not hire the applicant.

The 20-item questionnaire was analyzed to determine the effect that not reviewing the application blank prior to the interview had upon the quality and quantity of interviewer information. Significant differences were found between the interviewers with access to the application blank prior to the interview and those without. The 14 interviewers with the access processed more quality and quantity applicant information. Further, they also scored significantly higher on relevant versus irrelevant items. The interviewers with access to the application blank demonstrated a significant difference from those without in the application- and non-application-form items. Thus, the access interviewers had more information, including non-application information, upon which to base their decisions.

Summary Review of Research Study 3-3-A It has been suggested that a selection interview is more objective and permits more fact finding if the interviewer does not preview the applicant's application prior to the interview. This study found no advantage and some disadvantages in delaying a preview of the application blank. Interviewers, regardless of whether they were provided with an application blank, demonstrated no significant difference in time to reach a hire–no hire decision. However, interviewers with the application blank demonstrated more complete and relevant information upon which to base such a decision than did those without the application blank. Actually, those with the application blank obtained more non-application information than did the others. Apparently there was more time available to seek out additional information. Both groups of interviewers, application and non-application, expressed the same degree of confidence in their initial decisions. The non-application group was not more cautious in reaching a decision. The study suggests that the value of the application blank is in providing information not readily available elsewhere and in indicating areas that require further probing.

Research Study 3-3-B

What is the effect of previewing the application in gathering information? How does previewing affect the assessment of the applicant's personality and overall job qualifications?

Dipboye and others[2] studied these questions, using interviewers who conducted simulated interviews with two applicants for the position of assistant manager of a real estate office. The interviewers were 35 undergraduate students enrolled in psychology courses, who volunteered to participate for extra course credit. They were assigned randomly to one of three groups for a two-hour session.

Arriving at a session, the interviewer was told to assume the role of an interviewer of two other students for a fictitious real estate job as assistant manager. The job consisted of answering rental inquiries, explaining leases, and handling complaints and evictions. The qualifications for the job were that the applicant should be confident, ambitious, enterprising, one who takes initiative, enthusiastic, methodical, thorough, practical, understanding, tolerant, and able to communicate. Of the traits included in the job specification, half matched the self-descriptions of one applicant on the Adjective Check List and the other half matched those of the other. Other components of the job that appeared were written so that neither applicant would appear superior.

Twelve of the interviewers were to evaluate only on the basis of a face-to-face interview; another 13 previewed an application before interviewing; and in the control condition, interviewers were to base evaluations only on the application blanks. The interviewers were provided with six standard questions, but they were told they would have to go beyond these and formulate their own questions if they were to determine the applicant's personality. They were also told that the interview would last 20 minutes and would be videotaped. The two applicants for the assistant manager job were undergraduate women who were instructed to create a good impression and answer any questions honestly.

In the application-preview condition, the interviewers were provided with a four-page application blank containing information about family, education, employment, activities, health, and goals. The interviewers rated the applicants on a seven-point scale as to their impression of whether each would provide a good fit to the job and a description of things that would qualify and disqualify her. These impressions would then be tested in the interview. For the no-preview condition, the interviewers based their post-interview assessments only on the interview. In the control condition, the interviewers previewed and evaluated the applicants based only on the applications, with no interviews.

For those dependent measures that were related to information gathering, an observer, who was unaware of the experiment, scored the videotapes using ten items, including interview duration, number of question asked, and open-ended questions asked. Also, two raters who were unaware of the experiment evaluated the interviewer's performance on nine five-point scales. Another information-gathering technique was the coding of the applicant's answers to the interviewer's questions by two uninformed observers. The resulting list of compiled information was then rated as to job-profile relevance by three graduate students and one faculty member. A postinterview questionnaire completed by the interviewers asked for the answers given by the applicants to the six standard questions, plus many specific things that had been learned about the applicants. Correctness was determined by checking against the compiled information list.

After completing the interview, the interviewers rated the applicants on a seven-point scale as to whether they provided a good fit to the job profile. For the experimental condition, the interviewers rated the applicant on a seven-point scale as to how well questions were answered. The applicants' responses to the 300 adjectives of the Gough Adjective Checklist and 30 items from the Strong Vocational Interest Blank formed a composite of the applicant's personality. After the interviews, these instruments were completed by the interviewers as they believed the applicant would complete them. This was taken as an index of how accurately the interviewers judged personality. The differences between the applicant's self-rating and the interviewer's rating of the Adjective Checklist items were summed to arrive at a total accuracy score (TA). A second total accuracy score was obtained in a similar manner from the Strong Vocational Interest Blank (SVIB total accuracy). Four separate components of the total accuracy score were computed: Elevation accuracy (EA) reflected the agreement between the interviewer's response to the scales and those of the two applicants; stereotype accuracy (SA) indicated how successful the interviewer was in describing the mean response of the applicants; differential elevation (DE) demonstrated the interviewer's success in gauging the applicant's deviation from her own central tendency; and differential accuracy (DA) reflected the interviewer's success in estimating the unique responses of each applicant on each item.

The results of the study indicate that, for most of the information-gathering measures, there were larger variances within the preview condition than within the no-preview condition. However, there were no significant differences for the variances of the accuracy scores or the overall evaluations of the applicant. The preview group demonstrated significantly larger variances on all the information-gathering measures except for the number of yes-no questions (Do you like college? Do you like simple routine? and so on). An analysis of the objective and subjective information-gathering measures indicated that the interview lasted longer when there was a preview than when there was none. For objective measures, those interviewers with an application blank asked more double-edged questions (Do you like simple routine work, or work that is ambiguous and presents a challenge?) than did the interviewers who did not have an application blank. As for the subjective measure of information gathering, there was no significant difference between the application-preview condition and the no-preview group.

There was also no significant difference between the two conditions as to the mean number of application items mentioned by the interviewers. Yet the interviewers who previewed the application did gather significantly more non-application items than did the no-preview interviewers. The preview interviewers recalled more non-application items correctly than the no-preview interviewers did, although the difference was not at a conventional level of significance ($p = 15$). However, no-preview interviewers recalled more application items correctly than did the preview interviewers, for a significant difference. As control on the amount of information available, the proportion of each type of information recalled was computed, and the preview interviewers did not differ from the no-preview interviewers on the proportion of non-application items recalled. However, the proportion of application items recalled was significantly lower for the preview group than for the no-preview group.

An analysis of the assessment measures was made on evaluations of goodness of fit to the job and the interviewer's interview performance. For the goodness-of-fit rating, the interviewee main effect was significant in the no-preview group, but not significant in the preview group and application-only control group.

In regard to the Adjective Checklist (ACL), it was found that no-preview interviewers were significantly more accurate in estimating the self-descriptions of the applicants on the ACL than were the preview interviewers and the application-only control group.

For the ACL component scores for stereotype accuracy (SA) and elevation accuracy (EA), there was a significant effect for the preview interviewers. For stereotype accuracy, the application-only control group and the no-preview group did not differ significantly, and they were more accurate than the preview interviewers. However, for elevation accuracy, the preview interviewers were more accurate than the no-preview group, with the application-only control group being the least accurate. There was no significant difference among any of the groups as to differential accuracy (DA) and differential elevation (DE).

There were significant main effects of the applicant factor on most of the dependent measures. Applicant A was considered to have performed better than Applicant B, resulting in more time spent talking, longer interview time, and more questions answered. However, there were no significant interactions between treatment (previewing the application blank and not previewing) and interviewee, suggesting that the preview manipulation generalized across the two applicants.

Summary Review of Research Study 3-3-B   The act of previewing the application blank prior to the interview had a minimal effect on how the interviewers conducted themselves. The preview interviewers demonstrated nonsignificant effects on the subjective ratings of interviewer performance and most of the objective measures of interviewer information gathering. The preview interviewers obtained more non-application information than did the no-preview interviewers and also demonstrated a marginal ability to recall more non-application information.

For the assessment function of the interview, the preview made little difference and may have had some drawbacks. Although the preview increased ACL elevation accuracy, it also resulted in lower total accuracy and stereotype accuracy. The preview had no effect on differential accuracy or differential elevation. There was no difference between the previewers and non-previewers as to accuracy in determining individual self-descriptions on the ACL. But previewing resulted in substantially lower reliability in ratings of overall goodness of fit and of applicant interview performance.

When the interviewer functions as both information gatherer and judge, it may be best either to avoid previewing the application blank or to standardize the interview and evaluation procedures. This will help to ensure that the reliability and accuracy of the final decisions are safeguarded.

REFERENCES

[1]Tucker, D.H., and P.M. Rowe, "Consulting the Application Form Prior to the Interview: An Essential Step in the Selection Process," *Journal of Applied Psychology*, 62 (1977), 283–87.

[2]Dipboye, R.L., G.A. Fontenelle, and K. Garner, "Effects of Previewing the Application on Interview Process and Outcomes," *Journal of Applied Psychology*, 69 (1984), 118–28.

QUESTIONS

1. What are some advantages for the interviewer in studying the application blank prior to the interview? Explain.
2. What are some disadvantages in allowing the interviewer to study the application blank prior to the interview? Explain.
3. Should the interviewer function both as an application-blank information gatherer and as a judge of that information? Explain.
4. In regard to application-blank items versus non-application-blank information, what can be done to promote the gathering of non-application-blank information?

NON-EMPIRICAL RESEARCH ARTICLE ABSTRACTS

Abstract 3-1

- With regard to the questions on a job application form, do federal discrimination laws take precedent over state laws?
- What may be the problem with standard job application blanks purchased from a printing company doing national business?
- How does a company establish a bona fide occupational qualification so that it may appear on a job application blank?

These questions are answered in a 1983 article by Carl Camden, Cleveland State University, and Bill Wallace, Bowling Green State University.[1]

The authors point out that the majority of employers are aware of the past two decades of legislation designed to prevent discrimination in employment practices, including preemployment inquiries. However, many are not aware that laws in some states are more stringent than federal requirements. When this occurs, the more rigorous law applies even if it is the state law.

An example is the state of Ohio and BFOQs (bona fide occupational qualifications) that may intentionally discriminate, such as those for height and weight for firefighters. Federal regulations require employers to be able to justify these discriminatory preemployment practices; Ohio state law requires them to be approved by the Ohio Civil Rights Commission prior to their being practiced.

Being not guilty of either overt or systematic discrimination is not enough in Ohio; the company must not *appear* to be guilty. The becomes a straightforward issue, since Ohio prohibits questions on race, sex, marital status, national origin, age, and physical characteristics such as weight, height, and color of eyes.

The authors believed that many businesses could be unknowingly violating Ohio state law, so they requested current job application blanks from 100 businesses randomly selected from a large metropolitan area. The sample return consisted of blanks from 94 firms, representing large and small retailers, service industries, industrial manufacturers, civic institutions, and other employers.

The noncompliance of the sample group with the Ohio state equal opportunity regulations with respect to one or more illegal preemployment inquiries on the job application blanks was 73 percent. The most common illegal inquiries of applicants were with respect to physical characteristics, marital status, and dependent information.

One of the reasons for these widespread violations of Ohio state law is that many companies use standard application blanks purchased from national printing companies. In the study sample of 94 firms, 35 percent of the forms collected came from eight different national business-form companies. In a sample of job application blanks from the state of Kansas, these eight national printing companies accounted for 34 percent of the forms. These forms generally comply with federal regulations, but in many instances, they are illegal in particular states.

Another reason appears to be that companies who make up their own job application blanks use them in several states where they do business. Nine such firms were identified in both the Ohio and Kansas samples, and eight of them used identical forms. Companies operating in different states have difficulty in creating one form that will satisfy different state laws.

Further, some companies appear careless in complying with state laws. The Ohio state law does allow asking applicants a question relative to race or sex if such a question has been certified first by the Ohio Civil Rights Commission as being a BFOQ and the commission has certified such information for certain employment situations. Fire and police departments in Ohio are allowed to establish height and weight requirements as a result of appropriate testing and standardization. However, without certification from the Ohio Civil Rights Commission, it is illegal for other employers to ask about height or weight. Yet this study revealed many companies asking height and weight questions and identifying them as BFOQs without having received prior certification from the commission. In fact, none of the companies in the sample had registered any of their BFOQ questions with the commission.

Even though companies can attempt to obtain information for affirmative action purposes, and the otherwise illegal questions can be part of an affirmative action survey, such illegal questions must be detachable from the job employment application. Where this was being done in the sample group, the authors noted that some of the application blanks included surveys that were not detachable.

The final reason seems to be that even when the forms do recognize individual state laws and state that the applicant is not to answer certain questions unless told to do so, applicants are often told to answer all the questions; the authors report one incident in which a store manager incorrectly demanded that all the questions be answered. So people with responsibility for hiring must know the state law, as well as company policy.

The failure to comply with these state laws that are stricter than the federal laws can be costly. The Ohio Civil Rights Commission has said that by violating state law by asking illegal questions, a business could be sued for back pay for all the wronged parties who completed the forms. Then the U.S. Equal Employment Opportunity Commission could enter the case and sue in federal court for punitive damages.

The authors suggest having local and federal agencies review proposed job application blanks to identify any problem areas.

REFERENCE

[1]Camden, Carl, and Bill Wallace, "Job Application Forms: A Hazardous Employment Practice." From the March 1983 issue of *Personnel Administrator,* copyright 1983, The American Society for Personnel Administration, 606 North Washington Street, Alexandria, VA 22314.

QUESTIONS

1. How do the discrimination laws of the state of Ohio compare with federal laws? What does this mean to businesses in Ohio?
2. What may be the problem with standard job application blanks in Ohio that were purchased from a national printing firm? Any solution?
3. Some companies are careless about questions on their job application blanks. Discuss the Ohio state law regarding BFOQs.

Abstract 3-2

- Companies have been trying various programs over a period of years to reduce turnover. What has been the result?
- What is the role of statistical procedures in developing weighted application blanks? What do these statistical techniques contribute?
- How do the predictions of intuitive judgments rate with those of the weighted application blank? Do you have any explanations?

Lawrence, Salsburg, and Dawson of Bauer/Lawrence Associates, Inc., and Fasman of Wald, Harkrader and Ross,[1] addressed these questions in a 1982 article.

The authors say that as a partial result of equal employment programs, many companies have attempted to reduce turnover and increase performance through the use of various programs after a person has been hired. Yet despite these efforts, studies indicate that turnover rates continue to increase steadily. There is agreement that ineffective hiring is a significant business cost, but the problem remains of improving the selection process.

This article suggests that the development and use of weighted application blanks (WAB) offers the desired improvement. The instrument is described as determining personal history data and other variables of job applicants so as to improve their selection and success in specific job categories. Studies are cited in which weighted application blanks have successfully predicted tenure and have reduced turnover in a six-month period from 80 to 26 percent. However, despite the evidence supporting the weighted application blank, the vast majority of American businesses continue to use the standard, traditional job application blank.

The foundation of the argument supporting WAB development is that objective and quantitative information regarding job applicants exists that is predictive of their future behavior in a specific job or job family (different jobs requiring similar abilities) in a specific organization.

Using statistical techniques, the authors were able to determine in this study the factors that forecast an applicant's on-the-job behavior, the importance or weight of these factors, a predictive standard that permits a quantitative comparison, an objective basis for hiring, and specific items to be included on the application blank.

The following statistical terms and definitions were used to develop a WAB. The technique that measures and analyzes the relationship between two variables is called *regression*. When there are more than two variables, it is called *multiple/stepwise regression*. For the present study, the dependent variable was tenure/job performance, and other factors were considered independent variables. The line or curve that results from the regression technique describes the relationship between the dependent and independent variables. When a statistical relationship exists, there is *correlation* between the variables. However, this correlation or association is not necessarily a cause-and-effect relationship; there is no indication of causality or lack of causality between the dependent and independent variables. Usually the predictability can be improved if more than one information variable is used. This is called *multiple regression. Stepwise regression* results when the independent variables in the final equation explain a significant amount of the variation in the dependent variable. A problem in multiple/stepwise regression arises when two or more of the independent variables are correlated. This is called *multicollinearity.* The measure of the strength of the relationship between the dependent and independent variables is called the *coefficient of correlation.* It ranges from $+1.00$ to -1.00. The *coefficient of determination* indicates the percentage of variation of the dependent variable that is explained by the independent variable or variables. The prediction of the regression equation always includes the danger that the relationship between the dependent and independent variables results in part or wholly by chance. A *level of significance* indicates this probability.

The company in the study was a major daily newspaper in a major metropolitan city. Almost 70 percent of the paper's circulation resulted from home delivery, and the significant key was the route managers who managed the paper carriers. Over periods of time, high route-manager turnover had had a negative effect on overall circulation performance. For 1980, it was estimated that turnover cost the circulation division over $1 million.

After discussions with management, it was agreed that the essential ingredient in improving circulation performance was an analysis of the preemployment screening factors of route managers. One element the company recognized was that the traditional techniques of improved selection procedures, training programs, and multiple interviewing all had little effect on improving turnover.

The study project first made a determination of the working environment and a job analysis. Current and past managers were interviewed, and time was spent working on the job in an attempt to determine the conditions or environment under which the work was being performed. Also, meetings were held with management personnel to identify and obtain consensus on predictive profile factors to be included as potential independent variables. The result was identification of 29 potential independent variables.

A random sample of 243 current and former employees was obtained and was divided into four groups: 59 employees on the payroll less than three months, 184 current and former employees with tenure from 1940,

167 employees with tenure from 1968 or less, and 147 employees with tenure from 1975 or less. The first group of 59 employees was used for the initial revalidation with the other groups to test the hypothesis that the predictive profile factors would change over time.

The result of the statistical analysis and methodology was identification of the specific profile factors and their relative weights. The following are the profile characteristics and their relative weight importance on job tenure performance: experience as service representative (19.5); business school education (17.7); will live and work in same country (13.2); referral source an advertisement (11.6); high school diploma (11.6); experience doing strenuous work (10.3); experience working for another newspaper (9.0); one year college (7.6); experience in accounting, handling money (7.1); married (6.5); college degree (5.4); employed at time of hire (5.2); length of time unemployed, in months, when hired (2.6). The profile characteristics that had a negative effect on job tenure/performance were these: previously worked for XYZ Corporation (−17.6); experience doing sales work (−8.3); experience doing outside work (−7.2): number of previous jobs (−7.1); final salary on last job (−0.5); average tenure on previous jobs, in months (−0.2).

The key findings of the present study were that the predictive factors revealed significant changes over time from group to group in the three sample categories. Conventional value judgments, such as, "People with too much education don't last on that job," had little or no predictive value. Twelve specific factors that management judged were indicators of tenure performance were not validated by the study. Of the twelve, three had a small positive correlation, four had no predictive value, and five were negatively correlated with tenure/performance. The authors say that the more of these twelve factors the applicant possessed, the lower was performance and the likelier that the person would leave within the year. So much for intuitive judgments! The confidence level was in excess of 99 percent. As for the revalidation results, the authors accurately forecasted tenure in 83 percent of the cases.

It is the authors' contention that the use of the weighted application blank reinforces the goals of equal employment laws and is a useful device for defending against discrimination charges. The WAB is more defensible than the use of generic employment tests. However, as in any selection device, validation experience must be generated, especially if there is a negative effect on minorities. The authors' experience has been that no such minority effect has occurred as a result of using the WAB.

The conclusion of the article is that the WAB can yield substantial savings in turnover and improve performance. Also, it substitutes objective analysis for interviewer bias and subjectivity, and it provides statistically valid and reliable documentation for greater legal safeguards.

REFERENCE

[1]Lawrence, Daniel G., Barbara L. Salsburg, John G. Dawson, and Zachary D. Fasman, "Design and Use of Weighted Application Blanks." From the March 1982 issue of *Personnel Administrator,* copyright 1982, The American Society for Personnel Administration, 606 North Washington Street, Alexandria, VA 22314.

QUESTIONS

1. What does the weighted application blank weight? How are the items selected to be weighted?
2. What is the argument supporting the development of weighted application blanks? Are there any constraints or qualifications?
3. Management used twelve factors in its intuitive judgment of personnel tenure/promotion. According to the study, what would be the result if a person possessed all twelve factors?

CHAPTER FOUR

SELECTION: INTERVIEWING

INTRODUCTION

Once the recruitment process has established a satisfactory pool of applicants, the selection interview process begins. This is a function shared by many in the organization, but it is a basic responsibility of the human resource department. The selection candidates have indicated their desire to be hired, true, but some recruitment effort is still necessary.

The company's primary concern in the selection interview function is to obtain people who will be successful and make a solid contribution to organizational objectives. Some of the selection interview techniques used to predict the applicant's contribution to the organization are interviews, psychological testing, physical examinations, references, and application blanks. References and application blanks were discussed in the preceding chapter because of their importance in the employment process. Test scores of intelligence, personality, physical, or other characteristics that can be either estimated or measured are used as predictors of success in a job or related jobs. Then criteria are established, such as production records, peer ratings, supervisory ratings, and training-program scores. The degree to which a selection instrument such as a test either predicts or significantly correlates with important job behavior is indicated by criterion-related validity.

Two types of validity are related to criteria. The first, *concurrent validity,* produces predictor and criterion information at the same time from current employees. The second, *predictive validity,* requires testing applicants; after a period of employment, the criterion information is obtained. The relationship between the test scores and the criterion values is usually obtained through correlation methods, discussed in an earlier chapter. However, a repetition of the idea of validity may be helpful.

The validity of a selection instrument is how effectively it accomplishes what it is expected to do. The *content validity* of a selection instrument is how accurately it evaluates the particular job knowledge and skills being investigated. That is, a test for electrical engineers represents an electrical engineer's performance on the job, not that of a computer programmer. *Construct validity* measures a specific characteristic that is related to other measures of the same construct while having less relation to other constructs. For example, a measure of verbal ability must relate more to other measurements of verbal ability and less to, say, manual ability. *Synthetic validity* is used in situations in which the number of people performing a certain type of activity is small. It is based on the concept that different job elements may be found in a variety of jobs. Since each of these job elements is validated by a particular test, the task becomes knowing the elements of the job in question and then selecting from a group of tests those that validate those job elements. Different jobs then will have varying combinations of the same tests. Statistical validation requires a large sample size, and synthetic validation allows grouping a number of different jobs that have job elements in common to obtain a large enough group size.

To be of value, these predictors must result in a selection decision. Such decisions may be based on an analytical approach that considers how applicants "stack up" against the job perceptions of those doing the selection. This involves individual judgments of the predictors weighted for success importance in that particular job. Another decision approach that is less subjective and more objective is to first identify the most valid predictors and then evaluate them, using statistical techniques to determine appropriate cutoff points.

However, there are distinct limitations to the selection decision methods described above. An important consideration is that the available predictors are not perfect and may not always correctly identify the appropriate characteristics that determine job behavior. Further, the predictors do not consistently indicate the degree to which the characteristics are present in a person.

Regardless of which selection decision method is used, analytical or statistical, there is always the problem of human error. Although various training programs are helpful, the problem will still remain. Such errors may result from not understanding a statement made by the applicant or from improperly interpreting numerical data. And even when the selection process does function without error, the applicant may change after being hired. People do change physically, and some diseases gradually reduce effectiveness. Personal problems may surface, such as an unhappy home life or financial burdens, that take their toll of an employee's effectiveness. Periodic evaluations and counseling can reveal the early stages of such problems before they become a negative influence. Further, just as people change, so does the nature of their jobs, either through transfer, promotion, or downgrading or upgrading job skills. In this instance, a continuing program of job analysis will alert the human resource department to potential problems. Although these limitations are drawbacks to the present selection process, they do suggest some consequences of a less than complete organizational commitment to selection as an important factor in company success.

The application of equal employment to the selection process should be considered not a limitation but rather an emphasis on selecting better-qualified applicants. Equal employment legislation, as it relates to the selection process, comprises several federal laws and many state laws. The Equal Pay Act of 1963 covers employees engaged in interstate commerce and most federal, state, and local government employees. The law prohibits pay discrimination based upon the worker's sex. The Civil Rights Act of 1964, Title VII, prohibits employment discrimination based on race, color, religion, sex, or national origin. This act also created the Equal Employment Opportunity Commission (EEOC) to enforce the law. The Tower Amendment to Title VII permits the use of professionally developed ability tests. The Age Discrimination in Employment Act of 1967 prohibits discriminating against any person because of age between 40 and 70 years. However, a bona fide occupational qualification (BFOQ) allows age discrimination where it may be appropriate, such as in casting for a child's role in a TV commercial. The Equal Employment Opportunity Act of 1972 amended the Civil Rights Act of 1964 to cover more employees and strengthened the EEOC by allowing it to go directly to the courts for enforcement.

In 1978, owing to employers' uncertainty about the preceding laws, the *Uniform Guidelines on Employee Selection Procedures* was issued. It is a very important procedural manual for the human resource department. The *Uniform Guidelines* defines "adverse impact" as a significantly high percentage of protected groups who are considered for employment, placement, or promotion but are rejected. Adverse impact occurs when the selection rate for the protected groups is 80 percent (four-fifths) less than that for the group with the highest selection rate. This is called *disparate rejection.* Adverse impact also occurs when the organization's restricted policy in the selection method either intentionally or unintentionally excludes protected-group members. The final method of measuring adverse impact is population comparison, in which the percentage of the protected group in the local community is compared with the percentage of the group employed by the company.

The guidelines apply to practically all selection and promotion decisions. Included in the guidelines are the selection procedures: application blanks, interviewing, testing, probationary periods, work samples, training, and requirements for training and experience. Documentation by the employer is required as to records of selection rates by race, sex, and ethnic origin. Documentation of validation studies must also be maintained. Although the guidelines do not specify that each part of the selection process be documented individually, any selection process that has adverse impact must be shown to be predictive of future successful job performance. That is, the selection instrument being used must be job-related.

Another aspect of the scope of equal employment is demonstrated by the federal Office of Federal Contract Compliance Programs (OFCCP), which can require employers with government contracts of over $50,000 to initiate affirmative action programs to bring the composition of their workforce to represent the proportion of protected-group members in the local population. Federal courts may require such a program if an employer is found guilty of past discrimination policies.

The costs of an effective selection interview process can be very high as it attempts to satisfy both the organizational and legal requirements. Yet the time spent in careful selection interview procedures, including the validation of selection instruments, will prove to be in the long run cost-effective by matching organizational requirements and employee qualifications.

Probably the most important tool in the selection process is the selection interview. This is more evident today as equal employment regulations cause employers to abandon testing in favor of interviewing.

The process of interviewing is usually either informal or unstructured, or it follows a formal pattern of structured questions. The informal or unstructured interview follows an unplanned course, with the applicant encouraged to take the lead in discussing topics. The interviewer becomes a listener, even remaining silent during lulls in the conversation. When the interviewer does ask questions, they are so broad as to encourage the applicant to continue talking, thus permitting the interviewer to discover opinions, feelings, emotions, and attitudes that might not otherwise be revealed. This style of interviewing is similar to that used in counseling or at higher-level positions where the question of personal "chemistry" becomes more important. The informal or unstructured interview generates irrelevant information that is both favorable and unfavorable, and it runs longer than the structured interview.

The in-depth interview is similar to the informal or unstructured interview in allowing the applicant unlimited opportunity to talk. However, a series of questions is asked that relate to the applicant's life experiences concerning employment.

The formal or structured interview follows a definite set of questions asked of all applicants and asked in a certain sequence. This ensures that the desired information is obtained by all the interviewers, and it is very helpful in answering any charges of violating equal employment regulations. The structured approach helps to eliminate any inconsistencies in obtaining applicant information. Yet even this structured approach requires the interviewer to make subjective evaluations.

Among other techniques available to the selection interview process, one is the panel review, which requires the applicant to be interviewed by several people at once. A similar development is the stress interview, involving critical, rapid-fire questioning of the applicant's responses. Straddling the line between testing and interviewing are such methods as assessment centers and in-basket exercises. In the *assessment center,* the applicant or company employee is exposed to a variety of simulated work settings designed to select successful managers. The *in-basket exercise* can be part of the assessment center or it can be used alone as a selection interview tool. The applicant or employee responds to the contents of an in-basket of a hypothetical business manager, attempting to prioritize and act upon various memos.

Although the selection interview is an old technique, the thrust of current research efforts continues to refine its effectiveness without suggesting a viable substitute.

RESEARCH INCIDENTS

Research Incident 4-1:
Hugh Mills Tips the Scales

- How does information that contradicts the interviewer's initial opinion of the applicant affect the interviewer's final opinion?
- Will an interviewer be influenced in an evaluation by favorable or unfavorable interview information even if it is irrelevant?
- Does evaluating the level of ratings of high-quality applicants differ when the decision is made early or late in the interview?
- Does the intensity of body language affect the interviewer's ratings of applicants?

To Janet Uphill, it was like a dream. Here she was, practically in the front door of a super company. The position was at the junior-management level, with the promise of promotion to the conglomerate's head office. It was almost too good to be true. The company president had all but hired her; the local office of the Big Eight accounting firm had pushed her as its number 1 choice.

Yet she could not help feeling uneasy. The company president had told her that, at the last minute, the conglomerate headquarters office had stepped in and wanted to check her over before giving final approval. Her support group at the accounting firm said not to worry—it was just normal procedure for such an important entry position.

The interview started out well. The company president was there to introduce her to Hugh Mills, who represented a consulting firm used by the conglomerate. After the usual break-the-ice comments, the president excused himself and the interview began. Experience: What experience do you have for this position? Your previous employment record listed on your résumé: What experience did you gain there that applies to this position? Education: What specific courses did you take in college that relate to this position? What were your grades in these courses? Finally, the close: Why do you want this position? At last, Janet felt more comfortable; this question usually appeared in interviews.

"I am looking to broaden myself, gain more responsibility, and make more of a contribution to myself and society by performing in a demanding management role. I believe that I can begin to achieve these goals in the position here and perhaps be able to advance within the organization to the senior-executive level. Further, I want to do something more meaningful with my life than, say, peddling soap forever."

Hugh Mills looked up quickly and said, "I used to peddle soap."

The interview ended moments later. Janet vaguely remembers the dazed look on the company president's face, some meaningless comments, and the awkward moment as she left the office unhired.

RELEVANT EMPIRICAL RESEARCH STUDIES

Research Study 4-1-A

What effect does unfavorable information have on the interviewer? Does it matter whether unfavorable information occurs early or late in the interview?

Carlson[1] had a group of life insurance agency managers act as interviewers. These managers were attending a two-week agency management school and all had previously conducted interviews. The experimental material presented to them for evaluation closely followed the sequence of an actual selection system. The first item of information made available was the test results from the Aptitude Index Battery, showing that one-third of the applicants passed, one-third had not taken the test, and the other third had failed. These test results were presented on the top of the first page of the test booklet describing the applicant and on each of its succeeding pages. The second item of information was eight personal history data presented one at a time in the test booklet.

At the bottom of each page in the booklet, the managers rated the applicant on a seven-point scale as to potential success as a life insurance sales representative. Each applicant received a rating for the Aptitude Index Battery results and for each of the eight personal history items, for a total of nine ratings.

Four different types of hypothetical applicants were presented. The first type was constructed from the Aptitude Index Battery test results and eight items of favorable personal history. The second type of applicant was also constructed from the test results but with eight items of unfavorable personal history. The third applicant type was constructed from the test results with four items of favorable and then four of unfavorable personal history. The fourth applicant was the same as the third except that the four items of unfavorable personal history were presented first and the four favorable items last.

The results of the study would seem to indicate that all the variables and their combinations produced some effect on the manager interviewers' evaluations. However, by using a statistical treatment, it was found that three treatment conditions appeared to have the most effect on the evaluations. The most important condition was the objective information of the Aptitude Index Battery test results, which accounted for 14 percent of the variance in the evaluations. The second condition was differences in the favorableness of the personal history data, which accounted for 12 percent of the evaluation variance. The third condition was the combination of differing amounts and types of information, which accounted for 11 percent of the evaluation variance.

It was also found that the first set of four pieces of favorable information had the same effect on the evaluations as the second set of four pieces of favorable information. That is, there was no primacy or recency effect for favorable information. However, seeing the four pieces of unfavorable information first had a significantly greater effect on the evaluation than seeing them second. So for the unfavorable information, there was a primary effect. With information that is inconsistent, such as half favorable and half unfavorable, when the unfavorable information is presented last, it produces a greater change in the evaluations. That is, there is a recency effect.

Summary Review of Research Study 4-1-A   The study found that for all test conditions (passed, did not take, failed), applicants with eight items of favorable information were rated most positively and applicants with eight items of unfavorable information were rated most negatively. However, for those applicants with a half-and-half allocation, the unfavorable–favorable sequence produced more positive ratings (regardless of the test results) than did the favorable–unfavorable sequence. Generally, it appears from the study that information that agrees with the interviewer's initial impression adds less to the overall impression than opposite information detracts from the overall impression. That is, information that was of opposite value to an initial impression produced a much greater change in rating than did information of similar value. For instance, the evaluation of an applicant who has either passed or not passed the test was altered much more by unfavorable data than by favorable data.

Interestingly, although only a few items of unfavorable information were required to create a negative impression, the addition of further unfavorable information did not increase the negativeness of the original negative evaluation. The study suggests that the effect of unfavorable information is greater after a positive impression has been formed than is the effect of favorable information upon an already-established negative impression.

Research Study 4-1-B

To what extent does the interviewer respond to relevant or irrelevant information, whether it is favorable or not?

Constantin[2] considered these questions in a study, using a sample of 112 college students enrolled in an organizational behavior class. The experiment required groups of students to be assigned to listen to one of four taped interviews, each different in regard to relevance of math ability. There were two job descriptions; one included the requirement to perform mathematical calculations, and the other did not. After listening to one of the taped interviews, the students rated the person being interviewed on a seven-point instrument as to their willingness to hire the person and the applicant's ability to perform the job. After completing the first instrument, the groups completed a second one to rate the applicant on specific job duties mentioned in the interview tape.

One finding of this study supports Carlson (see Research Study 4-1-A), in that unfavorable information received greater weight in evaluating the applicant. However, the present study found that interviewers were able to distinguish the appropriateness of irrelevant information. Specifically, they discriminated between unfavorable information that was relevant and unfavorable information that was not.

Yet in an unusual twist, the study found that favorable information was considered favorable regardless of whether it was relevant or irrelevant. The students responded favorably to the mention of the applicant's good math performance regardless of whether it was stated as a duty in the job description.

The study also found that whether information was favorable or unfavorable, if it deviated from the social norms, it received greater weight in the decision-making process. Information that was favorable and relevant received the highest evaluation, and unfavorable information that was relevant received the lowest.

Summary Review of Research Study 4-1-B   The student judges gave more extreme evaluations to information that deviated from accepted social norms than to information that did not deviate. When the student judges responded to unfavorable information that was relevant, they rated the applicant lower than when the information was irrelevant. In responding to favorable information, they rated the applicant high regardless of the relevance of the information. It appears that information judged acceptable within social norms is of little value, whereas deviant information receives greater weight. There seems to be an information value in negative data. Further, the student judges were able to distinguish between unfavorable information that was relevant and that was irrelevant in evaluating the applicants.

The study also found that the applicant providing favorable information received a favorable evaluation regardless of the relevance of that information. That is, the judges responded to favorable math ability in a positive way whether it was needed or not. Perhaps, in a job description, duties that are not required should be listed in an attempt to eliminate this occurrence. It should be noted that the student judges may have responded to other factors in determining a willingness to hire.

Research Study 4-1-C

Does the length of time of an interview have an effect on the actions of the interviewer? What effect does the quality of the person being interviewed have upon the actions of the interviewer?

Tullar and others[3] exposed a sample of 60 experienced employment counselors, half of whom were male and half female, to one of two videotaped job interviews for a sales position. One tape was of a high-quality applicant and the other of a low-quality applicant. The employment counselors were divided into two groups; one group was told the interview would last 15 minutes, and the other was told it would last 30 minutes. Actually, both groups saw a videotape lasting 15 minutes.

Prior to viewing the videotape, the counselors were provided with a job description, a description of the company, and a standard form résumé, which they studied for 15 minutes. While viewing the videotape, the counselors marked their hire or no-hire decisions on a rating sheet while being timed with a concealed stopwatch. After seeing the tape, the counselors were asked to complete a questionnaire on the applicant's intelligence, motivation, self-assurance, sociability, and overall acceptability for the job.

The study found that the counselors did perceive a considerable difference between the high-quality and low-quality applicants. The questionnaire indicated that acceptability had the strongest effect, and motivation, intelligence, and self-assurance followed, all being significant at .001. Sociability had the least effect and was not statistically significant. The time-expectation manipulation (15 versus 30 minutes) had no effect upon the ratings. It is of interest to note that there was a sizable halo effect (ratings are biased by a general impression) on the ratings by the employment counselors.

Generally, the high-quality applicant received high ratings and a long decision time, and the low-quality applicant generally received low ratings and a short decision time. Also, in the low-quality presentation, the counselors who waited longer to make a decision gave higher ratings, and in the high-quality presentation, those counselors who waited longer to make a decision gave lower ratings. There was no effect of sex on decision time or the amount of time needed for the information to have "clinched" the decision. Eye contact appeared to be part of the decision; counselors who made an accept decision generally mentioned eye contact as good, and those who rejected generally mentioned eye contact as poor.

Summary Review of Research Study 4-1-C   This study suggests that in an interview, the decision time can be manipulated by the situation. For instance, the quality of the applicant is an important factor in determining how long it takes for a decision to be made. Another factor appears to be the length of time allocated for the interview. Those employment counselors who made early reject decisions on the low-qualified applicants tended to give them higher ratings than did the counselors who made later reject decisions. With the high-qualified applicants, those counselors who made early accept decisions tended to give lower ratings than did those who made later accept decisions.

The study also indicates that applicant quality and expected interview length do affect the decision time. Although the quality of the applicant was not a manipulatable variable, since the counselors were able to discriminate in this, the length of the interview was manipulatable. It would appear that increasing the allocated time for an interview may make the interviewer less likely to make a premature judgment. Variables not considered in this study that might be considered in future research include the effect of interviewer training, interviewer experience, and interview structure.

Research Study 4-1-D

Does body language have an effect on interviewers? Would it matter if the interviewer were male or female?

Sterrett[4] presented to a group of 160 mid-level life insurance managers, routinely involved in hiring, videotapes depicting an employment interview with a young male using body language. After viewing one of eight randomly assigned videotapes demonstrating either high or low body-language intensity, the managers rated the applicant from 1 to 10 (highest rating) on eight scales: ambition, motivation, self-confidence, self-organization, responsibility, verbal ability, intelligence, and sincerity. The eight videotapes demonstrated either high or low intensity for eye contact, hand gestures, dress, and pause length in answering the interviewer's questions. The determination of the level of intensity (high or low) was obtained from the average intensities demonstrated by 100 subjects in an earlier study by Sterrett.

Since the sample of 160 managers was composed of 100 males and 60 females, any difference in scoring was also investigated. The study found that there were no significant differences owing to body language, whether of high or low intensity, or whether the manager was male or female. However, there was a significant difference between high or low intensity and male or female, owing largely to the ratings on the ambition scale. The male managers rated the applicants higher on ambition for the high-intensity body language than for the low-intensity. The female managers' reaction was the opposite, with the low-intensity videotapes receiving a higher rating for ambition than the high-intensity tapes. Sterrett wonders whether ambition was equated with aggression, which the female managers may have found to be threatening, resulting in the low rating.

Summary Review of Research Study 4-1-D   The intensity of the body language did not significantly affect the ratings of the eight scales—ambition, motivation, self-confidence, self-organization, responsibility, verbal ability, intelligence, and sincerity. However, the finding that ambition ratings varied by interviewer sex was significant. It appears that the female interviewers' perception of ambition decreased, and the male interviewers' perceptions of ambition increased, with high-intensity body language. It is possible that the interviewers of both sexes equate ambition with aggression, and whereas the males found it positive, the females possibly found it threatening.

REFERENCES

[1]Carlson, R.F., "Effect of Interview Information in Altering Valid Impressions," *Journal of Applied Psychology*, 55 (1971), 66–72.

[2]Constantin, S.W., "An Investigation of Information Favorability in the Employment Interview," *Journal of Applied Psychology*, 61 (1976), 743–49.

[3]Tullar, W.L., T.W. Mullins, and S.A. Caldwell, "Effects of Interview Length and

Applicant Quality on Interview Decision Time," *Journal of Applied Psychology,* 64 (1979), 669–74.

[4]Sterrett, J.H., "The Job Interview: Body Language and Perceptions of Potential Effectiveness," *Journal of Applied Psychology,* 63 (1978), 388–90.

QUESTIONS

1. With respect to the research incident, how would you rate Hugh Mills as an interviewer? Explain your position.
2. What should the president of the company have done or not done? Why?
3. Was Janet Uphill a victim, or did she deserve her fate? Any advice?
4. With regard to the interviewer and the interview system, what are your observations, pro or con?

Research Incident 4-2:
Dick Biggs Smokes His Pipe

- When interviewers are allowed to choose the order of information being presented by the applicant, is the most important information obtained at the beginning, middle, or end of the selection interview?
- How important is it to the applicant in making an employment decision that the interviewer show familiarity with the job in question?
- What is the effect on employment interview ratings of varying the sequence of low- and high-suitability applicants appearing before the interviewer?

The résumé that Dick Biggs held looked very interesting. It wasn't often that Mountain Insurance Company received inquiries from the Ivy League, let alone an M.B.A. It was in Dick's department that the vacancy existed, and it was his job to land the new recruit, assuming no warts. Apparently, the company president was impressed, so Dick could offer more than the usual starting salary.

The interview started out on time, and the applicant looked sharp—perhaps too sharp for Mountain Insurance and the available position. Dick, while doing his best to present the company in the best light, didn't feel very sharp himself today. Working a full-day schedule at the company and then attending law school at night was beginning to tell. The company was paying the tuition at law school and had even encouraged Dick to study at the office when he wasn't busy, which was rather frequent.

The M.B.A. was loaded with questions, and Dick felt his eyes start to droop. Quickly he pulled out his pipe and, after the filling and lighting ritual, puffed away. However, with the warmth of the pipe, the pleasant taste, and the smoke softly swirling, his eyes twitched some more. The pauses lengthened as finally the M.B.A. began to run down. Dick had lost track along the way; in asking more questions of the applicant, he got the impression he was repeating himself. Somehow, the interview ended, with the applicant once again in the hands of the human resource manager, being escorted through the company chain of command. Dick Biggs sat at his desk wearily wondering if he could make it to class tonight.

RELEVANT EMPIRICAL
RESEARCH STUDIES

Research Study 4-2-A

What is the difference between an interview in which the interviewer controls the order of information received and one with uncontrolled or random presentation of information? How is the final decision affected by evaluating information as it is received during the interview as opposed to waiting until the end of the interview to summarize an evaluation?

Johns[1] had 32 employment interviewers evaluate a hypothetical applicant for a management position. The applicant was constructed from 30 items of information, including biographical data, academic items, and statements that might be made during an interview. At the start of the study, the employment interviewers were asked to estimate what percentage of 100 applicants accepted in their company for a lower-level management position would be successful on the job. This became the base rate or standard job success by which to judge items of applicant information. Then the interviewers were presented with 127 items of information, in which the previously mentioned 30 items were randomly included. They were instructed to estimate the percentage of successful job applicants based on the information contained in the 127 items of information.

The next phase was the stimulus for the evaluation of the applicant. There were 30 strips of paper, each containing one of the 30 items of information describing the applicant on one side. On the other side was a relevant question that was "answered" by this item of information. Those interviewers who were permitted to order input were restricted to these questions. The 30 strips of paper were placed before the interviewers, who randomly assigned each paper to one of four experimental conditions that included two levels of information order (subject's choice versus random) and two levels of frequency of evaluation (after every item versus summary only).

The study found that interviewers who received information in a random order processed that information more competently than did those who chose the order of information items. The frequency with which the applicant was evaluated did not affect the processing competence. Interviewers who controlled the order of information items chose to terminate the interview earlier than did those receiving information randomly. There was no indication of primacy in the frequent rating condition.

As a group, the interviewers were faster in remembering information encountered in the first half of the session; and this ability to remember faster was greater for the interviewers who were able to control the order of the information processed. It appears that this faster recall of information given early in the interview was due to the fact that the recalled information was considered more important than the latter information. Those interviewers who recalled more information about an applicant were in agreement in evaluating that applicant less favorably.

Summary Review of Research Study 4-2-A The study found that when the interviewer chose the order of information, the facts were processed less competently than when a random presentation was permitted. Those interviewers exercising control selected the most important information at the beginning of the interview, were quicker to recall that beginning information, and desired to terminate the interview sooner than in the case of the random interviewers. The two levels of evaluation frequency (after every item versus random) were not differentiated. Johns had hypothesized that the evaluation of information immediately after it was presented would be more competent. This hypothesis was rejected.

Another finding, which supports earlier research, is that those interviewers who remembered more of the characteristics of an applicant tended to evaluate that applicant less favorably.

Research Study 4-2-B

Are the impressions made by the interviewer upon the applicant important to the applicant's final decision?

Schmitt and Coyle[2] mailed a questionnaire to a sample of Michigan State University undergraduates who had used the services of the university placement office. The questionnaire asked the students, of whom 237 responded, to answer questions designed to obtain their perception of and any decision or impressions about their last employment interview. The sample was 68 percent male, with 51 percent business or management majors and 28 percent engineering majors; the average age was 22. The questionnaire consisted of three parts: The first part asked students to report on their perceptions of the interview via a Likert format of 74 items. The second part contained nine questions constructed as dependent variables to determine impressions or decisions resulting from the interview. The third part contained demographic variables, such as sex, parent's occupation and income, expected income, major study field, and past work history.

The results of the study indicate six factors to be considered of importance. The factor accounting for most of the variance was the degree of warmth and thoughtfulness of the interviewer. The second factor was how the interviewer conducted the session: duplication of questions, clarity of the questions, and the directness of the interviewer's replies. The third factor was the degree of self-confidence and forcefulness displayed by the interviewer, and the fourth related to the interviewer's speech pattern, thought presentation, and correctness of behavior. The fifth factor was the job information given: the salary, advancement, and job characteristics of the position being offered. The final factor was the manner in which the interviewer expressed opinions and attempted to determine the interviewee's opinions. The demographic variables, such as past work history, age, sex, expected salary, and parent's salary, were not significantly related to the impressions or decisions resulting from the interview.

Summary Review of Research Study 4-2-B   The most important factor to the interviewee, accounting for most of the impressions, was the personality of the interviewer. A good interviewer was described as a dependable, thoughtful, cooperative, nice person. Apparently the job applicant is sensitive to the human relations ability of the interviewer, and that significantly affects the employment decision. Of relative importance were the interviewer's mannerisms during the interview. Although the job applicants were aware of the aggressiveness and self-confidence of the interviewer, these appeared to have little positive or negative influence in the decision process. A relatively important consideration, however, was the interviewer's knowledge of and familiarity with the job itself. This factor is of interest, since it is not interpersonal in nature and is not part of the interviewer's personality.

The authors conclude that the interview situation is an important consideration with regard to job acceptance, perception of the company, and perception of the interviewer. Further, the applicant appears to form an impression of the interviewer—whether that person is "good" or "bad"—and this impression is an important factor in the employment decisions.

Research Study 4-2-C

How important is the frame of reference used by the interviewer in evaluating an applicant? Could acceptance or rejection of an applicant depend less upon that person's qualifications than on the qualifications of the previously interviewed applicants?

Wexley and others[3] asked 80 undergraduate psychology students to watch videotaped interviews of applicants for the job of office-system salesman and to rate each applicant. Prior to viewing the tapes, the students were given a detailed description of the sales job and an evaluation guide consisting of a series of questions about an applicant's qualifications that should be considered before assigning a rating. The videotapes were structured to show the applicant as having either high, average, or low suitability for the job. However, of the three tapes the students viewed, the first two would always be of the same suitability, resulting in a particular frame of reference. For example, the first two tapes might show the applicant as being of average suitability, and the third might show low suitability.

The authors found that when the student raters first saw two low-suitability tapes, they would rank the third higher than if the first two tapes had been of higher-suitability applicants. So it appears that a frame of reference had been established by the first two tapes, which then affected the rating of the third. Further, a low-suitability applicant received lower ratings when preceded by two high-suitability tapes than when preceded by two low-suitability tapes.

Although these results are statistically significant, they still account for only 1 or 3 percent of the total variance in the ratings when a high- or low-suitability tape is shown in the third position. What happens when an average-suitability tape is shown in the third position? The ratings for the average-suitability tape were significantly higher when preceded by two low-suitability tapes than when preceded by two high-suitability tapes. In fact, the contrast accounted for a substantial 80 percent of the total variance in ratings. The study suggests that the types of applicants preceding another applicant can be an important source of error in employment interview ratings.

Summary Review of Research Study 4-2-C   When applicants are of intermediate suitability, the contrast effects between applicants can be an important source of error in employment interview ratings.

The contrast effects were found to be the largest for average or neutral applicants. A possible explanation is that there is a ceiling on the high ratings and a floor on the low ratings. In a low-low-high (LLH) condition, the high-suitability applicant could not be rated much higher than in the HHH condition. Also, the low-suitability applicant in the LLL condition could not be rated much lower in the HHL condition. However, when the average-suitability applicant appeared in the third position, the ceiling-and-floor problem was not present, allowing more room for an upward or downward shift in ratings.

Further, the average-suitability applicant might have been a more ambiguous stimulus than the H or L, since people (including raters) tend to focus on what is novel. Although the average-suitability applicant is both suited and not suited for the job, the raters might have selectively focused on those characteristics that contrasted with those of the other applicants. So in the LLA condition, the average-suitability applicant emerged looking more suited for the position.

As possible limitations on this study, the subjects were students with relatively little interviewing experience, and there were no actual interviews—only observations of videotapes of simulated interviews.

REFERENCES

[1]Johns, Gary, "Effects of Informational Order and Frequency of Applicant Evaluation upon Linear Information-Processing Competence of Interviewers," *Journal of Applied Psychology*, 60 (1975), 427–33.

[2]Schmitt, N., and B.W. Coyle, "Applicant Decisions in the Employment Interview," *Journal of Applied Psychology*, 61 (1976), 184–92.

[3]Wexley, K.N., G.A. Yukl, S.Z. Kovacs, and R.E. Sanders, "Importance of Contrast Effects in Employment Interviews," *Journal of Applied Psychology*, 56 (1972), 45–48.

QUESTIONS

1. In the research incident, how well did Dick Biggs do in conducting the interview? Indicate both good and bad points.
2. From the information in the incident, how well did the M.B.A. perform in the interview?
3. As a new human resource specialist at Mountain Insurance, what suggestions would you make to improve interviewing procedure?

Research Incident 4-3:
Richard Bjorklund Finds Time to Think

- The situational interview is based on questions resulting from critical work incidents collected in job analysis. How valid is this selection interview technique?
- How effective is the assessment center in predicting promotions?
- Does performance on an in-basket test relate to actual on-the-job performance?

It was early Saturday morning, and for once, the human resource office was quiet. So Richard Bjorklund eased into his chair and surveyed his domain. The office arrangement was open, with no partitions, and Richard smiled as he viewed the untidy desks covered with stacks of paper. Perhaps production would have been a better game to be in, Richard thought; no other company function can have such a large paper flow as human resource.

That brought to mind the purpose of this early-morning visitation, a reply to a memo from the newly hired vice-president of human resource and labor relations, requesting an update on the company's selection procedures. A reasonable and innocuous request, but Richard had decided it was worth a quiet Saturday morning in the office to mull over and, he hoped, circumvent any potential problems.

Richard was well aware of the human frailties involved with interviewing techniques, and the human resource department conducted periodic training sessions in an attempt to reduce some of the problems. However, for the past four years, the company had started to rely on situational interviews and assessment centers as selection techniques rather than other processes that were solely dependent upon interviewing methods. Fortunately, some data were available, and as Richard scanned the computer printout, it appeared that those employees selected under the situational interview or assessment centers were staying with the company longer and were also moving on a faster track for promotions. Very interesting.

Well, let's get on with the memo. Richard checked his golf-trophy desk clock and wondered whom the gang had found to replace him in today's foursome.

RELEVANT EMPIRICAL RESEARCH STUDIES

Research Study 4-3-A

How reliable is the situational interview for selection purposes? Is it as valid as more costly selection methods, such as assessment centers?

Latham and others[1] regard the past selection interview research as lacking reliability and validity. Their study was based on Locke's theory of goal setting, that intentions are related to behavior; that is, that what people say correlates highly with what they do. The authors believe that the situational interview may reduce the need for expensive written aptitude tests and costly assessment centers.

In the present study, a systematic job analysis was used in perfecting the performance appraisal instrument and the selection interview. There were actually three studies: Studies 1 and 2 were concurrent validity studies of an industrial setting in the northwestern United States for an entry-level job and first-line supervisor; study 3 was in the rural South.

The first study involved 49 union hourly sawmill workers who were randomly selected from 207 employed in a mill. They were male, 44 were white, and the mean age was 29.4 years.

In the second study were 63 first-line foremen, white males, mean age 43.3 years, with a 5.4 mean number of years on the job.

A critical-incident technique was used in the job analysis, resulting in four performance criteria or behavioral observation scales (BOS). Every BOS contained from four to 13 behavioral items on a five-point Likert-type scale.

For the hourly workers, the job analysis yielded nine BOS, each containing from two to twelve behavioral items. Each behavioral item was rated on the Likert-type scale, and the rater made a global rating on a nine-point scale as to the person's overall effectiveness on each criterion.

The situational interviews for both the hourly workers and the foremen were developed by three to five company supervisors who had had experience in interviewing and supervising. They examined the critical incidents collected in the job analysis for such job areas as attendance, safety, interaction with peers, work habits, and so on. The procedure was for each superintendent to pick one "best" incident that represented the particular criterion and turn it into a question. This question was then read aloud to the group. By consensus, only one or two questions were selected, to ensure that the interview would last only one hour. For each question selected, the superintendents selected a benchmark answer that they had actually heard in an interview to represent the points on the Likert-type scale. Thus, a 5 represented an answer from a person subsequently judged outstanding, a 3 an answer from mediocre performers, and a 1 an answer from poor performers. A group consensus was reached for each benchmark answer.

The situational interview for the hourly workers contained 17 questions, and the interview for the foremen contained 16 questions. For each interview, a concurrent validity study was conducted. During the interview, one person read the question and two or more recorded the answer.

The interviewers were scored by 20 superintendents working in pairs and unaware of the interviewee's identification. The study 1 group superintendents participated in a 20-minute group discussion with one of the authors on ways to minimize rating errors such as contrast effects, halo, similar to me, and the like. In the study 2 group, the superintendents received an eight-hour in-depth training course on minimizing errors and evaluating others. The two study groups worked independently of each other.

The results indicate that the interjudge reliabilities were significant for both the hourly-worker and foreman interviews. Also, the internal consistency was significant for both groups.

For study 1, the hourly-worker interview scores correlated significantly with each of the nine performance criterion items on the behavioral observation scales. They also correlated significantly with the global rating as to the overall effectiveness of the person on the criterion, as they also did with the total BOS scores. Removing the effect of experience did not significantly reduce the correlations.

In study 2, the interview scores for the foreman interviews correlated significantly with three of the four BOS. They correlated with safety, work habits, and organizational commitment but did not correlate with interaction with subordinates. The interview scores also correlated significantly with the total BOS score and were not significantly affected when experience was partialed out.

For study 3, the predictive validity of the situational interview was investigated. This study took place in the rural South in an area of strong affirmative action that permitted a determination of the effectiveness of the situational interview in selecting females and blacks. The sample was 56 applicants for entry-level work in a pulp mill, all of whom were hired. The applicants were black, 30 were females, and their mean ages were 31.5 years for the females and 30 years for the males. The procedures were identical to those in study 1 for developing the interview questions and the performance appraisal instrument. Ten questions were agreed upon for the situational interview.

The mean interobserver reliabilities of the rating on the situational interview were significant, as was the internal consistency. The supervisors received the same training for minimizing rater errors as that given the study 2 group. After twelve months on the job, the employees' job performance was evaluated by the supervisors, who were unaware of how the employees were rated in the situational interview. A composite job-performance rating was determined for each employee. The correlation between the situational interview performance and performance on the job for twelve months was significant.

Summary Review of Research Study 4-3-A　In this study, the situational interview was used as a selection technique based on a systematic job analysis using a critical-incident approach. Supervisors turned the incidents into interview questions, with the interviewees indicating how they would behave. These responses were rated by two or more interviewers based on a scale agreed upon by the supervisors. For studies 1 and 2, there were significant interobserver reliability coefficients, significant internal consistencies of the interview questions, and significant concurrent validity coefficients.

For study 3, the mean interobserver reliabilities of the rating on the situational interview were significant, as was the internal consistency. Also, the predictive validity coefficients were significant for both the black males and females.

This suggests that intentions do correlate with behavior and indicates the effectiveness of the situational interview in the selection process.

Research Study 4-3-B

How accurate is the predictive validity of the assessment-center method? What is the effect long-term? How does the assessment-center rating compare to that of general management?

Hinrichs[2] noted that from the early 1960s to ten years later, an estimated 1,000 or more organizations used the assessment-center technique. Hinrichs's study was an eight-year validation follow-up of a large electronics company's assessment center that evaluated marketing personnel in its field organization. It also investigated the relationship of the assessment-center ratings to those of a more "natural" management evaluation of management potential.

The original research in 1967 involved 47 people in an attempt to predict advancement in management. These people were assessed by an assessment center and by two management representatives. The management representatives independently evaluated all available data in the personnel files of the 47 and, without any knowledge of the assessment-center evaluations, made their own evaluations of the management potential. This procedure was similar to the one routinely used by the organization in recommending people for promotion, although this time, a long-term prediction of management potential was included.

The overall assessment-center rating correlated .46 with the management-potential evaluation, suggesting an area of overlap between the two ratings. Further, there was a partial correlation of .37 with the overall assessment-center rating and the relative salary standing that was controlled for the management ratings. This could mean that the assessment-center evaluation does provide significant additional information regarding potential success beyond that provided by the manager's evaluation of data in the personnel files.

With the preceding as background, the present study investigated the predictive validity of the assessment-center method and compared it to the predictive accuracy of the "natural" manager evaluation.

The procedure was to follow up eight years later on the 47 people in the 1967 study and to determine whether the assessment center or the managers' evaluation proved more accurate in the long term. Neither prediction had been referred to during the eight-year period, so the data were not contaminated. The criterion used was the actual positions the 47 had attained in the organization as defined by the formal job-evaluation system. Of the original 47, data were available for 30, since 14 had terminated and data for three were not available.

The results indicated that correlations for the two predictors, starting with the initial position at year 1 and comparing the level attained eight years later, were more highly correlated at year 8 than at year 1. When year 1 was controlled for, the partial correlations suggested that the relationship at year 8 was not completely the result of year 1 differences being perpetuated over time. Also, the prediction by the two managers based on the review of personnel data predicted the eight-year criterion more significantly than did the assessment center. However, the change in position level from year 1 to year 8 was not predicted significantly by either the assessment center or the two managers. Further, neither the assessment center's nor the managers' prediction was related to turnover, either voluntary or involuntary.

Twelve characteristics were evaluated by the assessment center at year 1 with position level. At year 8, many of these characteristics significantly correlated with the level at year 8. Those characteristics included aggressiveness, persuasive and selling ability, oral communications, self-confidence, interpersonal contact, decision making, and resistance to stress. The characteristics not correlating significantly included energy level, administrative ability, written communications, planning and organization, and risk taking. Most of the characteristics demonstrated a greater correlation with the level at year 8 than at year 1. For instance, the largest correlation was for aggressiveness, which increased from .27 at year 1 to .69 at year 8. The next largest was for persuasive and selling ability, increasing from a correlation of .29 to .59.

During the assessment-center evaluation, certain objective tests were administered. The partial correlations of these test scores with the promotion predictions indicated some interesting trends. There were significant positive relationships for the Ascendency scale on the Gordon Personal Profile, the Self-Assurance scale on the Self-Description Inventory, and the Economic and Political scales on the Study of Values. However, several scales had negative correlations with the predictions: both scales (Consideration and Initiating Structure) on the Leadership Opinion Questionnaire, the Social and Religious scales on the Study of Values, and the Responsibility scale on the Gordon Personal Profile. Apparently, characteristics that indicate a methodical approach to organizational life and a degree of social awareness were detrimental to success in this company.

Summary Review of Research Study 4-3-B   In an eight-year follow-up, the assessment center in this study demonstrated significant predictive validity in predicting promotions. Assessment characteristics that were validated included aggressiveness, self-confidence, selling skills, oral communications, interpersonal contact, decision making, and resistance to stress. Test scales of ascendency, self-assurance, and political and economic values were also important. The picture of the successful person is of a hard charger, socially insensitive and upwardly mobile. The relationship between these assessment data and job-level increases, over the eight years of the study, further supported the predictive validity of the assessment center. Yet a provocative finding of the study is that the "natural" prediction of the two managers reviewing data in personnel files predicted the promotional level more significantly than did the assessment center.

Research Study 4-3-C

What is the procedure in designing an in-basket test? How should the responses be scored? Who determines the activities to be scored?

Brass and Oldham[3] conducted a study to determine whether the performance that is measured in an in-basket test corresponds to the observed performance under actual management conditions. The authors say that the past disappointing results in validating in-basket tests as a selection technique may have been caused by scoring categories that did not accurately reflect effective management activities. They suggest that in-basket scoring be on behavioral activities that have been shown to reliably predict managerial and subordinate work performance.

In the present study, the authors used six specific leadership activities that had been empirically tested by Oldham in his reported 1976 research. These activities included personally rewarding (a pat on the back or a smile), personally punishing (verbal criticism or a frown), setting goals (produce 40 product units in two hours), placing personnel (assign subordinates challenging tasks), designing job systems (enrich jobs with autonomy and responsibility), and designing feedback systems (subordinate receives more complete information). The authors believed that a more accurate prediction of a person's management performance will be obtained if the in-basket responses were scored on these six leadership activities.

The research was conducted in a large manufacturing company in the Midwest. The data were obtained from 71 first-level male foremen who completed the in-basket test. The foremen supervised from six to 21 subordinates. The criterion or evaluation data were obtained from eleven department superintendents who supervised the foremen.

The design of the in-basket test represented a comprehensive simulation of the first-level foreman's job in that organization. Data were obtained by observing the foremen at work and interviewing them over a one-month period. Emphasis was given to the actual correspondence received in their in-baskets. This resulted in 28 items that were designed to be ambiguous enough to require personal judgment, to require a wide range of solutions, and to occur in normal job activities.

The in-basket test was administered in small groups. The foremen were told that the results would be confidential and that the test was not to evaluate their performance but that it might be used later to select and train future foremen. The test lasted 2½ hours and the foremen assumed the role of a person recently promoted to first-level foreman. Only six of the foremen failed to respond to all 28 items in the in-basket within the time limit.

Their responses were scored according to the six leadership activities described earlier. The authors developed a scoring manual with specific rules for each of the six leadership activities in relation to the 28 items of the in-basket. The scoring was based on the belief that each of the 28 in-basket items provided the foreman with the chance to use one or more of the six leadership activities. However, only one leadership score was indicated for each item, so that the maximum score for a single leadership category would be 28. The responses were recorded by the author and two research assistants.

Upon completion of the in-basket tests, the eleven department superintendents rated the foremen in their units on the following eight dimensions: product quality, training, employee welfare, corrective action, technical ability, customer job demands, manpower productivity, and administrative duties. These eight effectiveness measures were rated on a seven-point scale ranging from "very ineffective" to "very effective," which represented critical incidents obtained from the department superintendents and categorized by them as ineffective or effective behavior. Ratings of the eight measures were averaged, forming a composite foreman effectiveness rating.

The results demonstrate the reliability of the scoring procedures. There was substantial agreement between the first author and the two research assistants as to the extent that the foremen used the six leadership activities. Also, the six leadership activities were positively related to one another, although only the correlation between "personally rewarding" and "setting goals" was significant.

The relationship among the six leadership activities and the eight effectiveness measures showed that four of the leadership activities were positively and significantly related to the composite foreman effectiveness rating: personally rewarding, personally punishing, setting goals, and designing job systems. The placing of personnel and designing of feedback systems were not significantly correlated with the composite effectiveness rating.

The amount of variance that all six leadership activities account for in the composite effectiveness measure was examined. It was found that a substantial amount of the effectiveness variance resulted from the leadership behavior demonstrated by the foremen while taking the in-basket test.

Summary Review of Research Study 4-3-C   It appears that a person's performance on an in-basket test can correspond to an actual on-the-job work performance if the appropriate in-basket scoring categories are used. This study found that foremen who were rated effective performers by their supervisors performed certain behaviors during the in-basket test: personally rewarding employees for good work, personally punishing subordinates for poor work, setting specific performance objectives, and enriching their subordinates' jobs. The authors caution that the present study's results are substantially stronger than those of previous research, suggesting that this study's focus on using scoring categories having to do with leaders' controlling certain parts of their subordinates' work environment might account for the promising results that were obtained.

REFERENCES

[1]Latham, G.P., L.M. Saari, E.D. Pursell, and M.A. Campion, "The Situational Interview," *Journal of Applied Psychology,* 65 (1980), 422–27.

[2]Hinrichs, J.R., "An Eight-year Follow-up of a Management Assessment Center," *Journal of Applied Psychology,* 63 (1978), 596–601.

[3]Brass, D.J., and G.R. Oldham, "Validating an In-Basket Test Using an Alternative Set of Leadership Scoring Dimensions," *Journal of Applied Psychology,* 61 (1976), 652–57.

QUESTIONS

1. What support can we offer to validate the effectiveness of the situational interview as a selection technique?
2. Is the assessment center for managerial evaluation a more effective predictor of long-term promotional performance? What evidence can you provide to support your position? Discuss.
3. What is required to obtain an accurate prediction of a person's management performance from the results of an in-basket exercise? Explain.

NON-EMPIRICAL RESEARCH ARTICLE ABSTRACTS

Abstract 4-1

- How reliable and valid is the unstructured selection interview?
- In a structured selection interview, how closely should the interviewer adhere to the standardized questions?
- What is contained in the interview log, and what is its purpose?

These questions are addressed by Terry W. Mullins, University of North Carolina–Greensboro, and Ronald H. Davis, Carolina Steel Corporation, in a 1981 article.[1]

The authors say that although the selection interview is the most widely used of all selection devices, numerous research studies show it to be unreliable and invalid. Their suggestion is a systematic strategy for managing the selection interview to increase its utility and reduce claims of unfair discrimination.

One problem with the selection interview is that although the human resource department has the responsibility for the effectiveness of the interview process, most of the interviewers do not report to the human resource department. Another problem is the lack of consistency used in unstructured selection interviews in which the same interviewer uses varying approaches with different applicants. The result is poor reliability or low agreement among the interviewers.

Some of the specific problems with the unstructured selection interview are these: The interviewer may become overconfident, developing a sense of infallibility that encourages hasty judgments without supporting information; interviewers often spend more than half the interview talking themselves, rather than gathering job-related information from the applicant; with the interviewers all asking varying questions of the applicants, decisions may be based on irrelevant information; some raters evaluate all the applicants as average, committing the error of central tendency; one characteristic may receive undue weight, overshadowing other characteristics, which is the halo effect; if the interviewer talks first to several poor applicants, a mediocre applicant following may receive an undeserved high rating; some interviewers give all high ratings, and others give all low ratings, committing leniency and strictness errors; interviewers may have a stereotype of the ideal applicant that may be invalid; some interviewers allow their personal biases to affect the interview; many interviewers ask trick questions so that they can play psychologist; and reviewers often ask inappropriate questions that are not job-related.

Although the problems above indicate the need to manage the selection interview, the authors suggest a more important reason to do so: The unstructured interview is subject to EEOC charges that it discriminates because it is unstandardized and subjective. This is ironic, since many companies stopped using employment tests in favor of interviews, believing that these would avoid equal employment problems. However, the authors say that the EEOC classifies the interview as a test, so it must meet the criteria as any selection device would.

Validation of a paper-and-pencil test is difficult, but it is far more difficult to validate unstructured selection interviews. If an organization tries to provide validation, it must have a systematic procedure for conducting interviews and recording their outcomes.

A suggested approach to systematizing the selection interview in order to avoid the problems discussed above would be, first, to use job analysis as the basis of developing a structured interview format, then to establish a training program for interviewers to prevent rating errors and poor questioning techniques, then to validate the new interview procedure and reviewer accuracy, and finally, to develop a record system of data collection that monitors the interview process.

An approach to structuring the selection interview is to require the interviewer to ask a standard set of questions of each applicant. The questions should deal with the skills, abilities, and interests required for that particular job. These questions, when written down, become an interview guide, and with every interviewer carefully following this guide, the problem of poor and inconsistent questions is reduced. However, even with the interview guide, the validity of the interview will not be increased unless the standard questions do discriminate between successful and unsuccessful applicants.

The job-analysis technique provides a list of the skills, tasks, and personal characteristics required to perform a particular job. The job analysis results in a job description and a job specification. These are used to form job-related questions that make up the interview guide. For the interviewer, following the guide carefully does not preclude asking follow-up questions to obtain elaboration from the applicant.

Four major benefits result from a standardized interview guide, as suggested by the authors: (1) Since the applicants are asked the same questions in the same order, reliability is increased and collection of data is consistent; (2) validity is increased, since the questions being asked were generated from a job analysis; (3) the standardized format reduces inappropriate and unnecessary questions; and (4) there is less opportunity for the interviewer to talk too much, resulting in hasty decisions.

Most interviews with a high potential of unfair discrimination are conducted not by the human resource department but by other company people, who ask questions regarding the applicant's age, marital status, ethnic background, or religious preference. Therefore, everyone engaged in the interviewing process needs interviewer training, not just members of the human resource department. This includes the supervisor, who will probably make the final hiring decision. Such a training program must consider what attributes of the interviewer need to be changed to avoid the rating errors of halo, central tendency, strictness, leniency, and contrast effects. The effectiveness of such a training program should be measured to determine changes in interviewer skills, knowledge, and behavior.

Since EEOC regulations recognize it, the interview must be validated if it has an adverse impact upon protected groups. This requires the services of professionally trained evaluation research specialists. The general requirements include reliability of the interviewing process. This can be achieved by correlating the ratings of several interviewers for a group of applicants. If the correlations are positive, there appears to be agreement regarding applicant suitability for a particular job. However, these positive correlations must be above .6 in order to obtain high enough reliability estimates if the interview process is to be validated.

To obtain the validation of the interview process, the interviewer's ratings of the applicant must correlate with actual job performance. If the number of minority applicants is substantial—say, 40—then the EEOC guidelines require a separate validity estimate for them. With validity established, poor selection decisions should decrease significantly, and documentation should be easy.

The interview selection process should also be monitored through the use of the interview guide and an interviewer log listing outcomes. The interviewer log should contain the name of the interviewer, the name of the applicant, the EEO-1 classification, the title of the job, the outcome of the interview, and job-performance ratings of those hired. Also to be included are statistical reports of adverse impact by job classification and interviewer, interviewer reliability reports, and interview validity reports by job classification and interviewer. These data should be retained permanently for all applicants hired and for five years for those not hired. Thus there is a record of the questions asked, the answers given, and how the answers were evaluated.

The statistical reports will indicate areas of the interview selection process that need examination. For instance, certain interviewers may be the cause of errors or personal biases. Training and counseling will probably be able to resolve these problems.

The authors identify the unstructured interview as the major culprit in poor decision making during the interview. They support a structured, job-related interview based on a job analysis. This approach should improve selection and reduce unfair-discrimination charges.

REFERENCE

[1]Mullins, Terry W., and Ronald H. Davis, "A Strategy for Managing the Selection Interview Process." From the March 1981 issue of *Personnel Administrator,* copyright 1981, The American Society for Personnel Administration, 606 North Washington Street, Alexandria, VA 22314.

QUESTIONS

1. Relative to the EEOC, what problem or problems does the selection interview share with testing?
2. Even with the interview guide, what may be a validity problem resulting from the standardized questions?
3. Why use job analysis to help formulate the standardized questions?

Abstract 4-2

- Why has the selection interview become more important today than it was in the past?
- What relationship between ability and motivation is the interviewer interested in?

- What are some of the benefits to the company in following a prescribed selection interview format?

The questions above are answered in a 1983 article by Charles G. Tharp of the Pillsbury Company.[1]

The author indicates that some of the reasons the recruiting and screening of applicants have become more important are the equal employment laws, a shortage of high-tech applicants, the immobility of career couples, increased staffing owing to turnover and promotion, and the increased costs of poor selections. Since selection is the most critical function affecting success, a logical and structured approach is needed.

Selection interviews are the only process by which managers can evaluate candidates to predict future job success. One such predictor category is past work experience. As a primary screening device, it allows the interviewer to determine the similarity between past work and the requirements of the new job; qualifications and skills from past work that apply to the new job; performance and accomplishments in similar positions; similarity to the new job of the situation and organization background of the job where the experience was gained; and the ability of the applicant to add to past experiences.

Another category for predicting applicant success is intelligence and education. The author does not equate intelligence with IQ, but rather with quickness of thought, verbal skills, and ability to solve problems. Education indicates whether a person has mastered a career field, such as law or engineering. The key areas to investigate relative to intelligence and education are these: problems solved and data analyzed in previous jobs; planning and conceptualizations in previous jobs; ability to articulate ideas and experiences clearly; grade point average, particularly in the major; and performance on standardized testing instruments. Yet ability alone does not predict success, since motivation must also be present.

A third category for predicting success is the match between the applicant's career expectations and the ability of the organization to develop and provide appropriate promotions. The following factors help the organization determine the applicant's motivation and career expectations: need for direction in previous jobs; extra job assignments and ideas suggested; nonwork activities pursued and achievements; independence and proportion of educational expenses personally paid; realistic timing of career plans and objectives; and present satisfaction with career progress.

The author suggests that in addition, the interviewer should spend enough time to establish "gut feelings" or interpersonal "chemistry" evaluations, by asking questions about family background, social experiences, and outside interests.

Tharp suggests that the job interview should last from one to one and a half hours, following this format: (1) Explain your organizational role and that of the position. Also discuss products, production facilities, geographic locations, employee population, human resource philosophy, the organization's strategic plan, and the responsibilities of the other interviewers who will be met. (The purpose here is to put the applicant at ease and provide a background of the organization.) (2) Review the résumé information. (The purpose is to ensure a logical sequence.) (3) Probe early family experiences, educational accomplishments, part-time jobs, and extracurricular activities. (The purpose is to learn the applicant's achievement orientation, interests, intelligence, social skills, and adjustment.) (4) Probe job progression after graduation as to reasons for leaving and for accepting the next job. (The purpose is to learn about career orientation, decision ability, whether job changes were voluntary, and the applicant's ability to plan, maturity, and personal learning curve.) (5) Review the preceding three jobs as to work environment, applicant performance, contributions, and results achieved. (The purpose is to learn about the applicant's performance in different situations and to predict performance in the prospective organization.) (6) Present a job-related problem to be solved. (The purpose is to determine the ability to conceptualize and search for solutions.) (7) Probe career plans and aspirations; ask for reference points the applicant uses in determining success. (The purpose is to determine internal and external reference points, self-confidence, self-image, and how much the applicant contributed to success.) (8) Ask about feelings of strengths and development needs with past work-related examples. (The purpose is to reveal the applicant's openness, self-confidence, assertiveness, and self-development activities.) (9) Wrap up the interview by asking for two or three things the interviewer should know about the applicant but failed to ask, and for any questions the applicant may want the interviewer to answer. (The purpose is to offer the applicant the opportunity to learn more about the company and to discuss personal qualities.)

The author concludes that the length of the selection interview will be adequate to establish a "gut feeling" about the applicant, and that such an interview format will result in greater reliability and effectiveness in selection while also being more enjoyable. The major benefits of this format are reduced turnover, higher employee career satifaction, increased performance resulting from better matches, fewer equal employment problems, and more management attention to job requirements and performance. Although this format requires more discipline, it should yield far greater benefits for the time involved.

REFERENCE

[1]"A Manager's Guide to Selection Interviewing," by Charles G. Tharp, copyright August 1983. Reprinted with the permission of *Personnel Journal,* Costa Mesta, California; all rights reserved.

QUESTIONS

1. What is the most critical function affecting the success of an applicant in an organization?
2. In the selection interview format, step 5, the applicant is asked about his or her last three jobs. What is the purpose?
3. How do you interpret the author's position on "gut feeling"? As a prospective selection interviewer, what is your position?

CHAPTER FIVE

PERFORMANCE APPRAISALS

INTRODUCTION

Most organizations maintain some type of procedure for evaluating their employees. The results of such performance appraisals are used to determine eligibility for promotion, justification for pay raises and job changes, and the rationale for retention or discharge. The person responsible for the performance appraisal is usually the employee's supervisor, although the human resource department is directly involved.

Properly completed performance appraisals provide employees with feedback as to their performance. When there are deficiencies, the performance appraisal serves as a basis for instituting change through training programs to correct poor work habits and provide adequate job knowledge.

The performance appraisal is represented in a variety of formats that evaluate the employee in reference to a selected group of desired behaviors. These behaviors are selected to represent actions that contribute to the profit effectiveness of the organization. As in any appraisal, each format has certain standards of measurement that differentiate the contributions of individual employees.

In most measurement systems, potential errors and biases must be recognized and controlled in order to produce valid evaluations. One such error is the *halo effect,* which is the rating of a person either favorably or unfavorably on most of the items in the appraisal format because the evaluator is unduly influenced by some previous impression. Halo error may be indicated when all the individual measurements of the evaluation format are high. *Constant* or *leniency error* results when a supervisor's appraisals are much the same for all subordinates despite individual differences. Thus, one supervisor may consistently evaluate subordinates high and another may consistently rate them low when, in fact, both groups are very similar. These differences are not due to differences in performance but to differences in the supervisors' standards.

Recency error results when the most recent behavior of the person being appraised is remembered by the evaluator, who then considers it to be representative of the person's total behavior. The error of *central tendency* occurs when the supervisor tends to appraise all subordinates within a narrow band of evaluation scores. The effect is to minimize the difference between the best performer and the worst. Another error that frequently occurs and is difficult to detect is the *personal biases* of the evaluator. This is reflected in a variety of personal values, prejudices, and stereotypes. The result is a performance appraisal inappropriately based on such items as manner of dress or physical attractiveness, neither of which may be representative of job performance. However, there is evidence that training programs, even of short duration, have been helpful in reducing the aforementioned errors.

There are many performance appraisal formats, but the procedure remains basically the same; the evaluator makes a "temperature" rating on a scale measuring a particular skill or behavioral characteristic representative of successful job performance. One such format that is straightforward is rating scales, in which the evaluator merely marks one of several values ranging from high to low. However, because of its simplicity, this format permits most of the errors mentioned previously.

Another performance appraisal format is employee comparison systems. These differ from the rating format in that they do not utilize absolute values. Instead, they call for evaluations of an employee based on other workers' attributes. One such format is alternation ranking, in which the "best" person is selected first, the "worst" person second, the next "best" person third, and so on. This technique has the advantage of capitalizing on the obvious differences between the top- and bottom-ranked people, with only the middle ranking requiring more difficult selections. Also, ranking eliminates the errors of central-tendency and constant error, since the employees being ranked are spread out over the whole range of performance.

The paired comparison is another employee-comparison performance appraisal format. Employees are compared against each other, with the best employee receiving the highest rating. For instance, employees are listed in alphabetical order, horizontally and then vertically. Next, each employee is compared to each of the other employees according to whether he or she is "better" than each. After the employee has been compared to all the others, the number of "betters" is counted. When all the employees have been ranked, the employee with the most "betters" is the best employee, the one with the second most "betters" is the second best, and so on. The variable that the employees are being compared by may be just one overall classification, such as effectiveness, or several characteristics deemed crucial to job success.

A problem with that format is that although it is effective within groups, comparisons between different groups becomes difficult because of the ranking procedure itself. If one group has many outstanding employees and another is more average, the ranking of both groups together would be unfair to members of the average group.

One performance appraisal format that attempts to identify several performance factors by using specific behavior items is the behaviorally anchored rating scale (BARS). It usually consists of several vertical scales, each representing an important part of a job as indicated by critical-incident job behavior. This behavior represents either unusual success or failure on the job. The evaluator then indicates the value on the vertical scale for the type of behavior that best represents the person's performance. Since these scales are usually developed by committees, they are generally accepted. However, the development of an appropriate BARS is a time-consuming and costly process.

Other performance appraisal formats are the forced distribution and forced-choice checklist. The forced distribution is similar to rating, although it tends to eliminate constant errors and errors of central tendency by requiring evaluators to place employees in predesignated categories. For example, the top 10 percent of high scorers would be in one category, the next 20 percent would be in another, the middle 40 percent in another, the next 20 percent in another, and the low 10 percent scorers in the bottom category. The forced distribution is not indicative of performance level, since the 10 percent of low scorers could still be satisfactory employees, merely representing the lowest scorers of the group.

The forced-choice checklist presents to the evaluatee the opportunity to choose between two behavioral descriptions, both of them about equally favorable. The problem from the standpoint of the evaluator is that only one of the two is actually associated with successful job performance, despite their apparent similarity. The forced-choice checklist tends to eliminate most sources of errors, although the evaluators do not know whether the interviewee is being rated favorably or unfavorably, since they do not know the difference between the two behavior descriptions.

The in-basket exercise and assessment-center management simulations were presented in the preceding chapter as possible tools in the selection interviewing process. They are also useful in the appraisal process, since their "appraising environment" is the same for all those being evaluated and is free of extraneous factors such as supervisor bias, peer pressure, working conditions, and the like.

Performance appraisals tend to meet resistance from both the evaluator and the person being evaluated. Most evaluators find it difficult to present bad news, and most evaluatees do not like to receive it. A part of the problem is that managers have many duties to perform besides performance appraisals, so a direct connection needs to be made between accurate performance appraisals and positive rewards. For the person being evaluated, the performance appraisal feedback session should be a blueprint for betterment, not a putdown. Since overcoming resistance is a continuing problem, the human resource department should review all ratings by managers to detect early any indications of rating errors. Also, cumulative performance appraisal data should be reviewed with individual managers in feedback sessions.

The performance appraisal process is a potential equal employment danger point, since evaluation decisions so directly and openly affect employees. Title VII of the Civil Rights Act allows the use of a bona fide merit system as a guide for management decisions, but the organization must ensure that the performance appraisal system being used is bona fide. This requirement is usually met by a legally defensible performance appraisal system that is based upon job requirements known to all concerned. Further, the component parts of what constitutes job performance should be clearly defined and be equitably rated, based on objective behavioral data that have been validated. In the event that the person being evaluated disagrees with the appraisal, a procedure should be available to that person for appeal purposes.

Whereas the equal employment laws are concerned with the selection process, performance appraisal systems receive special emphasis in the *Uniform Guidelines on Employee Selection Procedures.* The emphasis is on the use of job analysis to determine the important job-related performance measures and to provide evaluators with appraisal instruments designed for objective appraisals. The important point to remember is that race, sex, national origin, and religion cannot be allowed to enter into performance appraisal decisions. Otherwise, certain types of people will be rated lower than they should be, thus denying them desired promotions and pay raises.

The corrective action may be court-ordered back-pay awards and even perhaps extremely expensive class-action judgments.

RESEARCH INCIDENTS

Research Incident 5-1:
Grover Rodich and the Unexpected Response

- During a performance appraisal, what effect does the biographical similarity or lack of similarity between the appraiser and the appraisee have upon the appraisal outcome?
- Will the personality of the appraiser affect the final evaluation of the employee being appraised?
- What is the effect of the final appraisal, either good or bad, upon the employee's acceptance of the appraisal process itself?
- What can be done to improve the effectiveness of appraisers? Would goal setting be effective?

Grover Rodich studied the appraisal report on Eddy Flame and felt that the committee had once again made an appropriate, balanced, and objective evaluation. There were many accolades and only one area noted for improvement. This, he thought, should be a relatively easy and painless review session, especially compared to some of today's sessions. In fact, Grover looked forward to the next hour of review with Eddy as a welcome relief.

After the usual introductory remarks to Eddy, Grover quoted to him the well-done comments. At first, Eddy was a little tense, sitting rigidly in the chair opposite Grover, but as the list of well-dones continued at length, he appeared to become more at ease. However, when Grover mentioned the one area of needed improvement, Eddy stiffened in his chair so quickly that Grover found himself repeating that it was only one area, and really a minor one: Eddy needed more involvement outside the company in civic affairs, perhaps a civic organization, giving a speech to a civic group, something of that sort.

However, to Eddy Flame it was the final indignation. "How in the hell do you expect me to do that? . . . Working the hours I do! . . . I need an assistant to get this load off my shoulders. . . . Four back-breaking years, and I get this bull! . . ."

Ten minutes after Eddy marched out of his office, Grover was still in shock. He could not believe Eddy's reaction. Flame was an excellent manager, and the company needed more like him, not fewer. Yet the criticism was justified, and he had presented it to Eddy in his best "I am behind you 100 percent" attitude. What went wrong? Was it him or Eddy Flame? Or was it the system?

RELEVANT EMPIRICAL
RESEARCH STUDIES

Research Study 5-1-A

Does a relationship between the personal characteristics of the rater and the ratee affect the favorability of the rating?

Rand and Wexley[1] used a simulated employment interview to help answer that question. Although the employment interview and performance appraisal are two separate aspects of the human resource function, they have a similarity that seems appropriate to the question. The subjects in the study were 160 undergraduate students who volunteered to complete a questionnaire measuring interests. This resulted in four subgroups of 40 students each, divided equally among high- and low-interest members. The students then viewed a videotape of an interview in which twelve questions were asked of the applicant. In each of the high- and low-interest groups, half viewed an applicant who was biographically similar and half viewed an applicant who was biographically dissimilar. After the viewing, the applicant was rated on a 25-point hiring and interpersonal judgment scale.

The results indicated that biographical similarity was the major factor in the evaluation outcome. The ratings on job suitability, intelligence, personal attributes, and attraction increased with similarity. This result occurred regardless of the race (white, black) of the applicant, or the level of racial prejudice, or the affiliation needs of the student interviewers.

Some limitations of the study include the simulation approach, with the problem of external validity, and the fact that some of the black stereotypic statements may have caused negative reinforcement of dissimilarity.

Summary Review of Research Study 5-1-A   The study clearly indicates that the major factor in the evaluation of the job candidates was the biographical similarity between the evaluator and the applicant. Similarity increased the valuations for intelligence, personal attributes, and candidate attractiveness, regardless of the race of the applicant or the level of race prejudice and the affiliation needs of the interviewers. However, highly prejudiced interviewers awarded lower job-suitability ratings to all the applicants, regardless of their race.

The study seems to show that interviewers fail to distinguish between their evaluations and their rating of interpersonal attraction. The authors suggest a "similar to me" effect that causes the errors, since people attempt to evaluate information that is similar as positive because of the reinforcement it provides them.

Research Study 5-1-B

What effect do the characteristics of raters have upon their evaluation of the person being rated?

Lord and others[2] studied a group of volunteer college undergraduates consisting of 54 males and 42 females assigned to four-person mixed-sex groups. Since these groups had no formal leader, any one of the four in a group could assume that position.

During group tasks, the behavior of each group member was measured from videotapes of the interaction, using a procedure developed by Lord. The subjects also completed questionnaires measuring locus of control and least-preferred co-worker. After completing four tasks in which high and low combinations of jointly produced outputs and common external information to solve a problem were manipulated, members of each group rated each other on perceived leadership, influence, and social power.

The results suggest that for the locus-of-control measure, those who believed the control of events rested beyond their control rated other members significantly higher on perceived leadership and the social-power aspect of expert power than did those who believed events were within their control. Also, the sex of the rater was significantly related to the dependent variables of leadership exhibited, task contribution, solution influence, activity control, expert power, referent power, and reward power. In all the dependent-variable categories, females provided higher ratings than males. The least-preferred-co-worker scale demonstrated a significant positive relationship with legitimate power. Significant amounts of variance in person perceptions were indicated in rater sex, locus of control, and least-preferred co-worker. Thus it appears that rater characteristics did have a significant effect on interpersonal perceptions. This suggests the importance of rater personality, since differences among raters accounted for 17 to 44 percent of the variance in person perceptions, with up to 30 percent accounted for by individual rater differences.

Summary Review of Research Study 5-1-B Rater characteristics appear to have a significant effect on interpersonal perceptions. Apparently, the personality of raters needs further consideration with respect to the accuracy of their perceptions in evaluations of influence, leadership, and social power.

The study found several variables affecting the variability of interpersonal ratings. These variables included task behavior, group performance, and rater characteristics. However, the authors point out that other studies have reported different variables of ratee verbal behavior and group-member reactions to leader influence attempts. This suggests the many facets of raters that need to be considered in accepting their evaluations.

Some limitations of the study are a nonassessment of the quality of the ratee's task behavior, the relatively short interactions of the subjects, and the fact that the groups had no designated leader. This could affect generalization of the study results to hierarchical leadership situations or interactions of longer duration.

Research Study 5-1-C

How valid is the assumption that the only good appraisal is a favorable appraisal?

Dipboye and de Pontbriand[3] received 474 replies to a mailed questionnaire sent mostly to engineers, scientists, and technicians involved in research and development work. The questionnaire consisted of twelve Likert scale items and one request for employees to describe their last performance appraisal.

The results indicated several items that were strongly related to opinions of the appraisal session and of the appraisal system. These items were the perceived favorability, the relevance of what was evaluated, and whether plans and objectives were discussed.

The study shows that although the perceived favorability of the appraisal by the person being appraised is still an important correlation of acceptance of the appraisal system, other items are also important. The authors state that employees who receive negative feedback regard the appraisal system as being negative. However, it is suggested that employees will be more willing to accept negative feedback if they are allowed to participate in the feedback session, if plans and objectives are discussed, and if the evaluating factors are pertinent to their work. Interestingly, employee reports of the amount of talking done between the supervisor and the employee, or discussion of goal setting, did not change the perceived favorability of the appraisal by employees or their opinions of the appraisal.

Summary Review of Research Study 5-1-C   The performance appraisal was regarded by employees to be favorable or unfavorable depending on the extent to which they regarded the results as favorable. However, other attributes were found that appeared to be at least as important as the perceived favorability of the results. These attributes were the employee's perception of the devices used to measure the appraisal and any discussion of plans and objectives.

The authors caution that some limitations of the study include the low reliability and specific wording of the items; the correlations nature of the study, which prevented determining what caused the responses; and the facts that the study was a self-report measure and that favorability was measured by the employee without reference to the supervisor.

Research Study 5-1-D

How effective are training programs for improving raters' skills in performance appraisals?

A study was conducted by Ivancevich[4] of a research and development group in a large American company. Sixty team leaders, selected randomly from a population of 106 team leaders, were placed in one of three training conditions or in a control group. The three training sessions were a feedback condition, feedback plus assigned goal setting, and assigned goal setting. Each session required six hours and consisted of lecture, discussion, videotapes, critique, and role playing. A total of 203 professional subordinates of the 60 team leaders voluntarily completed a 23-item performance appraisal questionnaire designed to measure their perceptions of their most recent appraisal interview. These perceptions were classified as to equity, accuracy, comprehensiveness, clarity, motivational impact, anxiety, and degradation. The subordinates' responses to the questionnaire were subjected to a factor analysis procedure that found that five factors accounted for over 68 percent of the common variance and best represented the data. These factors were equity, accuracy, clarity, motivational impact, and anxiety.

Approximately two months after the completion of the training program for the 60 team leaders, the next cycle of performance appraisals began. After completing them, the subordinates again filled out the performance appraisal questionnaire with the same five factors best representing the data. The results of the study indicated that all three training conditions (feedback, feedback plus assigned goal setting, and assigned goal setting) were superior to the control group for subordinates' perceptions of equity occurring in the appraisal interview. The feedback-plus-assigned-goal-setting group was superior to the other training groups in regard to accuracy and clarity. It is interesting to note that there were no significant differences between any of the training groups and the control group in terms of motivational impact. Also, and perhaps of more concern, was the finding that in the two training conditions using assigned goal setting, the subordinates reported significantly higher levels of anxiety. The literature of occupational stress states that potential mental, physical, and organizational dysfunctions are related to high levels of anxiety.

Summary Review of Research Study 5-1-D The present study was designed to improve the performance appraisal interview abilities of team leaders. The data suggest that the appraisal interview reactions of subordinates were generally better when the leaders were trained to provide feedback and/or assign goal setting. However, the motivational impact of the subordinates did not significantly change as a result of the team leaders' training program. Further, in the two conditions in which the team leaders assigned goal setting, the subordinates reported significantly higher anxiety levels.

The author suggests that the results be viewed with caution, since the information was collected from questionnaires of subordinates involved in the appraisal process and may show response-response and memory bias. Also, the data might have been affected by the attention paid to the subordinates, the Hawthorne effect. Finally, the data were collected within two to four months, and the effect of such formal training may not last over time. Yet the team leaders who experienced the feedback and/or assigned goal training did improve their appraisal interviewing skills, as perceived by the subordinates, in the areas of equity and accuracy. Those team leaders trained in feedback plus assigned goal setting influenced subordinates' perceptions of clarity more than did the team leaders in the other treatments.

REFERENCES

[1]Reprinted with permission of authors and publisher from: Rand, T.M. and Wexley, K.N. "A Demonstration of the Bryne Similarity Hypotheses in Simulated Employment Interviews." *Psychological Reports*, 1975, 36, 535–44.

[2]Lord, R., J. Phillips, and M. Rush, "Effects of Sex and Personality on Perceptions of Emergent Leadership, Influence and Social Power," *Journal of Applied Psychology*, 65 (1980), 176–82.

[3]Dipboye, R.L., and R. de Pontbriand, "Correlates of Employee Reactions to Performance Appraisals and Appraisal Systems," *Journal of Applied Psychology*, 66 (1981), 248–51.

[4]Ivancevich, J.M., "Subordinates' Reactions to Performance Appraisal Interviews: A Test of Feedback and Goal-Setting Techniques," *Journal of Applied Psychology*, 67 (1982), 581–87.

QUESTIONS

1. In the research incident, what could Grover Rodich have done differently in the appraisal session with Eddy Flame? Explain.
2. What is your opinion of Eddy Flame's reaction? Was he justified? Explain.
3. What is your position regarding performance appraisals? Should we keep them or abolish them? What evidence do you have to support your position?

Research Incident 5-2:
Mr. Calderwood Is an Angel

- How do the personal attributes of raters, such as initiating structure or consideration, affect their evaluations in performance appraisals?
- What effect will training programs designed to reduce rater errors have upon the rater's long-term performance?
- Does the ability to observe certain behaviors during appraisal sessions vary among raters, and does it affect their final judgments of performance?

The performance appraisals were on the human resource manager's desk, and it was time, once again, to determine the allocation of raises. Somehow it seemed unfair to accept each department head's ratings as being compatible with the ratings of other department heads, especially since the work assignments in some departments were much more complex than in others. Then there was the question of contribution to the profitability of the company. The gang in engineering should certainly rank above those in the duplication department.

Well, thought the manager, next year these variables will have to be reconsidered, but for now, the wage and salary committee will expect me to sort out this mess and make some recommendations. Oh, my, here are George Calderwood's high appraisals for his group in the business department. That's an operation that needs to be run efficiently, but it's not the heart and soul of our high-tech company. Every manager is rated by George to be superior, with only one or two excellents. It's the same every year. George Calderwood is a nice, kind, and friendly guy; no wonder that bunch calls him an angel to work for.

*RELEVANT EMPIRICAL
RESEARCH STUDIES*

Research Study 5-2-A

Do factors external to a performance rating system affect the ultimate ratings? How does the personality of the evaluator affect the rating given an employee?

Klores[1] conducted a study of rater bias in a performance rating system. The setting was the chemical research division of a medium-sized chemical corporation. Ratings were obtained once a year, and a four-year period was observed. The rating instrument used by the company was a forced distribution, consisting of ratings on eight traits followed by a single summary performance rating. The rating categories were best 10 percent, next 20 percent, normal 40 percent, next 20 percent, and bottom 10 percent. The eight traits were amount of work, quality of work, cooperation and contacts, judgment, initiative, originality and imagination, planning and organization, and training and developing of subordinates (for supervisory responsibilities only).

In the chemical research division, there were two types of high-level people, the professionals who performed high-level technical functions and the supervisors who performed high-level administrative functions. Most of the supervisors came from the professional ranks. Also in the division were the nonprofessionals, without college degrees, who performed as skilled apparatus handlers and craftsmen, and the clericals, a small group of female secretaries. Groups of two supervisory high-level raters rated about 100 subordinates over the four-year period. Because most of the same raters gave ratings during this time, the independence of the data is reduced, but at the same time, the composition of the groups changed substantially through transfers. For instance, by the end of the four-year period, 80 percent of the ratees were being rated by different people from the ones who had rated them in the first year.

The data obtained on both the raters and ratees included job area (professional, nonprofessional, supervisory, clerical), job level, age, years with company, length of group membership, and education level. Data obtained on the ratees only were the ratings from the eight traits in the forced-distribution instrument described earlier. The data obtained on the raters only were from Fleishman's *Leadership Opinion Questionnaire*, to determine the emphasis each rater gave to initiating structure in the workplace or consideration for subordinates.

According to the results of the study, those raters who emphasized initiating structure gave significantly lower overall ratings than did those who emphasized consideration for subordinates. However, this lower rating was not because the initiating-structure raters were hard raters. Actually, they were more lenient than the rating instructions required. The difference resulted from the fact that the consideration-for-subordinates raters demonstrated a much greater leniency. In other words, both rater groups failed to enforce the intent of the rating instructions, but the consideration-for-subordinates raters were the greater violators, resulting in the highest ratings.

Also, the raters emphasizing initating structure gave overall ratings with a greater variance than did the raters emphasizing consideration. They gave significantly more weight to the trait of planning and organization than did the consideration raters.

Another interesting finding of this study is that within job areas, there was a strong, consistent job-level bias, with higher-level ratees getting higher overall ratings. Thus, those at the top level of a particular job category, such as professionals, received higher ratings than those at the lower levels.

Summary Review of Research Study 5-2-A   The high-level supervisory rater's leadership attitudes of emphasizing initiating structure or consideration, and the ratee's job-level rank in the rated group, had a very strong effect on the overall rating given on a forced-distribution performance instrument. The higher-level ratees were given higher overall ratings than the lower-level ratees were. Raters who emphasized showing consideration for subordinates gave higher ratings than those who emphasized providing structure. These high-consideration raters were also more lenient in giving the higher ratings. The ratings of the initiating-structure raters were more varied than those of the consideration raters.

It appears that performance ratings given on a forced-choice instrument are very biased in regard to the relative job level of the ratees and to the characteristics of the rater relative to expressing consideration for subordinates or of providing more structure in the work environment.

Research Study 5-2-B

How effective are training programs designed to eliminate or reduce rater errors such as halo and leniency errors?

Bernardin[2] studied 80 undergraduate college students who were randomly assigned to four groups. Group 1 received one hour of training on errors of leniency and halo effects. Group 2 was given a five-minute training session on the same errors. Group 3 members received no training but were informed of the importance of student evaluations and told that they would evaluate their instructors later in the semester. The Group 4 members first participated in another experiment, completing two short questionnaires in a situation downgrading the importance of ratings, before evaluating their instructors.

The time schedule of the study was four sessions, 14 weeks apart. At the start of the study during the first part of the semester, ratings of instructors from the preceding semester were collected from all four groups. Then groups 1 and 2 received the training, group 3 was given its instructions, and group 4 filled out the questionnaires. Fourteen weeks into the semester, ratings of instructors were collected from all four groups. At this point, half of group 4 received the one-hour training and the other half the five-minute training. The next part of the schedule occurred during the fourteenth week of the following semester, when all four groups evaluated their instructors for that semester. Group 4 did so again during the fourteenth week of the following semester. During the intervals, tests were administered to determine knowledge of the training material and its effect on the rating errors.

The results of the study were that the positive effects of the training sessions rapidly diminished to the point that after one 14-week rating period, those effects were practically nil. Further, there was a significant increase in the halo and leniency errors between the fourteenth and the twenty-eighth week. Thus it appears that by the twenty-eighth week, the positive effect of training may have completely disappeared. However, in the fourteenth week, there was a significant difference between the one-hour and the five-minute training groups relative to error. A difference was found between group 3 and 4 that the author attributed to the fact that for group 4, the importance of ratings had been downgraded. The suggestion is that the context in which the evaluation occurs is more important than the format used.

Summary Review of Research Study 5-2-B   The positive effects of a training program designed to reduce leniency and halo errors diminished within a relatively short period of time. Further, there was a significant increase in leniency error from the fourteenth week of one semester to the fourteenth week of the second semester for the groups receiving the training. This suggests that any positive effects of the training programs may have disappeared. A similar effect was noted for the increase in halo error over time. Of interest here is the fact that immediately after the training, the one-hour and the five-minute training groups did not differ in the quality of the ratings. When one group of raters was asked to hurry up and another group, participating for experimental credit, was not, the "hurry-up" group demonstrated a higher level of leniency error. Thus, the evaluation atmosphere and time constraints may strongly affect rating quality.

The authors point out that another study, in which a training program emphasized the error of leniency, resulted in ratings containing the error of central tendency. This suggests that before the value of a training program can be determined, there must be some measures of the validity of the resulting ratings.

Research Study 5-2-C

How does the ability of the rater to observe performance affect the judgments required in determining evaluations in a performance appraisal?

Murphy and others[3] studied accuracy in observing behavior in relation to the accuracy of the resultant performance rating. The authors' position is that there is a probable relationship between the two. They feel that accurate observation is a necessary precondition or requirement for accurate judgments. Yet they caution that raters who accurately observe behavior may also differ in their accuracy in evaluating performance.

In this study, 44 college undergraduates participated in the experiment in exchange for college credit. They viewed videotaped lectures delivered by drama students from a nearby university and evaluated them, using two types of rating instruments originally developed to measure the

lecture performance of graduate students. True scores of lecture performance were obtained from expert raters and were compared with those of
the raters in the study who demonstrated highly similar scores or validity.
The results of the study indicate that the frequency or number of performances and the evaluation of how effective such performance is are two
distinct parts of rating.

Frequency or number of occurrences is determined by clarity and
relation to the particular behavior; evaluation of that behavior requires
complex, abstract judgments about quality. There appears to be a relationship between the two. If the rater overestimates the frequency or
number of times the desired behavior occurs, the rater also tends to give
higher performance or quality ratings. The authors suggest that raters who
can accurately judge people in terms of frequency or number of desired
behaviors will also be accurate in judging between people within each of
several different behavioral dimensions. Thus, those raters who can accurately discriminate among a number of ratees in regard to the frequency of
a group of different behaviors will also be accurate in their judgments
about the level of the performance. Further, these raters will also accurately discriminate within the individual parts or dimensions that constitute
their performance evaluations.

Although the data suggest the relationship between frequency and
judgment, with each rating task the different degrees of accuracy are somewhat independent of each other. However, training raters to make accurate estimates in the frequency or number of desired behaviors may increase the accuracy of counting without having much effect on accuracy in
making discriminations as to the quality of those behaviors.

Summary Review of Research Study 5-2-C   Models of rating procedures
usually designate the observation and evaluation phases as separate steps in
the performance appraisal process. The authors point out that it is difficult
to separate the notation of the behavior observed from the evaluation.
However, it is the authors' contention that the act of noting the frequency
of certain behaviors and the evaluation of such behaviors are two different
aspects of the rating process. The frequency and notation of certain behaviors are made with respect to clarity and relevance; the evaluation of such
behaviors requires complex, abstract judgments of quality.

The study suggests that accuracy in observing certain behaviors is
related to accuracy in evaluating the quality of those behaviors. So training
programs designed to increase accuracy in observing behaviors may also
have the effect of increasing the accuracy of the ratings of their quality.

Some limitations of the present study suggested by the authors are the
problem that judgments about behavior made over long periods of time
may be affected by the accuracy of recall; that the rating tasks in the study
were simple compared to the complexity of real-life situations, which could

dramatically affect the accuracy of the reported judgments; and that, since the data are correlational, one cannot be positive of the study findings that training to observe correctly actually causes accuracy in performance evaluations.

REFERENCES

[1]Klores, M.S., "Rater Bias in Forced-Distribution Performance Ratings," *Personnel Psychology,* 19 (1966), 411–21.

[2]Bernardin, H.H., "The Effects of Rater Training on Leniency and Halo Errors in Student Ratings of Instructors," *Journal of Applied Psychology,* 63 (1978), 301–8.

[3]Murphy, K.R., M. Garcia, S. Kerkar, C. Martin, and W.K. Balzer, "Relationship between Observational Accuracy and Accuracy in Evaluating Performance," *Journal of Applied Psychology,* 67 (1982), 320–25.

QUESTIONS

1. You have just been hired by a company, and the human resource manager asks you to submit a report suggesting changes in the firm's performance appraisal format. What do you advise?
2. With respect to the research incident, what suggestions would you make regarding George Calderwood? Be specific.
3. The process of making accurate performance appraisals appears to be complex. What do we know about this process?

Research Incident 5-3:
Lance Masters Hears from the Roundtable

- What is the effect upon a rater who has made a positive evaluation of an employee when, later, negative information is introduced?
- Will a rater be more likely to change an evaluation because of knowledge of a negative act by a person being evaluated, or upon becoming aware of the negative outcome of the act?
- How should peer assessments be used in performance appraisals? Or should they?

When Lance Masters first became manager of the human resource department five years earlier, he had established a monthly meeting during the lunch hour for his four section heads. The usual fare was pizza (which Lance paid for) and personal beverages (which each person paid for) consumed around a large table in Lance's office. The table was oblong, but over a period of time it got to be called the roundtable, and that name stuck.

The agenda was determined by a section head's sending Lance an unsigned piece of paper the day before the meeting, indicating a topic. If none was received, Lance determined the topic. If more than one was received, the majority ruled. When there was no majority, Lance used an alphabetical system that everyone joked had no consistent basis of application.

Prior to today's meeting, Lance checked the "ballots." There were two, and both were marked "performance appraisals." Almost instinctively, Lance knew who the two section heads were. Two years before, the company had hired a new assistant comptroller, who had received top management's blessing to install a quarterly bonus system. The result was a simple plan for the blue-collar workers of a percentage for increased productivity gains. However, the plan for the white-collar personnel was more complex, based on supervisors' performance ratings of subordinate employees. Lance had not supported the assistant comptroller's plan, opting for a simpler percentage plan for all personnel, but was readily outvoted.

With the group assembled, the two section heads at the end of the table were acting uncharacteristically reticent. So the roundtable agenda was brought up earlier than usual, and Lance was right. Even though everything was discussed in the third person and involved other departments, Lance knew he was on the carpet. The complaints centered on the facts that the same white-collar people were benefiting from the bonus (favoritism?) and that the supervisors either did not have complete information or were overreacting to what information they had. Lance thought, "These are problems other department heads are suppose to have, not the expert in human resource." So, stalling for time to consider the problem in private, he maintained his best open and conciliatory manner, hoping to temporarily defuse the situation. One concrete suggestion brought up was the use of peer ratings. The idea seemed to have general support but no real champions, so it became an area for further consideration.

The roundtable meeting was over earlier than usual, and Lance was left alone contemplating his problem. Impulsively, he gulped down the last piece of cold pizza and suddenly realized he had another problem, indigestion.

RELEVANT EMPIRICAL
RESEARCH STUDIES

Research Study 5-3-A

What is the effect of a prior success upon the present performance evaluation? Does past recognition extend to unwarranted present salary increases? even to forecasts of future performance? Bazerman and others[1] studied the processes occurring within a rater making several judgments about a ratee.

The traditional view of performance appraisal assumes complete information about the ratee and an evaluation instrument provided by the company that directs the questions to be answered by the ratee. All the information obtained will be processed by the rater, resulting in a performance appraisal. Any errors result from rater biases, such as the halo effect, or are randomly distributed. One aspect of the present study was to determine the process that leads to these errors.

When the rater makes evaluations of the same person at different times, the expectation is that a new rating will be objective and unaffected by the previous rating. Past research indicates that this places psychological demands on the rater, who may respond in a nonoptimal manner and even give greater weight to confirming than disconfirming information.

The study sample consisted of 298 college business majors who participated in a decision-making exercise included in a course. They were randomly assigned to one of four experimental conditions. Each was given a written case and was asked to role-play the part of a vice-president who was either promoting and later evaluating an executive (the high-responsibility condition) or only evaluating an executive who had already been promoted by someone else (the low-responsibility condition).

The students were informed that the case was being used to study performance appraisal techniques. In an attempt to maximize their involvement, the students were told that their decisions would be helpful to the federal court of a nearby city that was following the procedures of private businesses in promotion evaluations.

For the high-responsibility condition, the performance appraisal case occurred in a hypothetical corporation. The vice-president whose role the student assumed had the responsibility of appraising the performance of three merchandise managers, the best ones in one region of the company's operations. The students were provided with a brief description of the managers and factual data on sales, earnings, return on investment, inventory turnover ratios, and past performance ratings. The role-playing students were then asked to determine which of the three should be promoted to regional director and to write a brief paragraph indicating why they selected that manager. Then they were given a second section of the case, dealing with the corporation two years later. This material provided negative data on the new regional director's performance during his first two years in office. The students were then asked to make a number of new evaluations.

For the low-responsibility condition, the students received the same set of materials, but they were told that the former vice-president had already appointed one of the three merchandise managers as regional director. An equal number of these students were randomly assigned one of the three managers as the promoted regional director and were provided with subsequent negative data irrespective of who had been appointed. They were then asked to make the same evaluation as that asked of the high-responsibility-condition students.

The dependent variable was the students' commitment to the previously promoted manager as indicated by the performance appraisal assessments. The dependent measures obtained were rewards, appropriateness of promotion/demotion, and forecasted future performance. The reward measure was obtained by having the students first set a percentage pay increase for the manager, knowing that the company average was 10 percent, and then designate the number of bonus vacation days to give this employee. The promotion/demotion potential was measured by three 11-point Likert items to determine the former manager's promotion potential within the next five years, current appropriateness for a demotion, and current appropriateness for a layoff if 15 percent of the corporation's manager positions were cut. The forecasted future performance was measured by asking students to estimate sales and returns for the former manager's region for the next three-month period.

The study examined whether the choice among the three managers affected the evaluations at the second decision point. The choice of manager did not significantly affect any of the seven dependent measures. Also, there was no clear pattern in the direction of the nonsignificant effects across these measures.

The effect of the experimental manipulation of responsibility, in the high-responsibility and low-responsibility conditions, on the seven dependent measures was significant. The high-responsibility students gave higher pay increases, more vacation days, and more positive evaluations of promotion potential. They were less likely to demote or lay off the former manager, and they forecasted higher future returns. They also forecasted higher sales, although the result was not statistically significant.

Thus it appears that the student rater was more likely to evaluate reward, assess promotion potential, and forecast future performance higher for a poorly performing ratee whom that rater had previously promoted than if another rater had made the promotion decision.

Summary Review of Research Study 5-3-A One viewpoint of performance appraisals suggests that raters who are provided negative information on an employee they had previously promoted will evaluate that employee more positively than if someone else had made the earlier promotion decision. In a study using 298 business majors, the experimental group selected one of three managers for a promotion, and the control group was told that the decision had been made by someone else. Both groups reviewed two years of performance data and were then asked to evaluate the promoted manager's performance. The experimental group that had selected the manager to be promoted evaluated him more favorably, provided larger rewards, and made more optimistic projections of future performance than did the control group.

Research Study 5-3-B

What is the effect of knowledge of the outcome of a subordinate's ineffective performance upon the superior's evaluation? Will it cause the superior to see an increased probability of the event's occurring again? Does the superior see the subordinate as more or less responsible?

A study by Mitchell and Kalb[2] investigated the effect of outcomes of a subordinate's ineffective behavior upon the evaluations made by a superior. Since all behaviors, good and bad, have outcomes, one may question to what extent the supervisor's knowledge of the outcomes affects the subordinate's ratings. Related to the supervisor's outcome knowledge is the degree of responsibility accorded the subordinate. Earlier studies suggest that supervisors ascribe more blame and more punitive responses to negative outcomes than to neutral or positive outcomes.

A group of graduate nurses was told that they would read two incidents describing a poorly performing nurse. Half read incidents that disclosed the outcome, and the other half read incidents that did not. The outcomes presented were either neutral or negative. The 41 incidents used of poor nursing behaviors were gathered from several hospitals.

In the study, each of 55 nurses in an advanced training program, assuming the role of supervisor, was given descriptions of two of the incidents and a questionnaire. For the nurses reading incidents with outcomes, half read outcomes that were negative (the patient fell out of bed), and half read neutral outcomes (the patient improved). Nurses who read incidents with no outcome were asked questions on the subsequent questionnaire relating to possible negative or neutral outcomes. There were four forms of the questionnaire:

1. Outcome present and neutral
2. Outcome present and negative
3. Outcome absent but probably neutral
4. Outcome absent but probably negative

The dependent measures were contained in six questions. Two questions evaluated the perceived probability of the outcome's recurring; two others measured the responsibility of the nurse's behavior in the incident; and the final two questions assessed the nurse's personal characteristics as causes for her behavior. The responses were recorded on a seven-point scale ranging from "extremely unimportant" to "extremely important." The results of the study indicated that outcome knowledge does increase one's perception of the outcome inevitability. Answers to the first two questions showed a significant effect for outcome knowledge as well as a significant interaction. Thus it appears that outcome knowledge increased the perceived probability of the outcome's recurring. Further, this increase was greater when the outcome was negative than when it was neutral.

It was also found in answers to the next two questions that outcome knowledge would affect the evaluation of the responsibility of the incident nurse's behavior. The incident nurse was seen as more responsible for her actions in the outcome-present than in the outcome-absent condition. A marginally significant effect ($P < .09$) was that knowledge of a negative outcome would result in judgment of the incident nurse as being more responsible than would knowledge of a neutral outcome. Thus, outcome knowledge increased responsibility for a negative outcome but reduced it greatly for a neutral outcome. This suggests that after a poor performance, a supervisor will not make a subordinate responsible for a neutral outcome but will blame the person for a negative outcome.

As for the final questions, there was no significant interaction between the results of question 5, that the nurses would ascribe the results more to internal factors in the outcome-present condition than in the outcome-absent position, and those of question 6, that there would be few instances of ascribing the results to external factors.

Comparing the negative and neutral outcomes in the outcome-present condition indicated that negative consequences resulted in the nurses' ascribing more internal causes than in the neutral condition. However, this was a marginally significant effect, $P < .08$. There were no differences for ascribing external causes.

Summary Review of Research Study 5-3-B   The study suggests that supervisors' judgments about an ineffective subordinate will be affected by knowledge of the outcome of the behavior whether it is negative or neutral. A group of 55 nurses were provided with descriptions of two incidents of poor performance. The nurses assumed the role of supervisor; half of them were presented with either a neutral or negative outcome, and the other half were not. Nurses with knowledge of the outcome, particularly of a negative outcome, rated the outcome as more likely to recur, felt that the subordinate was more responsible for the behavior, and ascribed the behavior more to internal causes than did those nurses with no outcome knowledge.

Research Study 5-3-C

How valid are peer assessments? Are they merely popularity contests? Is there any friendship effect on the validity of peer rankings and peer ratings?

Love[3] conducted a study of these issues. His first hypothesis was that in a comparison of peer nominations, peer rankings, and peer ratings, the peer nominations would have the greatest validity; his second, that peer ranking was expected to display the greatest reliability.

The subjects in the study were 145 police officers who acted as peer assessors and 33 police sergeants who provided rankings and ratings. They were all members of a municipal police department of a medium-sized southeastern city. Of those asked to participate, 70 percent agreed.

There were three phases of the peer-assessment process: nomination, ranking, and rating of fellow officers; rating of the friendship between the peer assessor and other assessees; and reaction of every peer assessor to each method of peer assessment.

Although the supervisor-assessment instrument was a duplicate of the peer-assessment form, it did not contain the nomination, friendship, and reaction sections. The squad supervisors provided rankings and ratings only for personnel in their squads.

All evaluations included nine performance dimensions: job knowledge, decision making, dealing with co-workers, use of equipment, dealing with the public, communication, reliability, demeanor, and work attitude. These dimensions were derived from a task-based job analysis on the position of police officer collected from the police department in the study.

The nominees were any police officers who performed patrol functions, excluding the peer assessors. For each of the nine performance dimensions, three officers were nominated who the peer assessor thought performed best on that dimension. The peers and supervisor assessors then ranked the performance of all squad members, excluding themselves, on each of the dimensions.

Then, ratings were gathered from the peers and squad supervisors for all squad members, excluding the rater, on each dimension. A nine-point behaviorally anchored scale (BARS) was developed within the department and used for each rating.

To determine friendship ratings, each person nominated, ranked, or rated by a peer assessor was scored on a Likert-type scale. This scale contained five dimensions of social attraction: contact off the job, contact on the job, knowledge of person, liking of person, and friendship with person.

Another measure was the peer assessor's reactions toward each type of peer assessment. These were measured on a five-point Likert rating scale ranging from "strongly agree" to "strongly disagree."

The results of the study indicate that the nine performance dimensions were significantly intercorrelated for all peer and supervisor assessments. The five components of friendship were also significantly intercorrelated.

Three random samplings were made of the squads, and within each, random assessor pairs were selected. A statistically significant interrater reliability was obtained for peer nominations. The peer-rating method had a significantly lower interrater reliability than that of peer nomination, whereas peer-nomination and peer-ranking methods were not significantly different.

As for the relationship between the peer assessments and supervisor rankings and ratings, all methods of peer assessment significantly predicted both supervisor rankings and ratings. The addition of friendship ratings as a predictor did not significantly increase the accuracy of prediction.

The supervisor assessors' reactions toward the peer-assessment methods indicated a general negative set toward all of them. Responses toward one assessment method were not significantly different from those pertaining to the other two. The supervisor assessors indicated that peer assessment was not fair, not accurate, and not liked by them, and should not be used in promotion decisions. The author suggests that this negative input results from resistance to any modification of a system in which management holds the sole right to performance assessment.

Peer nominations and peer rankings were significantly more reliable than peer ratings. However, they were not significantly different from each other. The peer nominations did not reveal a significantly greater relationship with the supervisory assessment instrument than did peer rankings and peer ratings. The peer nominations and peer rankings demonstrated significantly greater correlations with both supervisor rankings and ratings than did the peer ratings.

Although friendship between peer assessors and assessees was present, it did not bias the relationship between peer assessments and supervisor criteria. This lack of bias was consistent across the three assessment methods.

Summary Review of Research Study 5-3-C The study compared peer nominations, peer rankings, and peer ratings relative to reliability, validity, friendship bias, and user reaction. The peer-based methods showed significant reliability and validity. They were not significantly biased by friendship between the peer assessor and assessee. However, peer rankings and peer nominations demonstrated greater reliability and validity than did peer ratings. The supervisory reaction to all the peer-assessment methods was negative.

REFERENCES

[1]Bazerman, M.H., R.I. Beekun, and F.D. Schoorman, "Performance Evaluation in a Dynamic Context: A Laboratory Study of the Impact of a Prior Commitment to the Ratee," *Journal of Applied Psychology*, 67 (1982), 873–76.

[2]Mitchell, T.R., and L.S. Kalb, "Effects of Outcome Knowledge and Outcome Valence on Supervisor's Evaluations," *Journal of Applied Psychology*, 66 (1981), 604–12.

[3]Love, K.G., "Comparison of Peer Assessment Methods: Reliability, Validity, Friendship Bias, and User Reaction," *Journal of Applied Psychology*, 66 (1981), 451–57.

QUESTIONS

1. What is the effect of a favorable prior commitment by a rater upon the future rating given to the same ratee? What particular areas of the performance appraisal are involved? Discuss.
2. How does knowledge of the outcome of a subordinate's behavior affect the superior's evaluation of that person? What is the effect of negative or neutral outcome knowledge? Discuss.
3. What do we know about peer-assessment methods relative to performance appraisal? Indicate three methods and discuss reliability, friendship, and user reaction.

NON-EMPIRICAL RESEARCH ARTICLE ABSTRACTS

Abstract 5-1

- Do people prefer a more objective, directed performance appraisal to a subjective appraisal?
- How important are the results of the performance appraisal with respect to promotion and monetary rewards?
- Are gamesmanship and political connections associated more with the objective performance appraisal or with the subjective appraisal?

The questions above are treated in a 1983 article by Stuart Murray,[1] a consultant.

The author points out that there is continuing disagreement as to the most effective appraisal technique. Two techniques most often discussed are the subjective trait approach and the objective, results-oriented approach.

A traditional approach has been to evaluate performance on personality characteristics, traits, or behaviors. A list of traits is made up that affect the employee's performance. Then a graphic rating scale is used to evaluate the employee's traits. Such traits include reliability, cooperation, intelligence, maturity, and so on. This type of appraisal is simple and easy to use. However, a problem with the trait approach is poor reliability and validity.

In an attempt to overcome these problems, some organizations use a more objective, results-oriented program that compares the goals set by the employee and the results obtained during the evaluation period. Such results-oriented programs have been found to motivate people and increase performance while increasing the validity and reliability of the performance ratings.

The present study utilized a two-page survey questionnaire and personnel records. The questionnaires were sent to two engineering divisions of a large international petroleum company and were completed at work. The 163 respondents included 76 managers from an engineering division that was already using a subjective appraisal system, and 87 managers from another division that used the objective (management by objectives) appraisal system. The other data source was the respondents' personnel files, which were used to determine the discriminating power of the results-oriented appraisal system compared to the more subjective trait approach.

The respondent managers were evaluated at least once a year by their supervisor, who assessed performance for the preceding year. Although the subjective and objective evaluation methods are different, each manager was rated on a scale of 1 (poor) to 5 (excellent).

Since management had imposed standardization of policies, rules, salary levels, and the like, many variables in the two divisions were similar and thus controlled. The demographic variables of age, sex, educational level, and years with the company were not significant between the two organization divisions.

The results of the study indicated that the middle managers who were evaluated under the objective appraisal system were more significantly satisfied with the evaluation process than were the managers evaluated under the subjective system. When those appraised under the objective appraisal system (MBO) responded to a question of how they would evaluate it compared to the previously used subjective system, 91 percent said it was a moderate or great improvement.

The author suggests that a possible reason for the managers' dissatisfaction with the subjective appraisal system was that they did not perceive any link between performance and either pay raises or promotions. Those managers evaluated by the objective appraisal had a significantly better understanding of how they were being appraised and where they stood than did the subjective-appraisal managers, who also felt that their work and abilities were not being appreciated.

Another finding of this study was that the managers subjectively appraised believed that promotion and financial benefits were achieved through politics and gamesmanship, not performance.

Although both manager groups agreed that frequency of feedback affected their performance, the objectively appraised managers reported their feedback as being more objective than did the others.

When the managers' personnel files were analyzed, it appeared that the objective appraisal was more accurate than the subjective appraisal in assessing performance. Thus, 80 percent of the managers in the subjective appraisal were rated below average, compared to 56 percent in the objective appraisal. Yet 87 percent in the objective appraisal indicated that they were appraised accurately and fairly, whereas only 57 percent so responded in the subjective appraisal.

However, the author does caution that the results of this study, which favored the objective appraisal system, may be due to the fact that it is relatively easy to establish clear and concise goals in the field of engineering. This may not be the case in other, less-quantifiable career fields.

REFERENCE

[1]Murray, Stuart, "A Comparison of Results-Oriented and Trait-Based Performance Appraisals." From the June 1983 issue of *Personnel Administrator,* copyright 1983, The American Society for Personnel Administration, 606 North Washington Street, Alexandria, VA 22314.

QUESTIONS

1. Which appraisal technique suffers from poor reliability and validity, even though it is simple and easy to use?
2. Under which appraisal system were middle managers more significantly satisfied with the evaluation process?
3. Under which appraisal system were middle managers able to perceive a link between performance and either pay raises or promotions? Why?

Abstract 5-2

- What is contained in a training program designed to make supervisors more effective in the performance appraisal process?
- Are there specific techniques available to the supervisor that will make performance appraisal sessions more productive?
- How are the skills that are obtained from a performance appraisal training program applicable to other areas of human resource interest?

An article by Virginia Bianco,[1] Martin-Marietta Corporation, considers these questions.

The author points out that performance appraisals strike fear into the hearts of managers, because their organizations are not training them in the proper techniques. Adding to this problem is the secrecy in many organizations about performance and compensation. The solution, she says, is a training program to teach managers how to complete performance appraisals. Such training programs should be flexible as to length and content, depending upon the individual needs of departments.

A suggested performance appraisal training program for managers begins with an introduction outlining course objectives and defining performance appraisal and performance counseling. The performance appraisal is a formal meeting between the supervisor and the subordinate to determine how well objectives have been met during the preceding appraisal period, but it is also a measure of the supervisor's performance as a manager. Performance counseling involves periodic but informal sessions during the year between the supervisor and subordinate to determine goal progress and any necessary adjustments. The supervisory manager is expected to conduct both the performance appraisal and the performance counseling during the appraisal period.

The training program consists of five major areas. The first attempts to resolve the problem of evaluating while also attempting to do counseling. This problem is resolved through questioning the appraisal procedure and results in a problem-solving approach that emphasizes that the communication process itself is the boss.

Another training-program area considers equal employment laws that require measurements to be job-related and objective. The problem here is not in the measurable units but in the more abstract interpersonal practices. Thus, one does not say, "Does not get along with others," but rather, "Causes friction between people, requiring manager intervention." The training program utilizes actual lawsuits involving the company or related companies. The point of most lawsuits is the difference between what is done, such as dismissal, and what is written in the performance appraisal. There must be factual documentation for what is done.

A third area attempts to demonstrate the relationship between performance appraisal and other personnel functions, such as selection and placement, career development, long-range personnel planning, succession planning, and so forth.

The fourth area of the training program shows supervisors how to modify existing performance appraisal forms to fit the circumstances. Thus, instead of objectives being written for the whole year, they should be written for each project.

The final area teaches managers to openly communicate the compensation system and not operate in secrecy. For instance, compensation is usually based on other factors than just the person's performance, such as the department's performance relative to other departments, the value of the person's department, length of service, and the like. A person rated good may make more money than a person rated outstanding if the former is worth more to the organization. The subordinate must understand that even though there is a relationship between pay and performance, it is not a direct one; that is, it is not a one-to-one relationship.

Prior to the course given by the author, each participant received a performance booklet containing examples that were job-specific to that supervisor's particular department. Also included were two exercises to be completed before beginning the program. One exercise included actual performance appraisals that required the supervisor to determine what was wrong and then to propose corrective action. The other exercise required the supervisor to provide the necessary documentation for different parts of a performance appraisal session.

Ten areas were covered in the course: the orientation meeting for new and transferred employees; the maintenance of incident files to document employees' performance; the need for frequent counseling and feedback sessions; allowing employees to evaluate their own performance; ensuring that the supervisor and the employee understand the job responsibilities per the job description; the supervisor and employee both developing understandable objectives and standards; the need for job characteristics to be supported by job-related facts; filling in the need gaps in the employee's performance to meet present and future challenges; providing job-related objective documentation of material on the appraisal form; and making sure that the final performance review is consistent and provides justification for an overall rating.

The final process of the training program was to prepare the supervisor to conduct a successful performance appraisal session. This included setting an agenda and developing a performance review strategy illustrated by a slide/tape instruction format. Also, the supervisor learned six techniques for effectively communicating mutual goals. This was accomplished by having groups of supervisors view another slide/tape presentation, one that violated the six techniques, after which they rewrote the script and then played the roles of the participants. The rewriting was based on descriptive, not evaluative statements, using a problem-oriented approach to increase the employee's sense of control, demonstrate empathy, encourage equality and information sharing, promote the use of new ideas and creativity, and identify the causes of problems first rather than the conclusions.

The author believes this training program is less theoretical and directed more to the real world than others. Skills are practiced and appraisal sessions become interesting, lively exchanges. Further, these newly acquired skills can be applied to other human resource planning activities.

REFERENCE

[1]"In Praise of Performance," by Virginia Bianco, copyright June 1984. Reprinted with the permission of *Personnel Journal*, Costa Mesta, California; all rights reserved.

QUESTIONS

1. Why do performance appraisals strike fear into the hearts of managers?
2. The author suggests a training program with five areas. What is the fifth area attempting to accomplish?
3. How is the supervisor taught to prepare to conduct a successful performance appraisal session?

CHAPTER SIX

EQUAL EMPLOYMENT OPPORTUNITY

INTRODUCTION

For many years, the employment practices of American businesses were based on individual choice, without any infringement from government. These practices varied in different parts of the country as the result of local attitudes, religious preferences, and political considerations.

Today, owing to current federal and state legislation, any business policies or practices that adversely affect any protected group can bring regulatory action against the employer. The extent of federal and state antidiscrimination laws is inclusive, covering employment practices from advertising through retirement. Under the equal employment system, not only are all employees treated the same, all employees must also have equal opportunities.

It is interesting to note that laws against discrimination are not recent. The first federal legislation to prohibit intentional or overt discrimination in employment practices was the Civil Rights Act of 1866. This act extended to racial minorities the same rights white citizens had to make contracts, to sue, to engage in legal proceedings, and to benefit from the laws of the land. This legislation was followed by the Civil Rights Act of 1871 to plug some of the loopholes in the 1866 law. It outlawed discrimination because of race that was due to state law, custom, usage, or conspiracy between persons. However, these laws did not apply to sex discrimination or to employment. But after the passage of Title VII of the Civil Rights Act of 1964, the courts ruled that because the employment relationship was a contract, the 1866 statute would apply to all employment practices.

Prior to the Civil Rights Act of 1964, the Equal Pay Act of 1963 was passed as an amendment to the Fair Labor Standards Act of 1938; it prohibited paying different rates to workers of different sexes performing the same work. Such work must involve equal skill, equal effort, equal responsibilities, and similar working conditions. Firms covered under this law must be engaged in or affect interstate commerce, have two or more employees, and have a gross yearly volume of $250,000 or more. An employer may not comply with this act by lowering the wages of the opposite sex; the wages of those discriminated against must be raised. This law requires maintaining employee records of wages, work hours, and other work-related items for three years after the filing of any action.

The 1964 Civil Rights Act has the distinction of being the broadest of antidiscrimination legislation. The act prohibits any employment practice based on race, color, religion, national origin, or sex. This act, commonly called Title VII, applies to employers, labor unions, apprenticeship committees, employment agencies, and both state and local governments. The act covers all firms that employ a minimum of 15 people for a period of at least 20 weeks and affect interstate commerce. The Equal Employment Opportunity Commission (EEOC) is the enforcement arm of the act, and all discrimination charges must begin with the EEOC or a state referral agency. Title VII also protects majority groups, as in religious freedom, since the constitutional provision did not apply to employment practices. The law requires that job applications, payroll records, and personnel files be kept a minimum of six months or until any personnel action is resolved. Those employers with 100 or more employees must file annually the EEO-1 report inventorying employees' race, ethnic group, sex, job category, and pay. Unions must file a similar report, entitled EEO-3, with records kept one year after the report has been filed.

Charges of discrimination may be filed with the EEOC by an individual, and the EEOC may file its own charges that may involve more than one person. The party charging discrimination (the plaintiff) must present reasonable evidence of the event, usually offering some form of statistical data. Once reasonable cause is shown, the burden of proof is transferred to the one being charged with discrimination (the defendant). Now the defendant presents data to try to show that the employment practice being questioned is a business necessity or is job-related.

First, the EEOC must attempt to bring the parties together to obtain a voluntary, out-of-court compliance with Title VII. If this fails, the EEOC may bring charges in the federal courts. If the employer is found guilty, the EEOC may require reinstatement of employees, back pay of up to two years prior to filing, attorneys' fees, and an affirmative action plan (AAP).

The AAP shows the remedies offered and corrective measures to ensure that the discriminatory practices do not occur again. The EEOC also publishes guidelines that "suggest" how to comply with Title VII. Many employers regard these as compliance standards. The EEOC has issued guidelines covering selection, sex, religion, pregnancy, sexual harassment, and age discrimination.

Another antidiscrimination law is the Age Discrimination Act of 1967 (ADEA), which makes it illegal to discriminate on the basis of age against employees or applicants between 40 and 70. This law applies to employers with more than 20 employees and labor unions with 25 or more members. No employee may be forced to retire before age 70, unless it can be shown that the employee is unable to perform the job duties—although executives may be retired at age 65. However, exceptions are allowed in situations where age is a bona fide occupational qualification (BFOQ). For instance, a middle-aged person could legally be turned down for modeling children's clothes. For compliance with the law, the employee's personnel file, including employment records, must be kept for one year after any action is filed.

In 1972, the Equal Employment Opportunity Act was passed, amending Title VII of the Civil Rights Act of 1964. Title VII was amended to cover all private employers with 15 or more employees, public and private schools, state and local governments, labor unions, and labor–management apprenticeship committees. The 1972 act also added to the EEOC's powers by permitting it to go directly to the courts for enforcement. Further, regional centers were to be established, complete with legal staffs, to implement the law and enforce court decisions.

Although the emphasis of Title VII is on unlawful discrimination, it does recognize three discriminatory practices that are legal. First, BFOQs, mentioned earlier, can be used to discriminate on the basis of national origin, religion, and sex, but not race or color. So a women's fashion designer could legally discriminate against men and hire only female models. Second, employers may use tests for hiring and promotion purposes if those tests have been validated on job-related performance criteria. Third, employers may also use seniority and performance appraisal systems to discriminate among employees, provided that these systems have not been designed to inhibit the intent of Title VII and that they are based on job-related criteria.

In 1978 the Pregnancy Discrimination Act was passed, stating that pregnancy is a disability and that pregnant employees, like any other disabled employee, are entitled to benefits. Prior to this act, pregnant women might be forced to resign or take a leave of absence, and employers had no responsibility to provide disability or medical coverage. The act now requires employers to provide benefits to females because of pregnancy that males receive for other disabilities. However, the benefits for pregnancy need not be more than for any other type of disability.

The equal employment laws did not define discrimination, so it was left to the courts to decide that treating one class of people differently from others or denying them employment opportunities was unlawful unless a business necessity existed. After this ruling, the EEOC issued guidelines to determine discrimination or "adverse impact" through a mathematical formula using the percentage selection rates for minorities and nonminorities. The selection rate for minorities is divided by the selection rate for nonminorities, and if the resulting percentage selection rate is less than 80 percent, an adverse impact exists and there is evidence of a violation.

Included in equal employment regulations are executive orders. These orders indicate the position of the executive branch of the government on certain topics. Enforcement of executive orders is through the power of the executive branch to instruct government agencies not to transact business with enterprises violating the orders. If such executive branch action is deemed arbitrary and capricious by the enterprise, judicial review may be requested. The best-known executive order is Executive Order 11246 of 1967, which extended equal employment opportunity and affirmative action legislation to cover all contractors and subcontractors doing business with the federal government. Contractors receiving $50,000 worth of government business in one year and having at least 50 employees must file a written affirmative action program with the Office of Federal Contract Compliance Programs (OFCCP), which was established in the Department of Labor by Executive Order 11246 to enforce the intent of the order. Since action by the OFCCP is immediate, whereas extended time delays occur under Title VII, compliance with Executive Order 11246 occurred very quickly.

RESEARCH INCIDENTS

Research Incident 6-1:
Gerry Scherba and the Issue of Hugh Bowin's Age

- Which appears to be more potent in age discrimination, stereotyped age behavior patterns or stereotyped job characteristics, or are they equally potent?
- How do the ages of the rater and ratee influence performance appraisal evaluations?
- When do age stereotypes begin to adversely affect management personnel decisions?

The position of national vice-president for sales required many attributes. Experience carried the most weight, because the company's product line was varied and complex. Since many model changes were made each year, the national sales vice-president was expected to be not only a motivator but also an adept teacher, so that district sales managers could accurately extol the advantages of model changes to their sales staffs. Of course, plenty of travel was involved, since the company accounts were nationwide, including some Canadian accounts, and were not concentrated in any particular area.

Gerry Scherba pondered the final list of applicants. Actually, of the 24 original applicants, including four submitted by the headhunters, there were only two outstanding candidates. The process of selection shouldn't be too difficult; the committee had already ranked them, although the final decision was Gerry's. The committee had chosen Hugh Bowin as its selection for national sales vice-president. However, Gerry Scherba was hesitant in adopting the committee's recommendation. A confidential background check revealed that Hugh Bowin was 53 years old, eight years older than the second candidate.

Gerry agonized over the choice. He thought of the demanding physical effort required in managing a national sales force. He thought of the mental demands in analyzing customer requirements as they were affected by model changes. He thought of the stress, the long hours, the time-zone changes . . . and his father.

Gerry Scherba's father had been an aggressive life insurance executive, advancing to vice-president of operations just prior to his fiftieth birthday. But within a few short years, he had begun to age, not in a physical sense but in mental awareness. The result was early retirement at age 60 and, soon after, a full-service retirement home. The final years were not pleasant, and the memories of his funeral last year were all too vivid. Yet, despite his own personal experiences with the debilitating effects of old age, Gerry hesitated to capitulate to his own prejudices and continued to mull over the qualifications of Hugh Bowin.

He remembered that during the walk back from lunch, Hugh's stride was quick. He was still alert and physically active at the end of a demanding six-hour interviewing session. Gerry, uncharacteristically, leaned heavily on his desk and sighed. What to do, what to do?

RELEVANT EMPIRICAL
RESEARCH STUDIES

Research Study 6-1-A

Does a worker's age result in a stereotyped behavior pattern?

Cleveland and Landy[1] point out that a potential source of performance bias that has not been extensively researched is contextual variables such as the stereotype of a certain job. Past research has found sex stereotyping in personnel decisions. However, with the aging process now receiving more attention, the authors suggest that the phenomenon of age stereotypes may exist similar to that of sex stereotypes.

The passage of the Age Discrimination in Employment Act of 1967 acknowledged the problem of the older worker. Past research has shown that once unemployed, the older worker has more difficulty in finding work than younger workers do, and that once reemployed, older workers often take pay cuts and experience limited upward mobility. Also, there appears to be a bias against older people in recruitment for training programs, hiring, and selection testing. The issue is whether this treatment is due to real performance decreases or negative and inaccurate stereotypes of older people.

The authors cite studies that contribute to the stereotype of older workers as more passive, reserved, obsolete, and inflexible than younger workers. This negative stereotype appears to influence personnel decisions, since older workers receive fewer corrective instructions, are not often suggested for promotions, and are less likely to receive additional training.

In an unpublished study, the authors found that managers could classify some occupations by merely using the perceived age characteristics of people. So they propose that the occupational age stereotype (the situational variable) reacts with the worker's age-related characteristics (the person variable) to influence judgments and behavior. They also propose that the worker's age be established in two ways—chronological age, and behavior patterns reflecting either an older or a younger person.

The present study utilized two experiments; in one, subjects made award recommendations based on past performance, and in the other, recommended promotions were based on the prediction of future occupational performance. The subjects were 19 middle-level, salaried employees, ranging in age from 26 to 62 years, in a large manufacturing company.

The independent variables were age-stereotype jobs, target age groups (older, middle-aged, younger), performance patterns that represented a younger or older performance on ten different dimensions, and an importance rating of the ten dimensions using a five-point rating scale.

The dependent measures were performance ratings for all subjects prior to the awards recommendation, and overall rating. For the awards recommendation, each of the 19 subjects was asked to distribute award money among six hypothetical employees in each of the older (61 or 62), middle (40 or 41), and younger (27 or 28) age-typed positions. But before making the awards, the subjects rated each hypothetical employee on a six-point rating scale, with 6 representing excellent performance.

In the awards experiment, the largest difference in the amount of award money recommended between the younger and older performance patterns was found in the stereotype younger job, and the largest of these differences occurred when the worker was described as young.

The largest difference in overall performance rating occurred when the job stereotypes (older, age neutral, younger) were incompatible with the older and younger performance patterns. Again the largest of these differences occurred when the worker was designated as young.

It appears that people exhibiting younger pattern behavior in the younger job received more award money than did people exhibiting the older pattern behavior. Also, older pattern behavior was not viewed as more favorable than younger pattern behavior in the older-person job.

For the overall performance, an employee was rated higher when the stereotype pattern behavior matched the stereotype job. Also, people with a younger pattern behavior were judged to have a higher performance level than people with older pattern behavior in the younger job despite the equality of overall performance ratings.

In the promotion-decision experiment, the largest difference in promotability rating between the younger and older performance patterns occurred in the younger job stereotype. Further, the largest differences in overall performance ratings took place when the age characteristics of the job were incompatible with the young–old performance patterns.

By use of an Analysis of Variance test, the two experiments revealed that the age of the subject was not significant in either the awards or promotion exercise; the recommendations of the older and younger subjects did not differ. Also, the age of the hypothetical employee was not significant in the awards or promotion exercise. Further, regardless of actual age, those employees in the younger job who displayed the younger performance pattern received more award money and faster promotion than did employees displaying the older performance pattern.

Summary Review of Research Study 6-1-A   Two experimental studies investigated the effects of age on personnel decisions relative to a stereotype "older" job and a stereotype "younger" job. In one study, subject managers made award recommendations and evaluations on 18 hypothetical employees in three jobs that varied as to age stereotype. These 18 employees varied in age and also in regard to a stereotype older or younger performance pattern. In the second study, the experimental situation was the same, but this time the subject managers made promotion decisions for the 18 hypothetical employees. Generally, both experiments found that when either the young or old pattern of behavior was inconsistent with the age stereotype of the job, employees received lower ratings than when the pattern of behavior was consistent with the stereotype of that particular job.

Research Study 6-1-B

How do the ages of rater and ratee affect the performance appraisal process?

Cleveland and Landy[2] say that recent studies on the influence of rater and ratee characteristics in the evaluation process deal mostly with sex and race. But there is a growing concern with age discrimination, and some of the results of recent research are contradictory.

The present study attempted to overcome some of the recent methodological problems by using a large sample of actual performance ratings rather than simulated ratings.

In the first sample, data were collected on 513 upper-level, exempt managerial employees, all male, from a division of a manufacturing company. Ages ranged from 21 to 56 years. The 150 raters in this division had received extensive training in the use of a performance appraisal form, resulting in the 513 appraisals.

For the second sample, data were collected on 178 exempt employees from a different division of the same company, whose ages ranged from 22 to 64. The raters in this division had received only brief training in the use of the appraisal form.

The performance appraisal form contained 15 specific items measuring performance and another item for an overall rating of performance. The 15 items reflected six performance dimensions or criteria—use of time, problem solving, employee relations, interpersonal skills, self-development, and communication skills—plus "summed items" and "overall rating," for a total of eight criteria. The study used correlation analysis and regression analysis to analyze the data.

For six of the eight criteria, there was no significant rater or ratee age effect. When ages were then coded into younger (21–34), middle-aged (35–44), and older (45–65), the results showed older ratees receiving lower ratings in self-development than both the younger and middle-aged ratees.

In sample 2, ratee age was also found to significantly influence self-development ratings. The younger ratees received significantly higher ratings than older ratees for self-development, but middle-age ratees did not.

Further, in both samples, "interpersonal skills" was significantly influenced by ratee age. In sample 1, older ratees received marginally lower ratings than younger ones, and in sample 2, the ratings were significantly lower.

There was no significant rater-age effect in ratings of self-development in either sample. However, in sample 1, significant rater-age effect was shown in ratings of interpersonal skills; younger raters gave higher ratings than older ones did. This was not replicated in sample 2.

Both samples showed a rater-age and ratee-age interaction. All raters gave middle-aged ratees similar ratings, but the younger raters tended to give lower ratings to both the younger and the older ratees than did the middle-aged and older raters.

A finding in sample 1 that was not replicated in sample 2 was that although older workers generally received lower ratings in interpersonal skills, the younger supervisors gave them higher ratings than those of the older supervisors.

Other ratee age effects found in sample 2 but not in sample 1 were in the use of time, problem solving, the overall rating, and the summed performance rating. Generally, the younger ratees received higher ratings. Other rater-age influences revealed higher ratings given by the older raters for problem solving, communication skills, and summed performance rating. Failure to replicate these findings in both samples clouds their application to other situations.

The present study suggests that age influences ratings of self-development and interpersonal skills but does not have a major effect upon performance ratings. For the other six performance dimensions, there was no influence of rater age and ratee age. Where age influence was found, it accounted for only 1 to 4 percent of the rating variance. It appears in this study that rater age and ratee age did not have an extensive systematic distorting influence on performance ratings.

Summary Review of Research Study 6-1-B   The study investigated rater age and ratee age as they influence performance evaluations. From two samples of exempt managers from two separate divisions of a manufacturing company, two general performance criteria and six specific performance criteria evaluations were obtained. In the first sample, it was found that there were significant age influences on the specific performance measures of self-development and interpersonal skills; the older workers received lower ratings than the younger workers. Also, the younger raters gave significantly higher ratings than the older raters did on interpersonal skills. Significant age interactions were found in ratings of both interpersonal skills and self-development; these findings were partially replicated in the second sample, but others were not. The authors conclude that generally, rater age and ratee age have little consistent effect upon performance ratings.

Research Study 6-1-C

How widespread are age stereotypes held by management, and are they used to discriminate against the older worker?

An article by Rosen and Jerdee[3] points out that until recently, the discriminatory employment practices receiving the most attention were based on race and sex. However, age discrimination is now receiving more attention, and the authors cite studies indicating that owing to negative stereotypes associated with increasing age, older people are regarded as being deficient in job-related attributes.

In the present study, age stereotypes were investigated. Participants analyzed six hypothetical administrative incidents in which an employee's age might have affected management's decisions. A comparison was made of these management decisions with respect to younger and older workers in identical situations.

The subjects were 142 college undergraduate business students, 115 males and 27 females, and 99 percent between the ages of 21 and 29. The exercise was an in-basket simulation in which the subjects were asked to assume the role of a division manager and to respond to six items, presented in either letter or memo form, dealing with a managerial problem. Two versions of each incident were given, to control age as to young or old.

Age was manipulated in each incident by referring to the focal employee as either older or younger. Also, four of the six memos included personnel forms with pictures of a younger or an older man.

Of these six incidents, the first was concerned with the stereotype that older workers are rigid in their work attitudes and resistant to change. Another dealt with the need for creativity in a marketing position. The third incident investigated cautiousness and slowness of judgment. Still another examined an age stereotype of diminished physical capacities of older workers. The fifth incident centered on perceptions of older employees' desire and ability to stay abreast of technological change. The final incident dealt with the untrainability of older workers.

The subjects were asked the amount of difficulty they would anticipate in getting a worker to change. The difficulty rating was significantly higher for the older than for the younger worker. Regarding the suggestion of a talk as a means of a corrective strategy with the worker, 65 percent recommended that approach for the younger worker but only 42 percent for the older worker. As to replacing the incident worker with someone else, there was a significant difference; only 32 percent agreed to replace the younger worker, but 55 percent agreed to replace the older worker.

The authors had hypothesized that older workers would be regarded as less promotable to creative and innovative-thinking positions. This proved true: Of the subjects viewing the older candidate's record, only 25 percent recommended promotion, whereas 54 percent of the subjects viewing the younger candidate's record were for promotion.

The study found a significant bias against older applicants for positions requiring financial risk taking. Of subjects who viewed the older applicant's record, only 13 percent recommended promotion; of those who viewed the younger applicant's file, 25 percent recommended promotion.

It was also hypothesized that older people would be less likely to be transferred to a job requiring strenuous physical activity. The subjects rated the action to reject the transfer request significantly higher for the older than for the younger worker—and this despite the statement that the 52-year-old employee was in good physical health.

The subjects also indicated that an older employee was significantly less motivated than a younger employee to keep up to date on technological change. In addition, the decision to provide funds for an employee to attend a training session was influenced by age; there was a significant denial of additional training for an older employee than for a younger one.

In the final incident, the authors hypothesized that older workers with obsolete skills are regarded as less suitable for retraining and are considered expendable. The subjects evaluated a company-sponsored refresher course as significantly lower in suitability for a 60-year-old computer programmer than for a 30-year-old programmer. Also, they significantly recommended that an older employee, compared to a younger employee, be terminated because of obsolete skills and a qualified replacement be hired.

When negative job-related characteristics are equated with older workers and when these negative stereotypes are pertinent to work, these older workers are potential targets of discrimination, a statement supported by the findings of this study. Bias against older workers in personnel decisions was demonstrated in several of the incidents that made assumptions about the decline of their mental and physical capacities.

Age stereotypes characterized older workers as rigid and resistant to change. Further, it was decided not to attempt to correct the older worker's performance.

Several of the study's incidents demonstrated assumptions about older workers' decline of interest, motivation, and ability to improve job-related skills. As a result, there was no further training investment in the older employee, and a decision was made to terminate.

The present study of undergraduate business students indicates the extent of work-related age stereotypes as they may influence management human resource decisions. The authors suggest that these management decisions may actually reduce the older employee's motivation, since there are no opportunities for advancement or retraining. The low motivation may result not from aging but from management's biased attitudes in treatment of the older employee.

Summary Review of Research Study 6-1-C   An in-basket management simulation exercise investigated how age stereotypes affect management personnel decisions. Six in-basket items covered resistance to change, lack of creativity, cautiousness and slowness of judgment, lower physical capacity, lack of interest in technological change, and untrainability.

The subjects were 142 undergraduate business students who were presented with two versions of a hypothetical employee: a young employee and an older one. The results found negative age stereotypes present, with the subjects indicating that older employees are more resistant to management influence and less likely to improve their performance. The older employee was believed not to be creative, innovative, or willing to take risks. Other negative age stereotypes included declining physical strength, less motivation to keep current of technological developments, and unsuitability for retraining, with the only alternative being replacement.

The authors suggest that any lowered motivation on the part of older workers may result from the lack of opportunity and training caused by management's acceptance of negative stereotypes of age, not necessarily from their aging.

REFERENCES

[1]Cleveland, J.N., and F.J. Landy, "The Effects of Person and Job Stereotypes on Two Personnel Decisions," *Journal of Applied Psychology*, 68 (1983), 609–19.

[2]Cleveland, J.N., and F.J. Landy, "The Influence of Rater and Ratee Age on Two Performance Judgments," *Personnel Psychology*, 34 (1981), 19–29.

[3]Rosen, B., and T.H. Jerdee, "The Influence of Age Stereotypes on Managerial Decisions," *Journal of Applied Psychology*, 61 (1976), 428–32.

QUESTIONS

1. How does the older–younger performance behavior pattern affect such factors as money rewards and ratings of overall performance?
2. What is the effect of age, young versus old, upon the performance appraisal process of rating employees as to effectiveness?
3. When the older worker's skills are considered obsolete, how does the age stereotype influence management decisions on retraining?

Research Incident 6-2:
George Dalton and Racism

- What differences in evaluating intrinsic and extrinsic job differences are accounted for by race?
- How do race differences affect evaluations of work performance?
- What is the effect of race upon employee feelings of job satisfaction?

George Dalton entered the human resource office in the late afternoon and said, "I want to quit, and right now!" It was evident that he was upset and highly emotional. His request was handled in a neutral manner; he was told to return the next day at 3 P.M. to pick up his check and complete termination procedures. Upon his return, prior to receiving his final check, he would be interviewed by one of the specialists in the human resource department who would process the paperwork and also determine his reasons for quitting.

The company was a unionized manufacturing firm with an above-average pay scale. At this time, the local economy had a labor surplus, and good jobs were very difficult to obtain.

George Dalton was 30 years old, black, and a high school graduate, and he had been employed by the company for two years. The human resource specialist utilized the next morning to obtain further information before the meeting. Fred Johnson, the supervisor of the shipping department where George worked, was not aware of George's quitting, since it had occurred late in the afternoon. When told of it the next morning, Fred was surprised, since he felt that George had received a fair shake. He recalled that George had been hired initially as a temporary truck driver during a transportation strike and, after the strike was settled, was one of the few from the temporary workforce who were retained. Since George did not have enough seniority to remain as a truck driver, he became a relief man, filling in on various jobs because of absenteeism, sickness, or vacations. When the economy turned down and the company had a temporary layoff of employees, Fred hadn't wanted to lose George Dalton, so he assigned him as an extra worker. This involved a variety of job duties, since the department now had fewer men, but George would at least be working, and at the same rate of pay. Fred couldn't see why George had quit, but he wasn't going to worry about it.

The human resource specialist knew that Fred Johnson had a reputation as an authoritarian and task-oriented, so the mere fact that he had kept Dalton on the payroll during the layoff indicated that Dalton was a valuable employee. Since the company was an equal opportunity employer, the human resource specialist anticipated the afternoon interview with more than the usual concern.

George Dalton appeared at the human resource office promptly at 3 P.M. In the human resource specialist's office, some skillfully presented questions brought forth the reasons for his decision to quit. George felt that Johnson was prejudiced against his race and that that was why he was changed from a relief-worker to an extra-worker classification doing menial jobs. Apparently, Johnson had never thought to explain to George the valid reasons for the change of jobs. To prove his point that Fred Johnson was a bigot, George said he had spent most of the previous day shoveling sand into hoppers. Although this type of work was appropriate for an extra worker, Johnson had not mentioned this fact to George when the job assignment was made. After an extended discussion revealing the reasons behind the work changes, George Dalton was satisfied and returned to his job, still classified as an extra worker.

RELEVANT EMPIRICAL
RESEARCH STUDIES

Research Study 6-2-A

Although the issue of race in the work environment is a sensitive one, the research literature does provide the human resource specialist with helpful insights on the problem. How much input does race have in determining whether a person is likely to experience job satisfaction?

Moch[1] gathered information from a sample group of 466 employees from five departments of an assembly and packaging plant located in the South. Twenty years before, this plant had been segregated, but since 1958, those practices had been eliminated. (Approximately half the current employees had been hired by the company before 1958.) However, past social norms remained; members of each race ate together and preferred to remain in their current jobs rather than transfer to achieve racial balance.

The sample group completed a questionnaire, developed by the Survey Research Center of the University of Michigan, measuring intrinsic, extrinsic, and social factors, and measures of employee satisfaction. The study found significant differences between races regarding the importance of intrinsic factors such as doing something worthwhile, doing the things you do best, doing things that make you feel good about yourself, taking part in decisions, and developing skills and abilities. The black employees felt they were more likely to find another, comparable job than did either the Mexican-Americans or the whites, and the Mexican-Americans felt this way less likely than the whites did.

The employees' general satisfaction varied with race; the blacks reported less satisfaction than the whites, and the Mexican-Americans reported more than the whites. The author used regression analysis to determine whether structural, cultural, social, and social-psychological factors were responsible for the differences in job satisfaction by race. The statistical analysis revealed that race alone accounted for 53 percent, a surprising amount of the variance in level of job satisfaction. It appears that structural and cultural factors do not significantly affect the relation between race and job satisfaction, and the effect of social integration and deprivation is small. This study suggests that management practices may have only a modest effect upon the values that employees bring with them to work.

Summary Review of Research Study 6-2-A   The study found that the race of employees was a significant factor in whether they experienced job satisfaction. Other factors, such as work assignment, hierarchical position, and cultural factors, failed to significantly change that relationship. The author suggests that management efforts to alter racial differences in job satisfaction may result in only modest change, and that increased satisfaction can be attained only through broad racial and cultural change, not direct management policy.

An interesting finding was the difference in job satisfaction between the Mexican-Americans and the blacks. Both groups were underrepresented in management, relatively socially isolated, and not favored in terms of job assignment. But whereas the blacks were relatively dissatisfied, the Mexican-Americans were relatively satisfied. It appears that other reasons need to be researched to explain the apparent differences in job satisfaction by race.

Research Study 6-2-B

What effect do sex and race stereotypes have upon the rational judgments of raters in evaluating individual work behavior?

Hamner and others[2] investigated this issue in a sample of 36 volunteer undergraduate business students. The study was designed to determine what effect the sex and race of the rater and the sex and race of job applicants had upon the ratings. The raters were nine black males, nine black females, nine white females, and nine white males. They viewed a videotape of job applicants stocking grocery shelves for a position as stock clerk. The job applicants were black and white, female and male, high-performance and low-performance, for a total of eight. Each of the 36 raters received an instruction sheet prior to viewing the videotape and, at the conclusion of the videotape, received a rating sheet for each job applicant on which to indicate overall task performance.

The results showed the raters as able to significantly distinguish between high-performance and low-performance job applicants. Female job applicants were rated higher on overall task performance than were males. However, the black raters tended to rate the black job applicants higher than the whites, and the white raters rated the white job applicants higher than the blacks. The study found a tendency to favor a high-performing white job applicant over a similarly high-performing black one, but to favor a low-performing black job applicant over a low-performing white. Apparently, the bias toward the white job applicant shifted to the black when performances were equally low. Since the high–low performance levels were identical for the applicants, with no actual difference in objective measures of job performance, a bias was shown in the study, with females rated differently from males and blacks differently from whites. High-performing and low-performing blacks were both rated as average workers, low-performing whites were rated below average, and high-performing whites were rated better than average.

Summary Review of Research Study 6-2-B It appears that sex and race stereotypes do influence the ratings of behavior on a work task even when the objective measures are adequately defined. The task that was performed was low-level and relatively unskilled. It is interesting to note that the performance of the women was inflated rather than devalued relative to that of the males. Perhaps the job was one that males are expected to hold, so that when a woman performed equally well, she was regarded as the better performer. The authors cite other studies in which the task was at the managerial or professional level and the performance of women was devalued. They suggest that women may have a better chance for unskilled work and males a better chance for managerial or professional jobs.

The present study also found bias within the races, with higher ratings given to applicants of the same race. Also, the high-performing blacks were rated only slightly higher than low-performing blacks, yet high-performing whites were rated significantly higher than low-performing whites. This bias would work against the high-performing black relative to salary increases and promotions. There is also a question here of how appropriate supervisory ratings are as criteria by which to validate tests. The authors generalize that training is needed not only in performance evaluation techniques but also in applying objectively defined criteria.

Research Study 6-2-C

What can be said about job satisfaction and race? Do different races experience different amounts of job satisfaction?

Vecchio[3] investigated the relationship between job satisfaction and job quality for the majority cultural group (whites) versus the minority cultural group (blacks). The study group was 2,569 full-time male workers (2,303 whites and 266 blacks), who were surveyed in their homes by trained interviewers for the National Opinion Research Center over a six-year period (1971–77). The respondents were questioned as to demographic information—race, age, years of education—and as to how satisfied they were with the work they performed. In his article, Vecchio presents some statistical techniques that are complex and may be more at the level of students with training in advanced statistics.

The study showed that relative to white workers, the sample black workers were on the average less satisfied with their work. Also, the black workers held jobs of lower occupational prestige and were less well educated. The study also reported that as the age of the white respondents increased, so did occupational prestige; but for the black respondents, the reverse occurred, with occupational prestige decreasing as the age of the respondents increased. Perhaps the younger black respondents were better educated and more qualified for prestige jobs, and the older black respondents were not.

The next finding supports this position, since the study found that the black workers' age was more strongly inversely related to education than in the case of the whites. That is, in both groups, the younger workers were better educated than the older workers, but this was more apparent for the younger black workers.

Also, the relationship between the prestige of the job and dissatisfaction with the job was stronger for the white workers than the black. It follows then that black workers would express greater satisfaction relative to white workers for jobs of lower occupational prestige. On the other hand, the white workers expressed greater satisfaction relative to black workers for jobs of higher occupational prestige. Thus, for jobs such as automobile mechanic or barber, the white workers were more satisfied than the black workers, whereas for jobs such as file clerk or sign painter, the black workers were more satisfied than the white. In jobs that might fall between these two classifications of prestige, the black and white workers did not differ in terms of job satisfaction.

Summary Review of Research Study 6-2-C   Although the present study affirms previous findings of differences between blacks and whites relative to job satisfaction, occupational attainment, and educational attainment, there appear to be differences in the manner in which these are related. Relative to the inverse relationship between age and job prestige, it appears that young blacks rather than older blacks are the ones in positions of higher occupational prestige, whereas the reverse is true for whites. The inverse relationship between education and job satisfaction seems similar, with different levels of education, job opportunities, and career aspirations for younger versus older blacks. By contrast, the situation between younger and older whites is not so fluid. Apparently, that greater educational attainment results in more job satisfaction and prestige is truer for whites than blacks.

The author cautions that although individual differences exist in the relationship of job quality and job satisfaction as a result of worker alienation, the magnitude of these differences is not impressive, and that overlap exists, reducing any predictive utility in considering individual alienation relative to job selection or job assignment.

REFERENCES

[1]Moch, M.K., "Racial Differences in Job Satisfaction: Testing Four Common Explanations," *Journal of Applied Psychology*, 65 (1980), 299–306.

[2]Hamner, W.C., J.S. Kim, L. Baird, and W.J. Bigoness, "Race and Sex as Determinants of Ratings by Potential Employers in a Simulated Work-Sampling Task," *Journal of Applied Psychology*, 59 (1974), 705–11.

[3]Vecchio, R.P., "Worker Alienation as a Moderator of the Job-Quality/Job-Satisfaction Relationship: The Case of Racial Differences," *Academy of Management Journal,* 23 (1980), 479–86.

QUESTIONS

1. With reference to the research incident, what would you, as a human resource specialist, have done to prevent the George Dalton problem from occurring?
2. In the work environment, should the human resource manager expect difficulties to occur as a regular course of events where members of different races are employed?
3. In regard to Fred Johnson, does this situation suggest that any future action by the human resource department is necessary?
4. Was George Dalton's reaction justified? Explain your position.

Research Incident 6-3:
Edwin Mickle Meets the Law

- Which is the most effective affirmative action program, one that is threatening or one that is nonthreatening?
- How can discrimination be detected? Is it possible to construct a model that would eliminate discrimination?
- Does race affect an employee's preference for certain types of jobs?

The company lawyer was quite emphatic. Either the human resource department revised its present selection and promotion procedures to comply with the mandate of the EEO or the board of directors would adopt a resolution suggesting replacement of the staff. Since the lawyer was secretly referred to by many executives as "the law," his ultimatum was both real and ominous.

What triggered the visit of the company lawyer was a rash of discrimination complaints. Several of them appeared to have merit, creating an embarrassing situation for the company's national reputation as a progressive employer.

Edwin Mickle, head of the company's EEO department, immediately scheduled a meeting with his staff for the following afternoon. The agenda was identification of breakdowns in the selection and promotion process, preparation of appropriate action plans with definite deadlines, and submission of the findings to "the law." But 40 minutes into the meeting, it was apparent to both Edwin and his staff that there were no deficiencies in the company's selection and promotion procedures. The thick file folders that covered the conference table were all documented and verified as to each step of the lengthy, detailed procedures. There appeared to be no way that discrimination could occur, since a violation at any one of the procedural steps would be quickly noted and the person committing it would be clearly visible.

The current selection and promotion procedures had been formalized the preceding year, after a detailed study by Edwin's staff, working with a prestigious consulting firm that specialized in human relations. These procedures indicated that the company had a strong policy of complying with EEO directives, and the national publicity surrounding the company's announcement of those procedures had brought favorable responses from many minority and feminist groups. However, it was after the new procedures were initiated that the discrimination complaints began to surface.

Despite the consensus at today's staff meeting, Edwin knew there was a problem and answers were needed now. But where to look, and for what?

RELEVANT EMPIRICAL
RESEARCH STUDIES

Research Study 6-3-A

Which is "best"—a strong or a weak EEO policy? Are their effects on personnel who implement them different? What is the role of reactance?

Rosen and Mericle[1] studied different strategies designed to reduce or eliminate discrimination to determine whether affirmative action created manager *reactance*. That is, whether managers felt their freedom to make selection decisions was being unreasonably restricted. One strategy is to develop and initiate fair employment policies for all to follow. It might be expected that a weakly worded, nonspecific fair employment policy that only suggests compliance would have a limited effect on eliminating discrimination. A policy specifying compliance and providing explicit procedures of implementation might be expected to have a significantly greater chance of reducing discrimination.

The study investigated the effects of strong and weak fair employment policies on management selection decisions and salary recommendations. The authors hypothesize that discrimination is likely to be greater under weak policies with no follow-up of compliance. Also, under these conditions, male applicants will be selected more frequently than identically qualified females.

The authors suggest that strong affirmative action programs on selection decisions may be affected by manager reactance. When managers feel that their discretion and freedom are threatened or restrained, they may resort to reactance. This means that they will attempt to restore their freedom, and where this conflicts with management policy, they will resort to indirect strategies to reduce the reactance, such as recommending lower salaries for women, assigning them less-challenging tasks, and blocking opportunities for their development.

For purposes of experimental control, the authors limited the study to the reactance effects on salary recommendations. Their hypothesized position is that strongly worded fair employment policies provoke reactance among managers, resulting in lower salary recommendations for newly hired females.

The subjects in the study were 57 male and eleven female municipal administrators from a middle-sized southeastern city. The mean of their administrative experience was 9.4 years. They all participated in a decision-making exercise that was part of a management workshop on personnel policies. The exercise placed the subjects in the role of department administrators in municipal government who were to evaluate an applicant for a supervisory position. They received a job description, a statement of the city's equal employment opportunity policies, an application blank, and a decision form.

The two independent variables of fair employment policy statement and applicant's sex were manipulated in the decision exercise. The strongly worded policy statement indicated that the city was under considerable pressure and that selection decisions would be subject to review. The weakly worded statement said that the city was an equal employment opportunity employer and that administrators should use their best judgment.

The subjects then reviewed a standard application form for the applicant. Half the subjects reviewed a male application and half reviewed a female application with equal qualifications. The selection recommendations were made on a four-point scale ranging from "reject" to "accept." Those subjects who recommended hiring advised salaries ranging from $10,500 to $13,000.

The preliminary results found no significant main effects or interaction effects between the decisions of male and female subjects. Further, there were no significant effects based on comparisons of the subjects' years of administrative experience.

It had been hypothesized earlier that a strongly worded and enforced fair employment policy would counteract discrimination in selection decisions. Although the subjects were less likely to recommend hiring an applicant of either sex in the strong-policy situation compared to the weak situation, the difference was not statistically significant.

It was also found that selection decisions were similar for the male and female applicants in both the strong and weak fair employment policy situations.

In regard to salary recommendations, it had been hypothesized that the selection of females under the strong fair employment policy situation would provoke reactance on the part of management, resulting in lower starting-salary recommendations. This assumption was supported; the lowest starting-salary recommendation found was for a female hired under the strong fair employment policy, and the study revealed a pattern of relatively lower salaries for women hired under strong fair employment policies and relatively higher salaries under weak policies.

Summary Review of Research Study 6-3-A   The present study examined how fair employment policies influence selection decisions and salary recommendations.

It was found that fair employment policies did not significantly influence selection decisions. There was no evidence of sex discrimination in either the weak- or strong-policy situations.

The study results were consistent with a reactance-theory explanation. That is, management reaction against restrictions under a strong fair employment policy resulted in lower starting salaries for newly hired females.

The lowest starting-salary recommendations were for females in the strong fair employment situation. Interestingly, the highest starting-salary recommendations for females were in the weak fair employment situation.

It is suggested that care should be taken in developing fair employment policies so as to minimize management reactance.

Research Study 6-3-B

How can we determine whether a selection committee was prejudiced against certain people? Can we build a model that will allow us to validate discrimination claims?

A study by Maniscalo and others[2] suggests a method of resolving and also preventing claims of discrimination. The method is called *social judgment technology.* The situation analyzed was that of a graduate admissions committee rejection of an applicant who claimed he was refused admission because of being physically handicapped.

The graduate admissions committee in this study comprised three faculty members and one advanced graduate student. The admission process consisted of, first, rating of an applicant by two committee members. If the applicant received a high enough rating, then all four committee members evaluated the applicant. Of 210 applicants, 87 passed the first rating and 27 were finally accepted. Since the physically handicapped person did not pass the first rating, it was that part of the procedure that was analyzed.

The rationale for the analysis was the assumption that the committee members had weighted the relative importance of each information item and then integrated their weighted values to arrive at a numerical rating. If this was true, a regression approach could be used that would result in a model of the rating process. That is, the original rating procedure or policy would have been duplicated or captured.

Although it was not possible to reconstruct the thought processes of the committee, the model could assess the accuracy of the rating procedure. If the duplicated or captured rating procedure did predict the committee ratings accurately, then each applicant's rating by the committee could be compared to that generated by the duplicated or captured policy.

Thus, if an applicant's predicted rating was higher than the actual rating made by the committee, there would appear to be a basis for discrimination proceedings. If the predicted rating was equal to the actual committee rating but below the rating of admitted applicants, there would appear to be no case for discrimination. However, if the predicted score was substantially below the actual rating, it would appear that the admissions committee was giving the applicant a "boost" rather than discriminating.

To evaluate the discrimination claim, the study authors were allowed access to the application materials and other information, such as sex, race, undergraduate GPA, undergraduate GPA in major field, prior graduate attendance, and the Graduate Record Examination scores. The authors also obtained the committee's subjective comments about each applicant. These comments provided information on four other variables: letters of recommendation, an applicant interest statement, unusual features from the undergraduate transcript, and experience. It was necessary to code these four variables if they were to be used in the analysis. A three-point scale was used, ranging from negative to positive. The result of the factors above was a model of the actual committee's behavior.

Of the original 210 applicants, 50 were randomly selected for constructing a profile from their application information. These profiles contained eleven information items, which were put into booklets and given to four simulation committees composed of eight faculty members. They then made ratings on the same scale as the original committee.

The results of the study involved the adequacy of the linear modeling approach. It was found that for all the committees, the policy equations accounted for a large proportion of the judgment variance. The correlations demonstrated a consistency evaluating applicants and also a reasonable adequacy of the model. This means that it was possible to predict the applicants' ratings using the information described in the paragraph above.

Relative to the handicapped applicant, it was found that his predicted rating based on the model was lower than his actual rating. This suggests that there was no discrimination, but, in fact, the reverse. When all the applicants were evaluated through the application of the regression equation, the handicapped person's evaluation remained below that of the accepted group. One area of concern relative to bias is that the handicapped applicant received the lowest rating on the variable of letters of recommendation, which was a significant predictor. If his letters were evaluated poorly owing to his handicap, this would be undetected by the present analysis. However, the overall evaluation was that social judgment techniques using multiple regression analysis can be used to determine whether discrimination has taken place.

Summary Review of Research Study 6-3-B   The study analyzed the situation of a person rejected for a graduate program. The applicant claimed discrimination because he was handicapped. The policy of the admissions committee was captured or reconstructed in a linear model to determine whether discrimination had in fact occurred. It was found that the applicant's predicted rating by the model was actually lower than that awarded by the admissions committee. This suggests that there was no discrimination, but, in fact, the reverse. Further, the handicapped applicant's predicted rating was lower than the predicted ratings of those applicants who were accepted. The study suggests that a social judgment model is a useful technique for evaluating claims of discrimination.

Research Study 6-3-C

What effect does race have upon a person's preferences for particular positions? Do whites, blacks, and Hispanics exhibit different preferences for job tasks and job conditions?

A study by Ash and others[3] investigated possible differences among whites, blacks, and Hispanics in their preferences for clerical tasks and job conditions. The study subjects had applied to the state of Arizona for clerical positions: clerk, typist, and stenographer. The sample size was 600 applicants—200 whites, 200 blacks, and 200 Hispanics. They were 85 percent female and 15 percent male. The white and Hispanic subjects were chosen at random, but the sample of blacks represented almost the entire black clerical-applicant population.

To determine the test–retest stability of the instrument measuring job condition and task preferences, another sample of equal white, black, and Hispanic applicants totaling 150 was randomly drawn.

The instrument was the Clerical Job Condition and Task Preference Schedule, in which the applicant selected from a list of nine job conditions (standing/walking/bending/sitting/doing a single task, and so on) the three conditions liked most and the three liked least. After that, the applicant selected from a list of 19 job tasks (filing, sorting papers, taking shorthand, and so on) the six liked most and the six liked least.

To determine whether race was associated with the applicants' responses for each job condition and task preference, a computation was made by using a Chi-Square and an index of predictive association, the Lambda B. The Lambda B is a statistical technique that proportionately reduced the error of predicting the task and condition preferences of the particular racial group.

An assessment was made of any possible adverse effect on the racial groups of matching preferences for tasks and conditions. This required obtaining the frequency of occurrence of each job condition, which was then computed into an index of condition importance. Next, the weighted frequency of occurrence for each job task was computed and used as an index of task importance. The conditions and tasks were ranked separately for each racial group. A statistical comparison was made of the positive and negative preference rank orders for each racial group with the rank orders of both condition and task importance. The authors indicate that this technique measures the potential for adverse impact, not the existing impact.

The data for establishing the test–retest stability of the preference schedule were obtained with a second mailing to the original sample of 150 clerical applicants. Their preferences at time 1 were then compared to their preferences at time 2.

The results of the study indicate significant racial differences in preferences toward seven of the nine job conditions when the Chi-Square analysis was used. However, when the Lambda B index was applied to these results, the strength of association was found to be weak or nonexistent. The Lambda B index ranges from 0 (no reduction in error) to 1.0 (complete reduction in error or perfect prediction). The index for the seven job conditions was as follows: .093, .000, .000, .000, .000, .000, and .040.

The analysis for the job tasks was similar. Although nine of the 19 tasks demonstrated significant statistical associations between racial origin and preference toward the tasks, the Lambda B values were .000 for five tasks and a .012, a .041, a .055, and a .149 for the other tasks. Again, the association was weak.

In the comparison of the rank-order correlations of condition and task with overall positive and negative preferences by racial group, the relationships for all appear similar. However, they were slightly stronger for the Hispanic group, indicating that the matching selection process favored them. That is, of the three racial groups, the Hispanic applicants tended to like the tasks and conditions of the clerical jobs more and to dislike the most important tasks and conditions less. Thus, the Hispanics disproportionately preferred jobs in which they were told what to do next, were less desirous of jobs in which they might be responsible for planning their own schedules, and were less desirous of jobs in which they would have full responsibility for a clerical system. They preferred jobs in which they could assist people who have difficulty understanding forms or expressing themselves.

The stability of the preference schedule for each racial group was not statistically signficant. This finding was based on the return of the second mailing of 71 out of the 150 sample. Yet there was a trend indicating that the preference schedule was more stable for the white racial group. The low stability of the preference schedule was of concern regarding the study's findings but did not result from the elapsed time between the two mailings. It was found that the greater the clerical work experience, the more stable were the applicant's task and condition preferences.

It would appear that the small differences among the racial groups in the relationship between preferences and importance of job conditions and tasks indicates that the matching approach does not adversely affect the job opportunities of the racial groups. However, the matching selection process may tend to slightly favor Hispanic applicants.

Summary Review of Research Study 6-3-C   The study investigated whether a matching selection process used to hire applicants for a clerical position adversely affected white, black, or Hispanic racial groups. In a matching selection process, the applicant indicated preferences for job tasks and conditions, which were then checked for compatibility with existing openings.

Although there were many statistically significant relationships between task and condition preferences relative to race, their magnitude appeared to have little effect. This suggests little adverse impact or discrimination in the selection process.

Part of the study investigated the stability over time of the preference schedule instrument used to collect data. The result was an indication of low stability, suggesting caution in the use of the preference schedule as a predictor of job performance. However, stability did increase with more clerical work experience and was greater for the white racial group.

REFERENCES

[1]Rosen, B., and M.F. Mericle, "Influence of Strong versus Weak Fair Employment Policies and Applicants' Sex on Selection Decisions and Salary Recommendations in a Management Simulation," *Journal of Applied Psychology*, 64 (1979), 435–39.

[2]Maniscalo, C.I., M.E. Doherty, and D.G. Ullman, "Assessing Discrimination: An Application of Social Judgment Technology," *Journal of Applied Psychology*, 65 (1980), 284–88.

[3]Ash, R.A., E.L. Levine, and S.L. Edgell, "Exploratory Study of a Matching Approach to Personnel Selection: The Impact of Ethnicity," *Journal of Applied Psychology*, 64 (1979), 35–41.

QUESTIONS

1. What are the implications of reactance and fair employment policies? Discuss.
2. How does the social judgment technology model relate to discrimination? Explain. How does one construct such a model?

3. What is the effect on adverse impact of matching applicants' task and job-condition likes and dislikes with what is reflected in a particular job? Do all racial groups respond in a similar manner to the Clerical Job Condition and Task Preference Schedule? Explain.

NON-EMPIRICAL RESEARCH ARTICLE ABSTRACTS

Abstract 6-1

- How do the courts regard a company's adoption of a program that was not intended to discriminate yet whose results do discriminate?
- What authority do the courts have to change the provisions of a collective bargaining agreement to correct discriminatory practices?
- What power does the employer have relative to retroactive seniority under a collective bargaining agreement? where no union exists?

These questions are addressed in a 1984 article by Louis P. Britt III,[1] staff attorney for the city of Memphis.

The author points out that many people believed that a recent U.S. Supreme Court decision was the death knell for affirmative action. The decision referred to was *Memphis Fire Department* v. *Stotts,* which held that federal courts do not have the power to order an employer to lay off more senior white employees to protect minority gains under an affirmative action plan. However, the author contends that affirmative action is still alive, although the *Stotts* decision did offer restrictions and present questions for the future regarding affirmative action versus seniority rights in union and nonunion situations.

The background of the case occurred when the city of Memphis entered into two consent decrees in settlement of a class-action race-discrimination suit. One consent decree was with the U.S. Department of Justice in 1974; it provided for affirmative action hiring goals in many divisions of the city, including the fire department. The other decree was in 1980 and paralleled the first, but also included affirmative action for promotions.

About a year after the 1980 consent decree, the city of Memphis experienced financial problems and announced an attempt to reduce costs by a citywide reduction in personnel. These reductions were to take place under the policy of last-hired, first-fired seniority policy. Since most minorities were the last hired, they would be the ones who would be fired.

But before this seniority policy could be implemented, a federal district court enjoined the city from proceeding, on the grounds that even though the seniority system was not adopted with the intent to discriminate, the effects would be discriminatory. The court indicated that the proposed layoffs would hinder the purpose of the consent decree, since minorities would be the first group to be laid off, and this would reduce the minority representation. More-senior white employees would be retained, while less-senior black employees were either laid off or reduced in rank.

The city of Memphis appealed to the U.S. Court of Appeals for the Sixth Circuit and, losing there, sought the review of the U.S. Supreme Court. This appeal was based on the seniority rights of employees and the right of the court to change or modify the consent decree as previously agreed to by the parties involved.

The Supreme Court ruled in the *Stotts* case that the district court could not change the consent decree by imposing affirmative action remedies unless it first found that the protected groups were actually being discriminated against. It said that the lower courts may use remedial powers, including changing a consent decree, only to prevent future violations and to compensate discrimination victims.

This case did not resolve the question of a conflict between affirmative action and seniority. Yet it appears that if promotion is not covered by a consent decree, remedies cannot later be imposed by the court where seniority is the only determining factor for promotion.

Britt points out that under *Stotts* and other recent decisions, an employer is not free to change an existing seniority system resulting from collective bargaining. In one court decision, an employer had entered into a consent decree to maintain a percentage of female representation. However, the union contract had a seniority clause regarding layoffs. When layoffs occurred, the employer kept the less-senior females and laid off the senior males. The senior males filed a grievance, and an arbitrator awarded them reinstatement and back pay. The employer appealed to the Supreme Court, which upheld the arbitrator. In yet another case, an employer entered into an agreement with the EEOC to award certain employees retroactive seniority. The union objected, so the employer backed out of the agreement. The U.S. Court of Appeals held that without the union's agreement or a finding of discrimination, the employer could not award retroactive seniority, because of the detriment to other union employees.

In the *Stotts* case, the Supreme Court ruled that the union did not participate in revising the seniority system as it existed in the collective bargaining agreement, so the employer was not free to change it. However, in the absence of a union, an employer could unilaterally modify the existing agreement to comply with affirmative action requirements.

The effect of the *Stotts* decision restated that seniority rights cannot be changed by the courts to promote affirmative action without a finding of discrimination. It also limited the court in attempting to modify consent decrees. The author views the court decision as an attempt to balance conflicting interests. However, when a collective bargaining agreement exists, voluntary changes in seniority policies to comply with affirmative action require the consent of the union.

In the same issue of *Personnel Administrator* that the Britt article appeared in, another article concerning the *Stotts* case was featured. Lawrence Z. Lorber,[2] an attorney, pointed out that the *Stotts* decision does not mean the end of affirmative action in hiring or the end of timetables for hiring minorities and females. Instead, the decision merely restates that a bona fide seniority system cannot be altered by a court under an employment discrimination lawsuit.

The issue before the Supreme Court related only to the district court in modifying the existing seniority system. The Supreme Court ruled that a bona fide seniority system cannot be changed by a Title VII consent decree unless the union involved agrees to it. The author points out that the implication of the *Stotts* case as it applies to employers is unclear. The case does not end arguments regarding racial or sexual employment preferences. Nor does it deal with voluntary affirmative action or with hiring goals.

Lorber suggests that employers watch post-*Stotts* legal decisions to determine any fundamental change in the practice of affirmative action in permitting or requiring minority preferences in certain circumstances.

REFERENCES

[1]Britt, Louis P. III, "Affirmative Action: Is There Life after *Stotts?*" From the September 1984 issue of *Personnel Administrator,* copyright 1984, The American Society for Personnel Administration, 606 North Washington Street, Alexandria, VA 22314.

[2]Lorber, Lawrence Z., "Employers Should Not Take Precipitous Action in Affirmative Action Cases." From the September 1984 issue of *Personnel Administrator,* copyright 1984, The American Society for Personnel Administration, 606 North Washington Street, Alexandria, VA 22314.

QUESTIONS

1. What was the Supreme Court decision in *Memphis Fire Department* v. *Stotts?*
2. What freedom does an employer have to change an existing seniority system resulting from collective bargaining? Why?
3. Why does Lawrence Lorber state that the implication of the *Stotts* case as it applies to employers is unclear?

Abstract 6-2

- Given the importance of Title VII of the 1964 Civil Rights Act, may an employer legally enforce a bona fide seniority system?

- Why is discriminatory intent a more stringent requirement for the plaintiff than discriminatory effect?
- When may sex be used as an occupational qualification under EEO conditions?

A 1984 article by Ann Weaver Hart,[1] a high school principal, answers these questions.

The author says that for the past two decades, the philosophy of civil rights has been represented by Title VII of the 1964 Civil Rights Act, which prohibits discrimination in hiring, discharge, and compensation on account of race, color, religion, sex, ethnicity, or national origin. Although the act does not recognize any bona fide occupational qualification based on race, employers may enforce a bona fide seniority system, judge the quantity or quality of work, and apply professionally developed tests for employment, promotion, or compensation.

However, in recent years, the courts have been interpreting not only the effect of employment practices upon protected groups, but also the motives behind the formulation of such practices. An example is the conflicting standards that are developing in which some plaintiffs are required only to show a disproportionate effect upon a protected group, whereas other plaintiffs must establish proof of discriminatory intent. The author illustrates these two perspectives with two incidents.

Trailways Bus Company has a grooming code that requires all males in public contact to be clean-shaven to promote a company clean-cut public image. Even though the company was not intending to discriminate, this policy had an adverse effect upon male black employees. It appears that although less than 1 percent of white males suffer from a malady classified as "shaving bumps," 25 percent of black males are subject to this condition.

Since this policy had a disproportionate effect on black male employees, the U.S. District Court ruled against Trailways under Title VII. This is an example of plaintiffs successfully demonstrating a discriminatory effect of an employment practice. It is now the most commonly applied standard.

Another point of view is reflected in the immunity granted bona fide seniority systems. These systems perpetuate pre–Civil Rights Act discrimination, trapping minorities and women in low-paying jobs. In one court case, it was ruled that the plaintiff must show that such a seniority system was established with deliberate intent to discriminate. This thinking was represented in yet another case, in which a transfer to a more promising division of the company resulted in the loss of seniority. The plaintiffs argued that the system represented overt discrimination. However, since the seniority system lost whites as well as blacks their seniority if they transferred to the more promising company divisions, the court ruled that it limited all employees and was exempt from Title VII.

The author finds that plaintiffs' demonstrating discriminatory intent and direct evidence of that intent is much more stringent than their show-ing only discriminatory effect. This represents a significant change from decisions in previous Title VII litigation, since the standard of discrimi-natory effect favors the plaintiffs. This is so because it does not require showing the state of mind of the defendant, a more difficult and compli-cated task.

The author finds a trend in the courts to modify seniority systems through consent decrees that remedy past discrimination. Recent court decisions have prohibited seniority-based layoffs that would adversely af-fect protected groups.

In regard to employment testing for hiring or promotion, the courts and regulatory agencies have been strict in discarding any test, unless it has been validated, that has an adverse effect on protected groups. In one case, a written examination for the selection of supervisors, only 54 percent of the black candidates passed, whereas 80 percent of the white candidates passed. However, the employer countered that 22.9 percent of the black candidates were promoted and only 13.5 percent of the white candidates were promoted. The Supreme Court ruled discrimination, pointing out that Title VII protects individuals, not groups.

The EEOC developed in 1979 a series of 90 "Questions and Answers Dealing with Uniform Guidelines on Employee Selection Procedures," to discourage discriminatory effect. It requires test validity studies related to successful job performance, not to personal characteristics. In a U.S. Dis-trict Court ruling, a police department was ordered to develop a new agility test that would have less adverse effect on women, and to use fewer tests such as scaling a wall or carrying a dummy.

Discriminatory effect is also being used in cases of alleged religious discrimination, with emphasis on the employer's demonstrating a reason-able accommodation for religious beliefs unless it results in undue hard-ship. The EEOC currently supports some rather expensive options, such as staggered work hours, lateral transfers, and floating holidays. In one court decision, the plaintiff's religion prevented the payment of union dues, and the court ruled that the union must accommodate the person because it was not an undue hardship for the union.

Even when there is no intent to discriminate, employers cannot pre-vent bilingual employees from using their native language on the job when there is no business necessity such as safety or talking with the public. However, the court has ruled that requiring bilingual employees to gener-ally use English on the job does not violate Title VII. And the Supreme Court has supported a California requirement that all peace officers be U.S. citizens.

A major area of case law and regulatory agencies in the last three years has been in sex discrimination. The author cites conflicting opinions in different jurisdictions and a lack of direction by the Supreme Court. In one decision, the U.S. Court of Appeals found that the preferences and stereotypes of potential foreign customers did not justify an employer in practicing sex-based discrimination. Any policy that excludes women from attaining roles of authority is indication of discriminatory effect, regardless of motive or intent. The court also said that EEOC regulations identify sex as an occupational qualification only when it is a genuine and authentic necessity.

The author states that case law on comparable worth continues to develop. One U.S. Court of Appeals case did find that sex-based discrimination under Title VII is prohibited even if jobs are different. The concept of equal pay for work of comparable worth to the employer is still too new to have been resolved. The same can be stated for the unresolved questions of discrimination in pensions and other benefits, such as maternity benefits. However, the presence of discriminatory effect is generally sufficient to prohibit the discrimination.

The EEOC guidelines of November 10, 1980, prohibit sexual harassment as a violation of Title VII. The responsibility is the employer's when it is known or should have been known that sexual harassment occurred. Such responsibility can be avoided only if the employer can show that immediate corrective action was taken. In a U.S. Court of Appeals case, it was not necessary for the plaintiff in a sexual-harassment action to prove the actual loss of employment benefits in order to receive the relief offered in Title VII. Further, even if harassment is not from the employer or the employer's agents but results from an employment practice, that practice is prohibited under Title VII. The author also says that sexual harassment exists when demands are made of an employee because of his or her sex when such demands would not be made of another employee of the opposite sex.

REFERENCE

[1]"Intent vs. Effect: Title VII Case Law That Could Affect You (Part II)," by Ann Weaver Hart, copyright April 1984. Reprinted with the permission of *Personnel Journal*, Costa Mesta, California; all rights reserved.

QUESTIONS

1. The author points out that in recent years the courts have gone beyond interpreting the effect of employment practices upon protected groups. What is her point?
2. Why does the standard of discriminatory effect favor the plaintiffs?
3. What has been the direction of the Supreme Court in the past few years regarding sex discrimination? Give some examples.

CHAPTER SEVEN

WOMEN

INTRODUCTION

The arrival of women in the business world at both the worker and management levels is an established fact. The demographics of our society indicate that the number of women in the world of work will continue to increase. Indeed, enrollment in schools of business across the country shows increasing female interest, women in some instances making up over 50 percent of the enrollment.

Not only are such upward trends expected to continue; by 1990, 61 percent of all the women in the United States will be in the labor force. In 1975, this percentage was 46 percent. Perhaps most significant is that of the estimated 19.6 million employees to be added to the workforce by 1990, it is expected that 11 million will be women.

The extent of the change that has already occurred is shown by the fact that in 1900, the percentage of women in the total U.S. labor force was 17 percent, and by 1979, it had grown to 41.5 percent. This increase was not necessarily the result of low-skilled employment, since 9,000 women were in skilled-trades apprenticeship programs in 1978, representing an increase of 52 percent enrollment. Further, in 1970, 4.8 percent of the lawyers in this country were women, and by 1980, that figure had increased to 13.8 percent. These increases are attributed in part to the facts that 60 percent of today's families have two or more wage earners; that we have seen a decline in the fertility rate of the 1980s, with women having fewer children and later in life; that women enter the work force earlier; that more women are continuing the educational process; and that women are continuing to work after children arrive. But in spite of these increases, 80 percent of the women in the workforce are employed in only 20 of the occupational classifications designated by the U.S. Census Bureau, out of a total of 427 listed occupations.

The future role of women in business careers appears unlimited. However, when there is a changing of the guard or the introduction of a new element into an existing group, the question of qualifications or "fitness" seems to arise. Although such topics as age differences, regional differences, and race differences may be discussed with some reasonableness, the topic of sex differences is quite volatile. Fortunately, the empirical literature is up to the task, and previous, less-rigorous research has been replaced recently with more sophisticated studies.

Even though the more recent empirical studies are less inclusive, sex differences do exist. It is our responsibility as human resource professionals to avail ourselves of this knowledge to assist both the individual and the organization in attaining appropriate goals. Most sex differences are the result of family training and the socialization process of our society, and knowledge of them permits the human resource professional to utilize them and, where appropriate, to provide training avenues.

Generally, the more recent empirical research has discarded several unsupportable "beliefs" regarding differences between males and females. There appear to be no consistent differences relative to self-esteem, analytical skills, sociability, suggestibility, achievement motivation, and rote-learning ability. The research does support male–female differences in regard to males excelling in mathematical and visual-spatial ability and being more aggressive, whereas females demonstrate greater verbal ability. When male and female practicing managers are compared, few differences are shown in assertiveness, competitiveness, dominance, and managing motivation. And the available evidence suggests that equally trained men and women do not differ in meaningful ways relative to the labor market or management careers.

Yet one fact is clear relative to the monetary compensation of women. Even in those occupations considered to be female, such as clerical, since 1960 male earnings have been consistently higher. It appears on the average that a female with four years of college can expect to earn about the same as a high school dropout male. A study of 391 occupations revealed that only in the occupation of kindergarten teaching were women paid more than men. Still another nationwide study of 1,500 management, technical, and professional workers showed that 48.6 percent of the females each received $3,500 less than males of similar backgrounds.

With women now moving into jobs once dominated by males, the old barriers are falling, as are outdated myths and misconceptions. It is the responsibility of the human resource professional to ensure that the process is guided by knowledge and the results of empirical research, thus promoting the effectiveness of the individual and of the organization.

RESEARCH INCIDENTS

Research Incident 7-1:
Trainee Dick Still and Manager Mary Gough

- What is the effect of a stereotype sex role upon the ability of a person to function in a position of authority?
- Does the classification of an occupation as either masculine or feminine affect the significance of the occupation to prospective jobholders?
- How do a male evaluator's attitudes affect his evaluation of a female? Or do they?

After his discharge from the service, Dick Still found employment at Security Life Insurance Company. He was 32, was married with two children, and had been graduated from college with a B.A. degree in management. At Security Life, Dick was placed in the customer service department as a trainee. This was the usual procedure for the company; most management personnel were first employed in that position before advancing up the promotion ladder. The manager of the department was Mary Gough, aged 50, a 20-year employee, and highly regarded by her employees and management. Since the nature of the work in customer service was quite exact, Gough was responsible for personnel training and maintained a close but not oppressive contact with the trainees.

At first, Dick Still performed adequately, but after three months, he demonstrated a serious lack of interest and purpose in his work. This troubled Mary, and she attempted to communicate with Dick but was unsuccessful. She tried for several weeks to resolve the problem, but Dick's motivation had become so poor that it was beginning to affect the other members of the department. With a sense of urgency, Mary contacted the human resource office and suggested that Dick be terminated. Upon hearing all the facts, the human resource officer suggested a meeting with the company psychologist, who was employed on a consulting basis. The decision was based partly upon the company philosophy of not terminating employees and partly to check the company's selection procedure for inconsistencies.

The psychologist's report indicated that Dick Still was capable of performing at a higher level of work, so his immediate problem was not one of intelligence. Apparently Dick's relationship with his mother had been unsatisfactory, and he maintained a great deal of hostility toward her. This factor would be evident in his relationship with any female supervisor, resulting in inappropriate behavior.

A decision was reached to transfer Dick to the underwriting department, where the supervisor was a male. The work in underwriting was considerably more complex than that in customer service, and some company personnel viewed the move with skepticism. Within the first week, there was an obvious change in Still's behavior. He was interested in learning his duties and more committed to performing satisfactorily. Six months later, the supervisor of the underwriting department notified the human resource officer that Dick Still was doing very well and should be considered an employee with future promotional potential.

RELEVANT EMPIRICAL RESEARCH STUDIES

Research Study 7-1-A

The position of manager is a difficult one, and women may find themselves in a stereotype sex role that is not supportive of authority. Is personal authority a masculine sex characteristic?

Israeli and others[1] studied women executives in multinational corporations. The sample was 111 host-country managers, 107 men and 4 women, who interacted with the subsidiary of a multinational corporation. The study's dependent variable was the attitude of host-country managers toward women as top managers of multinational corporation subsidiaries. The independent variables were the host country, the host industry, and the degree of preference for those culturally and ethnically similar to the respondents.

In the first stage, to determine attitudes toward senior women executives, the respondents were asked, "Can a well-qualified woman successfully head and manage a multinational corporation subsidiary?" The second stage was an unstructured personal interview in which respondents explained their views, which were then subjected to content analysis. The study failed to find any significant difference among host countries, host industries, and high or low preference for cultural and ethnic similarity to the question of a woman's being a successful subsidiary head. A significant majority gave an affirmative response to the question. But during the interviews, the respondents, while not questioning women's gaining recognition for competence, perceived the problem of gaining legitimacy in the executive role. Personal authority was viewed as a masculine sex characteristic. Further, exercising formal authority was seen as part of the male sex role. A woman exhibiting the characteristic and performing the role, they felt, would lack the credibility or influence of her male counterpart. Those respondents who agreed that women could be senior executives usually added, "Only at the second or third position of command, and then only if unusually talented."

Summary Review of Research Study 7-1-A The problem of a woman's managing a subsidiary of a multinational corporation goes beyond the issue of gaining recognition of her competence; it centers on the legitimacy of women in the executive role. Personal authority and the exercise of formal authority were seen as part of the male sex role. Women were viewed as lacking credibility, and this would undermine their authority position, so that they should be considered only for the second or third hierarchal manager slot, and then only if unusually talented. There is also the problem of women's lower social status. Since the number 1 manager slot reflects the importance with which the multinational corporation regards the assignment in the host country, social status requires a male. Host countries are also concerned that women would have less local autonomy and would exert less influence with the home office.

The authors suggest that the preceding may not be totally dysfunctional, since, if a woman is appointed to the number 1 slot, the opinion will be that she must have superior qualities to have earned the position, resulting in subordinate respect and cooperation.

Research Study 7-1-B

How do males regard the importance or status of occupations that may be classed as being feminine?

A study by Garland and Smith[2] investigated the occupational achievement differences of 81 female and 80 male students in undergraduate psychology classes. The students completed a personal-attributes questionnaire and were then classified as masculine (high male value and low female value scores), feminine (low male value and high female value scores), androgynous (high male and high female value scores), and undifferentiated (low male and low female value scores).

The students also completed an occupational aptitude questionnaire to determine their interests, their estimates of their scores, their interest in taking an aptitude test, and the likelihood of their success in different occupations. The results indicated that the male students had significantly higher standards for masculine occupations than did the female students. Also, there was no significant difference in standards between males and females for the occupations classified as feminine or androgynous. The masculine males demonstrated significantly lower standards for the occupations classified as feminine than for the masculine and androgynous occupations. On the other hand, the feminine female students showed significantly higher standards for feminine than for both masculine and androgynous occupations. These preferences demonstrate that even though males and females did not differ on expected positive success in masculine and androgynous occupations, the females did expect significantly higher positive success in feminine occupations than did the males.

The males indicated significantly more interest than females in future choice of masculine occupations, and the females indicated significantly more interest than males in future choice of both androgynous and female occupations. In regard to high- to middle-prestige masculine occupations, the males responded with a significantly higher possibility of choosing these occupations than did the females. Also, both males and females indicated a higher likelihood of choosing the high-prestige masculine occupations, but the males indicated a significantly greater likelihood of choosing middle-prestige occupations than did the females. There was no sex difference within the high-prestige occupations.

In regard to success, those students classified as undifferentiated anticipated the highest negative view of success across all the middle-prestige occupations. All the students expected significantly greater negative consequences of success in the middle-prestige masculine occupations than in the feminine or androgynous occupations. Although the males anticipated higher negative consequences of success in the female occupations than the females did, there was no sex difference relative to expected negative consequences of success in masculine and androgynous occupations. The students expected more negative consequences for success in the middle-prestige masculine occupations than in the high-prestige masculine occupations. The males demonstrated more interest in taking masculine-occupation attitude tests than the females did, and the females were more interested than the males in taking feminine-occupation aptitude tests. All students indicated more of a desire to take high-prestige than middle-prestige masculine-occupation aptitude tests. However, the males were significantly more interested than the females in taking aptitude tests for middle-prestige masculine occupations.

Summary Review of Research Study 7-1-B   There appear to be sex differences in achievement motivation, with each sex being motivated toward sex-appropriate occupations. The males obtained higher scores than the females for the middle-prestige occupations and also reported more interest in taking aptitude tests for these occupations. On the other hand, in regard to the feminine occupations, the females had more interest than the males as to future choice and desire to take aptitude tests.

Of interest is the closeness of the males' and females' responses to the high-prestige masculine occupations. The authors suggest that the lack of high-prestige feminine and androgynous occupations may require a female to choose the masculine stereotyped occupations if she is to attain high prestige.

The undifferentiated males and females reported the lowest positive and the highest negative consequences of success with the lowest standards. However, the masculine and androgynous males and females demonstrated the highest positive and lowest negative consequences and the highest standards. This may suggest that the former have low self-esteem and the latter high self-esteem.

Research Study 7-1-C

How does a male's general attitude toward women in management affect his evaluation of the success or failure of a female manager?

Garland and Price[3] investigated this situation with a sample of 123 undergraduate males enrolled in a sophomore-level college course on human behavior in business. One subject group of 25 read a description of a female assistant who was successful, and another group of 23 read a description of a failure. Both groups then completed the Women as Manager Scale (WAMS). There was no significant difference between the WAMS scores of the group reading the success description and the group reading the failure description. The groups' general attitudes toward women did not appear to be significantly affected by either the success or the failure descriptions they had read.

Continuing the study, another group of 75 subjects completed the WAMS, and again, there followed either a success or a failure description. However, this time the subjects were asked to consider certain possibilities in the success or failure of the female manager. The success of the successful manager was considered more the result of ability, hard work, and luck, and less the job itself, than was failure. There was a positive correlation between WAMS scores and the attribution of success to ability and hard work. However, there was a negative correlation between WAMS scores and attributing success to good luck and an easy job.

The study suggests that males' general attitude toward women affects their interpretation of the female manager's success. Those with positive attitudes toward women found success to be the result of internal factors (ability and hard work), whereas those with negative attitudes found success to be due to external factors (good luck and an easy job). The fact that the WAMS scores were not significantly affected by the success or failure descriptions shows the difficulty of changing preconceived attitudes.

Summary Review of Research Study 7-1-C The male attitudes in this study were not affected by either the success or the failure description of women in management. The reasons given for the success or failure were definitely related to the subjects' attitudes toward women. These male attitudes, as measured by the Women as Managers Scale, indicated that males with positive attitudes found women's success to be the result of internal factors such as ability and effort. They did not agree that success resulted from external factors such as luck and an easy job. However, in the failure condition, neither positive nor negative male attitudes provided any significant relationships. The data suggest that biases against female managers may work against a female early in her career as well as later, without regard for a superior performance record. Since the male scores on the Women as Managers Scale were not affected by either the success or the failure description, they demonstrate how resistant male attitudes are to change regarding women in management.

REFERENCES

[1]Israeli, D., M. Banai, and Y. Ziera, "Women Executives in MNC Subsidiaries," © 1980 by the Regents of the University of California. Adapted from *California Management Review*, volume XXIII, no. 1, pp. 53 to 63 by permission of the Regents.

[2]Garland, H., and G. Smith, "Occupational Achievement Motivation as a Function of Biological Sex, Sex-Linked Personality, and Occupation Stereotype," *Psychology of Women Quarterly*, 5 (July 1981), 568–85. Copyright by the publisher, Cambridge University Press. Reproduced by permission of Cambridge University Press.

[3]Garland, H., and K. Price, "Attitudes toward Women in Management and Attributions for Their Success and Failure in a Managerial Position," *Journal of Applied Psychology*, 62 (1977), 29–32.

QUESTIONS

1. In the research incident, what could Mary Gough have done differently in this situation?
2. On the basis of limited information, what is your evaluation of Dick Still, particularly for a management career at Security Life Insurance?
3. Does this incident shed any light on the selection and placement policies of the human resource department? Indicate specific examples.
4. Discuss the problem of a department manager attempting to fulfill the responsibilities of the position while confronting a sex-role stereotype.

Research Incident 7-2:
Woman Repairperson in the
Meter-Repair Department

- How does "maleness" or "femaleness" affect a person's response to pressures to conform?

- Are male or female traits predictive of behavior? If so, which ones?
- When the same occupational role is being performed, does the sex of the jobholder affect the rating received?

The training committee had just completed another marathon meeting, and Delores Smethurst wondered whether her first assignment as the newest member of the human resource department was going to be a prune or a plum. She quickly positioned herself next to her supervisor, Eileen Bushman, and attempted to obtain more background information on the meter-repair department, whose foreman, George Freed, was characterized by everyone as primitive. Eileen, ready to rush off to another meeting, said that the proposed new training course was only tentative and that George Freed should be approached with respect for his many years of faithful service, but not with deference. After all, training was still the responsibility of human resources, and the buck stopped here.

The company was a medium-sized manufacturer of meters that were used in many industrial applications to measure the flow of varying viscosities of liquids. Accuracy was very important, and the company maintained a group of 25 male meter repairmen, who spent approximately half their time at customers' plants doing repair work and the rest in the repair shop at the home plant. The meter-repair work had changed very little over the years, and technological breakthroughs in meter construction appeared dim. A recent manpower planning study had shown that all the repairmen were over 55 years old, and 15 of them were over 62. This meant that within a few years, more than half the group would retire, and there were no replacements in sight, short of hiring experienced help away from competitors. The work was somewhat physical, requiring crawling and climbing to reach the meters at customers' plants, but the pay was quite high, reflecting more the ability of the local union than the skill requirements of the repairmen.

The company was below minority representation in many plant areas, particularly for women, so the training committee thought the meter-repair shop would be a good place to help correct the situation. When Delores Smethurst talked with George Freed, who was indeed primitive, she found that George did not agree with the consensus of the training committee. So at the next meeting of the committee, Delores presented some ideas on her agenda item relative to what is known about women in training roles—their psychological and special needs—vis-à-vis the situation in the meter-repair department. Eileen Bushman informed the committee that the meter-repair training program had been designated top priority by the company's executive committee, but she agreed that more research had to be done to come up with some needed new insights.

RELEVANT EMPIRICAL
RESEARCH STUDIES

Research Study 7-2-A

Sex-role stereotyping suggests different male and female behavior as a result of physical sexuality. Can this line of thinking be both misleading and self-defeating?

Brehony and Geller[1] investigated an alternative to viewing masculinity and femininity as opposite extremes of a continuum. This alternative is the concept of androgyny, a condition in which people do not adhere strictly to the role characteristics of their sex. (The Greek stem word for male is *andro-* and for female is *gyn-,* hence the word *androgyny*.) In this study, the authors looked into people's adherence to a sex-role stereotype and their perceived locus of control and social conformity.

The subjects were 734 college-student volunteers from classes in introductory psychology who were pretested on the Bem Sex Role Inventory, the Rotter Internal-External Control Scale, and the Personal Opinion Survey. The results were that 33 percent were classified as androgynous, 42 percent as stereotypic, 15 percent as undifferentiated, and 10 percent as cross-sexed. Four groups of 30 subjects each were then defined, based on higher-than-group-median scores, as to androgynous females, androgynous males, stereotypic females, and stereotypic males. These subjects participated in an experiment with the experimenter and one confederate who posed as a subject. The composition of the experiment group was randomly balanced, so that the confederate was a male half the time and a female half the time. The confederate and the subject were asked to predict the direction of stimuli that would be displayed on a screen by stating either "up" or "down." The experimenter signaled the confederate with a hand motion, so that the confederate predicted the correct stimulus direction in 50 percent of the trials for two trial blocks of 40 each, and in 75 percent for the last two trial blocks of 40 each. Both the confederate and the subject then completed an eleven-item scale to determine which personal characteristics of the experimental task pertained to them.

The results of the study were that the stereotypic females demonstrated the highest overall level of conformity. That is, they agreed most often with the prediction made by the confederate before the stimulus appeared on the screen. These stereotypic females also conformed significantly more often than did the androgynous females and the stereotypic males. However, they did not conform more often than the androgynous males. The stereotypic males demonstrated the lowest overall level of conformity.

Data from the eleven-item questionnaire indicated that androgynous females felt significantly less influenced than did stereotypic females, stereotypic males, and androgynous males. Further, androgynous subjects felt significantly less traditional than did stereotypic subjects. In regard to the locus of control, males scored more internal (had more control over their lives) than females did. On the Personal Opinion Survey, for factor 1 (achievement through conscientious effort), androgynous subjects scored more internal than did stereotypic subjects; for factor 2 (personal confidence in ability to achieve mastery), males scored more internal than females; for factor 3 (capacity of mankind to control its destiny versus supernatural power or fate), males scored more internal than females; for factor 4 (successful planning and organization), androgynous females scored more internal than stereotypic females; for factor 5 (self-control over internal processes), males scored more internal than females, and androgynous females scored significantly more internal than stereotypic females; for factor 6 (control over large-scale and political events), androgynous subjects scored more internal than stereotypic subjects; and for factor 7 (control in immediate social interactions), stereotypic females scored more external (less personal control and more influences beyond personal control) than androgynous females, androgynous males, and stereotypic males, and the androgynous females scored more internal than androgynous males.

Summary Review of Research Study 7-2-A The study found androgynous females to be the least influenced by the confederates in the experimental situation. The authors believe that differences between males and females will decrease in favor of conforming behavior. They suggest that early female conformity studies may have resulted from a large number of stereotypic females in the sample. The fact that androgynous females reported less conformity than androgynous males may indicate overresponses to avoid stereotypic sex-role expectations. A sex difference was noted for locus of control, with males scoring more internal than females. An unexpected finding was for factor 7, control in immediate social interactions, with androgynous females scoring significantly more internal than androgynous males. The results also indicated that the androgynous females were less conforming and more internal than the stereotypic females.

Research Study 7-2-B

Is there a relationship between a person's sex role orientation and his or her performance or reaction in certain interpersonal situations?

Kelly and others[2] investigated the distinctions in the male–female sex role. For instance, males are presumed to represent ascendent, instrumental, and cognitive characteristics; females are regarded as emotional, warm, sensitive, expressive, and self-subordinative. The presence of both male and female traits, such as replying in both forceful and emotional or both instrumental and expressive ways, is considered androgyny. When there is an absence of both male and female traits, the sex role is considered undifferentiated.

The authors believed that a variety of behaviors would be necessary in conducting successful interpersonal relations: In one situation, a person should be able to warmly compliment others when the occasion calls for it, and in other situations, the same person should be able to stand his or her ground in the face of unreasonable demands. It was the authors' expectation that the androgynous types would possess both the warm and forceful characteristics, achieving appropriate behavior, the male types were expected to be aggressive and handle the stand-one's-ground situation, and the female types would respond best in the compliment situation. The undifferentiated would be expected to exhibit problems in both situations.

The study sample consisted of 47 male and 47 female undergraduate college students. They were administered the Bem Sex Role Inventory and assigned to a sex role: masculine-typed, feminine-typed, androgynous, or undifferentiated. Then 30 males and 30 females were randomly selected and assigned to one of the sex roles. The subjects listened to eight role-played audio taped sessions that required a reply to a statement made by another person. Four of the taped sessions were designed to have the subject respond so as to compliment, praise, and show appreciation to the person making the statement. The other four taped sessions were designed so the subject could respond more assertively, to refuse unreasonable requests, demands, or unacceptable behavior. After practice sessions, the subjects listened to the eight tapes and then completed an assertiveness scale to determine self-reported assertiveness.

The subjects' reactions to the tapes were rated on six components by two judges to determine praise and assertive behavior. The results were that the males in the four sex groups differed significantly in praise behavior as to loudness, overall assertiveness, and affect (flat tone of voice versus a lively tone). Also, the androgynous males were rated more effective than the undifferentiated males as to speech, loudness, affect, and praise assertion. The masculine-typed males surpassed undifferentiated males for appropriate loudness and assertion. However, the feminine-type males were rated more affectively warm than were undifferentiated males. For the females, the four sex groups differed on the refusal sessions for loudness and affect. The female androgynous types were considered more effective for refusal assertion than were the undifferentiated female types. Further, the androgynous females were rated more effective on the refusal assertion sessions than were the feminine-typed females in loudness, affect, and assertiveness. The androgynous females were also rated more effective in affect than the masculine-typed females were.

Summary Review of Research Study 7-2-B   The effectiveness of differentiating interpersonal behavior appears partly associated with sex-role styles. For instance, in the commendatory scenes, where one could compliment, praise, and show appreciation, the males yielded generally significant differences for the four sex-role categories. For the females, where refusal assertion was appropriate for the role-played scenes, there was differentiation among several of the sex-role characteristics. In situations where certain social responses are appropriate, such as commendatory assertion for the males and refusal assertion for the females, there were some apparent differences. Almost without exception, the androgynous and undifferentiated categories defined the extremes for the ratings of commendatory and refusal assertiveness. Androgynous males appeared able to utilize warm, complimentary behaviors where warranted. Androgynous females were better able to use refusal skills in unreasonable requests from others than were their undifferentiated and sex-typed counterparts. The androgynous roles appeared highly associated with social competence, and the undifferentiated roles were more socially inept. Interestingly, the feminine-typed persons did not compliment any more effectively than the masculine-typed, nor were the masculine types superior to the feminine types in refusal assertion. It appears that blending masculine and feminine behaviors into an androgynous pattern results in a more effective personal style.

Research Study 7-2-C

How do the ratings of females compare to the ratings of males doing the same work? Is there a bias in favor of the males? Or does the quality of the performance affect the general perception of the performance?

Abramson and others[3] investigated the "talking-platypus" phenomenon. That is, in rating the achievements of a talking platypus, what matters is not the profoundness of what is said, but merely that the creature can say anything.

The study subjects were undergraduate students, 126 females and 91 males, who volunteered as part of their introductory-psychology course requirement. The students were divided into four groups of approximately 50 students each. They received a one-page, single-spaced biography of a person whose sex and success were manipulated, so that half believed it was about a male and half believed it was a female. Further, half the subjects believed the biography was of an attorney and the other half believed it was of a paralegal worker. The biographies of the attorneys included parental background, employment records, extracurricular interests, college records (Phi Beta Kappa), law school records (*summa cum laude*), and employment record as a judge, and concluded with a statement about running for Congress or governor. The paralegal biographies were nearly identical, differing only in college record, postgraduate training, employment record working for an attorney, and probability of running for city council.

After reading the biographies, the students answered 14 short questions pertaining to the biography to determine their evaluation of the vocational and potential marital and interpersonal successes of that person. The students' responses to the questions were indicated on a seven-point Likert Scale, with 1 as "not very" and 7 as "extremely so." The questions were about how successful, how likeable, how satisfied, and so on. Certain question scores were combined to form a vocational success score, a potential marital success score, and an interpersonal success score.

The results of the study indicated that the manipulation of vocational success was achieved, since all the students, male and female, rated the attorney biographies as reflecting more vocational success than the paralegal biographies. The highest ratings of vocational success for the male/female, attorney/paralegal grouping were awarded to the female attorney biography by the female subjects. However, all the students rated the female biographies as having more vocational success than the male biographies. It was also found that the female students who read the attorney biographies (both male and female) had rated them more vocationally successful than had those females who had read only the paralegal biographies. In addition, the female students who had read only the attorney biographies rated them as being more vocationally successful than did the male students who had read only the attorney biographies and the males who had read only the paralegal biographies.

The students perceived the male paralegal as being more likely to be successful in marriage. The male students awarded higher ratings of marital success than did the female students. As for interpersonal success, only the male students rated vocational success in a positive direction for the female attorney and the male paralegal. Apparently, the more vocationally successful these two were found, the more the male students liked them. The female students rated vocational success as significantly related in a positive direction to interpersonal success for all the conditions except the female attorney. Also, the female students indicated that the more vocationally successful the male paralegal worker was, the more successful his marriage would be.

Summary Review of Research Study 7-2-C   A woman who performs creditably in a male-dominated profession is apparently seen as more competent than a man in that profession. In the present study, both men and women found the female attorney the most vocationally competent. It appears that this rating was inflated because of the constraints that would ordinarily prevent a woman from being successful. Although the female subjects might be assumed to be more sensitive to the obstacles preventing a woman from reaching success, all subjects, male and female, considered both female biographies as demonstrating more vocational competence than did both of the male biographies.

In regard to the question of whether a successful woman may be less marriageable or interpersonally attractive than a successful man, there appeared to be no difference as a function of sex or occupation. Even though males generally gave higher ratings of potential success, both men and women regarded the male and female attorney as being equal in their potential for successful marriage.

The female subjects found that the more vocationally competent the female attorney or the male or female paralegal worker, the more they liked them. As for the male subjects, the more vocationally competent the female attorney and the male paralegal worker, the more they liked them. Interpersonal attractiveness and marriageability are not solely the result of status or sex. Yet when a female achieves a vocational competence that is not anticipated, her achievement appears to be overrated rather than underrated.

REFERENCES

[1]Brehony, K.A., and E. S. Geller, "Relationships between Psychological Androgyny, Social Conformity, and Perceived Locus of Control," *Psychology of Women Quarterly,* 6 (Winter 1981), 204–17. Copyrighted by the publisher, Cambridge University Press. Reproduced by permission of Cambridge University Press.

[2]Kelly, J.A., G.G. O'Brien, and R. Hosford, "Sex Roles and Social Skills Considerations for Interpersonal Adjustment," *Psychology of Women Quarterly,* 5 (Supplemental Issue, 1981), 758–66. Copyrighted by the publisher, Cambridge University Press. Reproduced by permission of Cambridge University Press.

[3]Abramson, P.R., P.A. Goldberg, J.H. Goldberg, and L.M. Abramson, "The Talking Platypus Phenomenon: Competency Ratings as a Function of Sex and Professional Status," *Psychology of Women Quarterly,* 2 (1977), 114–24. Copyrighted by the publisher, Cambridge University Press. Reproduced by permission of Cambridge University Press.

QUESTIONS

1. What can be said about the uniformity of sex-role stereotypes? How would you differentiate? Explain.
2. Is there a sex-role difference in the ability to compliment and to be assertive? Within sexes, does this ability differ? Explain.
3. When a female achieves a measure of career success that is not expected, what type of performance rating does she receive? Would it be higher than that of a male in the same career field? Explain.

Research Incident 7-3:
Doug David and Women Supervisors

- What is the ability of females to do physical work in industry? Does it differ from that of males?
- How do characteristics of the boss affect the job satisfaction of female subordinates? of male subordinates?
- How do males and females differ on the importance of intrinsic and extrinsic job factors? Or do they?

The ad hoc Committee to Train Women Supervisors had just started its first metting. Seated around the table were Doug David, from the human resource department; his assistant on the project, Jerry Hammond; two uncomfortable foremen from the lawnmower assembly line; and one scowling shop steward. Doug passed around copies of the job description for the assistant-foreman position. Everyone appeared to agree that the description was accurate. The nature of the work was indicated correctly, the examples of the work were complete, and the section on knowledge, abilities, and skills was comprehensive. Basically, the assistant-foreman job required covering for the foreman during his many absences from the production floor, keeping a proper parts inventory, and maintaining production and quality standards utilizing a group of semiskilled male and female workers. The work required a knowledge of lawnmower motors, since on-the-job training was extremely important, and sometimes heavy lifting was necessary.

With that hurdle eliminated, Doug turned the next part of the meeting over to Jerry Hammond, who presented a basic outline of a training program designed to take current female employees from the production line and turn them into assistant foremen. The questions followed quickly, and it was apparent that the two foremen thought the human resource group had failed once again to understand the complexities of lawnmower motor assembly. At times it sounded as if they were talking about assembling nuclear reactors. The complaints centered on the shortness of the overall program and aspects of the assembly process that were ignored. Finally, a consensus was reached among the four of them; but the shop steward had not said a word and continued to scowl. The final result was a training program heavy on technique and light on supervisory practice, but Doug and Jerry thought the human resource manager would give his approval.

This session had already taken an hour and 40 minutes, so Doug suggested they quit and meet again in two days to okay the final draft of the training program and to select the trainees. For the past two weeks, Jerry Hammond had been interviewing female workers from the production line who had applied for the posted new position. Practically everyone had applied, so there was no lack of applicants. The initial sort had eliminated those who lacked adequate work experience on the lawnmower motor assembly line, and many had decided to voluntarily drop out of consideration when Jerry explained the psychological and physical demands the new position required. So when Doug sat down with Jerry to go over the applicants, the self-selection process provided just slightly more than were actually needed.

When the committee adjourned again, the group had approved the new training program with only a few word changes. However, two more meetings were required before some form of agreement was reached on selection of the applicants. The foremen's complaints were about taking the best production workers off the line, applicants' inability to perform the physical tasks, and general dissatisfaction with the applicants' ability to "take charge." Finally, Doug had to remind the group that top management expected this program to be implemented, and soon. Reluctantly, agreement was reached, and the meeting ended. Walking down the hall, Doug shook his head. Another all-male cast with not one female voice heard. Too bad Jerry wasn't a Geraldine.

RELEVANT EMPIRICAL RESEARCH STUDIES

Research Study 7-3-A

What is known about the ability of females to do physical work? Can women perform heavy work?

A study by Wardle[1] provides some answers, although with a very limited sample size. First, the author referenced earlier studies to show that nurses expend energy during an eight-hour shift that is similar to the energy required for an automobile mechanic, milling machine operator, locomotive operator, or bricklayer. Another source cited said that what is usually called heavy work is in reality only moderately heavy and that it occupies probably less than 3 percent of a workday. One study pointed out that everyone, regardless of age or sex, uses about the same amount of energy to perform an identical task. It is larger people with more aerobic capacity (intake of oxygen) who expend more energy while working.

With that information as background, the author investigated the physical work capacity of women performing heavy, very heavy, and unduly heavy work. (Occupations requiring moderate energy include mixing cement, plastering walls, and laying floors; heavy-work occupations include construction and blacksmithing; and unduly heavy work would be done by, say, movers carrying loads upstairs or loggers felling trees with an ax.) The work tests were conducted in a laboratory setting with a constant temperature of 68° F. and 38 percent humidity. The work equipment was a treadmill, controlled as to degree of incline and speed. The subjects were eight volunteer female college students who had responded to a bulletin posted on campus. Their ages ranged from 18 to 23, with a mean of 19.6 years, and they had a mean weight of 138 pounds. The students arrived at the laboratory at 8:00 A.M., were served a light breakfast, and then worked out on the treadmill for eight different periods of 45 minutes each, for a total of six hours. There was a 15-minute break at the end of each 45-minute period and a 30-minute lunch break. The students were monitored as to pulse rate and heartbeat, the latter with electrocardiograms.

The findings reveal that in the measurement of maximal work capacity based on norms developed for Scandinavian women, five students were average in aerobic capacity, one was fair, and two were good. The maximal heart rate in the present study was considerably higher than that reported in the literature, suggesting that the women in the other studies did not work as hard or were athletes with lower maximal heart rates. The maximal work rate continued until the student voluntarily terminated it. The results for the eight female students appeared quite compatible with the maximum work capacity of fit young men. The data collected during the workday indicated that the students completed most of the eight tasks. In fact, three of them completed all the tasks, and as an average of the eight students, they completed all but 15 minutes of the workday, equal to 95 percent of the total work.

An analysis of the effect of speed, grade, and load on the measure of work found that speed and grade had a significant effect. Load did not, and although it caused an increase in the amount of work performed, the difference was not significant. The energy requirements for the work in this study ranged from moderate to unduly heavy. In doing the unduly heavy work, the students performed at 50 to 80 percent of their maximal aerobic capacities.

Summary Review of Research Study 7-3-A   The results of this study suggest that women possess the energy requirements demanded in a variety of jobs. They can perform physical work that requires the ability to meet peak workloads. Also, women appear to possess the necessary long-term energy reserves to complete a full day of demanding physical work.

It seems that there has been a general tendency to overestimate the physical requirements of work in industry. At least for short periods, women can be expected to handle the heaviest workloads.

Research Study 7-3-B

How does the sex role of the supervisor affect the job satisfaction of female employees? Do female employees prefer a male or a female supervisor?

A study by Feild and Caldwell[2] considered female job-satisfaction differences that might be attributed to a female or male boss. The study subjects were 139 paid employees, 93 female and 47 male, of a library in a large southeastern university. They averaged eight years of work experience and 14.6 years of education, with the average age 30. Approximately half the sample was supervised by female division heads, the other half by male. Data obtained from the employees included biographical data and measures of job satisfaction from the Job Descriptive Index. This index presents an adjective checklist; the employee responds with a yes or no or question mark to a series of adjectives indicating satisfaction with supervision, pay, co-workers, promotion, and work. The index was administered to four different groups of employees while at work: female supervisor/female subordinate; female supervisor/male subordinate; male supervisor/female subordinate; and male supervisor/male subordinate. The male/female groups provided no significant differences as to years of education, years of work experience, or professional status. However, there was a difference in ages; the female subordinates were older than the male subordinates.

The results indicate significant group differences regarding satisfaction with supervision, co-workers, and work. However, the male and female group differences were rather minimal. Turning to the supervisor scale, the results suggest that female subordinates who were supervised by male supervisors were less satisfied with work than were those supervised by women.

In regard to satisfaction with their co-workers, those females working for males reported a lower level of satisfaction than did females who were supervised by females. Further, their satisfaction was lower than that of male employees who were supervised by female supervisors. However, females working for females reported a significantly higher level of work satisfaction than did the males who were supervised by male supervisors.

The authors challenge the contention that these differences may be the result of female dissatisfaction because of being placed in lower-level jobs with lower pay rates and few promotional chances. Their conclusion from analyzing the data was that no significant difference existed among the four supervisor/subordinate groups owing simply to the sex of the subordinates. It would appear that the previously indicated group differences are not to be determined simply by the sex of the subordinates. Rather, the authors find these differences to be the rest of an interaction between the sex of the supervisor and the sex of the subordinate.

Summary Review of Research Study 7-3-B   The study found that women supervised by men had less satisfaction with their supervision than did women supervised by women. Also, women who were supervised by men expressed less satisfaction with their co-workers than men who were supervised by men. Further, the women with female supervisors indicated more satisfaction with their work than did men with male supervisors.

The authors suggest that the perceptions of women supervisors as poor leaders may differ quite a bit from the actual positive experiences of working for a women supervisor. It appears that these negative attitudes may result from a lack of experience with women in leadership roles.

Research Study 7-3-C

There has been ample research concerning the importance or unimportance of extrinsic and intrinsic characteristics of work in relation to feelings of job satisfaction. How do these extrinsic and intrinsic characteristics affect females? What are the differences and similarities between females and males?

Voydanoff[3] investigated the problem in a national sample of workers. The study considered extrinsic characteristics—parts of the work environment considered to be caused by external events or by people other than the employee—to include working conditions, co-worker relationships, supervision styles, company policy, salary, and job security. The intrinsic characteristics included responsibility in the job, variety, personal growth opportunities, development opportunities, and feelings of pride and accomplishment. Such characteristics are involved in performing the job as it pertains to self-expression and self-actualization.

The data in the study were collected in 1969 by the University of Michigan Survey Research Center under contract with the U.S. Department of Labor. A national probability sample of 1,533 people was obtained, people 16 years old and older who were employed for pay and worked at least 20 hours per week. These subjects were personally interviewed, and data were collected directly from them. A series of questions to be asked the subjects was selected for the extrinsic scales of financial rewards/promotion, hard work, physical context, role strain, supervision, and working conditions, and for the intrinsic scales of enriching job demands and self-expression. Another part of the data collection required the subjects to sort item cards representing these extrinsic and intrinsic scales into piles designated as very true, somewhat true, not too true, and not at all true, as each category represented their own jobs. The self-expression scale was considered to be in both the extrinsic and intrinsic scales, since the author felt it loaded on both scales. This overlap shows some of the ambiguity present in attempting to delineate between the extrinsic and intrinsic job characteristics. The scales representing the perceived job characteristics were the independent variables. The dependent variable was overall job satisfaction and was measured by the answer to satisfaction with the job—very satisfied, somewhat satisfied, not too satisfied, or not at all satisfied.

For men, the study found the highest correlations of overall job satisfaction with self-expression, financial rewards/promotion, and working conditions, followed by role strain and supervision. The highest correlations for women were self-expression, role strain, and working conditions, followed by supervision and financial rewards/promotion. Thus, self-expression had the highest correlation with overall job satisfaction for both men and women. For men, financial rewards/promotion had the second highest correlation, with role strain second for women. Third for both men and women was working conditions, followed by role strain and supervision for men and supervision and financial rewards/promotion for women. Self-expression and role strain were the two most important variables for both men and women. Financial rewards/promotion was third for men and fourth for women.

Summary Review of Research Study 7-3-C   Both intrinsic and extrinsic job characteristics were shown to be among the most important contributors to the job satisfaction of men and women. An intrinsic factor, self-expression, correlated highest with job satisfaction for men and women. The extrinsic factor of role strain was second for women, and the extrinsic factor of financial rewards/promotion was second for men. Thus, the major men/women difference is the greater importance of role strain for women and of financial rewards/promotion for men. Both men and women had generally similar patterns of relationships between perceived job characteristics and job satisfaction, suggesting that to be satisfied with their jobs, they require similar job characteristics. This similarity of job characteristics to job satisfaction indicates that sex differences relative to satisfying work roles may be overemphasized.

REFERENCES

[1]Wardle, M.G., "Women's Physiological Reactions to Physically Demanding Work," *Psychology of Women Quarterly,* 1 (Winter 1976), 151–59. Copyrighted by the publisher, Cambridge University Press. Reproduced by permission of Cambridge University Press.

[2]Feild, H.S., and B.F. Caldwell, "Sex of Supervisor, Sex of Subordinate, and Subordinate Job Satisfaction," *Psychology of Women Quarterly,* 3 (Summer 1979), 391–99. Copyrighted by the publisher, Cambridge University Press. Reproduced by permission of Cambridge University Press.

[3]Voydanoff, P., "Perceived Job Characteristics and Job Satisfaction among Men and Women," *Psychology of Women Quarterly,* 5 (Winter 1980), 177–85. Copyrighted by the publisher, Cambridge University Press.. Reproduced by permission of Cambridge University Press.

QUESTIONS

1. How do physical-strength requirements relate to women seeking jobs in industry? What considerations should be involved in placing women in construction jobs?

2. What do we know about the job satisfaction of women employees? Does the sex role of the supervisor have any effect upon the level of job satisfaction? Explain.
3. Are the intrinsic and extrinsic characteristics related to a job valued more by the female or the male employee? What differences, if any, exist? Explain.

Research Incident 7-4:
Norman Zeller Admits a Knowledge Gap
and Seeks Help

- How does perceiving oneself as having been hired as a "token" affect performance—positively, negatively, or neutrally?
- What is the effect upon job performance of perception of one's career or noncareer goals?
- When does counseling the female employee regarding career goals become appropriate?

The complaints were becoming more numerous. Wherever Norman Zeller went in the plant, he was being buttonholed and asked "what he was going to do about it." A few more weeks of this and the executive committee would get wind of it and the bottom would fall out.

So this afternoon, with a bad case of heartburn, Norman decided it was time to act. As he began to review the personnel files, a disturbing trend emerged. Many files contained no test scores and none of the usual evaluations by the selection committee members. When they were in the files, many test scores were well below the usual cutoff points, and the evaluations were rather vague. Apparently, most of the employees had been hired without adequate screening and testing—a clear violation of company policies. Norman shuddered. He was glad that all this had occurred before his entry into the top spot of the human resource department, but he knew that any corrective action would be his responsibility and that pointing a finger at someone else would not get him off the hook, not in this company.

Starting from square one, Norman called the vice-president for human relations and industrial relations to set up an appointment. Since the V.P. was his mentor and had been responsible for Norman's being selected as the manager of the human resource department, it seemed the natural thing to do.

Seated across from the V.P., Norman began to unfold the story. Several years ago, owing to the urgings of a new member of the board of directors, the company had made a concerted push to hire female employees. The man Norman had replaced as human resource manager—he had retired—was a retread from the production department and was woefully weak in selection techniques. The result was the improper screen-

ing of a group of women, many of whom were now working in inappropriate areas. Apparently, they had never been counseled as to career goals. As
they began to obtain seniority, they were becoming eligible for salary increases and promotions. The "tokens" had come home to roost.

With that as background, the V.P. eased Norman out of his office and
said, "Good luck."

RELEVANT EMPIRICAL
RESEARCH STUDIES

Research Study 7-4-A

What happens when female employees feel that they have been hired
because of their sex, not their ability? Can the human resource function be
satisfactorily bypassed in an effort to satisfy Title VII of the Civil Rights
Act?

Chacko[1] investigated the effect of affirmative action programs on the
work attitudes of women. Specifically, the study was concerned with the
perceived preferential selection of women and its effect on organizational
variables such as commitment, role stress, and satisfaction. This represents
an area of new concern, since previous empirical research has focused on
either the effect of sex stereotypes on personnel decisions or male attitudes
toward women in male-dominated positions.

The study subjects were 70 women taking part in a management
development program dealing with time management. The program was
conducted in a medium-sized southwestern city, and the subjects were
either managers or supervisors in a variety of organizations. They were
asked to take part in a study of work-related attitudes and perceptions. All
the women agreed and were given a questionnaire to complete and mail
back in a provided stamped envelope. A total of 55 returned usable questionnaires, representing a response rate of approximately 78.5 percent.
Those replying averaged 33 years of age and had been in their current
positions for about three years. Some 62 percent had attended college, and
31 percent had bachelor's degrees.

A nine-point Likert-type scale was used to determine how the subjects
perceived the use of sex as a selection device. This information was obtained by asking how important certain factors had been in their being
hired. The factors were ability, experience, education, and sex, which they
ranked in terms of perceived importance. It was assumed that those subjects who perceived themselves as tokens would rate sex as having been
more important than ability, experience, or education.

On the Crowne and Marlowe Social Desirability Scale, the study found no difference between women who ranked sex as an important factor and those who ranked the sex factor as unimportant.

Commitment to the organization was measured by a nine-item scale developed by Porter, Steers, Mowdaz, and Boulian. Scales developed by Rizzo, House, and Lirtzman were used to measure role stress. The role-conflict scale contained eight items and the role-ambiguity scale six items. The Job Descriptive Scale by Smith, Kendall, and Hulin was used to measure satisfaction with the work itself, supervision, co-workers' pay, and advancement opportunities.

The results of the study indicate that the perceived importance of sex in selection was significantly correlated with the overall index of satisfaction. It was also significantly correlated with organizational commitment, role conflict, and role ambiguity, as well as with satisfaction with work, supervisor, and co-workers. With the exception of role conflict and ambiguity, all the significant correlations were negative.

The perceived importance of sex accounted for about 6 percent of the variance in organizational commitment, 7 percent of the role-conflict variance, and 19 percent of the role-ambiguity variance. Among the job-related factors of ability, experience, and education, only ability accounted for a significant amount of the satisfaction variance. The perception of ability as an important selection measure accounted for 8 percent of satisfaction-with-work variance, 7 percent of satisfaction-with-co-workers variance, 8 percent of satisfaction-with-pay variance, and 10 percent of overall-satisfaction variance.

A comparison was made between the mean scores of the women who ranked sex as the most important selection measure and those of the women who ranked ability as the most important. The women who felt that sex was an important factor in selection had significantly less organizational commitment, overall satisfaction, and satisfaction with the job itself or with supervision. They also experienced more role conflict and role ambiguity.

The use of sex as a selection measure appears not to increase one's sense of responsibility or importance to an organization and may imply tokenism. This could create difficulties with affirmative action and equal employment opportunity programs by creating a backlash by female employees to the preferential treatment of other women by the organization.

Summary Review of Research Study 7-4-A   This study investigated the effects on women employees of preferential treatment. Specifically, the study explored the relationship between the perceived preferential selection and such organizational variables as organizational commitment, role stress, and satisfaction.

It appears that women who believed they were selected because of their sex demonstrated less organizational commitment and less satisfaction with their work, with supervision, and with their co-workers. They also experienced more role conflict and role ambiguity than did women who believed sex was not important in their selection.

The suggestion is that difficulties may surface in equal employment opportunity programs where a sex preference in selection is present.

Research Study 7-4-B

What conflict, if any, results from a woman's pursuing a career as opposed to a job? Is there an effect on commitment?

Holahan and Gilbert[2] studied the role conflicts of career and non-career women. The authors believe that interrole conflict occurs when a person engages in two or more roles and conflicting and competing demands are perceived.

The study focused on four major life roles: worker, spouse, parent, and self as a self-actualizing person. Conflict was measured as being experienced between various pairs of these major life roles.

Whereas previous research had studied highly educated women in pursuit of high-level careers, the present study investigated the conflicts resulting from a job versus a career in a sample of mothers holding bachelor's degrees. The authors hypothesized that women perceiving their work as careers would experience greater role conflict than women who regarded their work as jobs. This increased role conflict would result from greater involvement and personal investment from pursuing a career.

The authors note that at the bachelor's-degree level of employment, there is considerable variation of responsibility that might affect a job or career designation. Also, the same level of occupation could be regarded by one person as a job and by another as a career. Thus, a self-classification of job versus career was used rather than relying only on a job title. Since previous research had shown that professional women possess a high degree of independence, self-confidence, and self-esteem, a second purpose of the study was to determine if there was any difference in these traits between the job and career women.

The subjects were a sample of bachelor's-degree-level married women who were full-time employees of a large state university. Their names and addresses were obtained from the staff directory, and they were mailed a questionnaire with a later follow-up letter. The subjects were all married, were living with their spouses, and were parents; their spouses were employed full-time, and neither spouse was a student. Of the 215 questionnaires mailed, 112 were returned and 41 were usable.

The measures used included a career versus noncareer determination. This was obtained by asking the subject to state her current position and then answer the question, "Do you consider your present position to be a job or a career?" Responses showed that 26 considered their work a job and 15 a career. Job responses were for such positions as secretary, clerk, and administrative assistant. Career responses were for occupations with more technical skill: systems analyst, editor, and lab technologist. The job group worked an average of 40.19 hours per week and had been employed in their present positions an average of 7.08 years. The career group worked an average of 42.6 hours per week and had been employed an average of 10.4 years. Another question was, "Does your spouse consider his present position to be a job or a career?" The job group's tally was 69 percent and the career group's 73 percent for the career choice. The two subject groups were comparable in education level; 46 percent of the job group and 42 percent of the career group held master's degrees or higher.

To determine work attitude, a seven-point scale was used to indicate level of work commitment, level of career aspirations, likelihood of working without financial necessity, degree of self-perceived work competence, and degree of emotional support received from the spouse in regard to work.

There were six scales developed to measure role conflict between pairs of the four major life-worker roles (worker, spouse, parent, and self-actualizing self). These scales measured potential conflict between worker and spouse, worker and parent, worker and self, and spouse and self, spouse and parent, and parent and self. The subjects indicated their responses on a five-point scale ranging from "causes no internal conflict" (1) to "causes some internal conflict" (3) to "causes high internal conflict" (5).

A seven-point scale was used to measure level of life satisfaction received from the roles of worker, spouse, parent, and self as a self-actualizing person.

The self-esteem measure was determined by nine items obtained from a study by Bachman, Kahn, Davidson, and Johnson.* This scale measures satisfaction with life and self-esteem on a seven-point scale.

The short form of the Personal Attributes Questionnaire (PAQ) by Spence and Helmreich measures psychological androgyny through masculinity (M) and femininity (F) scales. The M scale represents eight attributes that are considered socially desirable for both sexes but that males possess more than females (such as independence and self-confidence), and the F scale contains socially desirable attributes for both sexes although possessed more by females (such as emotionality and concern for others). Scores result in four categories: androgynous (high M and high F), masculine (high M and low F), feminine (low M and high F), and undifferentiated (low M and low F).

The results of the study relative to work attitudes were that the mean levels of work commitment and of work aspirations were significantly higher for the career group than the job group. The career group also showed a

---

*J. Bachman, R. Kahn, T. Davidson, and L. Johnson, *Youth in Transition*, Vol. 1 (Ann Arbor, MI: Institute for Social Research, 1967).

greater likelihood of working without financial necessity. There appeared to be a greater personal investment for the career group, which supported the validity of the self-classification system of designating oneself as either career- or job-oriented. There was no significant difference in the level of work competence; both groups reported very high levels. However, the career group reported a significantly higher level of support from their spouses than did the job group.

In regard to role conflict, a development occurred that was contrary to the hypothesis of the authors. The job group reported more role conflict on all six scales. Of these six, two scales involving the self role were significantly different: parent versus self, and spouse versus self. The mean difference between the two groups on the total role-conflict score was also marginally significant ($P<.054$).

These two significant role-conflict findings involved conflicts between the self and family roles (parent and spouse). So the authors analyzed the influence of spouse support on role conflict. The result indicated the crucial nature of spouse support for the reduction of role conflict for working women. It is suggested that if the job women received the same amount of spouse support as the career women, they would not experience greater conflict.

The career group appeared to have increased role demands, as suggested by their working longer hours; yet they managed to offset some of this stress through a sense of personal fulfillment. The results of the life-satisfaction scales indicated that the career group received significantly more life satisfaction from both work roles and self roles than did the job group. The career group received relatively high satisfaction from all four roles (workers, spouse, parent, and self-actualizing self). However, the job group received much less satisfaction from their work roles than from their family roles.

As for possible personality characteristics that would permit management of several roles, the distribution of the two groups among the four categories of the Personal Attributes Questionnaire was not significant. In fact, 62 percent of the job group and 80 percent of the career group were in the high masculine categories (masculine or androgynous). There was a marginal difference in self-esteem ($P<.10$) favoring the career group, but both groups reported high levels of self-esteem.

It appears that variations in spouse support, work commitment, and the nature of the job situation may contribute to the coping ability of married working women with children in responding to role conflict.

Summary Review of Research Study 7-4-B The study compared how career and noncareer married women with children experienced role conflict. The women responded to a questionnaire that measured, among other variables, the potential conflict between pairs of major life roles:

worker, spouse, parent, and self-actualizing self. It was found that the career group had a higher work commitment than the job group. This was also true for work aspirations. The career group was also more likely to work in the absence of financial necessity.

Contrary to the authors' expectations, the job group reported more role conflict on the six scales measuring conflict. Apparently, spouse support was present for the career group but not the job group. Both groups were highly masculine and reported high levels of self-esteem.

The study suggests the importance of spouse support, work commitment, and the job situation as contributors to how married women with children experience role conflict.

Research Study 7-4-C

What can be done to counsel adult women as they make the transition from job orientation to career orientation? What instruments are available that might provide the person as well as her prospective employer with insights into her vocational interests and vocational needs?

A study by Murray[3] investigates the problem of career counseling for adult women and the problems that may be encountered in using interest inventories. Of particular interest is the adult woman whose vocational interests fail to correspond with any of the instrument's specific occupational groups. A low profile on an interest-inventory occupational scale is a frustrating experience to the person with limited time, financial resources, and initiative, and it may prevent more extensive career option exploration.

The low-profile person's score on interest inventories has not received much empirical investigation. The author reports only 13 studies, of which two deal with women. These studies demonstrated very few differences between low-profile and high-profile groups, and there were no reliable findings for women.

The present study specifically examined how women with low profiles on the Strong-Campbell Interest Inventory (SCII) or the Strong Vocational Interest Blank (SVIB) female occupational scales differ from women who have high profiles. These groups were also examined as to differences in personality characteristics, as measured by the California Psychological Inventory (CPI), and in vocational needs, measured by the Minnesota Importance Questionnaire (MIQ).

The subjects had utilized the services of the group testing program offered by the Department of Extension Counseling at the University of Minnesota. They were women 25 and older who had taken the SCII or SVIB, the CPI, and the MIQ. These women had voluntarily requested the testing services and had paid a fee to participate.

The first step was to identify the low- and high-profile groups from the SCII and SVIB populations. A total of 508 women were then contacted for permission to use their test data in the study. Of the original group, 97.6 percent were located, and 91.9 percent, or 467, gave written permission for their test data to be used. The SCII sample was 153 low-profile and 162 high-profile, and the SVIB sample was 70 low-profile and 82 high-profile. The groups averaged two years of post–high school education, with the high-profile women averaging six months more. The SVIB group demonstrated no significant differences in typical occupations. There were no significant differences between the low- and high-profile groups as to employment, homemaker, or student status when they had originally completed the test battery.

The SCII measurement instrument contains 325 items, covering many occupations, school subjects, occupational activities, amusements, types of people, and self-ratings of personality and abilities. Most of these items require the respondent to answer "like," "indifferent," or "dislike." The SVIB for Women Form TW398 contains 398 items relative to the same topics, and they also require responses of "like," "indifferent," or "dislike." The CPI is designed to provide information on educational and career issues. There are 480 items to be responded to as either true or false. The MIQ is a 210-item paired-comparison instrument. It measures the strength of 20 vocational needs and also provides a total score that indicates how consistently the person responded to the MIQ items.

The CPI, MIQ, and either the SCII or the SVIB were completed by each subject within a one-month period. The SCII and SVIB profiles were used to indicate those in the low- and high-profile groups based upon a previously agreed-upon formula of the SVIB or SCII female occupational scales score.

The results for both the SCII and SVIB women showed significant differences for the set of 18 CPI scales between the low- and high-profile groups. In the SCII sample, the high-profile women scored significantly higher than the low-profile women on the CPI scales of dominance, self-acceptance, capacity for status, sociability, social presence, achievement via conformity, intellectual efficiency, responsibility, and psychological mindedness. The same differences occurred with the SVIB sample. For two of the CPI scales, self-control and femininity, the SCII low-profile women scored significantly higher than the high-profile women. However, these differences did not occur with the SVIB sample. For three of the CPI validity scales—sense of well-being, good impression, and communality—there was no difference between the low- and high-profile women in either the SCII or SVIB samples.

For the 20 MIQ needs, the differences between low- and high-profile women on the demographic variables had no effect on the differences. The differences between low- and high-profile groups were significant for both the SCII and SVIB women.

In the SCII sample, the high-profile women had significantly higher needs than the low-profile women for authority, creativity, responsibility, and advancement.

In the SVIB sample, the high-profile women scored significantly higher than the low-profile women on needs for responsibility, ability utilization, creativity, authority, recognition, and social service.

There were no significant differences for both the SCII and the SVIB women in the low- and high-profile groups for the Total Circular Treads Score validity scale. This result indicates the consistency of responses to the MIQ items. Only authority, creativity, and responsibility significantly differed in the low- and high-profile women for both SCII and SVIB groups.

Analysis revealed that 107 CPI items for the SCII group and 63 CPI items for the SVIB group significantly differentiated the low- and high-profile women. The items demonstrated a liking for oral and written communication and an enjoyment of leadership. A large portion of the response differences resulted from the high-profile women's indicating the response "like" more than the low-profile women did. The items that sharply distinguished the groups were writing, public speaking, law, politics, and managerial careers.

The greatest differences between the low- and high-profile groups for the SCII and SVIB Basic Interest Scales occurred for public speaking, law/politics, writing, performing arts, music/dramatics, and business management. The higher scores of the high-profile women demonstrate an interest in self-expression for the oral, written, and performing arts and in leadership.

In both the SCII and SVIB samples, the higher scores of the high-profile women were on professional occupational scales such as guidance counselor, army officer, English teacher, and lawyer. The higher scores for the low-profile women were on nonprofessional scales such as beautician, instrument assembler, and secretary. The low-profile women did not score as high on the SCII academic orientation or the SVIB academic achievement. Also, they preferred less people contact in work situations and responded "like" less often and "indifferent" or "dislike" more often to SCII or SVIB items.

The low-profile women appeared to be similar to professional women in general. They demonstrated average scores on most of the CPI scales. Any significant differences from the high-profile women in the SCII and SVIB samples were due to the higher scores of the high-profile women and not to below-average scores of the low-profile women.

CPI and MIQ information revealed that high-profile women are apparently more comfortable interacting with others, more ambitious, more assertive, more verbally expressive, and more willing to obtain higher leadership positions in which they assume responsibility for their own and others' actions. In comparison, low-profile women are only average relative to these characteristics.

The personality characteristics of the high-profile woman indicate that she behaves in a socially outgoing manner, assumes positions of leadership, desires success, wants to move up in society, and values autonomy.

Summary Review of Research Study 7-4-C The study analyzed how adult women with low profiles on the Strong-Campbell Interest Inventory or the Strong Vocational Interest Blank female occupational scales are different from women who have high profiles on these two instruments. These differences were reflected in scores on the California Psychological Inventory, which measures personality characteristics, and the Minnesota Importance Questionnaire, which measures vocational needs.

The low-profile women in the SCII and SVIB groups demonstrated a significantly lower score than did the high-profile women on the CPI scales of dominance, capacity for status, sociability, social presence, self-acceptance, responsibility, achievement via conformity, intellectual efficiency, and psychological mindedness. The low-profile women also demonstrated a significantly lower score than the high-profile women did on the MIQ for the needs of authority, creativity, and responsibility.

The high-profile woman seems to behave in a more socially outgoing manner, desires leadership positions, wants success and upward mobility in society, and values autonomy. On the other hand, the low-profile woman does not enjoy oral or written communication, leadership roles, or interacting with many people.

REFERENCES

[1]Chacko, T.I., "Women and Equal Employment Opportunity: Some Unintended Effects," *Journal of Applied Psychology*, 67 (1982), 119–23.

[2]Holahan, C.K., and L.A. Gilbert, "Interrole Conflict for Working Women: Careers versus Jobs," *Journal of Applied Psychology*, 64 (1979), 86–90.

[3]Murray, S.G., "Personality Characteristics of Adult Women with Low and High Profiles on the SCII or SVIB Occupational Scales," *Journal of Applied Psychology*, 66 (1981), 422–30.

QUESTIONS

1. When women perceive that they have been selected because of their sex and not because of ability, experience, or education, what is their reaction? What is the effect upon commitment, role conflict, satisfaction with pay, and so forth? Be specific.
2. What is the effect of role conflict upon career and noncareer married working mothers? How can the effect of role conflict be reduced? Develop a profile of the career group and job group of married working mothers.
3. How effective are the SCII and SVIB instruments in differentiating adult women? What do the CPI and MIQ measure? Describe in detail the low- and high-profile women in the Murray study.

NON-EMPIRICAL
RESEARCH ARTICLE
ABSTRACTS

Abstract 7-1

- Why are women better listeners than men?
- Who is better at understanding nonverbal cues, women or men?
- How may the process of socialization later adversely affect the female executive?

These questions and others are answered in a 1984 article by Melanie Booth-Butterfield,[1] a college instructor.

The author points out that an important job skill for both men and women is the ability to listen. However, in the past, listening was traditionally considered a feminine skill and implied submissiveness, dependence, and willingness to follow directions.

For instance, an item from a 1936 masculinity and femininity test asked whether the respondent heard easily when spoken to. A yes answer was considered feminine and a negative answer masculine. But today, it appears that everyone wants to be a good listener, and most feel it is a very important skill.

The author indicates that listening patterns of males and females do differ as to their goals in listening, whom they listen to, and basic listening abilities. The research on the listening responses of infants demonstrate no sex differences. But differences do develop later in life, with males more apt to suffer impaired hearing and deafness. Females retain their hearing facility later in life, although this may be accounted for by males' working in more hazardous and noisy work conditions.

Research has found females to be consistently better at understanding nonverbal cues, such as listening for tone, emphasis, rate, and vocal quality. The author notes that although these differences did not achieve statistical significance in every case, they were consistent.

Studies do indicate that women are better listeners than men. Perhaps this is because women see themselves as better listeners and others expect them to be, which then becomes a self-fulfilling prophecy. However, in one study, males scored higher than females, indicating that males can evidently also listen more intently.

Although there are few inherent differences, as children grow up, males and females learn to listen for different purposes and for different goals. This is a matter of task versus understanding, with males hearing the facts and females being more aware of the communication mood. Yet such differences do not appear to be the case in the helping professions, such as counseling or nursing, where understanding requires attention to cues and message emotional content. Then males become superior in listening for nonverbal cues.

Boys and girls also exhibit different patterns with respect to whom they should listen to. Throughout elementary school, teachers direct more positive and negative feedback to boys than to girls. Boys receive so much verbal information that they screen out much of what they hear and listen selectively. Girls in elementary school receive most of their positive feedback on nonintellectual topics, such as neatness, following directions, and penmanship. The result is their learning to listen to directions and receiving desired positive feedback. Conversely, 90 percent of boys' feedback concerns the intellectual quality of their work rather than appearance and following directions. This results in boys' regarding intellectual ability as internal and not related to following instructions.

The author suggests that the result of these developed listening patterns is that females are listened to less by other females as well as by males. However, the more "liberated" female is better able to decode the nonverbal cues of female sources, and more "traditional" women are better at decoding men's nonverbal cues.

Other studies have shown that in mixed-sex college dyads, females listened more than males, with males interrupting more and listening less. Further, the males were less able to recall what the females said. The females not only talked less but maintained more constant eye contact, whereas the males were less apt to look at the speaker, thereby missing nonverbal cues.

This process of socialization is repeated later in business life, when female executives may not be listened to as carefully as males are. Also, males may not be aware of emotional messages from their female peers until working relationships have been severely damaged.

The author suggests the need for training practices to enhance effective listening skills. Entry-level females may require informational listening training, such as attention focus, repetition, paraphrasing, and putting messages into more meaningful context. Also, asking questions may be required as a means to enhance listening effectiveness.

Entry-level males may need training to be aware of their tendencies not to listen to certain sources and to listen only superficially to females, and training in learning to listen effectively to females in spite of socialized behavior. However, as both men and women advance in the company, it can be expected that they will both adopt the "masculine" listening habits of selective listening, factual listening, and not responding to emotional or nonverbal cues.

The author concludes that although there are very few innate differences in the listening ability of males and females, differences result from socialization and mistaken teaching. Not all males and females are weak in the areas discussed, but many people in the workforce exhibit listening patterns representative of traditional socialization forces. However-er, these learned patterns can be changed through education and training programs. The result will benefit people in their work performance and their personal lives.

REFERENCE

[1]"She Hears . . . He Hears: What They Hear and Why," by Melanie Booth-Butterfield, copyright May 1984. Reprinted with the permission of *Personnel Journal*, Costa Mesta, California; all rights reserved.

QUESTIONS

1. What differences, if any, exist between males and females when it comes to listening patterns?
2. Are women better listeners than men? Explain.
3. How does the author suggest learned patterns of listening can be changed?

Abstract 7-2

- Why is the typical woman employee generally seen as lacking in management skills and an overview of the business?
- What special qualities do experienced women managers bring to business that men usually lack?
- How does a Female Advisory Committee (FAC) function?

The questions above are addressed in a 1983 article by Nancy R. Hammer,[1] head of a public relations firm.

The author says that an important part of successfully implementing an affirmative action program is communicating to women the commitment of management policies to the upward mobility of women managers. Women have been conditioned in their early years to play it safe and not take risks that may lead to failure, thereby missing out on job opportunities. This conditioning has caused women to conform and not question authority, and this contributes to a lack of negotiation skills and a poor self-image.

The older values of women's marrying and raising families have stunted the career development of many adult women managers, as compared to that of the future manager who makes a long-term commitment and plans professional goals of two, five, and ten years. These future managers have strong personalities, they make things happen, and they are self-starters with a sense of self-worth. They are competitive yet work cooperatively with a team to achieve. Their educational backgrounds include math, science, and economics. They enter business through a training program, obtain the support and counsel of a sponsor, then move up through a series of risk-taking jobs.

However, the typical woman has traditionally entered employment with a technical skill and rises to a supervisory level in a department producing a product. She is usually a good producer, and her department generally produces perfect work. Yet management sees her as without extensive experience and thus unqualified to move on to middle- and upper-management responsibilities. She is regarded as lacking management skills and an overview of the business.

To overcome these problems and develop women managers, many companies have adopted affirmative action programs. But if such programs are to be successful, special signals must be communicated to these women. The author suggests that placing women in key senior jobs serves to provide women managers at lower levels with highly visible role models. If a woman is not ready for promotion, management can take different pieces of jobs and create a job that fills in her experience gaps. Such jobs then become stepping-stone positions.

Special workshops are available in which male managers can learn what motivates women and how to help them. These workshops explore both sexes' values and create a communication environment. Since women have not grown up in a business tradition, they need understanding of politics, assertiveness training, career planning, economics, math, and accounting training. It has been observed by others that the younger women coming out of business school today are aware of business conditions, but that the women who have been in business for ten or 20 years need help.

The article also points out that experienced women managers bring to business special qualities, such as socialization abilities, creativity, sensitivity to the needs of others, and an open, straightforward style that is less political than that of men. If these special qualities are not appreciated, women will have to become clones of male managers, with the resulting loss to industry and society of mixed viewpoints.

The author presents an affirmative action program at a Virginia bank where senior management made a commitment to train its women managers. First, as a result of the policy, women officers received letters from the bank president. A Female Advisory Committee (FAC), composed of eight women managers, was formed to serve as the communication link between women officers and senior management. A result was a new rotation program designed to increase experience for women officers. Candidates volunteered and were selected by a committee of senior lending officers based on interviews and performance appraisals. Those selected rotated in different bank areas and then specialized. With the first program completed, two graduates were promoted to senior-level positions.

Other activities of the FAC included articles in the employee magazine, information on professional courses offered by local colleges, and the writing of a new career book detailing the bank operation and job opportunities.

The article concludes that clear signals are needed from top management to establish affirmative action commitments. With appropriate programs, women managers can be trained and prepared to eventually succeed to senior-management positions.

REFERENCE

[1]Hammer, Nancy R., "Companies Must Communicate Their Commitment to Promoting Women." From the June 1983 issue of *Personnel Administrator,* copyright 1983, The American Society for Personnel Administration, 606 North Washington Street, Alexandria, VA 22314.

QUESTIONS

1. What does the author say contributes to women's lack of negotiation skills and a poor self-image?
2. What special signals must be communicated to women managers, even in companies with affirmative action programs?
3. How did the Female Advisory Committee (FAC) function at a Virginia bank?

CHAPTER EIGHT

SAFETY

INTRODUCTION

The challenge of safety management presents the human resource professional with the opportunity to achieve humanitarian goals while obtaining significant cost reductions.

The suffering and trauma resulting from job-related accidents and deaths is probably impossible for the healthy to comprehend. Although these human costs are incalculable, the dollar costs in the United States of occupational accidents and disease are estimated by the National Safety Council to average $35 billion annually. Occupational accidents result in 10,000 deaths a year and 6 million injuries, and occupational diseases amount to 400,000 cases and 100,000 deaths annually. Not included in these dreadful numbers is the further toll from the resulting stress and lowering of the quality of life in the workplace.

That the figures above are so high is not due to a lack of effort by many organizations and concerned companies—such as the National Safety Council, insurance companies offering clients accident prevention programs, state safety inspectors, the American Society of Safety Engineers, the Industrial Medical Association, and the American Industrial Hygiene Association. Yet despite the activities of these groups, the accident rate in manufacturing continues to increase, as does the rate of occupational diseases.

Such conditions prompted Congress in 1970 to pass the Occupational Safety and Health Act (OSHA) authorizing the federal government, through the Department of Labor, to establish and enforce occupational safety and health standards as they apply to private business. OSHA functions as an agency within the Department of Labor and covers more than 4 million private business firms that affect interstate commerce. The law also established the National Institute for Occupational Safety and Health (NIOSH) in the Department of Health, Education and Welfare. NIOSH carries out safety experiments, sets criteria standards, and researches hazardous substances. It is interesting to note that after more than a decade of OSHA, the results are mixed; the number of nonfatal cases without lost workdays has decreased, but the number of lost workdays has increased.

As the earlier data indicate, the incidence of occupational disease is a large problem, and some experts predict it will become even more significant in the future. About 13,000 known toxic chemicals are now in general use, and approximately 500 new substances are being introduced each year. Unfortunately, OSHA has been slow to establish standards on these substances, owing to a lack of funding. It has been estimated that, based on the present progress of OSHA, it will take another 100 years to establish standards on *existing* chemicals, and progress in standards on the continuing growth of new chemicals is nonexistent. The range of health hazards includes physical, such as heat and noise; chemical, such as gases or dust; biological, such as bacteria; and psychological, such as stress.

Evidence suggests that internal stress, such as anxiety and worry, influences one's likelihood to have accidents, and low stress apparently motivates people to increase their performance and probably acts as a stimulus. High stress causes a marked decrease in performance as people focus their attentions and energies on reducing the stress. This results in such counterproductive behaviors as alcoholism, drug abuse, absenteeism, and aggression, which may result in accidents. Suggestions to counteract high stress range from counseling programs to help people to develop self-awareness to training programs designed to develop the desired safety-related behavior.

The extent of this problem is recognized by many states, which now allow worker's compensation payments for job-caused cases of mental disorders, anxiety, and depression that result in a disabling condition. However, extending coverage of worker's compensation beyond the physical and into the psychological environment creates a financial problem for the states. To overcome this problem, as reflected in limited amounts of disability income, the recent trend for affected workers is to seek protection under antidiscrimination legislation while continuing to work.

Studies have shown that certain industries experience a larger number of occupational accidents and disease than others do. Such industries include construction, transportation, and mining. The least-safe occupations are fire fighting, police work, and mining. But even in office work, there are numerous cases of back problems, headaches, digestion problems, and, with the recent advent of video display terminals, eyesight problems. The plastics, refinery, and chemical industries have high incident rates of lung cancer, liver cancer, leukemia, and anemia.

Although accidents and disease are related to high-risk industries, attention is often directed to the "accident-prone" person. This is a misnomer, since recent studies indicate that it is highly unlikely that people would go through a complete life cycle causing accidents because of their ineptness. What appears to happen is that some people are involved in accidents for certain periods of time, but either they mature or learn better job skills, or personal situations change, relieving stress-building encounters and allowing them to lead normal work lives. However, we do know that younger people have more accidents than older people and that some people are better than others in recognizing visual pattern differences, resulting in fewer accidents.

The human resource manager should consider the problem of safety maintenance in a broad perspective, taking into consideration the types of accidents, the particular physical and psychological profiles of the employees, safety problems representative of the technology, and the organizational culture of the firm.

In the design of any company program, the commitment of all management levels is the first priority. This is especially true in a safety maintenance program, where employees are being asked to change previous comfortable and successful work habits because of the possibility of some unlikely event. If it is deemed necessary to wear safety goggles in certain work areas, then everyone should wear them, regardless of title or status. Role-model behavior is still one of the most effective behavioral-change techniques.

Workers usually become involved in a safety maintenance program through membership in local-work-group safety committees. A member of each shop or section or department committee joins members of others to form a larger committee. Selected members of this larger committee are then placed on a companywide or division safety committee. It is through this bureaucratic process that safety policies are formulated, specific safety practices are approved, and communication channels are established.

At the work level, the implementation and effectiveness of the safety maintenance program is in the hands of the local-work-group safety committee representative. This person is the key to whether existing safety rules are followed and sensible new rules are developed as needed. Such a committee member must be respected by the work-group members and have the ability to communicate with them.

The problem of safety motivation is a local workplace problem. It requires that at the local work level, safety training take place through actual demonstrations or effective media techniques. Such training should be coordinated with the local-work-group safety committee member, whose active participation in the process is needed to obtain group commitment. As in any behavioral-change program, group feedback and exchange are necessary to achieve acceptance.

When programs require change and conformity to new behaviors, enforcement and discipline are always problems. Since the specter of OSHA inspections is always present, this is an added incentive for management to ensure that safety regulations are being followed.

Yet to assume that the local-work-group committee member should function as a kind of police enforcer is unrealistic and self-defeating. Democracy still remains a better technique for gaining the cooperation of the uncommitted. Much depends upon the skill and diplomacy of the local work-group committee member. Regular safety inspection tours by representatives of the companywide safety maintenance committee help to instill an organizational commitment to enforcement.

The use of an accident form prepared by the local supervisor not only provides the statistical data needed for accident reporting but also alerts the safety committee to areas needing correction. Further, the local supervisor becomes immediately aware of the problem and its possible implications for anxiety, stress, and the like. A similar report form, but of a different nature, would indicate near accidents—that is, situations in which employees narrowly escaped injury. This form would be valuable in pinpointing areas possibly needing reform.

Another form of enforcement, although less direct, is the use of safety posters, safety booklets, and safety contests. Safety posters are available from the National Safety Council. However, care should be taken; material that is too disturbing is avoided by most people. Posters are meant to attract attention and stimulate thinking; scare tactics fail to do so. Safety booklets may be helpful, but they tend to generate more rules, so that they become too comprehensive, and employees may ignore them completely. Contests have been successful, particularly between work units. Simple awards that are generously distributed to the winners are effective. However, sometimes at the end of a contest, employees relax, and an increase in accidents follows.

Industrial medicine is an important part of a safety maintenance program; it helps to identify aspects of jobs that may be beyond the qualifications of applicants, determines health hazards and acts to eliminate them, and, when medical problems do occur, acts to provide treatment. Today, industrial physicians and hygienists have become more aware of the hazards resulting from noxious fumes, noise levels, and radiation.

Although safety maintenance programs are costly, they serve both a humanitarian purpose and a cost-effective purpose that allows companies to be competitive. However, the process requires constant management commitment as working environments undergo changes in technology and techniques.

RESEARCH INCIDENTS

Research Incident 8-1:
Dick Arnold vs. the Stamping Machine

- What are the advantages and disadvantages of contests as they affect the participants?
- How can one determine the most effective training technique to teach safety behavior?
- When should discipline be used in teaching safe behavior? Or should it?

At 9:00 Monday morning, Dick Arnold put the phone down and rushed out of his office. There was another injury in the stamping department. The beast had struck again, the second time in two months. And all this despite the money the company had spent on posters, lectures, demonstrations, and engineering studies. Up goes the cost of medical insurance, ditto for the state industrial accident rate. The top floor would be all over him again on this one.

Dick reached the stamping department and saw that, in spite of the noise and confusion, the emergency first-aid procedures were working very well. The injured man, Hank Henry, a ten-year veteran of the department, was lying on a stretcher, wrapped in blankets, being attended by two employees who had stopped the flow of blood. The company nurse was two steps behind Dick. She immediately took charge, stabilizing the situation, and Hank Henry was soon off in the company van to the local hospital. The hospital reported later that Hank had smashed three fingers of his right hand and two of his left. Some fingers were so badly damaged that amputation was likely.

That afternoon, the accident safety committee met to discuss this latest accident. The procedure on the press that Hank operated required pieces of aluminum, ranging from 6"×48" to 24"×60", to be placed inside the press, which was then activated by a foot pedal that stamped out the inside of fluorescent ceiling-light fixtures. To be certain the employee's hands were out of the mouth of the press, the company engineering department had designed padded cuffs for each wrist, which would pull the employee's hands back, if the employee had failed to do so voluntarily, before the press impacted on the aluminum. The cuffs were not uncomfortable and had no physical effect on the employee if the hands were already retracted from the press. However, Hank Henry had removed the cuffs when his foreman went to lunch, and that was how the accident had occurred.

RELEVANT EMPIRICAL
RESEARCH STUDIES

Research Study 8-1-A

The use of contests to help change behavior and promote desired work habits is a well-accepted technique, but can contests also have undesirable side effects?

Hampton[1] investigated eight contests and found three major types of harmful behavioral side effects. In one large aerospace-products manufacturing company, a cost-reduction contest was introduced that returned to the submitting employee part of the estimated savings from an adopted suggestion. The response was overenthusiastic; employees neglected their jobs to make suggestions, causing other employees to neglect their jobs evaluating the suggestions. The end result was a sharp reduction in the company's production.

Another contest was held in a bank, to promote its credit and service. For every new credit-card customer who applied and was approved, the soliciting employee received points that applied to prizes. However, since certain bank employees, such as tellers and bank officers, had more direct contact with the bank customers than administrative personnel did, conflict and stress developed. Tellers and bank officers approached customers aggressively, causing ill feelings not only among them, but also in the beleaguered customer.

The final effect that Hampton noted for contests was the dishonesty factor. In a newspaper contest designed to solicit new starts, a sliding scale of prize money was offered for the top three producers, with a much lower amount for the remaining carrier participants. Since the majority of the carriers were in the latter category, many of them pooled their new starts with the top three producers, who then split the higher prize money with them. The result was that over half the new starts were turned in by three carriers. Although the cooperating carriers made more money individually by pooling, it cost the newspaper more money per new subscriber than if the pooling carriers had turned in their new subscribers at the lower rate. The carriers won, but the newspaper lost.

Summary Review of Research Study 8-1-A   Contests result in anticipated and unanticipated results. A contest has not one payoff, but a set of payoffs. These result in side effects that are considered costs to the organization. Such side effects include neglect of the product line to zero in on the contest items; unfair access by some to the contest payoff source, resulting in employee conflict; and bending of the contest rules in a dishonest attempt to win. The design and implementation of contests may reward activities that are not consistent with company goals. The author suggests that these side effects may be so disruptive that the original state of affairs would be preferable.

Research Study 8-1-B

How effective is applied discipline, such as a reprimand or loss of wages, upon safety behavior?

A study by Schuster[2] provides some partial answers. In cooperation with the Iowa Department of Public Safety, a sample of 337 problem automobile drivers were classified into three groups that varied as to the severity of the action taken against them. The procedure was for a highway patrolman examiner to have the problem driver in for a driver-improvement interview in which the official action was manipulated among the three groups of varying severity. After a period of 24 months, the driving records of these problem drivers were reviewed to determine the effect of the selected severity.

The three groups were found to be significantly different in the characteristics of their previous violations. The most important variable in predicting the amount of follow-up action the problem driver would require was the manipulated severity of the action group the driver was assigned to as a result of the driver-improvement interview and the previous number of accidents. As a possible explanation for the interaction between the manipulated severity and past driving record, the drivers might have felt that since the Department of Public Safety classified them as poor drivers, they might as well continue to perform that way during the 24-month follow-up period.

Summary Review of Research Study 8-1-B The study showed some interesting aspects of a driver safety program. It appears that the effect of punishment is the opposite of what is intended. The beginning problem driver who receives a severe punishment reacts as if he is being told that he is a bad driver and then confirms that decision by driving in an unsafe fashion. However, if the punishment is mild, the problem driver responds with a safer driving record.

Research Study 8-1-C

The traditional safety training methods include verbal instructions, written instructions, and demonstration of correct techniques. How effective would accident simulation be?

Rubinsky and Smith[3] conducted an experiment with 32 male college sophomore volunteers from an introductory psychology class. The students used a standard bench grinder to grind a series of ten steel rods. If the student stood in front of the grinder while grinding, a water jet was turned on and hit the student, thereby causing an "accident."

One group of students was given a standard safety training method used in industry, consisting of written instructions and a demonstration of safe operation procedures. A second group received the same instructions as the first, except that the simulated accident was shown and explained, with the instructor turning on the water jet. A third group received the same instructions as group 1, but the simulated accident shown to group 2 was omitted, and during a trial run, the students unexpectedly experienced a simulated accident; that is, when they stood in front of the grinder (incorrect position), they were sprayed with water. A fourth group received the same basic instructions as the other groups, and the simulated accident was both demonstrated and experienced by the students as they were sprayed with water.

One week later, the groups were tested again, and the number of accidents (standing in front of the grinder) was recorded. The mean number of accidents was highest for group 1, followed by group 2, then group 3, and group 4 had the lowest number of accidents. All results were statistically significant. It appears that experiencing the single accident simulation reduced the possibility of an accident.

The authors conducted further studies and noted little difference in accident reduction whether those exposed to the accident simulation were trained under intermittent conditions or two, five, or ten simulated accidents.

Summary Review of Research Study 8-1-C Accident simulation appears to be an effective and powerful training method for the safe operation of a power tool. The training method uses the following procedures: Unsafe acts associated with the power tool are identified, a simulated accident that could result from unsafe acts is devised and the simulation is installed on the power tool, then the trainee operates the power tool and experiences the simulated accident. If the trainee does not perform the unsafe act, the simulated accident is shown.

A limitation of the study is the use of subjects who were not familiar with the power tool and had not yet developed habit patterns that might need to be changed. Established habit patterns may be more difficult to change.

REFERENCES

[1]Hampton, D.R., "Contests Have Side Effects, Too." © 1970 by the Regents of the University of California. Adapted from *California Management Review*, volume XII, no. 4, pp. 86 to 94 by permission of the Regents.

[2]Schuster, D.H., "Two-Year Follow-up of Official Action Taken against Problem Drivers," *Proceedings*, Seventy-ninth Annual Convention, American Psychological Association, 1971, pp. 505–6.

[3]Rubinsky, S., and N. Smith, "Safety Training by Accident Simulation," *Journal of Applied Psychology*, 1 (1973), 68–73.

QUESTIONS

1. With respect to the research incident, what do you suggest Dick Arnold do to reduce accidents at the stamping machine?
2. In regard to accidents at work, is this an individual problem, or a problem related to the particular machine being used?
3. In the incident, was the accident caused by the stamping machine? What is your opinion?
4. As a personnel specialist, what do you suggest we do for, or against, Hank Henry? Be specific.

Research Incident 8-2:
John Otting Uses His Feet

- When applicants are being evaluated prior to entering a training program for an extremely dangerous job, what can be done to ensure their success?
- Does a manager's mode of operation affect group safety response?
- What behavioral-change techniques are available to induce safety behavior?

John Otting, 42 years old, had been working for the past three years as a clean-up man for the A.T. Wright Furniture Company. His employment application showed successful completion of the eighth grade and a stable work history of low-level jobs. The space on the application blank for "General Health" was marked "OK," and the space "Any Health Problems" was marked "NO." The assignment as clean-up man appeared to be compatible with the information on the application blank and the past work experience. Although he had little direct supervision, John performed his duties satisfactorily and complied with the company safety regulations in working around hazardous machinery.

Recently, an opening had occurred to run the chipper machine, and John was the only employee who asked for the job. Even though it carried no increase in pay, the chipper job was cleaner and was considered by the employees to be a better deal. The job required feeding scraps of lumber and imperfect furniture parts into the chipper machine, which then ground the material into wood chips for particle board. Occasionally, some pieces would be too long and difficult to handle, or too heavy, so John was provided with a power saw to cut such pieces into more manageable sizes.

Since the chipper was a hazardous machine, John's new foreman was careful to explain the use of the power saw and the proper method for putting the scraps into the machine. The foreman had been with the company several years since graduating from industrial technical school and was highly regarded by top management.

The next week, John injured his back while working at the chipper and was bedridden at home for two weeks. The accident report listed the cause as lifting a heavy laminated tabletop. The report from the doctor advised care to avoid possible recurrence of the back injury, which had existed prior to employment.

The week that John returned to work, the foreman noticed that he was struggling to lift a heavy table frame into the chipper. The foreman quickly interceded, cautioned John about the need for personal safety practices, and once again demonstrated the proper use of the power saw. Later the same week, the foreman observed John attempting to free some jammed pieces of wood in the chipper, while it was still running, by pushing them with his feet. The foreman rushed over, pointed out the extreme hazard, and then demonstrated the correct safety procedure. From there, he walked into the human resource manager's office and said, "I have a safety-related problem with one of my crew."

Research Study 8-2-A

Aside from expensive physicals to determine possible future problems with job applicants, what other techniques are available?

Gunderson and others[1] studied 293 navy enlisted men who had volunteered to become members of underwater demolition teams. This is an extremely dangerous military duty and requires extreme physical effort. Past experience had shown that certain physical-fitness tests were most predictive of success in completing the training program. The authors used two health questionnaires to gather data on the men. One was the Cornell Medical Index, consisting of a special subscale of 30 items, and the other was the Health Opinion Survey, with a 20-item symptom index. The sample was divided into equal gropus. The other sample group studied was 94 officers, also in training for underwater demolition teams. Certain physical-fitness tests, such as squat-jumps, pull-ups, and sit-ups, were significant predictors of success in completing the training program. The Cornell Medical Index demonstrated significant position correlation for success with both the officer and enlisted groups. However, although the Health Opinion Survey correlated positively with success for both groups, it was not statistically significant for the officer group.

Summary Review of Research Study 8-2-A   The appropriateness of
physical-fitness tests is well established in determining the success of appli-

cants for an underwater demolition training program that requires arduous physical activity. However, in the present study, two health questionnaires, the Cornell Medical Index and the Health Opinion Survey, were used to predict successful completion of the training program. The two questionnaires correlated positively with the successful training for both the officer and enlisted groups. But the correlation of the Health Opinion Survey was not significant for the officer group. Both questionnaires contained a psychiatric orientation, suggesting that emotional health is an important element in predicting underwater demolition training success. A limitation of the study was the possible distortion of the groups' responses to the Cornell Medical Index questionnaire.

Research Study 8-2-B

What effect does the manager's style of leadership have upon the subordinate's response to safety programs?

Dunbar[2] sampled a group of 52 forklift operators with a questionnaire consisting of 15 safety-related questions and one item asking the extent to which their manager was interested in their general welfare. The subjects were in two approximately equal groups; manager A was in charge of one group and manager B the other. Through the 15 questions, the subjects assessed their respective managers in regard to safety matters.

Manager B was characterized as emphasizing the formal aspects of safety somewhat more than manager A, and manager A was considered more approachable and concerned about safety. However, these differences were not statistically significant. The one question about interest in their general welfare revealed that manager A was significantly perceived as more interested in the general welfare of his subordinates than manager B was. The forklift operators in group A saw little relation between the safety-related behavior of their manager and the safety of the workplace. But the operators in group B who were aware of their manager's lesser interest in their general welfare linked the safety of the workplace to his behavior. In regard to personal safety, both groups' belief in the likelihood of being involved in an accident was strongly associated with their managers' behavior.

The findings of the study suggest that whether or not subordinates associate safety practices with the safety-related behavior of their managers may hinge on the degree to which they perceive the manager as being interested in their general welfare. Thus, the perceived support of the manager may significantly affect the way in which subordinates think about safety.

Summary Review of Research Study 8-2-B Managers believe that subordinates should take responsibility for safety matters themselves and not

It first came up at the executive committee's weekly meeting. The division was falling behind its deadlines in all departments in introducing a new, energy-efficient electric motor. One look at the PERT chart clearly showed that. So around the table it went, with department heads all looking outward, not inward. Finally the plant manager interrupted the bickering and suggested that the breakdown was in the drafting section. The drafting section? After more discussion, the committee finally agreed that all the complicated scheduling and planning work for the new motor depended upon an important function that had rarely been mentioned or even considered.

The drafting section's responsibility was to produce scaled, detailed specification blueprints for all the components of the new motor. The process was not complex but painstaking and very time-consuming. In the past, on other projects, this responsibility had been met with regularity and efficiency.

Now came the problem of what to do. Surely this was a production problem—or was it? Suddenly, John Miner, human resource manager, heard someone say it was a "people problem." All heads turned to John, and the plant manager looked expectant. This had happened before, usually when the situation was a hot one and the department heads did not have a ready fast fix.

So John Miner agreed to tackle the problem, not because of peer backsliding but because the solution might be out of the ordinary. Besides, he knew Jim Reinmuth, head of the drafting section, and Jim never dropped the ball. Something unusual might be going on there.

Back in his office, John checked the computer printouts for the drafting section and immediately saw that absenteeism was up dramatically for the past three months. However, everything else checked out—turnover OK, pay increases OK, age profile OK, staffing OK, experience profile OK, grievances OK, and days lost to accidents OK.

The next afternoon, John met with Jim, who appeared very tense. A glance around the office showed that almost half the drafting tables weren't occupied. Where were those workers? Jim produced a list: Of the ten people not present, three had doctor's appointments and seven were home suffering from accidents. Apparently, Jim's employees were being struck down as if in an epidemic. The accidents had all taken place off the job and ran the gamut from tripping over a garden hose to running into an open closet door. Nothing critical, but serious enough to keep them off work for several days.

John asked how long this had been going on. Jim replied, "Since about three months ago, when the new-motor project started and the computer was installed in this section to help with routine work." Then he blurted out, "It's all this stress and rumors—first the pressure of the new-motor project, then that computer, with enough power to replace the whole section, including me!"

The next morning, John Miner went to the plant manager's office to report his preliminary findings. As he waited, a question occupied his mind: This was a section with an excellent safety record inside the company gates, but outside, an accident epidemic—mainly attributable to stress?

RELEVANT EMPIRICAL RESEARCH STUDIES

Research Study 8-3-A

How can stress be determined within a group? Does stress vary between job groups? Is one job more stressful than another?

According to Shaw and Riskind,[1] it is a common belief that certain jobs are more stressful than others, and that employees in these more stressful jobs suffer greater risks of physical or emotional harm. An illustration was the 1981 strike of air traffic controllers, whose union, PATCO, argued that air controllers experience more stress than people in other occupations do. This statement was countered by others, who pointed out that teachers, police officers, and firefighters have equally stressful jobs, and they get lower pay and work longer hours than air controllers.

The authors say that recent reviews of the occupational-stress literature reveal relatively little research on differences of stress among various occupations. Although some studies do indicate that certain jobs demonstrate higher stress-related problems than other jobs, the results are tentative. This is because the studies are not clear as to whether the results occur because of job characteristics or because people with stress-related problems are attracted to these occupations. To determine successfully whether one job is more stressful than another, we need to know that employees in the studies do not significantly differ from each other in personal stress susceptibility and also that job characteristics are systematically related to the stress employees experience on that job.

The concept that particular jobs have characteristics that offer a greater possibility of employees' experiencing job stress was labeled in this study as the job stress potential. This suggests that jobs may be rank-ordered as to their potential for job stress, which in turn implies the ability to measure jobs objectively for potential job stress.

To study job stress potential, it was necessary to obtain two types of data: a measurement tool to measure the characteristics of a large number of jobs, with data collected from several sources; and job stress data representing a variety of stresses for large numbers of employees in jobs whose job-characteristic data were obtained.

Because it would have been too costly to perform a field study, the authors obtained data from archival (public documents) sources. The data on job characteristics were obtained from the Position-Analysis Questionnaire data bank at Utah State University. The data on job stress were obtained from three major research studies: Caplan, Cobb, French, Harrison, and Pinneau;* Colligan, Smith, and Hurrell; † and Milham.‡

Two requirements for a job-characteristics measuring device were that it must measure the job itself, not some evaluation of the job by an employee, and that it must have available large numbers of identifiable jobs from which data had been collected. The instrument that met both these requirements was the Position-Analysis Questionnaire (PAQ).

The PAQ instrument is a job analysis of 194 different job components that are used to obtain 32 different job dimensions. This information is stored in the PAQ data bank and provides the behavioral characteristics of a large number of jobs.

The large data sample needed in this study was provided by the previously mentioned three major research studies. The stress data represented a wide range of occupations: pulp mill workers, welders, salesclerks, physicians, and college professors. The stress data of the jobs was measured by physiological indexes such as stress-related mortality rates; by psychological indexes such as anxiety, depression, and job dissatisfaction; and by behavioral indexes such as dispensary visits and accidents.

The study measured job characteristics using the 32 job dimensions of the PAQ to determine the relationship between the job-dimension scores and the stress data from the three major research studies. Of the 576 correlations computed, 141 were statistically significant. The authors found a fairly strong relationship between the job dimensions of the PAQ and the stress data.

The job dimensions and stress data from the three major research studies were analyzed using the job-dimension scores to predict each of 18 stress variables: heart, hypertension, ulcers, cirrhosis, suicides, falls, complexity, conflict, ambiguity, responsibility, ability underutilization, anxiety/depression, irritability, dissatisfaction, dispensary visits, and cardiovascular, respiratory, and mental-health admissions. The result was a fairly high predictability level for all 18 stress types, with multiple correlations ranging from .288 to .851.

The authors indicate that the study results, by themselves, do not provide conclusive support for the concept of more stressful and less stressful occupations. However, the data did indicate a fairly strong rela-

---

*R.D. Caplan and others, *Job Demands and Worker Health: Main Effects and Occupational Differences*, U.S. Government Printing Office (Washington, D.C., 1975).

†M.J. Colligan and others, "Occupational Incident Rates of Mental Health Disorders," *Journal of Human Stress*, 3 (1977), 34–39.

‡S. Milham, Jr., *Occupational Morality in Washington State 1950–1971* (U.S. Department of Health, Education and Welfare, Public Health Service), U.S. Government Printing Office (Washington, D.C., 1976).

tionship among the PAQ job-dimension scores and several varied indexes of job-related stress. It is their position that the job stress potential concept does suggest that certain jobs demonstrate characteristics that increase the likelihood that workers in those jobs will experience stress.

Summary Review of Research Study 8-3-A The study investigated whether there is a reliable relationship between the physiological, psychological, and behavioral characteristics of a variety of jobs and the levels of stress experienced by workers in these jobs.

Data for the study were obtained from archival sources—the Position-Analysis Questionnaire (PAQ) data bank at Utah State University and three major research studies. The PAQ provided the data on 194 different job elements, and the three studies the data on job stress.

The study results generally indicated a fairly strong relation between the job elements and the stress data. Further, the job-elements scores were analyzed and demonstrated a fairly high predictability level for all 18 stress types.

Research Study 8-3-B

What type of stress-management programs are effective? Do any stress-management programs provide long-term relief?

Rose and Veiga[2] made a study to determine whether locus of control and anxiety level can be reduced for a long-term period through stress-management intervention.

The authors note that the recent rapid growth of stress-management programs providing change effectiveness is in programs based on only short-term duration, not long-term. They believe stress occurs when people are in an appraisal situation and find a substantial imbalance between what is expected of them and their perceived ability to respond.

The study indicated two types of anxiety: state anxiety and trait anxiety. A person in state anxiety has limited ability to process information, decreased sensitivity to information cues, and a confused pattern of decision making. The trait-anxiety person blames personal inadequacy on events beyond his or her control, which serves to exaggerate any potential threat. The study attempted to determine the extent to which locus of control and the two anxiety levels can be changed by a stress-management intervention program, the duration of any change, and the effect of such a program on the behavior pattern of type A people. (Type A people are aggressive and competitive; type B are relaxed, "laid back.")

The authors decided to incorporate into the stress intervention program of this study three major stress-reduction techniques found in the literature: relaxation techniques, such as progressive muscle relaxation and cue-controlled relaxation, the use of self-produced cue words to reduce anxieties; coping-skills training, which identifies anxiety cues and then develops responses to eliminate tension; and cognitive modification, which focuses on the relationship between cognitions and the behavioral response. The study intervention program consisted of six two-hour instruction sessions, meeting twice a week for three weeks, in which the subjects identified anxiety cues and practiced cognitive skills and relaxation skills.

The study subjects were 48 undergraduate business students attending a large eastern university and enrolled in two separate one-credit courses in stress and career planning. Most were seniors, the average age was 22, and 54 percent were males and 46 percent females.

At the first meeting, all the student subjects were administered the following tests: Rotter's locus-of-control scale, the state-trait anxiety inventory, and the Jenkins activity survey (Form T), which classifies people as type A or type B. Equal numbers of types A and B male and female students were randomly assigned to the experimental and delayed-treatment (control) groups.

Four days after the initial test-completion meeting, the control (delayed-treatment) group was told that because of the large enrollment, the class had been divided in half, so that their group would start the career-planning course first and take the stress-management course in three weeks. The experimental group began the stress-management course immediately, and both groups, three weeks later, took the same battery of tests again.

To determine the sustained effects of the treatment, all experimental-group members were interviewed and administered the same test battery during a common stress period—their midterm examination week, which occurred approximately one month after the training program was terminated.

The Rotter locus-of-control scale consists of a 26-item I-E (Internal-External) scale that assesses the generalized belief that people exercise control over their reinforcement relative to their behavior. The state-trait anxiety inventory, or STAI (Spielberger, Gorsuch, and Lushene),* has two 20-item scales. The A-Trait scale asks you to describe how you generally feel, and the A-State scale asks you to describe how you feel right now. The Jenkins activity survey (JAS) contains 50 items designed to measure type A and type B behavior. Past research has shown the JAS to be a valid predictor of coronary heart disease. Other studies using the JAS have found type A college students to be more competitive, impatient, and aggressive than type B students.

The study compared type A and type B pretest means and the pretest means of the experimental and control groups on the three dependent

*C.D. Spielberger and others, *STAI Manual* (Palo Alto, CA: Consulting Psychologists Press, 1970).

variable scores, with the following results: (1) There were no significant differences between type A and type B subjects on state anxiety, on trait anxiety, or on locus of control; (2) there were no significant differences between the experimental group and the control group on state anxiety, trait anxiety, or locus of control. Thus, the groups appeared equivalent at the pretest stage of the study.

An analysis of the effects of the treatment on the experimental and control groups, on the type A and type B behavioral types, and on the three dependent variable scores over time found no significant interaction between treatment, behavior type, and the pre/post measures for state anxiety, trait anxiety, or locus of control.

The study did find statistically significant interactions between the treatment group and the measures of state anxiety and trait anxiety. However, there was no significant reaction between treatment and the repeated measure of locus of control. On state and trait anxiety, the experimental-group scores dropped from pretreatment to posttreatment, whereas the control-group scores remained fairly constant.

The authors suggest these interpretations of the data above: First, experimental treatment did significantly reduce state and trait anxiety compared to the control group but had no effect on modifying locus of control; and second, the treatment effects were not mediated by behavior type A or B.

The data were then evaluated to determine if any changes in anxiety or locus of control attained through the experimental treatment were maintained. There were significant differences among pretest, posttest, and during-stressful-event measures of state anxiety and trait anxiety. However, there were no significant differences between behavior type and repeated measures of state anxiety, trait anxiety, or locus of control.

It is clear that the significant differences between the pretest and posttest measures indicated that the reductions in both state and trait anxiety were maintained during a later stressful midterm examination event. Yet the experimental treatment failed to induce significant increases in the subjects' expectation of control over their lives (locus of control), with particular reference to perceived threatening life events.

Summary Review of Research Study 8-3-B This study investigated whether locus of control and anxiety level could be modified by stress-management intervention and whether the modification could be later sustained in a stress real-life event.

Two kinds of anxiety were investigated: state anxiety, which results in limited information-processing ability, decreased sensitivity to information cues, and confused decision-making patterns; and trait anxiety, in which the person blames some personal inadequacy on externalities, leading to exaggeration of a threat. Another aspect of the study was to explore the effect of any modification upon type A and type B behavior.

Three major stress-reduction techniques were used: relaxation techniques, including muscle relaxation and cue-controlled relaxation; coping-skills training; and cognitive modification. The measuring instruments included the I-E scale, state-trait anxiety inventory, and Jenkins activity survey. The subjects were undergraduate business students, divided into an experimental group and a control group.

The study demonstrated that state and trait anxiety could be reduced through the study's stress-management program and that the reduction could be sustained at a later real-life stressful event. However, the study treatment failed to increase the subjects' locus of control—control over one's life, with emphasis upon situations perceived to be threatening.

Research Study 8-3-C

How can a manager determine whether an employee may incur health problems as a result of job-related stress or tension? Is there an instrument available that allows an accurate prediction of one's susceptibility to stress?

Matteson and Ivancevich[3] utilized an instrument first used to study air controllers in an attempt to determine its external validity to other work groups.

The authors point out that the question is no longer *whether* stress is related to negative health consequences, but rather how general the relationship is. Thus, any instrument that offers to identify ahead of time those most likely to incur health problems in a stressful environment would be highly valuable. This is particularly pertinent in the light of an estimated cost of stress-related incidents of $100 billion annually.

The instrument chosen by the authors for this study is a predictor of psychological and physical illness called the tension discharge rate scale (TDR). This is a six-item scale developed by Rose, Jenkins, and Hurst* to study the stress and health change of air controllers. The TDR six-item scale uses a seven-point evaluation response format ranging from "completely false" to "completely true." The TDR supposedly measures the rate at which a person dissipates job-related tension. The idea is that leaving one's job tensions quickly behind at the end of the day is healthier than bringing them home to ponder over. The adaptive person efficiently discharges job tensions, but nonadaptive people have difficulty doing so. This nonadaptive coping may result in apathy, depression, or even suicidal behavior.

Previous research, say the authors, has shown that the TDR discriminates among a number of health, personality, and life factors. Since the

*R.M. Rose and others, *Air Traffic Controller Health Change Study: A Prospective Investigation of Physical, Psychological, and Work-Related Changes* (Austin: University of Texas Press, 1978).

TDR scale is short, easy to complete, and nonthreatening to participants, it is an appealing instrument for research and diagnostic purposes.

The initial study sample was 682 medical technologists who responded to an invitation in the *American Journal of Medical Technology* to participate in a research study. The final sample was 388 medical technologists, 86 percent female, who participated in the initial and second round of data collection. The TDR instrument was completed in the first round, and approximately eight months later, eight other measures were collected: TOTP, number of health problems; ILLH, work days missed because of health; BPAR, days not up to par; DOCV, visits to a physician; ASPR, amount of aspirin; TRNQ, amount of tranquilizers; cigs, amount of cigarettes; and ALCO, alcohol consumption.

The TDR scores were divided at the median to form a rapid-tension-discharge group and a slow-tension-discharge group.

The results of the study indicate that the two groups, rapid discharge and slow discharge, differed with respect to at least one of the eight measures (criterion variables). Further analysis attempted to determine which of the eight criterion variables were different in the rapid- and slow-discharge groups. There were significant differences in six of the eight variables; cigarettes and alcohol were the only differences not significant. In the six significant differences, the rapid-tension-discharge subjects had fewer health problems, fewer workdays missed for health reasons, fewer doctor visits, fewer aspirin used, fewer days not up to par, and fewer tranquilizers used.

The authors concede that their findings are tentative and incomplete, and further research with the TDR scale appears warranted.

Summary Review of Research Study 8-3-C   This study investigated an instrument that had shown promise in earlier research to be a predictor of psychological and physical illness—a six-item scale called the tension discharge rate (TDR), which had been used successfully in an earlier study of air controllers to predict their health status. The authors believe an adaptive person is able to release work tensions efficiently, whereas a nonadaptive person has difficulty in releasing work tensions and brings them home. The TDR scale was used in the present study to provide data on people's effectiveness in releasing tension rapidly. Eight criterion measures included number of workdays missed and number of visits to a physician.

The sample subjects were 388 medical technologists, 86 percent female, who completed the data collection. The study found significant differences between the rapid-tension-discharge group and the slow-tension-discharge group on six of the eight criterion measures.

The authors note that the findings are tentative, and they believe the TDR scale justifies further research.

REFERENCES

[1]Shaw, J.B., and J.H. Riskind, "Predicting Job Stress Using Data from the Position-Analysis Questionnaire," *Journal of Applied Psychology,* 68 (1983), 253–61.

[2]Rose, R.L., and J.F. Veiga, "Assessing the Sustained Effects of a Stress Management Intervention on Anxiety and Locus of Control," *Academy of Management Journal,* 27 (1984), 190–98.

[3]Matteson, M.T., and J.M. Ivancevich, "Note on Tension Discharge Rate as an Employee Health Status Predictor," *Academy of Management Journal,* 26 (1983), 540–45.

QUESTIONS

1. What value has the Position-Analysis Questionnaire in determining job stress in different occupations? Explain. What predictive power, if any, does it have? Answer in detail.
2. How do stress-management programs affect anxiety? Include in your answer state and trait anxiety. What is the effect of a stress-management program on different personalities, such as type A and type B?
3. How does the adaptive person resolve the problem of work stress? What is the tension discharge rate scale (TDR), and what does it do?

NON-EMPIRICAL RESEARCH ARTICLE ABSTRACTS

Abstract 8-1

- How is the problem of company trade secrets related to information regarding safe working conditions?
- What is the position of unions with respect to collecting employees' health information and the Freedom of Information Act?
- When does an employer have to communicate with an employee about exposure to "harmful physical agents"?

A 1982 article by Joyce Asher Gildea,[1] vice-president of a consulting firm, deals with these questions.

The author points out that safety on the job means more than freedom from injury, since millions of workers need protection from exposure to dangerous substances. A problem arises as companies collect a great deal of personal and medical employee information and provide these data to the Occupational Safety and Health Administration (OSHA) to show that the workplace is safe. Some of this information may reveal trade secrets, which may come to the attention of competitors through the Freedom of Information Act.

Such a problem occurred in 1978, when OSHA's Review Commission ruled against the Oil, Chemical and Atomic Workers' Union and for the Olin Corp. To protect trade secrets, Olin wanted only union representatives to review safety monitoring records of employees, not the employees themselves.

Another concern is whether the results of medical tests will be used against an employee. Unions maintain that if an employee is exposed to some disease, this information will prevent the employee from being promoted or from being employed by another company in the same industry.

With genetic testing becoming routine, companies take the position that knowledge of an employee's genetic susceptibility to certain substances will help to protect the worker. However, unions question this assumption if the person is not hired, or is fired, or is not promoted, or is not placed in a job because of medical test results or refusal to take such tests.

The question is, Is the employer's effort to protect both itself and the employee an invasion of privacy and/or job discrimination? This problem is further complicated by any data base upon which to compare test results, and a lack of court decisions.

OSHA did issue a rule on August 20, 1980, which is being contested in the courts, declaring certain conditions under which companies must make medical and toxic-exposure records available to OSHA and employees. The standard also allows employees to designate others to see the records, although OSHA may see them at any time. It provides some protection of trade secrets, with possible limitation of access to only those agreeing in writing not to reveal such secrets.

The problem is one of record access. Unions believe that their rights should be equal to OSHA's and that they should not have to ask their members' permission before seeing the records. The employers' response to the standard is that it invades company privacy and that it will damage their health-surveillance programs.

One aspect of the standard that affects the employee is that if employees have been exposed to toxic substances or "harmful physical agents," employers must communicate this fact to them at least once a year. Such a communication must include the location and availability of such records. Employees have the right to know who is responsible for maintaining these records and granting access to them. Such records must be kept for 30 years.

The author suggests that employers take the necessary steps to communicate these provisions to their employees. Since employees will have strong opinions on these matters, employers must demonstrate an attitude of favoring equitable resolutions through their commitment to open communications. More cooperation between employer and employee should reduce the intervention of government and labor unions.

REFERENCE

[1]Gildea, Joyce Asher, "Safety and Privacy: Are They Compatible?" From the February 1982 issue of *Personnel Administrator,* copyright 1982, The American Society for Personnel Administration, 606 North Washington Street, Alexandria, VA 22314.

QUESTIONS

1. What is the unions' fear in regard to company knowledge of an employee's genetic susceptibility to certain substances?
2. How do the unions regard their right of employee-record access as compared to that of OSHA?
3. With respect to employees' health records, there is the problem of employees' invasion of privacy by a company in an effort to protect itself and the employees. Discuss other problems that arise.

Abstract 8-2

- What is the difference between genetic screening and genetic monitoring? What do they reveal?
- How do relevant legal precedents affect the future of genetic testing? What are your recommendations?
- What would be the best case in which to use the manifestation theory? the exposure theory?

These matters are taken up in a 1984 article by Olian, an assistant professor, and Snyder, a public health engineer.[1]

The authors mention the significant progress of genetic engineering in the last ten years. Scientists are now able to predict some occupational diseases in an adult from genetic information obtained at birth. Also, a person's genetic endowment may help to predict susceptibility to disease from job exposure to toxins.

Two potential human resource management applications of genetic testing are *genetic screening* (GS) and *genetic monitoring* (GM). GS is a one-time testing of applicants to determine any genetic traits that could cause health problems when the person is exposed to certain chemicals. This information would assist in the applicant–job match; people would not be placed in work situations that would pose special hazards to them. GM would routinely test employees periodically, and if any changes were found in the genetic material of exposed people, the toxic agent could be removed from the production process, or engineering controls could be installed, or the people could be transferred.

The authors report a survey, by the Office of Technology and Assessment (OTA), of 366 respondents in six companies currently using genetic tests, 17 that had used them previously, and 59 that were planning to do so in the next five years. With respect to actions taken regarding genetic test results, eight companies had informed the employee of the test results, five had transferred the employee, three had added personal protection devices on the job, two had installed engineering controls, and one company had changed the product. These survey results suggest a cautious interest in introducing genetic testing into the workplace.

At this point, GS devices are not accurate and reliable predictors of hypersusceptibility, although future research may correct this problem and permit more accurate placement. Also, since the results of GS are beyond the control of the applicant, such information may be best used for placement purposes and not for a nonhiring decision. GM results could also be used for placement decisions.

A human resource management problem resulting from genetic testing is to develop fair and inexpensive job placement and transfer policies. This could involve the Equal Pay Act and the Civil Rights Act. If GM showed that some employees were hypersusceptible to certain toxins and these were within OSHA limits, an outplacement of these employees might be necessary. It is interesting to note that GS results indicating that an employee is hypersusceptible to certain acceptable low levels of toxins might minimize employer liability in later cases of occupationally related diseases.

To date, there are no direct relevant legal precedents for genetic testing. OSHA does require an employer to provide a workplace free from recognized hazards, and two specific standards that do exist relate to lead and vinyl chloride levels at work. Considering the intent of OSHA, if an employer had negative information resulting from GS and GM that was not acted upon, this might be violating the spirit of the law. In regard to the Rehabilitation Act and similar state laws, people diagnosed as genetically impaired would be considered handicapped and entitled to employment protection.

The worker's compensation (WC) system presents a problem, since eligibility for benefits requires establishing a cause–effect relationship between the workplace and the illness or injury. This is difficult to do with toxic agents and subsequent disease.

There are two contradictory legal theories regarding WC liability. The *manifestation theory* limits the employer to the active term of the WC policy. The *exposure theory* covers work-related diseases throughout life, regardless of whether the WC insurance has expired. Under the first theory, GS might be able to indicate an employee's predisposition to a disease, a benefit to the employer. But under the second theory, the employer is liable regardless.

Since both GS and GM are invasive tests that provide information for many decisions, the employer must protect the employee's rights so that genetic information is not used for nonjob situations. Although there are no such federal laws, OSHA provides for employees to see their medical records except what a physician decides may be damaging for that person to know.

The authors tell us that nine states require "right to know" labels on chemicals used at work. Other legal precedents imply that employers must not conceal medical data on workplace exposure, at the risk of punitive damages.

The general-duty clause of OSHA can be interpreted to require a GM program. Such a program must protect the employee's privacy rights and be limited to the job, and if the corporate physician deems it necessary, there must be a genetic counseling program. Such counselors need to be trained in nonthreatening but informative feedback.

The actions to be taken by an employer on GM information depend upon the validity of the data, the seriousness of the hazard, the feasibility of eliminating or controlling the hazard, and how general the hazard is to the workforce. OSHA has encouraged engineering controls in hazardous situations, at great cost to employers. However, in some circumstances, only certain susceptible employees may need to be removed and transferred to other, less personally dangerous jobs. In smaller firms, this becomes a problem, since there may be no other jobs to be transferred to. In such cases, employers should obtain consent agreements from affected employees who choose to remain on the job despite the health hazard. Such agreements will minimize any potential damages against the employer, but not eliminate them.

Although it is preferable not to place hypersusceptible applicants in hazardous work situations, even with their consent, the problem of excluding applicants may become a problem under Title VII. This is because if genetic screening results in unequal racial acceptance, it may be considered indefensible unless validity data are available.

The authors suggest that firms collect GS information for purposes of basic research that may someday provide the necessary validity evidence to allow selection and placement decisions.

REFERENCE

[1]Olian, Judy D., and Tom C. Synder, "The Implications of Genetic Testing." From the January 1984 issue of *Personnel Administrator,* copyright 1984, The American Society for Personnel Administration, 606 North Washington Street, Alexandria, VA 22314.

QUESTIONS

1. Why do the authors state that genetic screening (GS) information may be best used for placement purposes and not for a nonhiring decision?

2. What is the problem under the worker's compensation system of establishing eligibility for benefits as a result of toxic agents?

3. In some circumstances, certain susceptible employees can be removed and transferred to other, less personally dangerous jobs. However, in smaller firms there may be no other jobs available. What can the smaller employer do?

CHAPTER NINE

LABOR–MANAGEMENT RELATIONS

INTRODUCTION

The long history of labor–management relations has been one of turbulent confrontation, with the result that unions became more and more powerful. However, recent trends have reversed this past progression; the union movement, while still powerful, has entered a period of declining influence. This is evident in the numerical data that reveal a decrease in union membership as a proportion of the labor force, from a high of almost 25 percent in 1970 to less than 19 percent in 1984. Work stoppages today are fewer than in 1960. The number of elections to decertify existing unions has doubled in the past ten years, with 75 percent of such elections resulting in the removal of the union.

However, the union movement is far from becoming an unimportant factor in the world of work. In some manufacturing industries, such as steel and automobiles, union membership is still close to 45 percent. Even in the nonmanufacturing segment of the economy, union membership is about 20 percent. Union ability in organizing the growing number of white-collar workers is further indication that the union movement continues to be a significant factor in future management–employee relations.

The labor movement became a significant force in the economy as a result of federal and state legislation that forced employers to recognize and bargain with groups representing their employees and that protected employees from retaliation by employers. The first major federal legislation as the Railroad Labor Act of 1926, allowing railroad and airline employees to determine by election whether they wished to be represented by a union. Further, the law provided that employees could legally engage in union activity without fear of retaliation.

The next major federal legislation was the Norris–La Guardia Act of 1932. This law had little effect in promoting union growth in the private sector; it did not require employers to bargain with groups representing their employees, nor did it prevent employers from retaliating against those employees who were involved in promoting union membership. However, it did prevent employers from coercing employees to sign "yellow-dog contracts" specifying that the employees would not join unions or they would be fired. And the act did prevent federal judges from issuing injunctions to stop lawful union activities such as strikes unless they presented a danger to life or property. Prior to the Norris–La Guardia Act, if employees went on strike, the employer could obtain an injunction to prevent the strike, with the result that the employees either returned to work or were fired.

It was not until the passage of the Wagner Act of 1936 (National Labor Relations Act) that union membership began its phenomenal growth and its influence upon the national economy. The importance of the Wagner Act was that it made it legal for workers to organize and to be free of employer harassment. The act also defined several employer unfair labor practices, such as coercing employees, interfering with organization activity, firing or discouraging employment because of union activity, and refusing to bargain. Another part of the legislation was the establishment of the National Labor Relations Board to conduct union selection elections and to investigate unfair labor practices.

In an attempt to correct both management and union practices that abused employees, the Taft-Hartley Act of 1947 was passed to amend the Wagner Act. Management had formed its own unions to avoid outside unions and then entered into wage contracts (sweetheart contracts) that favored the company. This practice was now prohibited by the Taft-Hartley Act. The act also required that unions represent all employees in the bargaining unit whether or not the employees were union members. It said that employees outside of a union shop (one in which all employees must join the union) cannot be discriminated against because of nonmembership in the union. Further, the act established the Federal Mediation and Conciliation Service to assist in resolving labor disputes by providing arbitrators.

The Landrum-Griffin Act of 1959, resulting from labor racketeering, established certain rights for union members that had been denied them by their union leadership: nominating candidates, voting for candidates, and attending and participating in union meetings. The act said that unions must submit an annual financial statement to the Secretary of Labor, and union officials must be bonded. Employers and labor consultants must report any funds spent to influence employees on their bargaining rights.

The legislation cited above provided a positive environment for unionization, but the basic process starts with either a group of employees or a particular union. Once the union organizing campaign begins, at least 30 percent of the employees must be persuaded to sign authorization cards before a representative election can be called. Once the necessary percentage of signed cards has been obtained, the National Labor Relations Board is petitioned and an examiner is appointed. If the examiner decides that the signatures are valid and the bargaining unit has been determined, the NLRB schedules the election. When the balloting is over, the board counts the ballots and certifies the election results. If the union has won the election by a simple majority, the union officials are authorized to negotiate a bargaining agreement with the company.

The bargaining agreement usually contains sections on wages and working conditions, employee and union security, management rights, and the time span of the agreement. If the union officials and management agree to the terms, the contract must be submitted to a vote of the union membership before it can become binding on both parties.

In the event of an impasse in collective bargaining, the final act for the union is to strike. Since this is a costly act for both labor and management, most agreements contain alternative solutions—either grievance procedures or arbitration.

The grievance procedure is designed to resolve what one party views as a violation of the contract. Either the employees or the employer may bring the charge, but the grievance procedure is usually used as a device to defuse employee complaints before they reach the level of strikes. The usual grievance system begins when a disturbed employee contacts the shop steward; if the problem seems legitimate, the employee and the shop steward meet with the supervisor involved. Generally, about 75 percent of the problems are settled at this level. If not, the next step is involvement with a professional from the human resource department. If failure is again encountered, the third step is taken—a formal process, with the alleged violation typed and presented to a group representing top-level management and union officials. If the problem is not settled at this level, most agreements provide for arbitration.

The first step in arbitration is the selection of an arbitrator acceptable to both the union and management. Either the Federal Mediation and Conciliation Service or the American Arbitration Association is contacted for a list of available arbitrators. The union and management each indicate those arbitrators acceptable to them, and eventually, through a process of elimination, one arbitrator is selected and agreed to by both parties.

There are several forms of arbitration, such as final-offer, in which both sides present their final offers and the arbitrator chooses one; but the usual course is for each side to present its case, and the arbitrator makes a decision based upon the merits of the facts presented. The cost of arbitration, which is shared by both parties, is high, averaging about $1,500 per case. However, the grievance procedure and the arbitration process do present a system for resolving problems while avoiding the cost of the ultimate confrontation, the strike.

Contemporary challenges to labor–management relations are many. The unions are faced with changing characteristics of their membership. The interests of older and younger members differ; older workers prefer increased benefits, whereas younger workers are more interested in wages. Minorities and women are not interested in seniority systems that hinder promotions and wage increases. Members of some professional groups value their status as individuals more than they do communal membership in a union.

Management finds itself faced with the prospect of low-cost international competition as it attempts to satisfy the financial and motivational needs of its employees. The recent advent of quality circles and increased emphasis on participation are attempts to satisfy these needs.

The success of unions and management in resolving what are, in the final analysis, mutual problems will indicate the future course of union–management relations as to confrontation or cooperation.

RESEARCH INCIDENTS

Research Incident 9-1:
Sharon Lefferts and Carrot Allegery

- How does the perception of the authority given to an arbitrator affect the behavior of participants in a grievance proceeding?
- What is the effect on grievance participant behavior when the arbitrator decides on the final offer for individual issues, as opposed to a decision on one final package offer?
- Does the fact that the arbitration procedure is conventional or final-offer affect the aspirations of the parties to the arbitration?

As a human resource specialist, David Kenyon was not particularly satisfied with the selection of the arbitrator. However, from the list sent by the American Arbitration Association, it was the only name that management and the union both found acceptable. There was something else about this arbitration that made David somewhat uneasy. This was the first time he had been involved in final-offer arbitration. In the past, under conventional arbitration, both sides presented their arguments and the arbitrator decided the amount of the award for the winner. Under final-offer arbitration, each side makes an offer, and the arbitrator chooses the one that appears the most reasonable under the circumstances.

The other day, it had seemed like a clear case of employee insubordination subject to termination. Sharon Lefferts refused a direct order by her foreman to work on the carrot-processing line, claiming she was allergic to carrots. She was brought to the human resource office by the foreman, where her file revealed no mention of allergies. Besides, everyone on the carrot-processing line wore rubber gloves, so no one even touched the carrots. Sharon had stormed out of the human resource office, left her work station, and gone home before management could locate the shop steward. Now, after many hours of unsuccessful meetings according to the company grievance procedure, the final step of arbitration was about to begin.

David Kenyon wondered whether the arbitrator would consider management's decision to fire Sharon Lefferts unreasonable.

RELEVANT EMPIRICAL RESEARCH STUDIES

Research Study 9-1-A

A criticism of conventional arbitration is that both parties present extreme positions, which permits the arbitrator to split the difference. Anticipation of this by both parties creates a chilling effect, since neither side really tries to reach a solution. What support is there for this position?

A study by Grigsby and Bigoness[1] investigated the effects of anticipated mediation and the type of arbitration on bargaining behavior. The authors recruited 84 male undergraduate business students and told them they would be taking part in a collective bargaining simulation. They would receive a minimum of $3 for just participating, with the possibility of $5 depending on their success in bargaining. Each student was randomly assigned a management or union role and then paired with a student taking an opposite role. They were then given a booklet and 20 minutes to become familiar with union—management background information. The next step was a brief oral instruction period to ensure understanding of the procedures.

The bargaining was done face to face over issues of a vacation plan, a hospital and medical plan, wages, a cost-of-living clause, and a night-shift differential. The process began with the union making a written demand on the five issues. Bargaining then lasted for 30 minutes, after which the participants submitted their final offers.

An independent variable that was measured concerned the presence or absence of anticipated mediation. In the no-mediation bargaining, participants were told that if, at the end of 30 minutes, all five issues were not resolved, they would be given a few extra minutes to submit a final offer. In the mediation bargaining, participants were told that if complete agreement had not been reached in 30 minutes, they should write down their final positions and await a mediator. The mediator would attempt to help the parties reach an agreement, although the mediator's suggestions would not be binding.

The other independent variable was the type of arbitration anticipated. For conventional arbitration, the participants were told that a third party would determine the issues. In issue-by-issue arbitration, participants were told that a third party would choose one position or the other on each of the five issues. The total-package arbitration group was told that a third party would accept one position or the other in its entirety. The no-arbitration (control) group was told that if there were no agreements, there would be a strike.

The results indicated that groups anticipating mediation were just as cooperative in the bargaining session as those that did not anticipate mediation. The type of anticipated arbitration had a significant effect on the number of issues left unresolved for both the mediation and no-mediation bargaining. Those groups that anticipated mediation prior to arbitration left a significantly larger number of issues unresolved under conventional arbitration than did the other groups. In fact, total-package arbitration, issue-by-issue final-offer, and no-arbitration did not differ significantly at all. In regard to the no-mediation condition, fewer issues were left unresolved in the total-package final arbitration and the no-arbitration condition than in the conventional arbitration and issue-by-issue final arbitration.

Summary Review of Research Study 9-1-A   The study supports the concept of the chilling effect of conventional arbitration. The total-package final-offer arbitration reduced this chilling effect as the parties made a real effort to reach agreement. Further, the issue-by-issue final-offer arbitration was not as effective as the total-package final-offer arbitration in reducing the chilling effect of conventional arbitration. It appears that the participants were influenced more by the aspect of final conflict resolution than by the mediation process. In the no-arbitration situation, there was no expectation of mediation. The conventional arbitration situation resulted in the greatest number of unsettled issues when the participants expected mediation.

It would appear that anticipated mediation promotes bargaining under some types of anticipated arbitration, but it may be a negative factor under other types. The authors suggest that, in the light of the present findings, when it comes to third-party intervention, the unique contributions of total-package final-offer arbitration should be considered.

Research Study 9-1-B

What is the effect of final-offer arbitration on an issue-by-issue presentation as opposed to a total-package final-offer arbitration that covers all the issues? That is, suppose that, rather than a final offer for each separate issue, the award is based on the final offer for all the issues—a kind of "winner takes all."

Subbarao* set up an experimental design that involved 88 volunteers undergraduate students enrolled in collective bargaining classes. The students were placed in two-member teams of whom one was assigned as the union negotiator and the other as the management negotiator. They were provided with appropriate comparative data for negotiating the percentage increase of annual salaries and a reduction in work hours for firefighters in a fictitious city. Since each student negotiator received a grade based on the number of points accumulated at the expense of the other negotiator, it was assumed that the participants would be motivated to succeed.

These two-member teams were each assigned to one of four experimental conditions: a final-offer selection, in which a neutral third party must base the reward on one final package offer; an issue-by-issue last offer, in which a neutral third party would make an award by selecting for each issue one or the other party's last offer; an open award, in which the neutral third party would make the award without any regard for the parties' final positions; and a compromise award, in which the neutral third party would split the difference between both parties' final positions.

The study found that the amount of concessions and the amount of the terminal outcomes were significantly different for the final-offer selection and the last offer by issue. The terminal outcome was defined as the sum of the difference in salary and hours of work resulting from the union's and management's final bids. The means of the combined concessions between the union and management negotiators were highest in the final-offer selection and lowest in the last offer by issue of the four conditions. Also, the mean terminal outcomes were the lowest in the final-offer selection and highest in the last offer by issue of the four conditions.

Summary Review of Research Study 9-1-B   The final-offer mode of arbitration appears to create an atmosphere of genuine negotiation, whereas the last offer by issue appears to subvert the collective bargaining process.

*Subbarao, A.V., "The Impact of Binding Interest Arbitration on Negotiation and Process Outcome," *Journal of Conflict Resolution*, 22 (1978), 79–103. Copyright © 1978 by Sage Publications, Inc. Reprinted by permission of Sage Publications, Inc.

Concessions by the union and management were highest in the final-offer mode and lowest in the last-offer-by-issue mode of arbitration. The differences between the parties' final bids relative to salary and work hours were lowest for the final-offer selection and highest in the last-offer-by-issue mode. These differences suggest the possibility that uncertainty as to the amount of the award in the final-offer-selection mode may have led to genuine negotiations between the parties. For the last-offer-by-issue mode, the high last offers between the parties suggest that they were not negotiating in earnest but rather expected the neutral third party to award first one then the other. It is the author's position that final-offer selection creates a real bargaining situation and last offer by issue prevents free negotiations.

Research Study 9-1-C

Does prior knowledge of either conventional arbitration or final-offer arbitration affect the expectations of the participants?

Starke and Notz[2] devised a study using 160 male and female students enrolled in an introductory business course, who received points toward their course grades and were also paid based on their performance.

Each subject functioned as either the plaintiff consumer lawyer or the defendant company lawyer in two separate cases. The object was to negotiate an out-of-court settlement in a damage suit by a consumer claiming to have been injured using the company's product. There were two independent variables: the level of trust (high or low) that existed between the bargainers, and the type of third-party intervention. The four interventions included conventional arbitration, conventional arbitration with mediation, final-offer arbitration, and final-offer arbitration with mediation. The study included three dependent variables: the aspiration level of the bargainers, the dollar differences separating the bargainers at the conclusion of the session, and the bargainers' level of commitment as to attitude and behavior.

Prior to the study, the bargainers were given complete background data about the case and completed a test designed to measure trust. They were not told what the test was measuring. Two days later, the experiment began, with each bargainer receiving a biographical data form on his or her opponent and that person's score on the trust test. Half were told that their opponent had a high trust score and the other half their opponent's trust score was low. They were also told their specific bargaining procedure, with an explanation of the rules.

The results of the study show that the bargainer pairs who expected final-offer arbitration had less difference in their level of aspirations prior to the bargaining and in their offers at the close of bargaining than did those pairs who expected conventional interest bargaining. Also, those bargainers who were exposed to final-offer arbitration were more committed than those exposed to conventional interest bargaining. Finally, the conditions of mediation and trust produced a disappointing lack of results.

Summary Review of Research Study 9-1-C   The study showed a difference in the aspirations and behaviors of bargainers relative to whether they expected final-offer arbitration or conventional arbitration. If both parties, the consumer lawyer and the company lawyer, expected final-offer arbitration at the conclusion of their bargaining, there was less difference between their aspirations prior to bargaining and between their final offers at the conclusion of bargaining. However, this did not occur if they expected conventional arbitration. Also, final-offer arbitration did not create any negative effects; the bargainers were more committed for negotiations than their conventional-arbitration counterparts.

The relationship between bargaining behavior and commitment is an important and a complex one, as witnessed by the lack of results for the effects of mediation and trust. The authors suggest caution regarding the design of the study, recognizing that external validity is a problem for laboratory research, in that the experimental circumstances were not consistent with the real world.

REFERENCES

[1]Grigsby, D.W., and W.J. Bigoness, "Effects of Mediation and Alternative Forms of Arbitration on Bargaining Behavior: A Laboratory Study," *Journal of Applied Psychology,* 67 (1982), 549–54.

[2]Starke, F.A., and W.W. Notz, "Pre- and Post-intervention Effects of Conventional versus Final Offer Arbitration," *Academy of Management Journal,* 24 (1981), 832–50.

QUESTIONS

1. What position would you recommend that David Kenyon, in the research incident, take in attempting to resolve the Sharon Nefferts grievance? Why?
2. If you were a human resource specialist in grievance situations, would you prefer conventional arbitration or final-offer arbitration? Discuss.
3. Do you agree with management's position in terminating Sharon Nefferts over the carrot incident? Explain your position.

Research Incident 9-2:
Gary Barnes and Harvest Time

- Do union members' perceptions differ during a strike and after the strike is settled?
- How accurate is management in making assessments of strikes?
- What are the factors that affect our ability to make sound judgments? Can we improve that ability?

Gary Barnes looked at his watch; it was 1:30 A.M. He had been in the final negotiations of a contract with the local Teamsters Union since 7:00 A.M. yesterday. It had taken two weeks of intense bargaining to reach this stage. There appeared to be one last issue to be resolved, and then both sides could wrap it up.

Gary was a labor relations specialist representing a large gropu of fruit and vegetable growers that were spread across several states. His adversaries were a group from the Teamsters Union who, over a period of time, had demonstrated a willingness to strike—a tactic that had produced a series of wage and benefit increases. When Gary had joined the association of growers five years before, he had discovered that all the contracts expired either before or during the harvest season. Such was the case in the present negotiation, in which Gary represented George Markoff, the manager of a frozen-food plant that processed row crops. George had been ready yesterday to process the already-ripened stringbean crop; any more time spent in negotiation sessions and the bean crop would spoil in the fields. Gary felt that George had reminded him of that fact a hundred times during the last 18½ hours.

On the surface, the last hurdle seemed simple enough, especially when compared to some of the other, resolved issues. The union wanted the birthday of each employee who had been employed full-time for one year to be a paid holiday for that worker. Just as the bargaining session adjourned for a half-hour break, the local Teamsters president, Jamel Hassan, remarked that this benefit would cost George Markoff only $17,000 a year.

Back in the motel room, George told Gary that he would lose over $100,000 this year if the stringbean crop was lost. "Let's settle this now. For $17,000, it isn't worth it," sighed George.

But Gary saw the ploy. "Next year," he warned, "it will be a wedding anniversary off with pay, and something else the following year, and so on." Gary also pointed out that, if they gave in on this issue, the other Teamster locals would demand the same from the other association members.

But with the half-hour break now over and Gary still arguing to stand firm, George Markoff said, "Seventeen thousand versus $100,000—I'm going to agree to it."

RELEVANT EMPIRICAL RESEARCH STUDIES

Research Study 9-2-A

Perhaps George Markoff was fearful of the adverse effect a strike might have upon the attitudes of his employees. What happens to the perceptions of union members when they are faced with the crisis of a strike?

Stagner and Eflal[1] studied a sample of United Automobile Workers members from Ford, General Motors, and Chrysler through the beginning and ending of a strike at Ford. The sample contained 1,182 union members, of whom 405 were strikers (Ford) and 777 nonstrikers (GM and Chrysler). With the cooperation of the union and the automobile companies, a 101-item questionnaire was mailed to the homes of the union members. There was no difference between the strike and nonstrike groups regarding the strike effect and other pertinent variables, and the two groups were not significantly different on demographic variables such as job classification, sex, age, education, union seniority, company seniority, marital status, dependent status, type of community lived in while growing up, and leadership roles in the union. The questionnaire was mailed prior to the strike, then again during the strike, upon settlement of the strike, and seven months thereafter.

The results suggest that the leaders of the union acquired additional prestige and influence over the striking members during the strike, but seven months after settlement, this had vanished to a negative factor. This same phenomenon occurred for militant attitudes and felt membership cohesion, which decreased from a high point to a negative factor (relative to mean score standardized to 0) seven months later. The strikers' willingness to help the union increased up to the strike date, but it decreased rapidly thereafter and at seven months vanished. Interestingly, during this period, the mean score of the nonstrikers' willingness to help the union standardized to zero, was negative, and became increasingly negative at the end. Both the strike and nonstrike union members valued the gains won by a strike more than those gained without a strike. However, this study suggests the generalization that the attitudes and perceptions of the striking union members were not those of the nonstriking union members.

Summary Review of Research Study 9-2-A   The study found that union leaders obtained more prestige and influence over striking members during a strike. The militant attitudes toward the employer increased, along with cooperation in union activities. Further, the gains won by the strike were valued more than similar gains obtained without a strike. However, after a period of seven months from the strike settlement date, the overvaluation of the leadership and of the benefits attained had practically vanished.

Research Study 9-2-B

The incident "Gary Barnes and Harvest Time" represents a situation in which the union is in power. If the delay continued, the processing plant would shut down. What factors are perceived by management as advantageous in a strike settlement?

Shirom[2] investigated strikes involving 100 or more employees in single-plant manufacturing companies, each having a single union bargaining unit. The sample consisted of 51 struck plants selected from background information obtained from state departments of labor in the Northeast and Midwest. All the struck plants were heavily unionized, with 85 percent or more union members. In all cases, the chief negotiators representing management during and after the strike were interviewed, having been contacted no earlier than eight weeks after strike settlement. They were told that a second management representative and two unknown spokespersons would also be interviewed.

The data were slightly skewed, with 25 percent of the settlements being considered by the chief management negotiator to be more advantageous to the union, 34 percent considered a compromise, and 41 percent thought more advantageous to management. The results indicated that the past frequency of strikes, the duration of strikes, and the involvement of a mediator were not significant predictors. Management's perception of an advantageous settlement was positively affected by the breadth of the strike, as represented by more than 250 strikers. This accounted for 6 percent of the advantageous variance. The other predictive factor was management's ability to resist the strike by keeping the plant operating. This was by far the most significant predictor, accounting for 21 percent of the variance of being advantageous.

A final finding suggests that unions are not generally successful in attempts to identify companies that will be the most vulnerable, in having no will or ability to operate a struck plant.

Summary Review of Research Study 9-2-B   The study found that management's perception of a strike settlement as advantageous was positively affected by having a large number of strikers involved and by success in keeping the plant operating during the strike. In 62 percent of the strikes, management attempted to operate the plant, and it was generally successful in 30 percent of the cases. In 70 percent of those cases, strikebreakers were used to keep the plants operating.

However, from the union's point of view, favorableness of a strike settlement is only part of a more complex social psychological outcome. For instance, the union may regard the display of resolve and credibility and the reduction of membership tensions as value benefits of a strike.

The authors suggest that, contrary to another study, unions are not successful in identifying managements that have no will or ability to operate a struck plant.

Research Study 9-2-C

Contract negotiations may become a complex situation involving months of effort. Sometimes, decisions made under such conditions do not reflect the best judgment.

This phenomenon was examined in a study by Pitz[3], who was concerned with the thinking deficiencies resulting from unaided human judgment. It appears that when people are faced with conflicting values, uncertain outcomes, and complex information, they become highly selective in using information. This results in biased and inconsistent decisions that lead to markedly nonoptimal behavior. So the author suggests that decision making will be improved if the decision maker uses the methods of decision analysis. The analysis requires breaking the problem into its separate parts, having the decision maker respond to each part, and then using mathematical rules to combine the separate judgments into one decision. These mathematical rules are based on the principle of expected utility, that one should select the option with the largest expected utility. This approach ensures that every choice and outcome will be considered, although assessing probabilities and utilities is subject to the same biases and inconsistencies of other methods.

Two problems were used in this study, one with a fixed outcome and the other with two possible outcomes. The problems had two independent variables: base-rate probabilities, such as that of passing a test; and logical connections, such as that two separate events must occur before a third event occurs. The author was interested in finding out whether a judgment made directly or one based on an analytical prediction is more sensitive to the independent variables that ought to affect the choice. The processing of selective information usually results in a poor decision, since the selection process leaves out potential information. If the potential information is more complex, the processing will be more selective.

The present study was conducted as part of a lecture on decision making in an undergraduate course on the administration of organizations. The sample was 237 volunteer students, who completed two problems representing a direct judgment and an analytically derived judgment. The study found that people making unaided judgments are insensitive to information (the variables) that should affect their judgments. This insensitivity can be changed if the person makes judgments of the individual parts of the problem. So the smaller the problem part, the more sensitivity.

An important finding was the insensitivity of direct judgments and of judgments resulting from a composite of event probabilities. Apparently, some type of averaging occurs in combining single-event probabilities. Thus, a sizable bias in judgments resulted from the inappropriate combination of single-event probabilities. Finally, the more analytic the level of judgment, the greater was the sensitivity toward the variables.

Summary Review of Research Study 9-2-C   The author suggests that one approach to assisting people in making rational, complex decisions is to use formal methods of decision analysis. The idea is to respond to smaller elements of the problem, assign appropriate probabilities to these elements, and select and combine these probabilities to arrive at an integrative judgment. The study indicated that the more analytical the level of judgment, the greater was the sensitivity to the data.

However, a problem arises when people begin to combine single-event probabilities into a composite-event probability. Apparently, some type of averaging occurs, resulting in an insensitivity to the data. The present study showed a sizable systematic bias in judgments resulting from an inappropriate combining of single-event probabilities. Thus, as more levels of information are integrated, sensitivity to that information decreases.

REFERENCES

[1]Stagner, R., and B. Eflal, "Internal Dynamics during a Strike: A Quasi-Experimental Study," *Journal of Applied Psychology*, 67 (1982), 37–44.

[2]Shirom, A., "Strike Characteristics as Determinants of Strike Settlements: A Chief Negotiator's Viewpoint," *Journal of Applied Psychology*, 67 (1982), 45–52.

[3]Pitz, G.F., "Sensitivity of Direct and Derived Judgments to Probabilistic Information," *Journal of Applied Psychology*, 65 (1980), 164–71.

QUESTIONS

1. In the research incident, how susceptible was Gary Barnes to the demands of the local Teamsters president, Jamel Hassan?
2. Who was the rational decision maker in this incident—Gary Barnes, who wanted to hold out, or George Markoff, who decided to give in? Discuss.
3. You are management's negotiator, Gary Barnes. What would you have done that morning at 1:30? What would be the consequences of your decision?

Research Incident 9-3:
Dubin, Vigen, and Ingersoll—It Sounds Like
a Law Firm

- What is the effect of people's personalities on their behavior in union–management relations?
- Why do people join unions?
- When does sex stereotyping affect judgments in resolving grievances?

The company was a medium-sized, nonunion manufacturer of plastic parts, some of them preassembled, that were sold to larger electrical manufacturers. The product line was varied and constantly changing, resulting in a great deal of involvement by the employees as to techniques and layouts. Generally, the employees were a creative group and appeared to enjoy meeting the challenges of production.

But lately there seemed to be trouble brewing in the moulding and trim department. Bob Dubin, the company's human resource manager, had met yesterday over lunch with Jim Vigen, who was in charge of that department. They had agreed that the behavior of Ginny Ingersoll, one of Jim's employees, was becoming a serious problem, in that it was attracting what Bob felt was the wrong kind of attention—not only in some of the company's other departments but also in the community.

Two factors appeared to be related to the problem. First, Ginny was attending the local community college at night, taking a course dealing with consumer protection, taught by a local activist, Don Parker. Then, last month, the group in moulding and trim had elected her their representative.

Although the company was nonunion, its employees did have an organization, complete with a constitution and by-laws, whose purpose was to meet with management about any employee concerns. This association functioned very informally, mostly as the clearinghouse for company activities, such as the bowling, basketball, softball, and volleyball leagues, birthday parties, weddings, and the like. However, the association's by-laws did include a grievance procedure, and that involved the department representative, who, in a union shop, would have been called the shop or union steward.

Since Ginny's election, Jim had been besieged with complaints concerning alleged injustices and inequities in the moulding and trim department. Most of these complaints were quickly and satisfactorily resolved, although several required Bob Dubin's intervention. Bob and Jim were getting together so often to resolve Ginny's allegations that a company wag had suggested they all go to law school together and form a law firm—Dubin, Vigen, and Ingersoll—specializing in grievance resolution.

The latest injustice Ginny was protesting involved two employees who had worked on a Saturday and received the usual time and a half. However, that Saturday had happened to be the birthday of Abraham Lincoln, and Ginny believed the company should recognize it as a holiday, thus paying triple time. There was no legislation declaring that day a holiday, nor was it specified as such in the by-laws, but Ginny felt it would be an appropriate gesture.

Somehow, Ginny's community college instructor, Don Parker, had become involved on this issue and had notified the local TV station, which had featured the story in its news program the night before. And if that wasn't bad enough, one of Bob's union cronies had telephoned him this morning to tell him that Don Parker was somehow involved with the Teamsters Union.

RELEVANT EMPIRICAL
RESEARCH STUDIES

Research Study 9-3-A

What is the effect of a shop steward's personality on the number of grievances filed? Are the needs of the shop steward a factor in grievances?

Dalton and Todor[1] point out the lack of empirical research in the general area of labor–management relations. In particular, they note that despite agreement that the union is an important part of the grievance procedure, the literature has ignored the effect of the shop or union steward.

The authors suggest that individual differences in the personalities of union stewards, rather than those of the employees doing the filing, may account for varying degrees of grievance-filing behavior. Further, it may well be the individual differences between union stewards, not employees, that affect whether or not a formal grievance will be filed.

They hypothesized that the union steward's personal needs are the critical determinants that account for the substantial variance in grievance-filing behavior—that the number of grievances filed by a steward and the number informally settled with supervisors prior to formal filing may reflect the steward's needs for achievement and dominance. Thus, filing many grievances may be equated with achieving behavior, whereas discussion prior to formal filing is equated to a power shift in which the steward temporarily becomes at least equal to the supervisor.

The study sample was 62 union stewards who represented 3,450 union members in two western communications companies. Researchers administered a questionnaire to these stewards on union premises.

The stewards' company and union tenure ranged from less than one year to over 21 years, resulting in a mode of 11–15 years. Their weekly pay ranged from $126 to $350; the modal age was 26–35 years; 41.7 percent were female and 58.3 percent male; 70 percent were white, and the remaining 30 percent were either black, Spanish-surnamed, Asian, American Indian, or those choosing not to indicate.

The questionnaire used in the study, the Manifest Needs Questionnaire, was developed by Steers and Braunstein and measured needs of achievement, affiliation, autonomy, and dominance. The shop stewards indicated their preferences on a seven-point Likert scale of behaviorally based items. Three other items were asked to determine the number of grievances filed, number of consultations with supervisors, and number of interactions with potential grievants.

The results of the study showed that nearly 12 percent had not filed a grievance within the preceding year, 46.7 percent had filed more than ten grievances, nearly 30 percent had never counseled an employee not to file a grievance, and 62 percent had counseled an employee not to file less than 5 percent of the time.

As to interaction with supervisory personnel, 25 percent of the stewards reported that they had solved potential grievances by discussing them with supervisors only 5 percent of the time. However, 20.7 percent of the stewards had discussed potential grievances with supervisors to solve them over 50 percent of the time.

In analyzing the data, it was found that dominance was significantly related to the number of grievances filed and to discussion with supervisors that had led to an informal solution of the grievance. Further, the need for affiliation was significantly correlated with frequency of supervisor discussion to obtain agreement. However, although need for autonomy was significantly correlated with frequency of supervisor discussion and need for achievement was significantly correlated with the number of grievances filed, another statistical test substantially reduced the number of these associations, causing the authors not to include them in their further analysis.

The study supports the earlier hypothesis that the personal needs of union stewards are related to their grievance behavior. Apparently, a large percentage of stewards do not consult with the union member about the grievance or discuss any potential settlement with the supervisor. The steward's need for dominance appears related to the number of grievances filed, and the need for affiliation is related to the number of resolution discussions held with the supervisor.

Summary Review of Research Study 9-3-A   The study investigated 62 union stewards to examine the association between their grievance behavior and their personal needs. Previous empirical literature has chosen to ignore any such relation.

The authors hypothesized a link between personal needs and grievance behavior for the stewards as to the number of grievances filed, consultations with union members, and informal resolution discussions with supervisors. Significant relationships were found between the stewards' achievement needs, dominance, affiliation, and autonomy and their grievance behavior.

The study concludes that the needs of union stewards are related to their behavior in the grievance resolution process.

Research Study 9-3-B

What are the factors that cause employees to join unions? Are economic or noneconomic factors more important? Are attitudes toward the national union more significant than those toward the local union?

A study by Schriesheim[2] analyzed the effects of economic, noneconomic, and attitude factors in a representative election to determine union certification.

The author says that although evidence is lacking, the general conclusion appearing in published material is that employees vote to be represented by unions primarily for economic reasons, such as higher wages, fringe benefits, and job security. However, this material measures only satisfaction of working conditions and does not consider other, noneconomic or quality-of-work reasons.

The sample subjects in the present study were 59 production workers in a well-automated, medium-sized plastic injection moulding plant in the Midwest. Most of these workers had high school diplomas.

The author distributed a questionnaire, the morning after the vote, to 64 employees who had voted in a union representation election. Election results were not announced until the questionnaires had been completed and returned. The questionnaires contained no information that might identify the subjects. Groups of ten to fifteen employees gathered in the company lunchroom, and both company and union officials requested their cooperation in completing the questionnaire, stressing confidentiality. Of the 64 employees, two refused and three indicated either that they did not vote either way or that they could not remember how they voted.

The questionnaire attempted to measure satisfaction factors, as well as attitudes toward unions in general and toward the local union. The measure of job satisfaction was obtained with the Minnesota Satisfaction Questionnaire (Weiss, Dawis, England, and Lofquist).* Of the 20 different job aspects that the instrument measures satisfaction in, eight were selected, four noneconomic and four economic. Noneconomic aspects were independence, variety, creativity, and achievement; economic were satisfaction with security, company policies, pay, and working conditions.

The union attitudes were measured by two scales: a 20-item instrument of affective attitudes toward unions in general, and a seven-item instrument of affective attitudes toward the local union in the election. Both scales were developed by Uphoff and Dunnette.†

The results of the study indicate that voting for union representation is strongly related to attitudes toward unions in general and toward the local union. The measure of total job satisfaction revealed a substantial negative correlation with pro-union voting.

For all measures, the highest correlations with pro-union voting were produced by the four economic factors, and these were significant. Also,

---

*D.J. Weiss and others, *Manual for the Minnesota Satisfaction Questionnaire (Minnesota Studies in Vocational Rehabilitation 22)* (Minneapolis: University of Minnesota, Industrial Relations Center, 1967).

†W.H. Uphoff and M.D. Dunnette, *Understanding the Union Member* (Minneapolis: University of Minnesota, Industrial Relations Center, 1956).

the correlation for total economic satisfaction was significantly higher than the correlation for total noneconomic satisfaction. Interestingly, a point not mentioned by the authors was the significant negative correlations between pro-union voting and the noneconomic measures of independence satisfaction and achievement satisfaction. Although the noneconomic measures of variety satisfaction and creativity satisfaction also demonstrated negative correlations with pro-union voting, they were not significant correlations.

The author regards these results as a major indication of a closer relationship of pro-union voting to economic factors than to noneconomic factors. Further, there is the indication of a strong relationship of pro-union voting to attitudes about unions and total job satisfaction. Apparently, employees react strongly to such economic job factors as job security, company policies, pay, and working conditions. The author notes that the reasons that employees vote for or against union representation probably change over time, so continual monitoring of voting factors should take place.

Summary Review of Research Study 9-3-B This study measured the effect on pro-union voting in a representative union certification election of economic job satisfactions, noneconomic job satisfactions, attitudes toward unions in general, and attitudes toward the local union.

The sample was 59 production workers in a medium-sized plastic injection moulding company. The data were obtained from questionnaires filled out after the election had taken place but prior to notification of the results.

The results indicated that pro-union voting is more strongly associated with dissatisfaction with economic than with noneconomic job factors. Economic factors included security, pay, working conditions, and company policy. Noneconomic factors included independence, variety, creativity, and achievement. The pro-union vote was strongly related to a positive affective attitude toward the local union and unions in general. There was a strong negative relationship between total satisfaction and pro-union voting.

The author stresses the continuing importance of economic factors to employees and the need of employers to be aware of them.

Research Study 9-3-C

What role does the sex of the grievant play in the amount of attention management gives to the grievance? Is a pleading or a threatening approach more effective? Are the strategies for seeking redress the same for males and females?

A study by Rosen and Jerdee[3] examined a situation of nonlitigable sex discrimination—a situation in which biased or condescending treatment of female employees exists but there is no established standard of treatment of males for comparison that would serve as the basis for a litigable grievance. This type of grievance is usually found in one-of-a-kind situations.

There would appear to be optimal coping strategies for seeking redress of the discrimination, and they would probably differ for females and males. For instance, in the case of a female, a meek, mild, pleading approach, according to attribution theory, might be regarded as the appropriate stereotype behavior and might evoke a mild degree of concern. An aggressive, threatening approach by a female might be seen as at variance with sex-role expectations, resulting in extreme agitation and developing into a litigable case. This threatening approach could be more productive for the female. However, such a response could also cause the manager to react in self-defense with further oppression of the complainant.

Perhaps for the wronged male, such stereotypic expectations are less restrictive, since a demonstration of agitation is of less consequence, owing to the view that the male employee is worthy of greater concern.

The study examined the male-versus-female source of the complaint and the threatening-versus-pleading behavior of the complainant as they affect management's response for justice. The two types of nonlitigable injustice examined were (1) failure to take supportive action, as in a case of missed opportunity for career development; and (2) status inequity, as in a case of an inappropriate desk placement.

The authors hypothesize that a male complainant would receive better treatment than a female, based on the stereotype that males are more valuable and females are more expendable; and further, that soft, pleading appeals would be ignored for females, and that threatening demands would increase management's receptivity to nonlitigable grievances.

The sample subjects were 73 male and 28 female bank employees attending a college management seminar. In the bank, they represented the following management levels: top management, 10 percent; middle management, 71 percent; and supervisory, 19 percent.

The experimental materials used in the study were incorporated into an in-basket exercise. Two employee grievance items were written in four versions so as to manipulate the sex and threat variables. Each of the subjects received only one of the two grievances and was unaware of the other.

The grievance item regarding the missed opportunity for career development was from either a male or a female in the bank's marketing department and indicated the injustice of not being allowed to attend a training conference. The grievant said that on past occasions, other members of the marketing staff had attended, including one of less seniority. In the threat grievance, the male or female used expressions such as, "I insist," "deserves immediate attention," "expect to hear from you," and, "taking immediate action." For the pleading version, the terminology was, "very grateful," "thank you," and, "your consideration."

The other grievance item, of status inequity, was from either a male or a female bank cashier, who complained about a desk location among clerks of lower status. The position taken was that the desk location hindered respect from subordinates and relationships with other officers. The terminology of the threat grievance included, "will not hesitate," "I want action," and, "immediately." The pleading grievance included, "I wonder," "anything can be worked out," and "any possibility."

These two grievances were evaluated by the subjects on two scales: justification for the complaint, and favorableness of reaction to the request. Both scale evaluations were summed to form an eleven-point index of management reception to the grievance.

For the case involving the missed opportunity for career development, the hypothesized main effect for the sex of the grievant was affirmed. When the grievant was a male employee, the management reception to the grievance was significantly better than if the grievant were a female employee.

If a subdued, pleading grievance was attributed to a male employee, it was significantly very well received, whereas if the same approach was attributed to a female employee, it received a significantly low reception. However, a threatening grievance from either a male or a female was only moderately well received.

For the status inequity grievance, there was no significant difference in management reception whether the grievant was male or female. However, the significantly lowest receptivity scores resulted from a passive, pleading appeal from a female employee. In the case of threatening, aggressive demands from a female, higher receptivity scores were observed than those resulting from a threatening demand from a male employee.

The results of the two grievance issues demonstrate that management's reception to grievances is a function of both the form of the grievance and whether the source is male or female. When a male grievant makes a polite, pleading appeal, it is favorably received; an aggressive, threatening appeal is less effective, but it is still well received. Male employees appear to have considerable flexibility in appealing for just resolution of grievances. Management receptivity to grievances from females in an aggressive, threatening appeal is quite favorable, whereas a polite appeal is much less well received.

The authors believe that behavior contrary to role expectations (attribution theory) conveys more information about a person than does more normal behavior. The threatening behavior by the female is inconsistent with the stereotype sex role and thus indicates to management the intensity and seriousness of the grievance, resulting in the more favorable reception.

Summary Review of Research Study 9-3-C   This study investigated the influence of a grievant's sex and the type of appeal used upon the recipitivity of management to the appeal.

The subjects were 101 bank managers who reacted to the grievances in an in-basket exercise. There were two grievances: missed opportunity for career development, and status inequity. They were written in four forms, so as to manipulate the grievance's sex and the type of appeal.

When the grievant was a male and the grievance was made in a polite, pleading appeal, it was very favorably received by management; an aggressive, threatening appeal was fairly well received.

When the grievant was a female and the grievance was made in an aggressive, threatening appeal, it was quite favorably received by management, but a polite, pleading appeal was much less well received.

The authors attribute this to the attention received when a person acts differently from a perceived sex-role stereotype.

REFERENCES

[1]Dalton, D.R., and W.D. Todor, "Manifest Needs of Stewards: Propensity to File a Grievance," *Journal of Applied Psychology,* 64 (1979), 654–59.

[2]Schriesheim, C.A., "Job Satisfaction, Attitude toward Unions, and Voting in a Union Representation Election," *Journal of Applied Psychology,* 63 (1978), 548–52.

[3]Rosen, B., and T.H. Jerdee, "Effects of Employees' Sex and Threatening versus Pleading Appeals on Managerial Evaluations of Grievances," *Journal of Applied Psychology,* 60 (1975), 442–45.

QUESTIONS

1. What do we know about the personal needs of union stewards as they affect their behavior in the grievance resolution process? Be specific. How do the results of the Dalton and Todor study relate to grievance procedures?
2. How do employees regard economic job factors versus noneconomic job factors in voting for or against union representation? What does your answer to that question suggest to the human resource professional relative to the employee work environment?
3. What effect does a grievant's sex have upon management's reception of a grievance? Should a grievant use a threatening or pleading form of appeal?

NON-EMPIRICAL RESEARCH ARTICLE ABSTRACTS

Abstract 9-1

- What is the relationship of the arbitration clause to a no-strike provision in the bargaining agreement?

- When does a court use the coterminous principle?
- How can management use the bargaining agreement to legally discipline union officials as a result of workers' striking?

These questions are answered in a 1984 article by Gary L. Tidwell,[1] an attorney.

Section 7 and Section 13 of the National Labor Relations Act (NLRA) state that employees have the right to engage in concerted activities (strikes). The act also gives employees the right to picket and to honor other unions' picket lines. However, certain types of strikes are not protected. These include sit-down strikes, wildcat strikes, and strikes involving violence. Strikes considered unfair labor practices, such as jurisdictional strikes or secondary boycott strikes, are also not protected.

The federal labor law does allow employees to waive their right to strike, and employers seek to have such a waiver included in collective bargaining agreements. The employer usually agrees in exchange to arbitrate a wide range of grievances. The Supreme Court has held that a no-strike provision can be implied to be part of the bargaining agreement by the inclusion of an arbitration clause. However, even if there is a no-strike clause in the bargaining agreement, strikes may be permissible. The employer's defense against the strike is a court injunction stopping the strike and requiring the employees to report for work.

The purpose of the NLRA is to promote industrial peace. Arbitration of disputes is the substitute for industrial strife. Any doubts as to whether particular grievances are arbitrable are resolved in favor of arbitration.

An employer may seek an injunction against no-strike-clause violators in the federal courts, using Section 301 of the Labor Management Relations Act of 1947. This may occur despite the prohibition against injunctions contained in Section 4 of the Norris–La Guardia Act if certain conditions are met. Perhaps the most troublesome condition for the employer is that the work-stoppage dispute must be arbitrable. If it is not, workers may strike despite the no-strike clause in the bargaining agreement.

A principle used in the courts to determine whether or not an issue is arbitrable is the *coterminous principle;* that is, the principle that the no-strike clause is only as broad as the arbitration clause. One court held, to the detriment of the employer, that damages for a sympathy strike that breached a general no-strike clause could not be collected, since the union can waive its right to strike only when arbitrable issues are involved.

In one such situation, a union engaged in a boycott of Soviet cargo following the Soviet invasion of Afghanistan. The employer used a Section 301 injunction to stop this boycott until an arbitrator's decision could be obtained as to whether the strike was in violation of the no-strike clause in the bargaining agreement. The court ruled against the employer because the labor dispute was a political protest against Russia and could not be resolved by arbitration. The result was that the employer had bargained something away to obtain a no-strike clause that was not effective in preventing all strikes. Employers are now advised to negotiate a provision that would prohibit sympathy strikes.

Employers may discipline employees who engage in a strike violating the no-strike clause. However, even though the NLRB does support selective discipline of employees, this may end up in arbitration in which the employer has the burden of proving "just cause." One approach to this problem is to include such discipline in the bargaining agreement and limit the issues while establishing a more lenient burden-of-proof provision.

The employer may discipline union officials but should be careful to avoid the charge that the discipline was solely the result of their union status. Recent court decisions have placed greater responsibility upon union officials, permitting more severe discipline on them than on the rank-and-file strikers. However, this can occur only when the bargaining agreement states that union officials have an affirmative duty to prevent work stoppages.

Sympathy strikers may be disciplined if workers have waived their right to participate in such strikes in the bargaining agreement, even though this is a protected activity under the NLRA. Without this waiver, the employer will have to rely upon the bargaining history and facts surrounding the contract before disciplining sympathy strikers.

The author points out a recent court decision in which it was found that the no-strike clause in the bargaining agreement was in a separate section from the arbitration clause. To the court, this represented a functionally independent no-strike clause, so that the employer was able to discipline sympathy strikers.

Section 301 permits civil suits to recover damages for a breach of a no-strike provision if the union instigated, supported, ratified, or encouraged the strike. However, Section 301 does not allow damage action against individual union officers or members when it is the union that is liable for violation of the no-strike clause.

In a wildcat strike, the employer cannot seek damages from the union. The courts have continued to protect the parties involved in wildcat strikes from liability. A rare exception was an employer who proved union liability through the agency theory. A union meeting had taken place on the first day of the wildcat strike, and the court viewed this act as demonstrating union support for the strike. This occurred despite the fact that the local union had ordered the strikers back to work and that no vote was taken. It was held that the union authorized the strike by making a collective decision not to return to work. Further, the local union president had sent a telegram asserting that the strike was outside the scope of the bargaining agreement and that the employer's actions violated the employees' rights, and the court considered this act as ratifying the strike. Yet the Supreme Court has acted to shield the parent union from liability and exempt individual workers from civil liability.

Wildcat strikes are very difficult to control from the standpoint of management. For management to recover damages, probative evidence of the union's ratifying the strike must be shown. The author suggests clauses in the bargaining agreement requiring the union to pay for losses and to control wildcat strikes through internal union discipline. This requires separating the no-strike and arbitration clauses and using specific "boiler-plate" language prohibiting sympathy strikes and establishing liability.

REFERENCE

[1]Tidwell, Gary L., "The Meaning of the No-Strike Clause." From the November 1984 issue of *Personnel Administrator,* copyright 1984, The American Society for Personnel Administration, 606 North Washington Street, Alexandria, VA 22314.

QUESTIONS

1. Since federal labor law allows employees to waive their right to strike, what does the employer usually agree to exchange for inclusion of a no-strike clause?
2. What is the problem facing the employer with a no-strike clause in regard to work stoppages?
3. The author suggests employers take certain steps regarding wildcat strikes. What are those steps?

Abstract 9-2

- How difficult are bargaining agreements to read?
- What are some of the available instruments to determine readability?
- Why may some bargaining agreements be purposely written by management and the union to be difficult to read?

A 1984 article by Suchan and Scott,[1] two assistant professors, addresses these questions.

The authors point to the increased strain developing between unions and management, which requires collective bargaining agreements to clearly indicate areas of agreement in order to avoid future conflicting interpretations that will only further increase bad feelings.

Three time-tested readability formulas are used in this study to determine how effectively bargaining agreements are understood by employees, shop stewards, and supervisors. A computer search of the literature revealed only three previous readability studies of bargaining agreements, two in the 1950s and one in 1981. The 1950s studies used the Flesch reading ease formula, designed to determine how easily readers can understand what they are reading. The result showed that the bargaining agreements were difficult to read. The 1981 study used another readability formula, the Gunning Fog Index; however, the authors found that the research was not extensive enough to report on.

The present study obtained 196 collective bargaining agreements from the Bureau of Labor Statistics, with selection based on specified criteria to obtain uniformity. In each agreement, three clauses were analyzed—seniority, discipline, and grievance. These three were selected as being representative of most agreements.

Three formulas were used to measure the readability of the 196 agreements: Flesch, Farr-Jenkins-Patterson, and Gunning. The authors say that although these formulas were selected because they provide an accurate measure, critics have argued that they do not consider specialized knowledge or such factors as graphs and charts. However, linguists and rhetoricians have proved that the variables measure affect reading comprehension and information retention.

The variables used in the three formulas were average number of words per sentence, number of sentences per 100 words, number of syllables per 100 words, number of single-syllable words per 100 words, and number of words having three or more syllables per 100 words.

The three formula results indicate that the clauses for seniority, discipline, and grievance fall into the very-difficult-to-read category. For readers to understand these clauses easily, they would at the very least need the reading skills of a college graduate. The authors believe that most of the rank and file, shop stewards, and supervisors would experience great difficulty in understanding these clauses.

Another result of this study was that many clauses registered negative Flesch scores, which means that they were virtually incomprehensible. The Gunning scores show that to understand the agreement language, readers would need almost 19 years of education.

The authors suggest that the difficulty of understanding the agreements may be either unavoidable or deliberate, owing to the process of writing them out. Sometimes language acceptable to one party is not acceptable to the other, so in an attempt to reach agreement, both parties settle on vague and complicated sentences. Also, time constraints and fatigue during negotiations may result in complicated phrasing.

The authors conclude that the rank and file would have difficulty in reading the typical bargaining agreement, since only those with a college education would find it readable. Further, there has been no progress toward simplification in the past 30 years. The evidence presented in the study indicates that management and union negotiators have much progress to make if bargaining agreements are to be made understandable to the rank and file.

REFERENCE

[1]Suchan, James, and Clyde Scott, "Readability Levels of Collective Bargaining Agreements." From the November 1984 issue of *Personnel Administrator,* copyright 1984, The American Society for Personnel Administration, 606 North Washington Street, Alexandria, VA 22314.

QUESTIONS

1. What is a general criticism of the three readability formulas discussed by the authors?
2. What did the authors find regarding the readability of many clauses as measured by the Flesch formula?
3. What do the authors think of the process of simplifying collective bargaining agreements in the past 30 years?

CHAPTER TEN

TRAINING

INTRODUCTION

The training of employees to be efficient producers of the company's product is an important element of a successful enterprise. The cost of training both old and new employees can be estimated at over $137 billion annually. This should not be surprising, since more than 1.5 million young people enter the labor market each year, and most of them need training.

The most basic and perhaps the simplest training program is orientation for new employees. Usually, very little job-related material is presented; the emphasis is on introductory information and "housekeeping" procedures. The purpose is to make employees feel comfortable in adjusting to the new work surroundings, particularly in the department where they are assigned.

When training goes beyond the orientation phase, it becomes a complicated process of technique and motivation, as employees are persuaded to discard inefficient skills and learn new, more productive skills.

A logical point at which to determine training requirements is the labor planning process. However, since labor planning is not a formal process in most companies, the organization's overall planning and objectives provide a general point of departure to determine organizational needs. This is accomplished through job analysis, which defines appropriate knowledge and skill areas, and performance appraisals, which indicate how adequately these have been attained.

Another approach to determining training needs is to review other organizational records, such as accident reports, grievances, production reports of utilization and product defects, and customer complaints. Other inputs include employee attitude surveys, assessment-center results, and skills tests.

Once the training-needs analysis has been completed, the question of priority arises. Even with unlimited financial resources, the human resource department will be able to cope with only a specific number of training programs. When the priorities have been determined, the next step is to choose the appropriate training methods.

Perhaps the most widespread training method is on-the-job training (OJT), usually conducted by the new employee's supervisor. OJT was developed by the War Manpower Commission during World War II, and that training program is the one usually followed today. Pretraining steps include establishing a timetable to learn the skills, breaking the job into learnable segments, having all the necessary materials available, and arranging the workplace as the employee would find it. The training steps that follow include putting learners at ease and determining present skill levels, presenting the material to be learned by questioning and repeating, having the employees perform the steps and explain them, putting the employees on their own, and continuing to check them on a tapering-off schedule.

OJT requires little special attention; it is flexible and is related to the work the employee will be performing. However, some drawbacks may be poor training, high accident rates, and a disruption of regular work routine.

Another form of OJT is internships, which combine on-the-job training with classroom instruction ranging from trade schools to the university level.

Vestibule training also combines OJT with instruction, but the on-the-job training occurs at a place separate from the actual work area but with similar equipment. Usually there is no pressure for production, and instructors are well trained. However, old and worn-out equipment can result in the learning of poor work habits and increase the possibility of accidents.

Apprentice training is similar to vestibule training, in that it is both on- and off-the-job learning. The training is for skilled work occupations, with the apprentice agreeing to work for a wage well below that of a skilled worker. Such programs last two to five years; most are registered with the Department of Labor, and they usually take place in cooperation with a particular union. A local apprenticeship committee determines the training content, which includes classroom courses and on-the-job experience. The results obtained are excellent, although there is criticism that the programs take too long to complete and that they include unnecessary material. It appears that apprentice programs are too rigid in their content and fail to respond to the changing technology in many occupations, thus producing workers skilled in inflexible occupational categories.

A more individualized form of training allows learners to proceed at their own speed, using materials especially designed for such programs. One such individualized procedure is programmed instruction, which organizes training material into a series of frames, each frame more difficult than the last and building on the information contained in the preceding frame. These frames are usually presented as a series of slides in a teaching machine utilizing multiple-choice questions designed to provide both feedback and positive reinforcement.

Programmed instruction has yielded good results and appears to produce more rapid learning than conventional methods do, but it does have some problems. Although retention is about the same as in other approaches, there is no evidence of superior performance at the end of the programmed instruction period. Also, since the cost of writing the individual frames is very high, this approach requires a large number of employees to be trained before it is cost-effective.

Computer-assisted instruction and programmed instruction are very similar. Most computer programs adjust the instruction to the level of the student, and material is selected to provide the student with the most beneficial format. This flexibility is probably the major advantage, although the cost factor must be carefully considered.

Two relatively new training programs are for retraining and for the culturally disadvantaged. The increasing rate of technological change and the wave of increased international competition, both abroad and in our home market, has resulted in a need to retrain present employees. A serious problem is that many of the employees to be retrained do not have the necessary educational backgrounds to learn new job skills. Similar problems are found in training the culturally disadvantaged person. The federal government has assumed training responsibilities through such representative legislation as the Comprehensive Employment and Training Act of 1973 and the Department of Labor Job Opportunities in the Business Sector (JOBS) program, but the problem of adequate skill preparation remains.

Any training program must utilize the concepts of learning theory if it is to be effective. One of the first steps is to motivate the student to want to learn. This is accomplished by determining what is important to that person—for instance, status, achievement, recognition, or advancement.

Once motivation is established, the new material being learned must be reinforced. Behavior that leads to a reward or satisfies a motive is usually learned, and behavior that does the opposite is not. Thus, we reinforce the desired behavior through rewards or satisfied motivation.

Related to reinforcement is the immediate confirmation or knowledge of results. Employees need to have an understanding of their progress so as to sort out the "bad" behavior from the "good." Without such immediate confirmation, the person may later have to unlearn something that was learned wrong.

"Active practice" is another way of saying "repetition." The employee who is to learn a skill will require repetition and practice. This demands attention and concentration. The successful result is immediate response to the new requirements of the job.

Sometimes the learning of whole self-contained units is preferred to learning only parts of the segments. However, opinions differ on this concept; it appears to be affected by the person's intelligence and the complexity of the material to be mastered.

Another learning-theory concept is the timing of practice directed toward the new task. It appears that spacing out the practice sessions, rather than massing them together, helps people to retain the new material.

After the training program has been completed by means of the appropriate learning-theory concepts, the final step is to evaluate what has been accomplished. A training program should have taught the desired knowledge, and the new skills should result in the anticipated outcomes at the workplace. Evaluation can be accomplished very simply, by taking a measurement before the training and then another at an appropriate time after the training to determine any difference. The cost benefits of the new skills can be compared to the cost of the training program to determine a rough approximation of benefits.

The billions of dollars spent annually on training by business is an indication of the importance ascribed to this function and of the responsibility assumed by human resource professionals for its success. With increased technological change, the aging of our working force, and continuing international competition, the need for training expertise will continue.

RESEARCH INCIDENTS

Research Incident 10-1:
Howard Rudd Asks, Is It the Trainees or the
Training Program That Went Wrong?

- How do different trainers process identical information?
- Which is the most beneficial for trainer improvement, a highly structured training program or a nonstructured training program?
- What role should encounter groups involved in sensitivity training play in developing trainers' complexity of conceptual ability?

Howard Rudd had never received a memo direct from the desk of George Hacker, vice-president of human resources and industrial relations. As manager of the training division, Howard was a small part of the human resource function organizational chart. Yet there the memo lay, smoldering on his desk, awaiting Howard's reply (via a memo, naturally).

The company was launching a new bonus compensation system that was eagerly awaited by the employees. So suddenly, the old procedure of performance appraisals that had been going on for years on end had received the attention of top management; and the result was the present new training program to improve the accuracy and reliability of performance appraisals. But the memo from Hacker informed Howard of management's dissatisfaction with the new program.

The next day, Howard met with his training group, and after 90 minutes there appeared to be no easy answers. The trainees were a diverse group; every one of them was college-educated, was somewhat individualistic, and utilized a wide variety of training methods that were current and in vogue.

Returning to his office, Howard found a note saying that the human resource manager had phoned and wanted Howard to return the call as soon as possible.

RELEVANT EMPIRICAL
RESEARCH STUDIES

Research Study 10-1-A

Do different types of training programs offer different results? Specifically, does a certain type of training program designed to increase rater accuracy result in more efficiency than other well-qualified techniques?

Zedeck and Cascio[1] designed a study to examine both the effects of the purpose of a rating on rater accuracy and rater strategy (the latter defined as the processes raters use in evaluating information—weighing, combining, integrating), and the effects of training and purpose on rating accuracy strategy policy. For example, the accuracy/strategy policy should reflect a difference between those trained and those not trained.

The subjects were 130 undergraduate students in psychology and business administration. Participation in the study was part of a class exercise. Their ages averaged 24 years; 50 percent were males, and 65 percent were Caucasians, 30 percent Asians, and 5 percent blacks or foreign students. There were two independent variables—training (versus no training), and purpose of the appraisal (developmental, merit raise, and retention). The 77 students receiving the training were randomly assigned to the three purpose groups. Their rater training consisted of five hours of instruction in the most common rating errors—leniency/severity, central tendency, halo, and first impression. An additional two to three outside readings were assigned concerning rater training and the performance appraisal process. The purpose of this training was to increase the discrimination power of the raters. These sessions utilized role playing and feedback. While the training was taking place, the nontrained group of 53 students, also randomly assigned to one of the three purpose groups, spent the week in classroom discussion of general issues in management and organizational behavior.

Approximately three weeks later, the experimental material was distributed to both the trained and nontrained groups. The material consisted of 33 one-paragraph descriptions of checkstand performance by supermarket checkers. Each of the paragraphs contained information relating to performance dimensions such as ability to organize checkstand work, knowledge and judgment, human relations skill, monetary transactions skill, and bagging skill. The supermarket checkers' performance was then evaluated by the subjects on a scale of 1 to 7, in their roles of managers of a large supermarket chain. Instruction to the subjects relative to completing the booklet varied as to the purpose of the appraisal (developmental, merit raise, or retention).

The study found that the purpose of the appraisal affected the discrimination of the checkers' performance; less discrimination was shown by the raters in evaluating the ratees for a merit increase. It appears that evaluations differ as a result of their purpose, and that training does not influence the evaluation. In this instance, the difference was strongest between merit-raise and development and retention purposes.

The study also supported the expectation that regardless of training or purpose, the raters would be accurate in their evaluations. Thus, raters would evaluate average performance as average, and those checkers who were described as giving a more positive performance were also evaluated more positively for development, merit-raise, or retention purposes.

Another finding was that the strategy of evaluation differences was not represented by the training/no-training conditions but rather by the purposes of the rating—merit-raise versus development or retention purposes. Apparently, the strategy employed by the merit-raise group relied mainly upon the performance dimension of human relations skill, followed by organizing checkstand work. However, the development and retention groups relied equally upon the dimensions of organized checkstand work and bagging skill. These policy-capturing clusters suggest that the evaluation decisions were made from an organizational and consumer viewpoint. Further, the most homogeneous groups were the development and retention groups, an indication that they were more similar in their use of information than was the merit-raise group. There were no real differences between the trained and nontrained groups.

Summary Review of Research Study 10-1-A   The study suggests that the variability in the ratings of supermarket checkers might have been more the result of the purpose of the rating (developmental, merit raise, retention) than of whether the raters were trained or not trained regarding performance appraisals and common rating errors. Those raters evaluating the checkers for merit pay raises exhibited significantly less discrimination than did raters evaluating for development or retention purposes. It also appears that the rater strategy (how the rater weighs and combines the data in determining evaluation) varies with the purpose of the rating. Identical information was evaluated differently depending on whether the purpose was for a merit raise or for development or retention. The authors state that the purpose of the evaluation is a significant factor in understanding its results.

Research Study 10-1-B

What is the effect of the trainer's style upon the functioning of the group being trained? Does it matter to trainees whether the trainer is a directive or nondirective type?

Ivancevich[2] studied the effect of two different trainer styles upon group development in a formal training program whose object was expanding the knowledge range of the trainees. Two training groups, each of 32 first-level managers from a six-plant manufacturing company, were observed over a five-day period as they participated in a management and organizational behavior training program. After each of the eight sessions, the managers recorded their observations of the group and the training program. Four areas relative to group development were studied: group cohesion, conflict between members, amount of open communication, and degree of productive work. Another variable concerned with trainer–trainee interaction was monitored throughout the program. Trainee attitudes toward the trainer were collected at the end of each of the eight sessions.

The 64 managers were each assigned to one of the two groups by company officials and the author to ensure that they were not well acquainted with others in the same group and were similar in regard to age, educational level, tenure, and salary rates. The eight sessions were in approximately four-hour instruction blocks. The instructional material, the same for both groups, included a text, articles, cases, role playing, in-basket material, and a communication exercise.

The style of the trainer was different for each of the two groups. For one group, the trainer style was structured and task-directed. This group was referred to as the training group structured. The trainer generally lectured at the start of each of the eight sessions, specifying the learning expectation and the methods by which it would be accomplished.

The other group trainer adopted a distinctively different style, was less directive and functional, more of a facilitative role. Lecturing was minimal, free discussion periods were provided, and members were allowed to introduce any ideas they desired. Since the main difference was the amount of trainer control, members often presented the material themselves. This group was called the training group with minimum structure.

The training-group-structured leader reinforced good suggestions, provided immediate feedback, expressed his disagreement with members' ideas, and tightly controlled the time during the sessions. The leader of the training group with minimum structure was the opposite, showing minimum reinforcement, little feedback, and avoidance of disagreements with participants, and giving members control over sequencing of the sessions. Company officials observed the one trainer (the author) who performed the split trainer role for three full days and unanimously agreed that the sessions were conducted as described above.

The data for the study were collected by a 50-item questionnaire using a Likert scale and taking about six minutes to complete. The questionnaire attempted to measure group cohesiveness, interparticipant conflict, communication openness, session productivity, and the members' attitudes toward the trainer. After the questionnaire had been completed, ten members who were randomly selected by the director of industrial relations all correctly identified the particular trainer style used in their group.

The study data reveal that although interparticipant conflict was reduced in both groups regardless of the trainer's style, there was no significant difference between the groups with structured and minimum-structured trainers' styles. In general, there was an improvement in cohesiveness, conflict, communication openness, productivity, and attitudes toward the trainer for both groups. However, the group provided with structure demonstrated a significant difference in group cohesiveness, communication openness, productivity, and attitudes toward the trainer.

Summary Review of Research Study 10-1-B   The same trainer conducted a five-day training session for two groups of first-level manufacturing managers in a management and organizational behavior training program. One group was highly structured by the trainer, and the other group was not. The trainer's style seemed to influence several task activities and structure phases of the groups' development. Specifically, the highly structured group demonstrated more significant improvement in the areas of cohesiveness, communication openness, productivity, and attitude toward the trainer. Since these first-level managers all worked for the same company, the author believes the results achieved in the structured group to be beneficial. Apparently, the directive trainer style was more effective in the development of the group. However, the author points out that these results were obtained from only a relatively small sample of 64 managers.

Research Study 10-1-C

Would it be helpful for trainers to become more complex in their thinking? What benefits would accrue to the trainer? Gardiner[3] conducted a study of the information-processing characteristics of complex thinkers.

The theory involved, complexity theory, concerns the process of thinking rather than what is known. Those who are complex in their thinking tend to discover and use large amounts of information that lead to a variety of concepts. Previous studies had shown that complex thinkers are more creative, more democratic, more empathetic, and more capable of handling decisions in a complex environment. The opposite would be the simplistic person, who uses little information and forms few concepts. Generally, an increase in thinking complexity is accompanied by a greater ability to adapt to stressful or changing situations.

The present study investigated the learning and motivational change of a problem-oriented program, an encounter-oriented program, and a conventional program of instruction. In the encounter-oriented program, the college courses extended over three academic quarters in the junior year. These courses were structured around lecture sessions and weekly two-hour group meetings that had no formal purpose other than making the group into a community similar to that achieved in sensitivity training. The problem-oriented program, which also extended over three quarters, comprised formal lectures and release time for solving interdisciplinary problems in a business laboratory.

At the beginning of the quarter, all students were handed a problem statement with instructions to submit questions to a data-bank operator so as to form hypotheses or concepts relative to the problem. At the end of each quarter, each student submitted a single written laboratory report detailing hypotheses relative to the problem and presenting supportive course material. The course instructor checked the report for application of concepts, a staff psychologist checked for complexity.

The sample for the encounter problem program was 52 students; the sample for the problem program was 33 students; and there were two control groups totaling 58, one for the encounter and one for the problem group, who were enrolled in the regular business program. The reason for two control groups was that the encounter and problem courses were not run in the same year but in consecutive academic years. All students in the encounter and problem programs enrolled on a voluntary basis. The measuring instruments used in the study were the test of General Business Knowledge to determine the content acquisition, the Paragraph Completion Test to evaluate conceptual complexity, and a modified Thematic

Apperception Test that was used because of its demonstrated relationship to entrepreneurial success. Generally, all four groups completed these instruments at the start of the first quarter and again at the end of the third quarter.

The results of the study were that the encounter-oriented program students and the conventional program students were nearly identical as to gains in business knowledge, but the encounter group experienced a significant decrease in conceptual complexity compared to the control conventional program students. Although the encounter group also experienced more decrease in achievement motivation than did the conventional group, the difference was not significant. In a comparison of the problem group with its control conventional group, there was no significant difference in business knowledge at the end of the third quarter and also no significant difference in gains of conceptual complexity, although the problem group demonstrated a larger gain. However, the problem group showed a significantly larger achievement motivation gain than the control conventional group. Also, the problem group significantly outgained the encounter group on the business knowledge, the conceptual complexity, and the achievement motivation measures.

It is interesting to note that there was a significant positive relationship between changes in complexity and changes in achievement motivation in both the problem group and the encounter group. With the conceptual change scores in the encounter group predominately negative, faculty members were asked to rate how effective the participation of the students had been. The result was a tendency to rate those students decreasing in complexity as being more effective in the encounter-group sessions.

Summary Review of Research Study 10-1-C The study found that students in a special problem academic course could raise their level of conceptual complexity. Usually, increasing one's complexity of thinking results in a greater ability to adjust to stressful or changing environments. Those students in an encounter group similar to sensitivity training suffered a decrease in their conceptual complexity ability. They also exhibited a decrease in business knowledge and achievement motivation compared to a gain for the problem group. Although it was not part of this study, the author suggests that raters exhibiting complex thinking, as opposed to simplistic thinking, would be more effective.

REFERENCES

[1]Zedeck, S., and W.F. Cascio, "Performance Appraisal Decisions as a Function of Rater Training and Purpose of the Appraisal," *Journal of Applied Psychology,* 67 (1982), 752–58.

[2]Ivancevich, J.M., "A Study of a Cognitive Training Program: Trainer Styles and Group Development," *Academy of Management Journal*, 17 (1974), 428–39.

[3]Gardiner, G.S., "Cognitive and Motivational Development in Two Experimental Undergraduate Programs in Business," *Academy of Management Journal*, 17 (1974), 375–81.

QUESTIONS

1. What is the effect upon a rater's evaluation of an employee of the stated purpose of the evaluation?
2. You have the responsibility for training a group of trainers. Does your individual style have any effect upon the results of the training sessions? Explain.
3. Complex or simplistic thinking—which serves the trainer best? Explain.

Research Incident 10-2:
Stan Terry Has Heard It All Before

- How effective is computer-assisted instruction for training purposes?
- What is the role of sensitivity training in management development?
- Why should delayed appraisal be used in training programs? Or should it?

Stan Terry had just left the monthly meeting of the American Society for Personnel Administration. The luncheon speaker had been another one of those college professors specializing in personnel management. Of course, like all the rest of that Ivy League crowd, he had called it human resource management. The topic was "Trends in Training Programs." Stan had heard it all before; first it was on-the-job training, then vestibule training, orientation training, apprenticeship peer systems, simulations, groups, and now computers. He had seen them come and go over a period of 15 years, ever since he had been transferred from assistant plant manager to the top job in personnel. For Stan there was only one method of training, and that was on the job, where the watchful eye of the foreman provided the necessary motivation.

Strange, the group had certainly applauded the professor, almost as if they believed all that bull. However, Stan had other matters on his mind as he drove back to the plant. That recent merger with the high-tech company was stirring things up, what with talk of new products and revamping the product line. And then there was the new kid that corporate headquarters had sent down to help him with the paperwork that had suddenly multiplied. For a college graduate, the kid had certainly been considerate and polite, yet he was full of crazy ideas and energy. Stan fumed about corporate democracy as he searched for a parking space in the company lot, remembering the old days when he and the brass all had reserved spots up front. Perhaps that memo on his desk yesterday about early retirement at full benefits was something to look into. Too many new ideas, too fast.

RELEVANT EMPIRICAL RESEARCH STUDIES

Research Study 10-2-A

How effective is peer training? Is it effective in all circumstances? Should the grouping be homogeneous or heterogeneous?

Dossett and Hulvershorn[1] studied the effectiveness of peer training as an active learning source for students using computer-assisted instruction. They made a comparison of peer training via computer-assisted instruction with conventional classroom training and with individual computer-assisted instruction. Also, a comparison was made of the effectiveness of various pairings based on ability.

The subjects were male air force personnel trainees assigned to a 36-week course in principles of electronics. There were three groups: One group consisted of 55 conventionally trained students, a second was of 55 trained by individual computer-assisted instruction, and the third group was of 72 students who were sampled from the same population and paired on four relative levels of ability. The paired students were assigned to terminals where they trained jointly, with a supervisor available for questions and supervision. The individually trained computer-assisted-instruction students were trained singly at an assigned terminal.

Since the training was conducted in blocks, this study began in the third block of instruction for a period of two weeks. If either group completed its training in less than the one week allowed, it could skip the next week, returning the following week to start conventional instruction for block 4.

The study found no significant differences in ability, as measured by a special end-of-week examination among the three instruction groups. The mean training time for the computer-assisted-instruction group that was individually trained was significantly lower than that for the computer-assisted group that was peer-trained, and the time for the latter was significantly lower than that for the conventionally trained group. The variability in training time for the peer-trained computer-assisted-instruction group was significantly less than for the individually trained group.

Since the number of computer-assisted-instruction peer-trained students in the study presented a small sample size, 24 additional pairs of students were then trained as described above and added to the sample, for a total of 60 pairs. This larger sample was then paired into two ability levels that were heterogeneous. One ability or degree level paired ability level 1 with level 3, ability level 2 with level 4. The second ability level or degree paired ability level 1 with level 4. Another pairing was for homogeneous students.

The data for the enlarged sample showed that greater student ability significantly decreased training times. The students' training times appeared unaffected by the ability of their partners. Interestingly, the pairing of homogeneous level 2 students produced a significantly longer mean training time than did any pairing that included a level 1 student. However, if a level 2 student was paired with a level 4 student, the training time was reduced by over 3½ hours. The lowest training times resulted from the homogeneous pairings of levels 3 and 4 students; but when these level 3 and 4 students were paired with lower-ability students, their training time increased. As would be expected, those student pairings with greater ability required less instructor help, although even the slowest pairing, level 2 and level 2, required only 20 minutes of instructor time out of more than 18 hours of training time. The level 4 students were the only level generally able to train their partners without instructor help.

Summary Review of Research Study 10-2-A　　The study suggests the practicality of training two students at the same time on one computer terminal. Achievement scores were equal for peer-trained students, those trained individually with computers, and those trained in a conventional classroom. The peer-trained computer-assisted-instruction students demonstrated a significant reduction in training time and a smaller variance in training time, compared to the individually trained computer group. Relative to student pairing in the peer-training group, student achievement appeared unaffected by partners' ability-level differences. Yet total training time and instructor contact time reacted to student ability level as well as to the pair homogeneity/heterogeneity grouping. Level 2 students required the most instructor help and longer training time, but when they were paired with level 4 students, this time requirement was reduced. Homogeneous pairing appeared best for very low-ability students, with the best heterogeneous pairings being level 2 students with level 4.

The authors caution that the computer-assisted instruction was a relatively short one week, the computer training situation was artificial, and the heterogeneous pairs were actually very homogeneous. That is, the students were all enlisted air force personnel, male, and between 18 and 20 years old, and all had high electronics aptitude scores.

Research Study 10-2-B

How effective is sensitivity training or the T-group as a human resource technique? Is it being used in business organizations?

Kearney and Martin[2] studied the controversy over sensitivity training in management development programs by mailing a questionnaire to 300 U.S. business firms each employing 1,000 or more employees. The firms were drawn from each of the nine census regions in the United States in proportion to the number of firms employing 1,000 or more in each region. The response rank-ordered from 1 to 6 the effectiveness of quantitative analysis techniques (game theory, operations research), sensitivity training (T-groups), seminars, in-basket techniques, conferences, on-the-job experience and job transfers, role-playing, and any other techniques the respondents wished to indicate.

The study found that on-the-job experience and job transfers were perceived as clearly more effective than any other technique. The lowest-ranked technique was sensitivity training; of the companies responding to amount of time devoted to sensitivity training, almost half responded that they did not set aside any time in their management development programs for sensitivity training. Of the other half, 36.9 percent spent less than 10 percent of their training time on sensitivity training, 5.3 percent spent between 10 and 25 percent, and 1.7 percent spent over 25 percent. When asked whether the time devoted to sensitivity training would increase, remain the same, or decrease over the next five years, slightly over half said they believed the time allotment would be unchanged, and one-fourth believed it would increase.

The 99 personnel directors who said they used sensitivity training were asked whether there were any observable behavior changes in those managers who participated. Almost 45 percent reported observable changes, 15 percent said none, and 35 percent could not determine any change or felt there was some small change. The remainder did not answer the question. Perhaps even more important was the question about whether the personnel directors believed sensitivity training had improved managerial performance. Forty directors felt that the training had improved performance, 43 said it had not, and the rest either were unsure or did not respond.

The final question to the personnel directors asked whether they would recommend to other firms that sensitivity training be emphasized in management training programs. Of those who replied, 26.2 percent said yes, and 48.9 percent said no.

Summary Review of Research Study 10-2-B Sensitivity training ranks low as a management development technique in comparison with other approaches. The study suggests that it is not regarded as an important part of management development and perhaps is less effective than other techniques. Of those companies utilizing sensitivity training, only a small portion noted permanent behavioral change. As to whether it actually improves managerial performance, users of sensitivity training were about evenly divided, positive and negative. Nearly half the responding personnel directors would not recommend its use to other companies. It appears that sensitivity training is not now an important part of management development training nor does it appear that it will be in the future.

Research Study 10-2-C

How effective is role playing as a training technique in management development programs? What are the effects of goal setting and reinforcement in causing management training programs to be more effective?

Wexley and Nemeroff[3] studied the use of positive reinforcement and goal-setting techniques as a means to improve the supervisory skills of managers. Two programs were established, one using delayed appraisal sessions and goal setting, the other using delayed appraisal sessions, goal setting, and immediate reinforcement. The objective was to determine whether the programs would improve the consideration and integration skills of the managers, thereby increasing subordinate job satisfaction and reducing absenteeism.

A large urban medical center participated in a management development program involving nine departments: nursing, medical records, credit, office service, housekeeping, laundry, supply service, maintenance, and food service. First, the department heads were put through the training exercises to obtain their understanding and commitment. Then, 27 managers who were subordinate to the department heads entered the training program. These managers were five males and 22 females, mostly first-level supervisors, and aged 21 to 53 with two to 17 years' managerial experience. Their 114 subordinates, who averaged a twelfth-grade education and approximately nine years employment at the hospital, filled out questionnaires.

The 27 managers were randomly assigned to two experimental groups and one control group. Experimental group 1 utilized role playing with delayed appraisal and goal setting. Experiment group 2 utilized role playing with delayed appraisal, goal setting, and immediate reinforcement, called telecoaching. The control group received no positive reinforcement or goal setting. Each group was randomly assigned nine managers and three to six of each manager's subordinates, so that group 1 was composed of 37 subordinates, group 2 of 43 subordinates, and 34 subordinates in the control group.

The training for group 1 was in two phases, two 4½-hour workshops that took place on two consecutive days, with trainees participating in role-playing exercises. Each exercise required certain behaviors of effective and ineffective supervisors. The trainer was very specific as to the effectiveness of the trainees' behavior. In the delayed-appraisal sessions, criticism was kept to a minimum, and trainees were told how well they were doing and improving. Also, performance goals were assigned to the trainees.

After the workshop, trainees returned to their jobs and began the second phase. This required filling out a daily behavioral checklist that included items from the Leadership Behavior Description Questionnaire (Stogdill), the Leadership Opinion Questionnaire (Fleishman), and the Survey of Organizations (Taylor and Bowers). After the first and third weeks, the trainer met with the trainees to assist with any problems and to assign specific performance goals.

The training given to group 2 was similar to that of group 1, with the exception that telecoaching was added. Telecoaching is an attempt at changing behavior through verbal feedback—an ear microphone device by which the trainer verbally reinforces and shapes the trainee's behavior during role-playing exercises. The control group did not use this ear microphone, kept no daily checklist, and performed no goal setting. The role-playing exercises that were used lasted from 15 to 50 minutes. One exercise required the trainee to confront three subordinates who wanted the same vacation dates. The second required the trainee to tell a group of three subordinates that they were taking advantage of a flexible coffee break. Another required the trainee and two subordinates to organize a garment manufacturing company to maximize profit. A fourth exercise required denying subordinates' requests for deserved overtime. The fifth exercise was an interview situation regarding evaluations. For each role-playing exercise, lists of desired behaviors were constructed and were used by the trainer to assign performance goals, to conduct delayed appraisals, and for telecoaching. Subordinates used a list of 35 items from the Leadership Behavior Description Questionnaire to anonymously describe the leadership behavior of their immediate supervisor. Two scales from the Job Description Index (Smith, Kendall, and Hulin) were used by the subordinates to describe satisfaction with work and with the supervisor.

The results of the study showed that group 1 (delayed appraisal plus goal setting) and group 2 (delayed appraisal, goal setting, and telecoaching) were significantly better than the control group on consideration and integration scales of the Leadership Behavior Description Questionnaire. However, neither experimental group was significantly different from the other on these scales. As for work satisfaction, group 1 was significantly higher than either group 2 or the control group, between which there was no significant difference. It was also found that although the two training programs did not significantly differ from each other on absenteeism, they were significantly lower on this than the control group was.

Summary Review of Research Study 10-2-C   This study found that two training programs utilizing goal setting and positive reinforcement procedures, one using delayed-appraisal sessions and goal setting and the other using delayed-appraisal sessions, goal setting, and immediate reinforcement, were slightly more effective than the control group on measures of behavior and absenteeism. The program of delayed appraisal and goal setting was significantly more effective in increasing the work satisfaction of subordinates than was the program of delayed appraisal, goal setting, and telecoaching (immediate reinforcement). The assigned goal setting appeared to be effective.

The authors say that a limitation of the study is that there was no investigation of how individual differences interact with the particular training programs used. Their causal observation is that the telecoaching method worked best with younger and better-educated trainees.

REFERENCES

[1]Dossett, D.L., and P. Hulvershorn, "Increasing Technical Training Efficiency: Peer Training via Computer-Assisted Instruction," *Journal of Applied Psychology,* 68 (1983), 552–58.

[2]Kearney, W.J., and D.D. Martin, "Sensitivity Training: An Established Management Development Tool?" *Academy of Management Journal,* 17 (1974), 755–60.

[3]Wexley, K.N., and W.F. Nemeroff, "Effectiveness of Positive Reinforcement and Goal Setting as Methods of Management Development," *Journal of Applied Psychology,* 60 (1975), 446–50.

QUESTIONS

1. You are working on a computer-assisted training program. The training director wants you to include peer training. What should you be aware of? Explain.
2. Sensitivity or T-group training is not very popular with your human resource manager. What are the pros and cons? Discuss.
3. How do you implement role playing and immediate reinforcement without being disruptive? Has telecoaching been proven effective? Discuss.

Research Incident 10-3:
Virginia Mulcahy Tells Richard Robinson His
"Successful" Training Program Is Not Working

- How does trainability testing differ from the work-sample approach?
- What is the effect of feedback on safety performance when it takes place daily as opposed to once or twice a week?
- How do lectures affect the ability of observers to be accurate?

It was all too much for Richard Robinson to hear. The morning had started out with his most valuable trainer telling him of having received a generous offer from a nearby competitor. Then the new videotape on stress that had been scheduled to be shown this afternoon had been mis-labeled and couldn't be located. And now, Virginia Mulcahy had informed him that the recently completed training program in her department was a bomb. As head of the training section, Richard knew it was going to be a long day.

The next day, Richard met with Virginia to discuss the training prob-lem. Even as he sat down, he thought it was impossible that the program had failed—his best people had worked on it, and the company had spared no expense in its preparation and presentation. But Richard was a human resource pro, and he had learned long ago to keep his initial thoughts private, approaching events with an open mind. Besides, Virginia Mulcahy was one of the company's best production managers, and if past history was accurate, she would be well supplied with the facts and figures to support her position. Yep, history sure repeats itself, thought Richard when he saw the numerous graphs and computer printouts Virginia set before him, all of them complete with red circles and notations that seemed endless.

The story was simple. The latest data indicated that since the comple-tion of the training program, production was down, quality was poor, and costs were marching out of sight.

However, Richard had not come to the meeting unprepared. He countered Virginia's position with several sets of test scores on the training material presented to her group, and they were generally all very high. Further, her employees' comments on the Trainer-Session Appraisal Form were very complimentary regarding the thoroughness of the presentations and the appropriateness of the material.

So what had happened?

RELEVANT EMPIRICAL RESEARCH STUDIES

Research Study 10-3-A

How are employees selected for training? Do we waste training re-sources training those already competent? Are there techniques available to determine who will succeed or fail during a training period?

An article by Robertson and Downs[1] reviewed a series of statistically significant studies of trainability tests. The authors point out that many research articles on work sampling relate to people already trained and able to perform the work, and the test is designed merely to indicate the best applicants. However, the problem in many applications is the need to choose people to be trained to do the job. In essence, this study was an attempt to predict a person's ability to learn the job. The authors report that attempts to accomplish this through psychological tests have met with only moderate success, and that the predictive power of aptitude tests has also not been impressive.

A prime use of trainability testing would be to relocate older workers into proper jobs for retraining. An example would be the agricultural worker who wants to go into welding. The usual practice is to begin training for a probationary period to see if the applicant has the right stuff. But when failures occur, this experiment becomes costly in resources, energy, and time. One kind of trainability tests is those designed for carpentry and welding, which take about 30–45 minutes to administer and grade. The following is the general form of training: A standardized form of instruction and demonstration is used, with the instructor teaching the task and the applicant asking questions; the applicant then performs the task unaided, and the instructor records a rating of the applicant's potential success, using a standardized error checklist.

One study reported was used to assess the success of trainability testing in government (United Kingdom) training centers. The trades involved were carpentry, electric arc welding, sewing machine operation, fork-truck operation, electronic assembling, dentistry, metal using, fitting, electrical work, bricklaying, center lathe turning, and capstan operation. The trainees in the study, whose ages ranged from the early twenties to the late fifties, had chosen their trades before entering the skill center, and shortly thereafter, they were tested before having received any prior instruction. The trainees then continued the trade training program, with the results of the test unknown to the instructors. At the end of the usual three-week probationary period, the instructors assessed the trainees' performance on a five-point scale. The results revealed that the trainability tests were successful in predicting training progress.

One of the first steps in developing trainability tests is to determine the task to be used in the test. This normally requires a job analysis, which includes obtaining learning-behavior critical incidents from both good and bad trainees. These chosen learning tasks should be based on crucial job elements, should use only knowledge and skill obtained during the learning period, should be complex enough to permit observation of a range of errors, and should be completed in a reasonable amount of time.

Since the job tasks are supposed to be demonstrated to the applicants in a standard fashion, thus overcoming any ineffective individual styles of instruction, the authors suggest providing the instructors with a precise format. Such a format of instruction for task demonstration should indicate the tools, equipment, and materials needed; the sequence of operations to be followed; and an indication of points to be emphasized and of where the trainee should participate.

The trainees are judged on five-point rating scales. Although these rating scales are subjective, past practice has shown them to be as successful predictors as are objective and behaviorally anchored checklists. Also used is an error checklist that draws the instructor's attention to important items while also serving to improve the validity of the rating.

The trainability tests are similar to work-sample tests, in that both display high content validity and face validity. Since the test content is related to the job, the tests are favorably viewed by the trainee and the assessor.

Further, trainability tests provide the trainee with a more precise understanding of what the particular training program will involve. The authors report of one study in which applicants who scored poorly on a test for sewing machine operation were still invited to report for work. On a scale of A to E, only 9.3 percent rated A failed to report, but 76.9 percent of those rated E failed to report. Such a test allows a person some self-appraisal while also reducing the number of frequent quits.

Although trainability tests have been used only with psychomotor skills, the authors suggest that they are useful in a wider range of occupational areas, such as in training managers.

Summary Review of Research Study 10-3-A   This study considers the work-sample approach and the trainability-testing approach to personnel selection. Trainability testing differs from work sample in providing a structured learning period and a systematic observation of not only what is done but how well it is done.

The test is designed to predict training performance prior to the beginning of the training program. It requires a job analysis that includes the learning behavior of both good and bad trainees.

Training tests are useful in semiskilled manual tasks, including areas where written psychometric tests are poor predictors of trainability. Since the semiskilled areas have an increasing need for people to be retrained, training tests also serve as valid selection and counseling instruments.

The authors suggest that well-constructed trainability tests could prove useful in areas of social skills and management skills.

Research Study 10-3-B

Does training alone provide sufficient momentum to maintain increased performance on the job? Or does training only begin the improvement process, during which continual reinforcement is necessary to maintain the new levels of performance?

A study by Komaki and others[2] investigated whether training alone would substantially improve and also maintain job performance, or whether it would be necessary to provide feedback. The study differed from previous empirical studies in that the training aspect was presented by itself and the results recorded before the feedback element was introduced. Also, the data in this study were collected three to four times a week for almost a year, thereby providing an extended period over which to observe the effects. Finally, the sample population represented a more skilled group than had previously been studied.

The study took place in the vehicle maintenance division in a large western city's Department of Public Works. Although this division had one of the highest accident rates in the city, it was still comparable to the average rates of similar departments in other cities.

The vehicle maintenance division consisted of several sections: sweeper repair, with seven employees; heavy-equipment repair, with four; preventive maintenance, with 37; and light-equipment repair, with seven. These sections were very different in terms of their members' seniority and age. Heavy-equipment repair included both the oldest, with a mean age of 53.5 years, and the most experienced, with a mean seniority of 31.8 years. Light-equipment repair had the youngest and least experienced, with a mean age of 32 years and a mean seniority of 11.5 years.

To obtain study safety items, the accident logs for the preceding five years were analyzed. Items were collected, and the section supervisors were asked for suggestions. During this initial period, supervisors and workers were invited to eliminate inappropriate items. The result was four categories of items: proper use of equipment and tools, use of safety equipment, housekeeping, and general safety procedures. Since there were differences in the work requirements of the sections, items were tailored to each section.

People who had been trained as raters coded each appropriate safety item in full view of the workers. An observation would last a total of 60 minutes: The raters would spend five minutes in each of the three sweeper-repair sections, ten minutes in the heavy-equipment repair section, five minutes in four preventive maintenance sections, and, in the light-equipment repair section, ten minutes in one location and five minutes in another.

These observations occurred from four to five times each week for the first three phases. For the last two phases, observations were reduced to an average of three times a week. In all the phases, times were varied so that no two consecutive visits were the same. The result was a total of 165 observations taking place over a 45-week period.

A second observer was present for 21 observations to record agreement with the primary observer. This was a check on interrater reliability, with agreement reached on an average of 94.8 percent of the observations. A check of observer bias was also made, with approximately half the observations made by three persons who agreed on an average of 94.4 percent.

A behavioral analysis, or assessment of behavioral factors that contributed to unsafe practices, was conducted. It was found that newly hired workers did not receive formal safety training. There was little recognition of safe or unsafe practices; in fact, in some cases, unsafe practices were being reinforced.

Research Study 10-3-C

The Achilles' heel of any training group is the ability of the people involved to be accurate observers of the situation that warrants improvement or new directions. This requires the ability to detect what is needed, to perceive how things are progressing, and to recall accurately or recognize behavior that either supports or does not support what is supposed to take place. Can observer accuracy be increased? What form should such a training program attempt?

A study by Thornton and Zorich[3] suggests such a program. The author observe that the primary source of data is the human observer and that prior research has failed to distinguish between processes of observation and those of judgment.

The process of judgment includes categorizing, integrating, and evaluating information. Previous studies had attempted to improve the accuracy of the judgment process, but the present study was concerned with improving the observation process. This function is more basic and includes the detection, perception, and recall or recognition of particular behavioral occurrences.

According to the authors, observation accuracy is usually measured by interrater agreement. However, this analysis is sensitive only to random or unsystematic errors; systematic errors, which affect all observers in the same way to decrease observation accuracy, are not evaluated by interrater agreement. To correct this, the present study used a method to evaluate observer accuracy that is independent of interrater agreement.

The training program content in the judgment studies had emphasized improving observation of the information-gathering skills of detection and perception. The dependent variables were interrater reliability and rating errors such as halo, leniency, similarity, and contrast. In the present study of the observation process, the dependent measure used was the recall and recognition of particular behavioral occurrences.

The study attempted to evaluate two lecture training procedures that were hypothesized to increase the accuracy of observers. The first lecture was concerned with behavioral instructions; it emphasized the need to observe carefully, to be on the lookout for specific behaviors, and to take notes. The second lecture was concerned with error instructions; it contained the same material but also presented several systematic errors of observation. Systematic errors are the constant, nonrandom effects that people introduce into communications with others. They occur when we attempt to duplicate or transmit or translate information from a source and then offer a response. The observers were trained to avoid eight of the most relevant errors of interpersonal perception (introduced later).

The study subjects were 170 students enrolled in an introductory psychology course at Colorado State University. They viewed a 45-minute videotape of a leaderless group discussion by three male and three female industrial managers. The group was attempting to decide how to divide among six candidates an $8,000 discretionary salary increase. After individual presentations, each member of the group argued for his or her own candidate with the intent to allocate the money equitably.

To measure the representative behavior of the group, a questionnaire was developed regarding objective facts about the group members and the candidates. The correct answers were the actual behavior as demonstrated on the tape. The questionnaire items were to be evenly distributed over the tape; items about group members were to be proportional to their speaking time; the format was to be true-false, multiple choice, and matching; there was to be internal consistency with item categories; and the difficulty levels were to be equal throughout. The questionnaire was then given to an untrained group, which viewed the tape and then selected those question items that met the criteria above.

The procedure for all the study subjects was for groups of ten to twelve students to attend a two-hour research session in which they were presented with one of three randomly selected instruction modes. In Group A, the control, the students were instructed to watch the tape, to take notes, not to talk to anyone during or after the viewing, and to be ready to answer several questions about the discussion at the conclusion of the tape.

Group B, behavioral instructions, was told to observe the tape carefully and make a concerted effort to observe as many details as possible, to note specific verbal and nonverbal behaviors, and to make notes that included who said what to whom and when.

Group C, error instructions, was given the same instructions as Group B, plus a lecture that included labels, definitions, descriptions, examples, and avoidance tips on the eight systematic observation errors. These eight errors were loss of detail through simplification; overdependence on a single source, such as making snap judgments; middle-message loss; forcing observations into categories instead of remembering differences between ideas, called categorization error; contamination from prior information; letting the situation or the setting influence observations, called contextual error; prejudice and stereotyping; and being too influenced by one characteristic of a person, called halo effect.

The various sets of instructions lasted three minutes for Group A, five minutes for Group B, and 15 minutes for Group C. The tape was played first, then the questionnaire was administered.

The results of the study indicated a significant difference between groups A and B, B and C, and A and C. Both lectures increased the accuracy of observers. Behavioral training alone increased accuracy; but there was a further significant increase of accuracy with the additional training on how to avoid the eight systematic errors of observation. The authors believe the study results have application where observation is important in gathering information.

Summary Review of Research Study 10-3-C   The study investigated two training procedures that it was hypothesized would improve the accuracy of observers in gathering information.

The subjects were 170 college psychology students who were divided into three groups and trained via three different sets of instructions. All three groups watched a 45-minute videotape of a leaderless discussion group.

The subjects in Group A (control) watched the tape, took notes, did not talk to anyone, and were prepared to be asked questions after the viewing. Group B (behavioral instructions) received the same orientation, but they were also told to observe carefully, try hard to remember details, note specific verbal and nonverbal behavior, and take complete notes of who said what to whom and when. Group C (error instructions) received the same instructions as Group B, but they were also given a lecture stressing labels, definitions, descriptions, examples, and how to avoid eight systematic errors of observation. A questionnaire was developed to which the subjects responded after viewing the tape.

The results showed significant differences between the groups. Both lectures increased observer accuracy, but it was further enhanced by training to avoid the eight systematic errors of observation.

REFERENCES

[1]Robertson, I., and S. Downs, "Learning and the Prediction of Performance: Development of Trainability Testing in the United Kingdom," *Journal of Applied Psychology*, 64 (1979), 42–50.

[2]Komaki, J., A.T. Heinzmann, and L. Lawson, "Effect of Training and Feedback: Component Analysis of a Behavioral Safety Program," *Journal of Applied Psychology*, 65 (1980), 261–70.

[3]Thornton, G.C. III, and S. Zorich, "Training to Improve Observer Accuracy," *Journal of Applied Psychology*, 65 (1980), 351–54.

QUESTIONS

1. What is the difference between the work-sample and the trainability-testing approaches to selection? To be descriptive of good or bad learning behavior, what criteria should the learning tasks satisfy? Explain.
2. What are the components of a training program to achieve an increase in safety-related behavior? Explain. Indicate in your program the emphasis or deemphasis on feedback.
3. What is the "best" training method to improve observer accuracy? How is it

achieved? Name and discuss the function of the eight systematic errors of observation.

NON-EMPIRICAL RESEARCH ARTICLE ABSTRACTS

Abstract 10-1

- What is the relationship of the problem statement to a needs analysis of training?
- How appropriate to organizational problems is the training process?
- Under what circumstances does training failure occur?

These questions are treated in a 1984 article by Carol Haig, a staff development manager.[1]

Rather than relying on outside consultants or films to train employees, Haig says, a company can save money and time by using the line managers as its training resource.

The author believes that with their technical expertise, line managers who are given the proper guidelines, simple methods for deciding when to train and the best approaches, are capable of being effective trainers. First it must be decided whether training is needed, who should be trained, and what the goals of the training program are, and an outline meeting these goals must be made. The training program should accommodate changes in company procedures and provide a program evaluation to determine whether goals are met.

Training failure results from problems that cannot be resolved by training. To ensure that this does not happen, a basic needs analysis is completed that looks to training either to support a new product, procedure, or position, or to correct a performance problem. In either case, an accurate problem statement is needed, with the needs analysis identifying what is to be learned. A performance problem indicates the difference between the current performance and what is expected. The deviation between the two represents a good problem statement.

The author says that of the problems considered to be training-related, only 20 percent require training; the other 80 percent are due to other organizational issues. For instance, people may not need a remedial program if they once met standards. People perform substandard work for a variety of reasons, and lack of training might not be one of them. A clear problem statement will indicate this.

However, once a training problem exists, certain questions must be answered in designing and implementing a training program: What is the training problem? What knowledge and skills are needed? What has been taught in the past? Were there failures, and if so, why? Perhaps there is no past training history, and there should be compelling reasons not to proceed with a training program.

The author looks to training history as a key. If there have been past unsuccessful attempts, perhaps new efforts should not be pursued.

Determination of what needs to be learned can be very difficult. It may require examining individual behavior to find out what causes a person to fail. The problem could be as simple as failure to proofread material before committing it to final text.

Another decision is who is to receive the training. When the group becomes more diverse, it encompasses different levels of expertise. Those who will benefit most from the training become the target group. Once they are identified, a clearly defined objective of what they should be able to do as a result of the training is as important as the problem statement is to needs analysis. Such a well-defined objective consists of givens such as what the employee has to work with; the task, or what the learner will do; and the standard, a statement of acceptable performance.

The activities in the training program should all support the specified objectives. These objectives will define in measurable terms what the trainee will be able to do after the training, will establish a testing base, and will focus on an achievable goal.

Another step in developing the program content is to determine what the trainees need to learn, so that they can demonstrate their new knowledge. This requires listing the detailed applications of the particular work skill. Each revised listing of a technique, such as using a spell-check program or reading backwards, requires an estimate of the time to accomplish it and the necessary teaching methods.

The final step is to refine the training content outline as materials are added to the program. Program implementation requires consideration first of the methodology and the specific materials to be used. Rules to follow in presenting a program include using a simple and comfortable method, using successful learning methods, and determining an overall approach. Consider classroom, lectures, large-group discussions, small-group activities, and pre- and postwork assignments. Avoid boring details; use flip-charts, handouts, case studies, readings, manuals, chalkboard, slides, and video tapes. Also, assign unfamiliar materials to the trainees to do as their own responsibility.

One approach is to use a three-column worksheet, with column 1 representing starting and ending times, column 2 for activities you or the participants will do, and column 3 for your content outline.

In building a program, include measuring devices that allow you to set standards of trainee performance. In this way, you are able to measure the training results.

Sometimes even well-trained people lose their momentum or lower their performance level, so rewards and incentives are needed to keep participants working effectively.

In any training program, the three most important factors are to present the problem clearly, to make sure that training is the solution, and to recognize that most of the time, training will not be the answer.

REFERENCE

[1]"A Line Manager's Guide to Training," by Carol Haig, copyright October 1984. Reprinted with the permission of *Personnel Journal,* Costa Mesta, California; all rights reserved.

QUESTIONS

1. Why does the author believe that a company can save money and time by using the line managers as its training resource, rather than relying on outside consultants or firms to train employees?
2. What is an accurate problem statement? How is it determined?
3. When well-trained people lose their momentum or lower their performance level, what may be needed?

Abstract 10-2

- Why isn't the primary role of the training department to provide training?
- What is the danger of large training facilities and staff?
- Where should the training director and the training staff spend their off-classroom time?

Frank O. Hoffman, a consultant, answers these questions in a 1984 article.[1]

The author says that training is the personnel function least understood by personnel managers, training directors, and line management. Training is often judged by student reports, supervisor reports, and budget reports. These factors are irrelevant to the reason for the existence of training.

Perhaps the obvious reason for a training department is to provide effective training at an effective cost. Yet, if the goal is for training to make a significant profit contribution, this obvious reason is wrong. Training programs are presented whether they are needed or not and whether other, less costly solutions are available. Courses are established to justify the training staff and keep the training function alive.

The real purpose behind the existence of a training department is to determine whether training is the best solution to a problem. Sometimes a training department was established to satisfy a particular need that no longer exists.

When the purpose of the training department is to provide training, the result is an increase in budgets, since training facilities are built simply to perpetuate training. The author calls this approach "more is better," and says that the costs are large but the contribution is small.

To support his position, Hoffman says that some firms use a "training needs analysis" consisting of a selection of topics from a list of possible course titles. The list of course titles always corresponds to the interests of the training staff, and the titles receiving the most votes win. The needs analysis rarely begins with the organizational problems or opportunities. The catalog approach of offering the current topics of communication, stress, motivation, and assertiveness does not address the true needs of the organization.

Large training centers that duplicate the curricula of local colleges are topic-oriented and not needs-oriented. When offerings are not based on needs, the survival of such training is frequently dependent on popularity. The author says that there are hundreds of situations in which student ratings of instructors have little correlation to what was learned and applied. Classes become filled by managers given "quotas." Training is not supporting managers; rather, managers are supporting training.

The contribution of such training can be only inferred but costs can be measured. To control costs, a limit is put on what a day or hour of classroom time should cost. This can be altered by increasing class size to reduce the cost per student. Trainers on a salary can offer more courses, thus reducing the cost per course. This amortized cost also results in lengthening the duration of classes. Such attempts are not conducive to effective training.

One cost-effective approach is to put consultants on a declining per-student fee. This gives the consultant a higher day rate but results in a lower per-student rate. Further, consultants can then develop larger group instruction techniques, since there is no guarantee that smaller classes produce more learning.

Another cost-effective approach is to have the training department establish its own budget and objectives. This puts the responsibility on the trainers and not on the line managers. However, the budgets and training objectives should result from the plans of the line managers and not from the training staff.

One approach to determining how the training department regards its basic purpose is to see how the training director and staff spend their off-classroom time. If they are refining lessons and designing teaching aids, the primary emphasis is probably on training.

Personnel managers divert training from its real mission by ignoring the following guidelines: Don't judge training on the number of courses offered; don't set training objectives prior to consulting line management; don't overreact to student evaluations; don't judge the training director as a manager but as a training consultant to line managers; don't accept test scores and completed courses as the training department's contribution to profit; don't view training as personnel's responsibility but as the line manager's responsibility; don't have training "fix" a problem without first conferring with line management; allow the training department free access to managers without going through the personnel manager; and don't accept surveys and questionnaires as valid training needs.

The author repeats that the fundamental purpose of the training department is to decide whether training is the solution to a problem or an opportunity. Training must be need-oriented toward operational objectives. The true training need represents a problem or opportunity that is the active concern of line managers.

Training cannot be expected to "fix" in one day a problem of long-time duration. Neither should training teach people skills and knowledge they already possess.

A new partnership develops when the training manager stops selling courses to line managers and begins to help them achieve their department goals. This requires gaining the confidence of those managers to determine needs.

The training department that is aware of its mission will spend a large part of nonclassroom time in discussion with the line managers. This will result in line managers' achievement of their goals and create on-the-job reinforcement of posttraining.

REFERENCE

[1]"A Responsive Training Department Cuts Costs," by Frank O. Hoffman, copyright February 1984. Reprinted with the permission of *Personnel Journal,* Costa Mesta, California; all rights reserved.

QUESTIONS

1. What is the real purpose behind the existence of a training department?
2. The author regards one approach to training as "more is better." How is this illustrated?
3. What does the author suggest is the point of a company determining how the training director and staff spend their off-classroom time?

CHAPTER ELEVEN

JOB EVALUATION

INTRODUCTION

The purpose of job evaluation is to ensure that the method used to determine the relative worth of jobs does so on an equitable basis. This method must be fair and impartial in determining the worth of one job in comparison with other jobs.

The procedure usually begins with the information collected in the job description as the result of the job-analysis process. The job description provides data about job duties and responsibilities. The job specifications, which may be part of the job description or may stand by themselves, detail the knowledge, skills, and abilities that are required of the person occupying the position.

With this information available, the company needs to know what elements make up the wage that is being paid. These elements, called compensable factors, are accountability, mental effort, problem solving, working conditions, and any other elements that are part of the job environment. Once the compensable factors have been determined, they are assigned points or weights based upon their value to the company.

The next step in the job-evaluation process is to choose one system to evaluate the jobs from the several that are available, such as ranking or point. The point system was developed at Western Electric and then adopted by the National Manufacturers Association and the National Metals Trades Association. Point systems are generally developed for different job categories, such as sales, clerical, or factory. A number of factors are used: mental demand, job knowledge, responsibility, working conditions, and job hazards. When these factors have been identified, they are listed in a point manual and usually divided into five degrees. Then the degrees as well as the factors are described, briefly but adequately, to show the difference between the degrees. Each degree is assigned a number of points based on the difficulty it represents.

To use this manual, one compares the factors in the job specification with the factor description in the manual and determines the appropriate degree and points to assign to the factor. The point total for the job is then calculated, and the relative worth of the job is determined by that total. Although companies may develop their own systems, there are general systems available that may be used. Some systems use statistical techniques to assign points, but the point system, like other job-evaluation techniques, still remains a judgmental process.

Another job-evaluation technique is the factor comparison, which ranks the various parts of a job. Unlike the case with the point system, the parts of jobs are compared to those of key jobs that serve as the evaluation scale. Usually these job parts or components are skill, mental effort, physical demands, responsibility, and working conditions. After they have been determined, the next step is selection of a group of key jobs that appear to have a correct wage relationship. The key jobs are then ranked as to their job parts or factors. Then, in a judgmental process, the present wage being paid for a key job is apportioned among the parts or factors. Thus, a job paying $8.50 an hour might be factored as $2.80 for mental, $.75 for physical, $2.29 for skill, $1.70 for responsibility, and $.96 for working conditions. The effect is a ranking of the five factors for a particular job as the result of the money allocation to each factor. This ranking by money may be compared to the original ranking of the factors by difficulty for all the jobs. For instance, the mental effort for a common laborer may have been ranked as the least difficult of 20 jobs, so when the money amounts allocated to mental effort for the 20 jobs are ranked, the laborer's money allocation should be the lowest. Sizable differences might indicate that such jobs should be eliminated from the list of key jobs.

With the key jobs acting as benchmarks, a non-key job is placed in the comparison scale, with its placement determined by which key jobs it falls between. This approach allows us to see how the company has priced the entire job structure.

Other job-evaluation systems are not as precise as the point and factor comparison systems; one is the job grade or classification system, similar to

Now Hanks was at the water cooler again, and that was too much for Hal; tomorrow it would be time to chat with the boss.

The next day, Hal talked with his boss, who talked to the human resource manager, who talked to the person in charge of job evaluations, and then they all got together to discuss the problem.

The human resource department was using a factor comparison method to determine job worth. Hal was shown the key jobs that were selected as representing the correct relationship between wage rates, and he was shown how these key jobs were rank-ordered on five factors— mental effort, physical effort, skill, responsibility, and working conditions. He was shown how the wages paid for these jobs were proportioned among these factors, then he was shown how all this was applied to his job. Joe Hanks was being paid more for mental effort, skill, and responsibility; both were being paid the same for working conditions; Hal was being paid more for physical effort than Hanks. Hal quietly studied the numbers for a moment and then remarked, "It all adds up, but it still isn't right."

RELEVANT EMPIRICAL
RESEARCH STUDIES

Research Study 11-1-A

How accurate are the raters in job-evaluation methods? Are some job-evaluation methods more accurate than others?

Doverspike and others[1] investigated the point method of job evaluation as it relates to generalizability. The point method is popular; it rates jobs on a set of factors that represent money figures. For each of the factors there are several scales with a number of levels, and each level has a point value. These values are totaled, and wage rates are assigned accordingly, with reference to local conditions. In regard to generalizability theory, studies are designed so that each potential source of error can be studied. This allows a more precise and accurate determination of reliability.

In the present study, the generalizability of job-evaluation ratings to a group of ratings was defined in terms of three potential sources of errors: jobs, scales, and raters. Jobs and scales were the objects to be compared; raters and scales were considered sources of variation affecting the measuring of job-evaluation points.

The sample was five male and five female industrial and organizational psychology doctoral students with graduate training equivalent to a master's degree. They were enrolled in an seminar on equal pay that involved extensive training in job evaluation. Further training included a one-hour session on job evaluation and a one-hour session on the particular point system of job evaluation used in the study. These students were provided with a packet of 20 job descriptions, ranging from accounting clerk to secretary. They also received a job-evaluation instrument that consisted of four main factors: skill, effort, responsibility, and working conditions. Each of these four main factors had certain scales. Skill had four scales: education, previous experience, time to proficiency, and ability. Effort had two scales: mental and physical. Responsibility had three scales: financial, supervisory, and extra duties or tasks. Working conditions had two scales: work conditions and hazards. Each level on these eleven scales was assigned from one to five points. The students rated one job at a time on all eleven scales before proceeding to the next job. They took approximately four hours to complete the task.

The results of using the generalizability theory to access the point-method evaluation reliability utilized formulas relevant to the theory. It was found that the student raters' evaluations made only a minor addition to the total variance or difference. The major contributors to the total rating variance were the scale and the jobs. The study revealed that reducing the number of student raters from ten to one had a small effect on the generalizability coefficient. This coefficient indicates the dependability of generalizing from the present sample of student trainers to a larger group of trainers outside the study. Further, the coefficient remained practically unchanged when the number of student raters was reduced from ten to four and dropped only slightly when the number was reduced from four to one. When the scales were analyzed as to a potential source of error with jobs held fixed, the drop in the generalizability coefficient was minimal.

A computation was made to determine a confidence interval for the ratings that were obtained from one rater and also four raters; the result was that 95 percent of the time, the ratings would represent those found in the universe. When estimates were made of error variance and the scales were fixed with the student raters being the potential source of error, the estimates of error variances were small. Further, the student raters as a potential source of error made almost no contribution to the scale values, and most of the individual scale values were highly reliable. An exception was working conditions and hazards, both of which were highly intercorrelated, so that a relationship would be expected. There was no difference in ratings by males and females, as indicated by the high generalizability of the scores across the student raters. Another result was that reducing the number of scales from eleven to one reduced the correlation coefficient. When the scales were treated as fixed, the correlation coefficient increased for the student raters.

Summary Review of Research Study 11-1-A   The generalizability analysis demonstrated that when ten trained student raters with appropriate job information used a well-designed job-evaluation point system, they obtained adequate reliability levels in making job-evaluation ratings. Also, as the number of student raters was reduced from ten to one, the drop in reliability was only slight. This would indicate the interrater reliability in this study. Further, variations due to the student raters were very small, but substantial variation was due to the eleven scales and the 20 job descriptions. Since reducing the number of student raters had little effect on reliable job-evaluation ratings, four trained raters randomly chosen may be all that are necessary to obtain reliable ratings. Also, the number of scales, eleven in this study, cannot be reduced if rater reliability is to be maintained.

The overall result suggests that the point method of job evaluation is reliable. However, the authors caution that the external validity of the study may be questioned, since the raters were graduate students who had no contact with the real job environment. Also, there is no way of knowing if other job-evaluation methods would obtain such reliability, since only the point method was used.

Research Study 11-1-B

How effective are the newer statistical job-evaluation techniques as compared with those of a more traditional nature?

Gomez-Mejia and others[2] investigated the superiority of a policy-capturing approach to job evaluation over traditional methods such as ranking, point factor, and factor comparison. The statistical approaches included multiple regression on individual job elements and multiple discriminate analysis. The traditional methods included ranking, factor analysis, and point-factor rating. Also included was a "hybrid" method using regression analysis in the structure of a point-factor system. The value of the policy-capturing or statistical methods is that in a hierarchy of jobs, statistical relationships can be used to "predict" pay raters. This approach would be less costly than the more administrative approaches of the traditional methods. The predictive accuracy of all the job-evaluation methods was based on the correlation between actual and predicted grade level, percent relationship between actual and predicted grade level, interrater reliability, and the cross-validation of sample results.

The first part of the study required a questionnaire that would accurately describe a variety of management positions across a wide range of functions and levels. The result was the Management Position Description Questionnaire (MPDQ), containing 235 items classified into general information, financial and human resource responsibilities, decision making, planning and organizing, supervising and controlling, consulting and innovating, coordination, monitoring business indicators, know-how, overall ratings, and reporting relationships.

A sample of 657 managers, representing a cross-section of functional areas and management levels, was used to determine the accuracy of the job-evaluation methods. There were seven methods: three statistical, three traditional, and one hybrid. As for the multiple regression on factors resulting from factor analysis, nine factors were selected from the original 235 items in the MPDQ. Factor scores were obtained using an approximation procedure for computing factor scores. These factor scores and the grade levels were submitted to multiple regression, with the eventual result of a predicted grade for each position. The multiple regression on individual job elements used questionnaire-item responses, not factor scores, as predictors and entered them into the regression analysis. The result was 15 items that were combined into a predictive equation. The multiple discriminant analysis of MPDQ responses from a sample of 449 managers, selected because their positions represented benchmarks for each level, resulted in nine factors being identified. For the traditional methods, a group of 26 personnel managers met twice, using a delphi technique to select eight compensable factors and their relative weights, and using the MPDQ as a tool to collect data.

In the ranking method, scores were obtained by totaling all the compensable factors, which were grouped into a frequency distribution with 18 categories per the manager's score. The factor-comparison method used the rankings within the eight factors multiplied by the assigned weight to determine the manager's position within the rank. The point-factor system used a rating scale for each of the eight compensable factors by summing the responses on the items composing that factor. Then, multiplying by the weight produced a total weighted score. Each position was then assigned to the closest grade level. In the "hybrid" system, scores of the judgmentally compensable factors were obtained from a linear transformation using regression analysis. Factor scores were obtained for each position, and then predictions followed the traditional point-factor system.

The results compared the methods as to evaluation accuracy or hit rates (percent relationship between the predicted and actually assigned grade). All the traditional methods (65–68 percent) had higher hit rates on cross-validation than did either the multiple regression (60 percent) or discriminant analysis (66 percent). However, the hybrid method (73 percent) had a higher hit rate than all the other methods. For the traditional methods, none had an apparent advantage over the others. Yet among the statistical methods, multiple regression appears to have had the advantage. As to the factors, the eight compensable factors demonstrated higher correlations with grade level than did the statistical factors.

As part of the study, 43 compensation managers responded to a user-reactions questionnaire; they evaluated the hybrid method for evaluating jobs to be better than the other methods. Traditional methods were seen as time-consuming and costly, and statistical methods as difficult to understand and to explain to employees.

Summary Review of Research Study 11-1-B Judgmentally derived compensable factors proved to be quite different from those obtained via factor analysis. Yet they had a predictable relationship to the grade level of hierarchy positions. It appears that the traditional and "hybrid" systems are at least as accurate as statistical methods in predicting grade. Further, if one is selecting a statistical job-evaluation method, the study suggests that simple techniques, such as multiple regression, fare as well as, if not better than, more sophisticated models. The authors point to the user-reactions questionnaire that rated the "hybrid" method as equitable, and they see it as the superior job-evaluation method.

Research Study 11-1-C

How do we determine the worth of a job? Specifically, what is available to assign monetary figures to various management jobs?

Tornow and Pinto[3] investigated a behavior-based management group of tasks, independent of traits, abilities, or individual differences, that would be effective in job evaluation. From a 575-item Executive Position Description Questionnaire originally developed by Hemphill in 1960, the authors developed a 208-item Management Position Description Questionnaire (MPDQ). Of these items, 53 referred to position concerns and responsibilities, 43 were position demands and restrictions, and 49 were miscellaneous position characteristics. This instrument was given to 489 incumbent managers in six companies in three broad management levels: high, middle, and low. The final sample contained 212 high-management people, 172 middle, and 105 low. The six companies, all part of the same corporation, represented manufacturing, services, education, finance, and marketing. Management levels went from president to first-line supervisor in functional areas of sales, manufacturing, personnel, research and development, and general administration. The overall sample was split into two groups: a development group of 433 for developing the management classification system, and a cross-validation group of 56 to verify and evaluate the new system.

The results of the study were that a seven-, ten-, or 13-factor solution was the most complete solution to the analysis. Using a clustering procedure to determine how similar each of the management positions was to each of the others, the 433 cases were then merged into ten homogeneous groups. Variance increased drastically, indicating that even the next-best matching was not even close to the similarity provided by the preceding clusters. The ten-homogeneous-group solution best represented the sample in regard to similarity of scores. The scores for the MPDQ of the 56 managers in the cross-validation group were then compared against the original sample. The average hit rate across salary levels and functions was 73 percent. In other words, vice-presidents ended up in clusters previously reserved for top management, and foremen and section managers went into clusters for low management.

Summary Review of Research Study 11-1-C Thirteen independent position description factors were identified that were behaviorally defined rather than being anchored in terms of job titles. These 13 factors representative of management work have an important application in job evaluation. The authors point out that most evaluation plans use factors of responsibility, complexity, and degree of independence in determining job worth. However, these factors are usually arrived at rationally and are subjectively measured. The 13 MPDQ factors are objectively measured and describe behavioral job content. The management clusters in the study permitted the development of job groups of managers based on similarities and differences in the job content.

REFERENCES

[1]Doverspike, D., A.M. Carlisi, G.V. Barrett, and R.A. Alexander, "Generalizability Analysis of a Point-Method Job Evaluation Instrument," *Journal of Applied Psychology*, 68 (1983), 476–83.

[2]Gomez-Mejia, L.R., R.C. Page, and W.W. Tornow, "A Comparison of the Practical Utility of Traditional, Statistical, and Hybrid Job Evaluation Approaches," *Academy of Management Journal*, 25 (1982), 790–809.

[3]Tornow, W.W., and P.R. Pinto, "The Development of a Managerial Job Taxonomy: A System for Describing, Classifying, and Evaluating Executive Positions," *Journal of Applied Psychology*, 61 (1976), 410–18.

QUESTIONS

1. Is there an optimal number of raters in a job-evaluation survey? Is more better than few? Explain.
2. Would you recommend a statistical or more traditional job-evaluation method? Why? Which specific method? Why?
3. Can a behavior-based management job classification be created that is independent of worker traits, abilities, or other individual differences? Defend your answer.

Research Incident 11-2:
Ken McGowan's Successful Job-Evaluation
Survey—But Not Everyone Is Happy

- Why may the systematic job-evaluation bias regarding female jobs not work to the disadvantage of all female jobs?
- Who gives higher scores in the job evaluation process, male raters or female raters?
- When is it advantageous in job evaluation to use the observational technique?

The company's point method of job evaluation was considered to be a model of comprehensiveness and accuracy. It had been successfully adopted by many companies, several of them outside the industry. However, Ken McGowan, last year's local "Human Resource Personality of the Year," was looking at his first really baffling problem in 15 years as a human resource manager.

The irony of the present situation was that the company had a progressive reputation in the industry, always in the forefront of modern employee relations programs. Yet several departments were now in an uproar over the latest job-evaluation survey, and to complicate the issue, the complaints were all from the women employees. It was very pointedly emphasized at this morning's meeting of the executive committee that last week's production figures were down 10 percent, absenteeism was up 15 percent, and illness was up 12 percent.

Over the last five years, the company had steadily increased its proportion of women employees and until now had believed them to be loyal, committed workers. The cause of the uproar was the issue of comparable worth, pay rates based on the worth of the job and not on other, discriminatory factors. And it all rested on job evaluation. The charge was that the company's point method of job evaluation was perpetuating wage differentials that had existed for years.

Ken knew that the program was fair and that the raters were all highly qualified professionals with years of experience. No way was there discrimination, but then why the uproar?

RELEVANT EMPIRICAL RESEARCH STUDIES

Research Study 11-2-A

What happens to the job-evaluation process when it is subject to systematic sex-based errors? What technique can be used to identify such errors?

Schwab and Wickern[1] evaluated the consequences of systematic measurement errors in job evaluation using a multiple and reverse regression technique. The study points out that the concept of comparable worth is based on the idea that jobs can be measured as to their value to employers and that job evaluation is a suitable vehicle for determining that value. Job evaluation, then, can be a source of discrimination by establishing certain pay-rate differentials between jobs held predominantly by females and those held by males. The consequences of systematic sex-related bias were investigated as they relate to the evaluation of jobs and the wages used as a criterion in validation.

The authors used multiple regression to predict wage rates by treating the wage rates of key jobs as the dependent variable and the compensation factors as the independent variable. Their multiple regression model was simplified by the assumptions that only one compensable factor is considered, jobs are occupied by either females or males, and female jobs average lower levels of the compensable factor than male jobs. Using the multiple regression models, the authors found that if male jobs and all wages were observed without error and the female job scores were all undervalued by the same amount, then the non-key-job wages predicted from the male-jobs equation were inconsistent. Combining male and female jobs, the regression line indicated that jobs with higher evaluation scores were underpredicted and those with lower evaluation scores overpredicted. If the regression line used undervaluated female job scores and overevaluated male job scores, this led to non-key-job wage predictions that over- and underestimated true wages. Key-job wage criterion bias can result in underpaying female key jobs relative to the true wage, or overpayment of male key jobs, or both. If male key-job wages and evaluations were correct but female key jobs were underpaid by the same amount, the regression line would overpredict female-job wages compared to those obtained from using female-job data only. The multiple regression model would show that if overpaid male key jobs were extrapolated over correctly paid female key jobs, the female jobs would appear underpaid.

The authors continued their study with more calculations to show consequences of errors in both wages and in evaluation scores. Although the multiple regression model demonstrates that the results of systematic errors in wage and compensable variables can be predicted, the problem of identifying these errors remains. To this extent, the authors used reverse regression to demonstrate that systematic errors can be identified.

The results of the study indicate that systematic bias against female jobs may not operate in a negative sense, in that positive or negative systematic error in job-evaluation socres may not influence non-key-job wage predictions relative to true scores as long as the only data included in the model are from the group experiencing the systematic error. If female jobs are underevaluated and all data are included in the model, then predicted non-key wages will generally be in error, but not necessarily to the disadvantage of the females. Female non-key jobs may receive fewer job evaluation points and receive higher predicted wages than true score predictions. Downward bias in female key-job rates would depress female non-key-job-rate predictions. Also, downward female job bias, combined with male key-job rates upwardly biased, increases the underprediction of female raters at the lower part of evaluation scores.

Summary Review of Research Study 11-2-A   Bias against female key- or benchmark-job rates generally has a negative effect on predictions for female non-key-job rates. However, the systematic evaluation bias of female jobs does not necessarily work to the disadvantage of all female jobs. Although the use of reverse regression appears useful in identifying systematic errors, the authors remain skeptical about its benefits, owing to the need to eliminate errors in the data input, such as the measurement of wage rates. A problem in job-evaluation research is that it has received little attention in the last 30 years.

Research Study 11-2-B

How do sex-role stereotypes affect job-evaluation procedures? What is the effect of the sex of the job incumbent upon the rater?

Arvey and others[2] conducted a study to determine the influence of sex-role stereotypes in job-analysis procedures. The study featured a simulated job of an administrative assistant, using a verbal narrative with color slides of the person being evaluated. The simulation material consisted of six sets of slides, in which three females and three males each appeared as the job incumbent to be rated. One instrument to be completed by the raters was the Position Analysis Questionnaire. This instrument reflects the basic human behaviors in jobs, based on 194 job elements that are grouped into 32 job dimensions. The scoring also permits prediction of the nine aptitudes of the General Aptitude Test Battery and estimation of pay rates using multiple regression. The other instrument used in the study was the Gough Adjective Checklist, which measures personality dimensions.

The raters were obtained by posting notices on a college campus that participants were needed for a study dealing with job analysis; the study would last three hours and would pay $2 per hour with a guarantee of at least $6.60. The sample of student raters consisted of 22 males and 35 females. Almost all were college juniors, average age 22.3, with no significant differences between male and female students regarding age or educational major. However, they did differ significantly on the Gough Adjective Checklist personality scales; the males scored higher on intraception, and the females scored higher on counseling readiness.

The procedure for the study brought the raters together, and they were told they would be checking out the validity of a new job-analysis instrument. For familiarization, each student rated his or her last job on the Position Analysis Questionnaire. They were then asked to analyze a job and were shown the slides with the voice tape. After completing the instrument, the student raters completed a form, using a five-point Likert scale to rate the job incumbent's physical attractiveness, voice quality, and estimated age.

The study found no significant differences among the presentations of the male and female job incumbents as to physical attractiveness or voice differences. However, the male job incumbents were perceived as significantly older than their female counterparts. Using a statistical technique, the authors concluded that this estimated age variable would not result in a loss of precision.

Of the 32 job dimensions of the Position Analysis Questionnaire, there was only one item that was significantly different. The male raters gave higher scores to the dimension evaluating information from things than did the female raters. This dimension is described as having to do with activities involving the estimating or judging of quality and quantity. Apparently, the males perceived the administrative assistant position as involving more estimation and evaluation activities than the females did.

Other data suggest that the sex of the rater could have an effect on the Position Analysis Questionnaire. It appears that the only consistent effect found in the study was the sex of the rater, although even this was not considered strong. Correlations between the Gough Adjective Checklist and the Position Analysis Questionnaire found only six significant relationships out of a possible 684. This demonstrates no consistent or high relation with the scores on these instruments given by the raters. This suggests that neither the male nor female raters devalued or inflated their descriptions of the job, regardless of whether the incumbent was male or female. Yet the data indicate a tendency for the female raters to give consistently lower scores than the males did on the 32 job dimensions. Also, there were no differences between males and females as to aptitude requirements or estimated pay rate.

Summary Review of Research Study 11-2-B The Position Analysis Questionnaire was used as the job-analysis instrument to rate a simulated administrative assistant job via color slides and a voice tape. Only the sex of the incumbent jobholder was manipulated, by using male and female figures. The sex of the jobholder did not influence the questionnaire scores, although the sex of the rater demonstrated marginal but consistent effects. Regardless of the sex of the incumbent jobholder, female raters gave relatively lower scores across most of the job dimensions of the questionnaire than did the male raters.

The authors caution that the results were mostly marginal because the sample was small and that the results need to be confirmed using larger sample sizes. Also, only one job was used, at a fairly high level, and it was somewhat neutral as to either a female-only or male-only job. The one significant finding was that the sex of the rater was related to the questionnaire job dimension of evaluating information from things, with males giving higher scores than females.

Research Study 11-2-C

What can be done to improve raters' observations of job performance? Is it possible to obtain the same results from two observers at two different times?

Jenkins and others[3] studied the results of using standardized observations in measuring the characteristics of jobs. For standardized observations to be usable, they must demonstrate repeatability. That is, two observers should agree on what is observed of the same job at the same time, as well as what is observed of the same job at different times. Also, observations should be homogeneous, with agreement among the different parts of the same method as it measures a particular part of the job. Another aspect of the observations is convergence, the agreement of results between different measurements of the same thing. Finally, there should be discriminant validity; there should not be agreement of results for measures designed to evaluate different concepts.

The subjects were 448 employees from three organizations: an automobile-parts manufacturer, a printing concern, and four departments of a large hospital. Most of the jobs were in six categories: operative, clerical, professional/technical, service, craftsmen/foremen, and managers/officials. Seventy-five percent had completed high school, 36 percent earned over $10,000 per year, 91 percent were white, and 62 percent were male. The subjects were first contacted by a letter explaining the purpose of the study and asking them to participate. They were then contacted by phone for agreement to an interview of about two hours by a professional interviewer in their homes. The subjects were also told that observations would be made of them at work for the purpose of verifying working conditions, not how hard they were working. Most subjects agreed to the observation.

The interview itself was structured with 19 relevant job-description items: variety, autonomy, task identity, task feedback, worker pace control, comfort, resource adequacy, certainty, required cooperation, external feedback, and required skills and abilities. The observers were obtained from posted announcements and attended a two-day training session. These observers, 19 men and 16 women, were nonprofessionals, mostly upperclassmen, and they were paid $2.65 per hour. The observation instrument contained 59 questionnaire items that measured a wide variety of job factors. Most of the items were responded to on a six-point Likert-type scale, although some required a seven-point anchored scale. The subjects were observed on the job twice for an hour; the observations were made two days apart, at different times of the day, and by two different observers. Also, 48 observations were made by two observers at the same time on randomly selected employees to determine the repeatability of the measures.

The results of the study indicate that in regard to repeatability, there was empirical agreement between the observers when the observations or ratings were made at the same time on 32 of the 59 measures. When the observations or ratings were made at different times, only 19 of the 59 measures demonstrated acceptable agreement between observers. As for homogeneity, nine measures were reasonably homogeneous: variety, autonomy, rigidity, certainty, conflicting demands, cooperation, required skills and abilities, worker pace control, and effort. Homogeneity did not exist for the measures of external feedback, task feedback, task identity, comfort, work pressures, interruptions, and resources. As for convergence, the agreement of results between different measurements of the same thing, the authors found only six measures that could be meaningfully tested. Of these six, four demonstrated reasonable levels of convergence: variety, skills, autonomy, and pace control. The measures of certainty and cooperation did not demonstrate convergence between methods. It appears that what the observers regarded as certainty, the subjects viewed as measures of variety and skills. The data indicate that observers had difficulty in discriminating among the measures of variety, skills, certainty, autonomy, and pace control. Further analysis of the data reveals that the interview sessions satisfied the requirements for discriminant validity, but the observations did not.

Summary Review of Research Study 11-2-C   The observational technique for evaluating job characteristics was moderately successful. The measures did exhibit repeatability, homogeneity, and convergence. However, the study also revealed significant limitations of the observational technique, particularly in regard to halo error.

The authors suggest that limitations of the study include the instrument's length, which led to observer boredom, the fact that certain jobs lend themselves more to observation than others, and a lack of discrimination among job characteristics. Yet the observational technique does appear to be a potentially useful method to measure the characteristics of jobs.

REFERENCES

[1]Schwab, D.P., and D.W. Wickern, "Systematic Bias in Job Evaluation and Market Wages: Implications for the Comparable Worth Debate," *Journal of Applied Psychology,* 68 (1983), 60–69.

[2]Arvey, R.D., E.M. Passino, and J.W. Lounsbury, "Job Analysis Results as Influenced by Sex of Incumbent and Sex of Analyst," *Journal of Applied Psychology,* 62 (1977), 411–16.

[3]Jenkins, G.D. Jr., D.A. Wadler, E.E. Lawler III, and C. Cammann, "Standardized Observations: An Approach to Measuring the Nature of Jobs," *Journal of Applied Psychology,* 60 (1975), 171–81.

QUESTIONS

1. In the multiple regression model, what is the effect on female job rates if overpaid male key jobs are extrapolated over correctly paid female jobs? What advantages and disadvantages do you see in using the multiple regression model in a plant manufacturing plaster wallboard?

2. What does the Postion Analysis Questionnaire do? Does it make any difference whether the rater is male or female? Explain.

3. How effective is the observational technique for evaluating job characteristics? What are some of the strong and weak points of this technique?

Research Incident 11-3:
Ms. Vi Higgins Pulls John Lehman's Chestnuts Out of the Fire

- How can we measure the work values generally associated with the Protestant Ethic?
- What is the variable that distinguishes the "stayers" from the "leavers" in a company? Can it be measured?
- What is the discrepancy between job involvement and intrinsic motivation on the job?

It all started when the company's CEO and president attended a one-day conference at Very Prestigious University to hear about the positive effects of Japanese management techniques upon human productivity. The result was the memo that John Lehman, human resource manager, now held in his hand.

The memo was very simple, merely a statement that the company's job-evaluation method included worker commitment and loyalty in its computation and of the weight given these factors. The problem, it said, was that the job-evaluation method did not consider any subjective measures, only pragmatic factors that lent themselves to quantitative values.

John knew that if he responded accurately about the present job-evaluation method, he would spend several hours in the president's office engaged in a philosophical discussion, whose end result would more than likely be a dismantling of the present system, causing added responsibilities on the human resource department as it struggled to reinvent the wheel.

John Lehman's management style was to call his group supervisors together to discuss problems, so the word went out for an early morning meeting tomorrow. Besides, a major revision of the scope he envisioned meant all hands would be involved, since the human resource department was just too small for narrow specialists. It was a staff of only broad generalists, who, incidentally, did the work of narrow specialists.

The next morning, when John explained the purpose of the meeting and what the top company executives had brought back with them from Very Prestigious University, there were audible groans and hoots. But when the possible effect on the human resource department sank in, there was only silence and head shaking for a while. After about 15 minutes of panic discussion, Ms. Vi Higgins suggested a two-day delay in which she could gather information, so that the group could at least present a supportable position. John and the others were only too happy to agree; Vi had a proven reputation of handling hot chestnuts so no one got burned.

Two days later, the meeting started promptly. Ms. Vi Higgins passed around copies of a concise handout and took charge of the flip chart. After a brisk 15-minute presentation, the room was full of smiles and sighs. The request of the CEO and president could be met without disrupting the equity and balance of the present job-evaluation method. John Lehman leaned back and almost said out loud, "That was a smart move on my part when I hired her."

RELEVANT EMPIRICAL RESEARCH STUDIES

Research Study 11-3-A

Can we measure a person's work values? Can we measure the meaning people attach to their work roles?

Wallack and others[1] constructed a set of scales that measured areas of work values. The resulting instrument, called the Survey of Work Values (SWV), measured people's attitudes toward work in general rather than feelings about a specific job. This is different from job satisfaction, which is people's attitudes toward their own jobs.

The SWV was developed around the work values that seem to be closely associated with the Protestant Ethic: individualism, self-denial, and industriousness. Perhaps the most widely accepted index of the Protestant Ethic is concerned with the intrinsic aspect of work—that work is its own reward. Three dimensions or subscales were selected by the authors to satisfy the Protestant Ethic intrinsic aspects of work: the satisfaction and enjoyment of doing a job well, called Pride in Work; the personal preference of keeping active and busy on the job, called Activity Preference; and the interest taken in co-workers and in contributing to job decisions, called Job Involvement.

Although the Protestant Ethic emphasizes the intrinsic rewards of work, much value is also placed on extrinsic rewards. So the authors included the following extrinsic subscales: value placed on making money, called Attitude toward Earnings; and the effect one's job has on one's standing among others, called Social Status of Job. Two other subscales were included that did not seem appropriate for these classifications and were regarded as a mixed category. They were the desire to obtain a higher-level job with a better standard of living, called Upward Striving; and the realization that one must work and is dependent on oneself, not others, for support, called Responsibility to Work.

The precise items that were obtained to represent these subscales resulted from a review of the literature and suggestions from faculty and graduate students. The items were first checked for representation of the categories with an industrial sample. The retention of an item required a certain percentage allocation of that item to a single category by the sample. Then the retained items were exposed to further allocation to the categories by two undergraduate samples. Scale values for the items were obtained from another industrial sample and an undergraduate sample. These scale values were then rescaled by an undergraduate sample as a measure of stability. The attitude statements were finally submitted to another industrial sample to obtain endorsement of the work values.

Of the 91 items in the original pool, the exposure to the different samples indicated that 45 were to be retained. These items had been assigned to particular categories by an average of 84.1 percent of the judgments. The Responsibility to Work subscale was eliminated through this process, since it failed to meet standards. The Activity Preference items also failed, but only because the items were being allocated to the Responsibility to Work scale. The Activity Preference definition was then revised with new items.

The retained 45 items, plus 13 original statements from the Activity Preference that had failed earlier, plus 17 new statements, were exposed to two more sample allocations. Of the total of 75 statements, 67 were retained, with an average of 85 percent allocation to a single category.

The correlation between the two sets of scale values resulting from the industrial and undergraduate samples was .94. The total subscale scores were also highly correlated, at .98. The SWV was given to a sample of government employees, and an analysis of the values obtained showed their scores agreed closely with those obtained from the development sample. However, the homogeneity or internal consistencies of the subscales was not as high as one might expect or prefer as a result of all the prescreening that had occurred.

Several studies were conducted to determine whether the SWV did actually discriminate among occupations. One study suggested a blue-collar and white-collar difference, with the white-collar workers having a more favorable view of work-related activity than blue-collar workers did. Another study, of the work background and work values of unemployed persons, found an emphasis on the social rewards of employment but a devaluation of job involvement and job activity. By the use of different predictors and a sample of civil service employees, the subscales Attitude toward Earnings, Activity Preference, and Social Status of Job were found to be related to race, occupational level, area of the country that the person came from, and supervisory level. These predictors described a minority member, raised in the South, in a low-level nonsupervisory job, who places great value on earnings but has low preference for Activity at Work, and sees low status in being employed.

The authors believe the SWV is a useful research tool. Its six work values are distinguishable from one another, the items are well represented in what is being measured, and studies have shown it to discriminate also among occupational groups.

Summary Review of Research Study 11-3-A   This study details how a series of scales designed to measure attitudes toward work were developed. The result was the Survey of Work Values (SWV), based on the Protestant Ethic as it relates to the meaningful roles of work perceived by an individual worker.

The SWV was subjected to several sample studies to refine the validity of the items used. Its applications with different samples indicated that it discriminated among occupational categories and between the characteristics of employed and minority persons.

The authors believe that the present study supports the use of the SWV as a useful research instrument.

Research Study 11-3-B

Does job satisfaction or organizational commitment contribute more to an employee's willingness to give that extra effort? How do job satisfaction and organizational commitment affect the "stayers" and "leavers"? Can we effectively measure job satisfaction or organizational commitment?

A study by Porter and others[2] considered job satisfaction and organizational commitment as predictors of turnover. A value of this study is that it measured patterns of attitude change regarding turnover over a time period rather than obtaining one measurement at one time point. The study compared the predictive powers of job satisfaction and organizational commitment over a 10½-month period to determine turnover for a sample of psychiatric technician trainees.

The authors point out that organizational commitment may be part of the linkage between the employee and the organization that also includes member job satisfaction. Yet few empirical studies have investigated the relationship between organizational commitment and turnover.

The definition of organizational commitment used was the strength of self-identification and self-involvement in a particular organization. Such a commitment involves an acceptance of and strong belief in the goals and values of the organization, the willingness to give the organization one's considerable efforts, and the desire to remain a member of the organization. The authors predicted that people exhibiting these three factors would be inclined to stay with the organization and achieve these objectives.

Organizational commitment may be a more effective predictor of turnover in certain circumstances than job satisfaction is. The authors suggest that people dissatisfied with their pay or their supervisor may find that their high commitment to the organization overrules such dissatisfaction. And although money dissatisfaction may be important to a worker, satisfaction with other areas of the job may take precedence.

The subjects in the study were two groups of psychiatric technician trainees in a major West Coast hospital for the mentally retarded. Their training program lasted one year and included supervised clinical experience and classroom lectures. The tasks required of the trainees were varied, and they received a modest salary.

The two training groups were similar. There were no differences in regard to age, male–female ratio, or educational background. Selection procedures were identical, as were the training sequences, ward assignments, and instructors. Because of these similarities, the two groups were combined into one for purposes of analysis.

Turnover for psychiatric workers was high; rates for the first year ranged from 30 to 50 percent. At the start of training for both groups, there were 84 trainees, and approximately nine months later, when the study started, there were 60 remaining. Of this group, 27 more, or 45 percent of the sample, terminated during the study period.

Two instruments were used to determine the attitudes of the trainees. The Organizational Commitment Questionnaire, containing 15 items, was designed to measure the extent to which people feel committed to their place of work. Items included perceptions of loyalty to the organization, willingness to expend great effort to achieve organizational goals, and acceptance of the values of the organization. Responses were on a seven-point Likert-type scale ranging from "strongly disagree" to "strongly agree." The Job Descriptive Index (JDI) measured satisfaction with five areas of the job: supervision, co-workers, work, pay, and promotion. The sum of these five areas served as a measure of overall satisfaction. These instruments were administered at four intervals during the research study.

The results of the study indicated that the stayers and leavers were generally a homogeneous group with respect to demographic characteristics of education, male–female ratio, and income. Only the mean age of the stayers (31.9 years) was significantly higher than that of the leavers (23.9 years)—a relationship that has been found in other studies of turnover. Since this suggests that relationships between attitudes and turnover may be affected by age, it was controlled in the subsequent analysis of the data.

An analysis was made of each of the four time periods to determine any relationship between turnover and the variables of commitment to the organization, satisfaction with supervision, satisfaction with co-workers, satisfaction with the work itself, satisfaction with pay, and satisfaction with opportunities for promotion. For time periods 1 and 2, no significant discrimination was found between stayers and leavers. However, significant relationships were found in time periods 3 and 4 between turnover and several of the attitude measures. This suggests that any relationship between turnover and different attitudes is strongest when the person is closest to leaving.

The analysis of time period 3 reveals that 21 percent of the variance in organizational commitment and job satisfaction pertained to the decision to be a stayer or a leaver. The commitment to the organization was clearly designated as the most important variable distinguishing the stayers from the leavers. The next most important variables were satisfaction with opportunities for promotion and satisfaction with the work itself. In time period 3, the more positive attitudes were registered by the stayers, not the leavers. The one exception was satisfaction with pay; the stayers and leavers exhibited approximately equal group means.

For time period 4, 21 percent of the variance was related to turnover. Again, organizational commitment was the most important variable in discriminating between stayers and leavers; the other variables appeared to contribute little, if anything, to the relationship. The group means on the original instrument in time period 4 demonstrated that stayers expressed higher levels of organizational commitment and job satisfaction than the leavers did. Again, the one exception was satisfaction with pay; the two groups showed comparable levels of satisfaction.

The authors found the study results indicating that individual attitudes are predictive of turnover behavior, that leavers have less favorable attitudes than stayers. However, although it is clear that leavers have lower levels of commitment and satisfaction, the data were not designed to determine why these differences occur.

Summary Review of Research Study 11-3-B   This study investigated the effect of organizational commitment and job satisfaction on turnover. Organizational commitment was defined as a strong acceptance of the organization's goals and values, willingness to exert considerable effort on behalf of the organization, and a strong desire to remain an organizational member.

Two attitude measurements, the Organizational Commitment Questionnaire and the Job Descriptive Index, were administered at four separate times over a span of 10½ months.

The results indicated relationships between attitudes and turnover in the last two time periods. This suggests that the relationships are strongest as one approaches the time of leaving the organization.

The most important variable that discriminated between stayers and leavers was organizational commitment. It discriminated better than the other components of job satisfaction.

Research Study 11-3-C

What are the differences between a specific job involvement and a generalized work involvement? How is the Protestant Ethic related to either or both? What is the best method to use in measuring work involvement?

A study by Kanungo[3] took exception to the past psychological research in the area of job involvement, which Kanungo feels contained conceptual ambiguities and measurement inadequacies. He points out that past conceptualizations have confused the issue of job involvement with that of intrinsic motivation on the job.

The author says that there are two different contexts in which one can demonstrate personal involvement. One context is the specific or particular job, and the other is generalized work. Job involvement is not the same as involvement with work in general. Job involvement relates to one's present job and how adequately that job satisfies present needs. But work involvement is a learned belief about the value of work in one's life; it is more the result of one's past experiences.

Further, job involvement is also different from organizational commitment, which is a general attitude toward the organization as a whole. In fact, the Protestant Ethic may not be a necessary condition for work involvement to develop. Work involvement may result from experiences other than those of the Protestant Ethic type.

The author believes that job involvement and work involvement cannot be measured with existing instruments. The present study attempted to develop valid and reliable new measures of job and work involvement.

To obtain measures of specific job involvement and of general work involvement, three different formats were used: questionnaire, semantic differential, and graphic techniques. The questionnaire items were obtained by ten graduate students who searched the existing literature. They agreed completely on the inclusion of twelve items in the Job Involvement Questionnaire (JIQ) and nine items in the Work Involvement Questionnaire (WIQ). A six-point agree–disagree analysis was used, resulting in the dropping of two items from the JIQ and three from the WIQ scales.

Another six graduate students made an extensive search of the literature and dictionaries for key words that reflected psychological identification. These items were used to construct the Job Involvement Semantic Differential (JISD) and the Work Involvement Semantic Differential scales, each of which contained eight items.

Three graphic items representing psychological identification were prepared for each of the job and work contexts. Two items were finally selected. One presented two circles representing the job and work, with differing degrees of overlap. The other item presented an office desk and a figure representing oneself, with varying distances between them. These two items resulted in the Job Involvement Graphic (JIG) scale for the job context and the Work Involvement Graphic (WIG) scale in the work context.

A three-part questionnaire was designed. Part 1 contained the JISD, JIQ, and JIG scale items to measure satisfaction with 15 job outcomes and overall satisfaction with one's present job. Part 2 contained the three work-involvement scales—WISD, WIQ, and WIG. Part 3 asked for demographic information about the participant. The questionnaire was written in both French and English, for participation by 900 full-time French- and English-speaking industrial and government employees. The final result was completed questionnaires for 184 in French and 519 in English, for a total of 703. A parallel study was conducted at the same time with 63 employees for the purpose of establishing test and retest reliabilities of the measures.

The results of the demographic data for the original samples and the test/retest were heterogeneous. In the original sample, public- and private-sector employees were equally represented. Half came from large employers, and the rest from small or medium-sized organizations. Males represented 57 percent and females 43 percent. The sample mean age was 28 years; 37 percent were French Canadian, 41 percent English Canadian, and 22 percent other ethnic groups; 40 percent were married, 60 percent single; and nearly half the sample had tenure of two to five years. The test/retest sample was similar in composition.

The results of the study provide considerable support for the distinction suggested earlier between job and work involvement. All three job-involvement scales (JISD, JIQ, and JIG) and two of the work-involvement scales (WIQ and WIG) appeared to be satisfactory instruments. They had reasonable levels of internal consistency, test/retest reliability, and convergent and discriminant validity. However, the semantic differential measures demonstrated questionable validity regarding the measurement of work involvement.

Whereas previous researchers have used mostly questionnaires, the graphic techniques successfully used in this study suggest an application in cross-culture studies where language is a problem. The author believes the new scales to be appropriate for use in future research to measure job and work involvement.

Summary Review of Research Study 11-3-C   The author of this study questioned past research in job involvement as having problems of measurement inadequacies and suggests this is because job involvement has become confused with intrinsic motivation on the job. The result is that job involvement and work involvement cannot be measured with the instruments that had been used.

Several new instruments were developed to test for job involvement and work involvement. They included semantic differential, questionnaire, and graphic techniques.

Sample data were obtained from 703 employees from heterogeneous backgrounds to establish reliability and validity of the new measures. The results indicated that the questionnaire and graphic measures performed at an acceptable level. The fact that the graphic measures were able to overcome language barriers suggests applications in cross-culture situa-

tions. However, the semantic differential measures demonstrated questionable validity.

REFERENCES

[1]Wallack, S., J.G. Goodale, J.P. Wijting, and P.C. Smith, "Development of the Survey of Work Values," *Journal of Applied Psychology,* 55 (1971), 331–38.
[2]Porter, L.W., R.M. Steers, R.T. Mowday, and P.V. Boulian, "Organizational Commitment, Job Satisfaction, and Turnover among Psychiatric Technicians," *Journal of Applied Psychology,* 59 (1974), 603–9.
[3]Kanungo, R.N., "Measurement of Job and Work Involvement," *Journal of Applied Psychology,* 67 (1982), 341–49.

QUESTIONS

1. What information does the Survey of Work Values provide to the human resource department? What practical application does the SWV suggest? Explain.
2. How can we measure a person's loyalty toward an organization, willingness to expend a large amount of effort to achieve organizational goals, and acceptance of the organization's value system? What do we know about the attitudes of stayers and leavers?
3. Discuss any differences between job involvement and work involvement, and the role played by the Protestant Ethic.

NON-EMPIRICAL RESEARCH ARTICLE ABSTRACTS

Abstract 11-1

- What may be the problem today with the job-evaluation methods of the 1940s?
- Why do well-trained administrators in a point-factor job-evaluation system pose a problem in a centralized company?
- Where does the company's "personality" enter into the selection decision of a particular job-evaluation method?

These questions are answered in a 1984 article by Brett and Cumming,[1] consultants.

The authors say that the choice of a job-evaluation system is important because it supports the organization's human resource objectives, operational characteristics, and cultural characteristics. However, many times managers choose to use a point-factor system without considering the implications. Recently developed job-evaluation systems should be considered, for several reasons: Methods of the 1940s may be ineffective in today's work environment, the comparable-worth issue requires systems that are objective, and suitable market data have improved, resulting in more accurate pay comparisons.

The selection of a job-evaluation system is as important as the application if the organization is to avoid employee discontent and ineffective administrative techniques. The cultural climate of the organization must be taken into account; a job-evaluation system suited for a bureaucratic company would probably not suit a dynamic, unstructured company.

The authors suggest a list of "effectiveness criteria" to evaluate the present system or alternative job-evaluation systems. First, the employees must accept the system as equitable, and the management must believe that the system contributes to an effective operation. The system must be understood by those administering it and by the employees. Further, the costs must be reasonable, and the system itself must be objective.

The general approach arranges jobs in a hierarchy, using either a whole-job- or factor-evaluation method. The whole-job evaluates the job on its overall merits; the factor-evaluation analyzes the job on its characteristics.

In a centralized organization, the point factor requires well-trained administrators. In a decentralized organization, these well-trained administrative staffs will have to be duplicated to cover the many different business units, resulting in increased costs.

The administrative style also becomes a consideration, since for a point-evaluation system to be successful staff is required to provide input. However, in a line-dominated company, the staff will be accepted only if it does not interfere with other line priority objectives.

The authors tell us that there is now a wider choice than in the past for selecting a job-evaluation approach. One such approach is a computerized job-evaluation system that has the advantage of storing and quickly processing large amounts of information. Information can be gathered from job incumbents, scored, and correlated. However, some drawbacks are low face validity, because the computer, not the working of the system, is observed, and the fact that in a changing environment, the cost to change software may be high.

Another approach is scaling methods, like those used in the social sciences. Scaling requires the selection of certain predefined criteria such as compensable factors. A benefit of using compensable factors is that they do not require subjective decisions as to weighting. A compensable scaling system provides fewer levels than a point-factor system, resulting in more distinctions between levels. Once benchmark positions are evaluated, a table can be constructed for future job evaluations. The result is a simple system that is easily communicated.

Still another job-evaluation approach is the market-based/job-content method. Traditionally, this approach has been used with a ranking or other whole-job evaluation approach. But it has been improved by combining the market-pay-data approach with one of the factor-evaluation approaches. This requires a detailed market-pay-level determination for the benchmark jobs. Then all jobs are subjected to a job-content analysis and comparison to determine equitable relationships. The result is fully competitive salaries for all job categories.

The authors suggest that the selection of a job-evaluation system be based on the organization's personality. Recent changes in job-evaluation techniques now provide a company with a choice among relatively new, nontraditional, and traditional methods.

REFERENCE

[1]Brett, Edward C., and Charles M. Cumming, "Job Evaluation and Your Organization: An Ideal Relationship?" From the April 1984 issue of *Personnel Administrator*, copyright 1984, The American Society for Personnel Administration, 606 North Washington Street, Alexandria, VA 22314.

QUESTIONS

1. Why should managers reconsider the use of a point-factor system in favor of recently developed job-evaluation systems?
2. What are the "effectiveness criteria" the authors suggest to evaluate present or alternative job-evaluation systems?
3. One job-evaluation approach is scaling methods, which require the selection of certain predefined criteria such as compensable factors. What is a benefit of using compensable factors?

Abstract 11-2

- What determines wage levels—a concept of just wages, or the market?
- Under what circumstances should companies claim that job worth is substantially different from relative market worth?
- How do differences in individual wage midpoints occur, compared to market-value midpoints?

A 1984 article by Foster and Gimplin-Poris,[1] compensation analysts, addresses these questions.

Many job-evaluation plans are used to determine a defensible job structure of worth to the organization, but such plans have recently been called sexually biased. The issue appears to be whether the plans measure either compensable factors independent of the market or the market value of jobs.

The authors say that to prove that job-evaluation plans do in fact provide true measures of job worth requires the use of some outside market standard of value. Several sources are quoted to indicate that the concept of just wages is not supportable and that the real arbitrator is the market.

It is the authors' hypothesis that if the market theory is correct, a high correlation should exist between the salary-range midpoint and the average market-survey midpoint. However, if a job-evaluation plan based on compensable factors independent of the market is correct (the intrinsic job content theory), there should be little or only a modest correlation.

In testing the market-worth theory, data were collected on 25,000 managers in 250 defined jobs, from 277 companies that were divided into five categories based on annual sales. The average midpoints were calculated for the 250 defined jobs in the multi-industry sales group and for 125 narrowly defined jobs in a single industry group.

These midpoints were then converted into a Z-Score that indicated the standard deviation of each midpoint from the mean of a firm's salary grade. This permitted comparing ranking of jobs across firms without the effects of different pay levels. The standardized points were averaged for each job that developed a market value in points. Then correlation coefficients were obtained to show the relationship between the dollar midpoints and the market value in dollars.

The results indicated for all the survey groups a high correlation between the average midpoints in dollars for the job and the actual salary-range midpoint. The industry-mix and pay-level organizational differences affected the survey ranking correlation with the midpoint rankings. So the authors analyzed the individual companies and were able to neutralize the salary differences among them. The results demonstrated a strong relationship between actual midpoints and relative market values.

The authors conclude that job evaluation must and does account for the influence of the market. In fact, the data indicate that this occurs with great precision, since the average relative market value of jobs consistently has more reliable estimates of existing midpoint rankings than do those of subjective job-evaluation plans. Their conclusion is that job rankings using market value produce a better base from which to fine-tune job evaluations than do multiple evaluations using subjective plans.

Thus, companies should avoid claiming that job worth is substantially different from relative market worth. Such erroneous statements falsely imply some underlying criterion of job value that is not determined by the market. What companies should do is focus on jobs relative to the market and ignore the subjective and misleading job-evaluation systems. They can do this by using multiple regression to determine salary grades as shaped by the market for key jobs. The result is a model that identifies inconsistencies in the salary structure. Differences in individual midpoints from market value can be explained by differences in content of the job.

The authors conclude that change will be slow, since facts that conflict with existing theory are not readily adapted. However, job-evaluation systems need to be based on fact, not theory.

REFERENCE

[1]Foster, Kenneth E., and Sheryll Gimplin-Poris, "Job Evaluation: It's Time to Face the Facts." From the October 1984 issue of *Personnel Administrator,* copyright 1984, The American Society for Personnel Administration, 606 North Washington Street, Alexandria, VA 22314.

QUESTIONS

1. What appears to be the issue involving sexually biased job-evaluation plans?
2. Which produces a better base from which to fine-tune job evaluations: job rankings using market value or multiple evaluations using subjective plans?
3. How valid are company claims that job worth is substantially different from relative market worth? Explain.

CHAPTER TWELVE

WAGE AND SALARY

INTRODUCTION

Upon completion of the job-evaluation process and the compensation survey, the establishment of a wage structure begins.

The usual procedure is to price the job structure graphically by plotting the job-evaluation points on the horizontal axis and the wage rates on the vertical axis. Jobs are indicated on the graph at the current wage rates. A curve is then drawn through the dots, either freehand or using the least-squares method. The result is a wage curve that at any point represents the relation between the value of a job and its wage rate. The jobs that fail to cluster about the wage curve, being either too high or too low, are red-circled to represent jobs that are overpaid or underpaid. Another procedure would be to place the compensation-survey data on the vertical axis and the job evaluation points on the horizontal axis, with the wage curve then demonstrating the relationship between the job-evaluation points and the compensation-survey rates. In both procedures, job classes or job groups can be used in place of individual jobs. Besides finding the red-circled jobs, pricing the job structure also indicates pay discrepancies between jobs of equal or unequal point evaluations.

Since most jobs start at an entry-level wage and later peak at a maximum wage, this range of rates needs to be plotted to determine any relationships in a progression of jobs. The usual procedure is similar to that used in pricing the job structure, in that evaluation points are plotted on the horizontal axis and hourly rates on the vertical axis. Then the midpoint or median of the pay grades or wage classes are indicated on the graph and connected by a straight line. Since rate ranges may vary, a 50 percent overlap can be made with the next job grade or class. This means that a highly experienced person at the top of the wage range in step 5 will make more money than an inexperienced one starting at the beginning rate for step 6. This allows for recognition of skill and experience within a job classification while maintaining the distinctions between the classifications. The purpose of such distinctions is so that employees will prepare for and advance into more demanding jobs.

However, despite the logic and rationale of job ranges, a problem of pay compression may occur as a result of paying higher wages at the entry level because of either inflation or scarce labor. The solution would be more pay or class grades, or wider pay grades, or a larger percentage grade overlap.

In any wage structure, a distinction is made between wages as an hourly rate and as a regular salary. Salary has usually been equated with management and office workers; hourly wages are considered more appropriate to the factory. However, with the emergence of newer styles of management and factory technology, such distinctions have been changing. An hourly wage is generally paid for temporary employment where layoffs are frequent, or when overtime is a common occurrence. Yet in a more stable work environment, salaries for factory workers have met with a positive reaction from the workers and management. Although salary tends to minimize differences between work groups, it does not eliminate the issue of pay equity—that is, what people perceive they should be paid relative to what others are being paid. Dissatisfaction results when people perceive an imbalance between what the level of pay should be and what it actually is.

Such problems are resolved by a wage structure that resembles the pay of similar jobs outside the company, job evaluations that provide equal pay for jobs of comparable worth, a measurement of performance that is accepted as fair and equitable, a wage structure that is continuously updated, and a belief by employees that the company is looking out for their interests as well as its own.

A question of pay secrecy accompanies any wage structure. Some companies provide open salary administration, but most do not. Research into this area has provided no clear answers, but it appears that more open communication on wage-structure policies may provide a partial solution to this continuing problem.

Wage structure has always been part of the productivity issue. The question of attaching pay to performance has been around for a long time, but with only partial answers. And this question creates more questions: Is money important? Does money motivate? How does pay affect satisfaction? The position taken depends upon the person involved, the work environment, and the social/political/economic environment.

Yet the interest in and the proliferation of incentives as a means of directly relating earnings to output continues. Generally, in the case of individual or group incentives, a standard of performance is created, along with a formula to determine the earnings allocation.

Although incentive systems can be very complex, studies have shown that they can affect productivity positively if employees understand the plan, see the relation between effort and earnings, and trust management to be fair in executing the plan. General guidelines for implementing an incentive plan include anchoring the plan to performance so that employees understand and appreciate the relationship, recognizing the particular corporate culture, tailoring the rewards for individual preferences, and monitoring the plan for effectiveness.

Incentives are usually classified as individual and group. Individual incentives have been used in various forms over the past 75 years or more. The most frequent early application centered on time and motion studies designed by industrial engineers. Perhaps the oldest individual incentive plan is the piecework plan. Still in general use, it is joined today by the production bonus and commissions.

For the piecework incentive, the employee is usually guaranteed the minimum hourly wage for producing a minimum output. Anything over the minimum output is paid for at a price rate that is the result of time studies and collective bargaining.

Sales commissions are similar to piecework rates. The straight commission pays a certain rate for everything that is sold, corresponding to the straight piecework rate. A variation used in the retailing industry is payment of a small salary plus a commission.

Still another individual incentive is merit pay, a percentage pay increase based on recognition of the employee's past contribution. The usual basis for the reward is the assessment received in the performance appraisal, and the amount is a percentage that varies according to the person's current salary-range position.

Another incentive is the use of group plans, which may include production employees or department heads or the professional and staff groups. One example of a group incentive plan is the Scanlon Plan, which offers a bonus calculated from the savings in labor costs. However, the major intent of a Scanlon Plan is to obtain union–management cooperation to increase productivity.

Perhaps the most publicized group incentive plan is at the Lincoln Electric Company. This plan is very effective. It bases compensation on an individual time plan, but its many cooperative aspects make it a group plan.

It also includes a suggestion system that rewards production savings. Such a plan is sometimes referred to as gainsharing.

Another form of incentive system takes in the whole organization, rewarding all employees according to company profits for a given time period. Profit sharing is such an organizational incentive system, one in which the firm usually decides at the end of the year what percentage of the profits are to be paid back to the employees. Another form of profit sharing is the employee stock-ownership plan (ESOP); it establishes a trust in which employees are assigned stock shares based on seniority and pay levels. It can also be used by employees to prevent a firm from closing by buying the stock and becoming the owners. A form of ESOP is PAYSOP, a payroll plan by which the employer can contribute a certain percentage of payroll to purchase stock for employees that becomes available to them upon death, retirement, or separation from the company.

The allocation of executive compensation generally differs from that of lower-level employees. The executive level is the president and vice-president positions, although lower executive levels may be considered. The idea behind executive compensation is to reward executives if the company is profitable and is growing in value. The compensation package consists of salary, benefits, perks, bonuses, and stock options. A compensation committee composed of directors makes recommendations to the board of directors on compensation-package items. As sales volume increases, so does the executives' compensation, with the chief executive's compensation serving to set the upper limit. The second person in office rank usually receives 50 to 60 percent of the chief executive's compensation, and so on. Middle management's compensation is established more by the market and job-evaluation techniques.

A compensation issue that continues to attract active discussion is that of comparable worth. The issue results from equal employment legislation and has yet to be resolved. Basically, comparable worth attempts to reduce the earnings gap that exists mainly between the more traditional male and female jobs. The idea is that pay should be the same for jobs that, although dissimilar, are comparable as to skill, responsibility, and effort. If the concept is applied, the wages of some office jobs would have to be increased to the level of, perhaps, a carpenter's, since the jobs are comparable in these areas. The effect upon a human resource department of implementing this concept would be far-reaching.

Any presentation of wage structure must consider the effect of government regulations. The Fair Labor Standards Act (FLSA) of 1938 covers minimum wage rates, overtime payments, and child labor. There are also state laws covering these issues that may be more stringent than the federal legislation. The Equal Pay Act of 1963 is an amendment to the FLSA. The Walsh-Healy Act of 1936 enforces payment of the local prevailing wage rates for government contract work.

The designing of a wage structure is a complex process subject to many inputs, some controllable and others beyond the control of the human resource department. A vital factor in any compensation system is administration. The administration of a wage and salary program requires attention to costs and communication. Controls and budgets must be established to contain the compensation system within anticipated limits. Communication is necessary to help influence employee attitudes and behaviors to achieve company objectives. Since compensation is a major item of expense, management must manage it efficiently.

RESEARCH INCIDENTS

Research Incident 12-1:
Rodney Masters Brings Home the Bacon

- How does receiving an undeserved reward affect one's reciprocation with others?
- When is a strong demand for equity more effective than a nondemand request?
- What is the effect of a pay schedule that does not depend upon performance, work orientation, or work satisfaction?

Even the teller at the bank told Rodney that his company paid low wages. She should know; the bank branch was in the industrial district of town and processed a lot of workers' checks. That really wasn't the crux of Rodney's concern at the company—one bank teller at a branch office—but it was one of many pieces of information that indicated a problem.

Several weeks before, Rodney had stayed at the plant until 8:00 one night, plotting wage trend lines, first for the company and then for some key departments. The results were rather startling. For a two-year period, the overall company wage line showed an increase of about 2 percent, with some departments 3 percent, others 1 percent. No wonder those three workers from the forming department he had overheard in the washroom were so bitter. Wages at the company had become a negative factor.

So several days later, Rodney had met with the human resource manager, a company veteran of 18 years who had been promoted from quality control two years before. The result was rather unexpected; the "old fossil" agreed with Rodney, stating that he had a gut feeling worker dissatisfaction was running sky-high. The meeting had ended with Rodney scheduled to attend a two-day seminar on "The Equality Factor of Money as a Motivator," sponsored by a local private university.

Since Rodney had recognized some of the presenters' names from his college research studies, he was optimistic that this wouldn't be just another

juniors with the working managers might create a problem even though there appeared to be no differences on the major variables in the study.

Research Study 12-1-B

How rational are superiors' pay-raise recommendations? What effect do off-the-job considerations have? Does the employee response make a difference?

Freedman[2] investigated the criteria used by managers in allocating pay increases. The sample was 257 undergraduate business students at a southwestern university. The students were given a packet explaining that they were participating in a management exercise concerning subordinate pay and were to assume a manager role. The company was described as decentralized, with annual pay decisions based on performance reviews. The student managers were to assume that they were in charge of six subordinates, of whom only one was being considered for a raise. The decision on the new salary would be based on information contained in the packet. After they completed the task, the students filled out a questionnaire.

There were three independent variables—pay equity, equity off the job, and strength of demand—and two levels of pay-equity variables—pay equity and underpayment inequity. The students graphed the position levels and monthly wages of their six subordinates. The pay-equity condition for the subordinate being considered for a raise was at $1,400, which was in the middle of the pay range for that position. For the underpayment-inequity condition, the monthly wage was $1,225, well below the salary range for the position. The second variable, equity off the job, was manipulated through information in the subordinate's personnel file. For the disadvantageous inequity-off-the-job condition, the file said that the subordinate's house had burned down. The equity-off-the-job condition did not mention this fact. The third variable was the strength of the subordinate's demand for a pay increase. This was manipulated by including in the personnel folder a memo notifying the subordinate of the performance appraisal results and that a salary decision would be made within two weeks, and the subordinate's response, which was either a strong demand for a wage increase or just an acknowledgment that the memo had been received.

The student managers recorded their compensation awards on a salary action form that was provided. The postexperiment questionnaire was analyzed for manipulation checks on the independent variable, in order to determine the student manager's evaluation of the subordinate and perception of the required salary decision. For purposes of this study, the author decided to discuss only the manipulation checks and the raise in the questionnaire.

The study results showed that the student managers did find the subordinates in the inequitable-pay conditions to be underpaid. Interestingly, those subordinates who experienced the disadvantageous inequity off the job (house burned down) were seen as more underpaid than subordinates who had equity off the job. The subordinate who was underpaid and also had experienced inequity off the job was seen as much more underpaid. That is, inequity off the job made the pay inequity appear more important in the student managers' perceptions.

There was no mention of inequitable treatment in the subordinate demand situation, but those subordinates who had made a strong demand were perceived as less equitably paid than those who simply acknowledged receipt of the memo. Also, the students viewed the subordinate as making a significantly stronger demand when he made a demand than when he made no demand. The subordinate who was equitably paid was seen as more demanding than the underpaid subordinate. The student managers rated subordinates experiencing inequity off the job as being more unfortunate than those who maintained equity on the job, and those who made a strong demand were seen as more unfortunate than those making no demand.

The study also found that the student managers gave larger raises to subordinates who were inequitably paid than to those receiving equitable pay. The subordinates experiencing inequity off the job received larger raises than those with equity off the job, regardless of the level of pay equity and the strength of demand. This indicates that there was no triple interaction of the three independent variables (pay equity, equity off the job, and strength of demand). However, pay equity and strength of demand interacted; the students awarded larger raises to subordinates making a strong demand than to those making no demand when both were equitably paid. Yet when the subordinate was underpaid, strength of demand had no significant effect.

There was also interaction between equity off the job and strength of demand. Subordinates demonstrating equity off the job and also exercising a strong demand received a larger raise than the no-demand group. When inequity off the job was present, strength of demand did not affect the raise; similar raises were given in both demand conditions.

Summary Review of Research Study 12-1-B   The student managers gave larger raises to the underpaid than to the equitably paid employees. However, these raises did not restore complete equity, and differences continued to exist. Regardless of the level of pay equity (over- or underpaid), subordinates who experienced inequity off the job received larger raises than those with equity off the job. Under conditions of pay equity, the students gave larger raises to the strong-demand than to the no-demand subordinate. Under conditions of pay inequity, strong- and no-demand subordinates received identical raises. With inequity off the job, the no-demand and strong-demand subordinates also obtained identical raises. With equity off the job, larger raises went to the strong-demand than to the no-demand subordinates.

The study found reward allocation decisions to be influenced by subordinate pay equity, equity off the job, and the strength of the demand made by the subordinate.

Research Study 12-1-C

What is the effect of a reward upon the satisfaction of performing a task? Is motivation highest when there is task satisfaction and reward?

Pinder[3] conducted a study of E.L. Deci's theory of cognitive evaluation. Deci holds that the payment of a money reward (a wage) causes the justification for working to change from the satisfaction of doing the task to that of receiving the money reward. The money reward is an extrinsic reward, since it is external to the task being performed; the motivation that results from just performing the task is an intrinsic reward. Deci hypothesized that the adding of an extrinsic reward to an intrinsic reward might not result in increased motivation; that is, that the two rewards were not additive.

The study was conducted in a laboratory setting and compared four groups of subjects to four dependent variables: intrinsic motivation, extrinsic motivation, productivity, and task orientation. The two experimental variables that were manipulated for the study were task attractiveness (high versus low) and the mode of reward schedule (contingent upon performance versus noncontingent). The subjects were randomly assigned to one of four possible task/compensation conditions: Group 1 worked under both intrinsic and extrinsic incentives, group 2 under a contingent incentive that was also extrinsic, group 3 under an intrinsic incentive only, and group 4 worked under conditions that involved neither intrinsic nor extrinsic incentives.

The 80 subjects were recruited through newspaper ads and were either high school or college males with a mean age of 17.26 and a mean schooling of 11.76 years. They were told that the project was a study of problem solving. Two tasks were involved: The appealing task was constructing a large model car, using several dozen separate joints, and required about an hour's work; the nonappealing task required assemblying similar pairs of parts over and over again, with the fastest completion time being over an hour. The subjects were paid by either a contingent or a noncontingent schedule. With the contingent reward, as soon as a piece was correctly fitted, a five-cent coin audibly fell into a box in front of the subject. This reward schedule was immediate, continuous, expected, and conspicuous. For the noncontingent payment, the subjects were each paid $2.75 per hour, and it was emphasized that they would receive no more.

The experiment had the subject sitting in a work cubicle with a table containing the parts appropriate to the appealing or nonappealing work condition and then hearing a tape-recorded set of instructions explaining the task. After a period of 40 minutes, the procedure was interrupted by a planned phone call from the experimenter, telling the subject that the experiment would be shut down temporarily until the experimenter returned, but that during the interval, the subject could either relax or read a magazine or continue to work at the task; however, any work completed during this interruption would not be paid for. After five minutes had elapsed, the experimenter returned, announced that the experiment was over, and asked the subject to complete a questionnaire.

Intrinsic task satisfaction was measured by a five-point questionnaire item. Work orientation was measured by an item that ranged from the task itself to the money. Performance was measured by the number of pieces or parts put together. The behavioral measure of intrinsic motivation was whether or not the subject had worked at the task during the break. If he had, an item in the questionnaire asked whether this had been for intrinsic reasons (such as that he enjoyed the task) or for extrinsic reasons (such as working ahead to make more money).

The results of the study indicated that the orientation among the noncontingently paid subjects was more intrinsic; however, this difference was not statistically significant. The most intrinsic orientation took place in the task/compensation condition in which the work was performed under intrinsic incentives only. In a comparison of the group that worked under conditions of both intrinsic and extrinsic incentives with the group that worked under conditions of a contingent, extrinsic incentive, there were no reliable differences. A third comparison found no significant difference between a combination of these two groups and the group working under conditions of neither intrinsic nor extrinsic incentives.

The author says that these findings support Deci's concept that intrinsic and extrinsic incentives are not additive. Although satisfaction was higher in the group working under only intrinsic incentives, there were no significant differences in the other three groups—a mixed situation. Finally, as to the group working under intrinsic incentives versus the other groups, there was a significant difference. This suggests that intrinsic motivation to do the task in the absence of extrinsic inducements was strongest for those subjects working at the appealing task for noncontingent pay.

Summary Review of Research Study 12-1-C The study suggests that workers who are paid on a noncontingent schedule (not contingent upon performance) may have a more intrinsic orientation toward work and obtain greater work satisfaction than those paid on a contingent pay schedule. Yet the effects were not that strong, suggesting considerable individual differences. The data on the four dependent variables (performance, intrinsic motivation, task orientation, and intrinsic satisfaction) suggest that intrinsic and extrinsic incentives are not additive. However, the author cautions that this study does not offer unequivocal support for Deci's concept and suggests the need for further research.

REFERENCES

[1]Goodman, P.S., "Effect of Perceived Inequity on Salary Allocation Decisions," *Journal of Applied Psychology*, 60 (1975), 372–75.

[2]Freedman, S.M., "Some Determinants of Compensation Decisions," *Academy of Management Journal*, 21 (1978), 397–409.

[3]Pinder, C.C., "Additivity versus Nonadditivity of Intrinsic and Extrinsic Incentives: Implications for Work Motivation, Performance, and Attitudes," *Journal of Applied Psychology*, 61 (1976), 693–700.

QUESTIONS

1. What is the relation between a manager's perception of being fairly or unfairly treated by a compensation system and how that manager tends to reward subordinates? Explain.
2. Are the compensation decisions of managers rational or irrational? Support your position with empirical research data.
3. How important are intrinsic and extrinsic incentives to employees? What combination of them, or lack of them, would you suggest? Explain.

Research Incident 12-2:
Tom Hemphill Has Another Meeting with the New Plant Manager

- How do people perceive incentives—as guilt or reward?
- Will performance vary depending on the schedule on which employees are paid?
- What is the effect upon the recipient of receiving an unearned job title?

Tom Hemphill checked his appointment calendar for the next day and immediately saw that the day would be off to a fast start. The new plant manager had made an appointment to see Tom at 9:00 A.M. There would be no surprises—the agenda would be the same as in the last three meetings: increasing productivity and worker satisfaction through innovative wage and salary plans. If only the new plant manager and the vice-president of human resource and labor relations were not such good friends. Tom was the human resource manager, but the odds were against him.

The present situation was the result of a new manufacturing facility the company was building 25 miles away in a small rural farming community. Apparently, the new plant manager and the vice-president had decided that the new facility presented the opportunity to devise some nontraditional methods of compensation. Tom Hemphill was proud of the present system; it was equitable, labor strife was nil, and worker-attitude surveys indicated a high degree of job satisfaction. If it ain't broke, don't fix it.

At 9:00 the next morning, the plant manager arrived with his two assistants, both M.B.A.s fresh from a top university. One hour and eight minutes later they had left, taking their flip charts and slides with them.

Tom sensed the overkill and suddenly saw the handwriting on the wall. The vice-president of human resource and labor relations had just played his trump card in absentia.

RELEVANT EMPIRICAL RESEARCH STUDIES

Research Study 12-2-A

What happens when the reward is too large? Is there a point at which largess does not motivate?

Korman and others[1] studied the traditional use of incentives as a strategy for increasing motivation. The traditional approach is to direct people's behavior toward certain goals by offering them rewards. This suggests that the greater the reward, the greater the possibility of behavior change.

Specifically, the study investigated the effect on the motivation of civilian youths to enlist in the navy if the number and the amount of incentives to do so were increased. The sample subjects were selected from a national cluster sampling conducted by Gilbert Youth Research. The population was stratified within geographic regions according to age and school states. The result was a group of civilian males, ages 16–22, totaling 860 in the first study and 854 in the second.

A list of incentive statements was designed by the authors and then revised in discussions with navy personnel to ensure that the incentives would be appropriate to a naval environment. During recruitment interviews, prospective recruits responded to these incentive statements on a five-point scale of "less favorable" to "more favorable." For the first study, there were 17 incentives, divided into seven subsamples because of the impracticality of asking a prospective recruit about all 17 incentives. Generally, the incentives concerned vocational and financial satisfaction, integration of military and civilian life, self-determination or fate control in vocational life, reduction of perceived inequities, and self-determination relative to vocational/financial satisfaction.

In the second study, the five highest-rated incentives from the first study and ten new ones were used. The effects of increasing the number of incentives in the first study produced no significant difference between the best single-, double-, and triple-incentive packages. To test the effect of increasing the absolute magnitude of the incentives, two pairs of single incentives were used. The attractiveness of a $1,000 enlistment bonus was compared to that of a $3,000 bonus and, after four years of duty, two years of college was compared to four years of college. The mean attractiveness of the $1,000 bonus just fell short of being statistically significant; however, the count of those choosing the more favorable of the two bonuses was significant. The authors found that in neither case was more assumed to be better with respect to either the number or the magnitude of the incentives.

In the second study, the effect of increasing the number of incentives offered little more than a generalization. Out of 30 significant tests, it was found that the best double-incentive package was significantly more attractive than both the best single-incentive and triple-incentive packages. In the matter of the effects of increasing the absolute magnitude of the incentives, there was no difference between the attractiveness of the $1,000 enlistment bonus and a $1,000 bonus for each of three years. However, a bonus offer of 10 percent of base pay for good performance was seen as significantly more attractive than a 25 percent bonus. The authors note that more did not equate with better; in fact, more could be worse.

Summary Review of Research Study 12-2-A   The study suggests little support for the concept that more incentives are a better attraction. More may be actually regarded as worse, because of a feeling of distrust or of being bought. Increasing incentives may be perceived as a violation of individual equity norms or of guilt. There appears to be a perceived threshold level beyond which increasing the incentive results in no additional meaning or weight.

The authors suggest that attracting good employees or attempting to motivate them may not result from increasing incentives. The result may be only increased costs.

Research Study 12-2-B

How does the method of payment affect employees? Can the method of payment be considered a job-enrichment technique?

A study by Saari and Latham[2] explored employee reactions to continuous and variable schedules of reinforcement and compared employee performance under these schedules. The study subjects were twelve beaver trappers working for a forest-products company. The trappers were male, high school graduates, union members, and aged from 21 to 40. Both the company and the union agreed to the study, with the notation that it would not be a future negotiation issue. The subjects were paid $7 per hour both before and during the study.

A baseline was the number of beavers trapped for a period of four weeks prior to the start of the study. The trappers were randomly placed in two groups, a continuous and a variable-ratio group. These groups alternated weekly for the entire trapping season of twelve weeks. Under the continuous schedule of reinforcement, the trapper received $1 for every beaver caught. On the variable schedule, the trapper would present the beaver to his supervisor, and if the trapper could then successfully predict twice whether the roll of a die would be even or odd, the trapper would receive $4.

The senior author conducted one-on-one interviews with the trappers during the season to determine if the incentive program provided more motivation to trap, if the trapper believed either schedule was effective, and why he thought a schedule was effective or not. The trappers revealed several items that differentiated the two schedules, and these were developed into a 33-item questionnaire. Some of the items were these: takes the dullness out of my work, creates excitement, gets others' attention when I do well, causes friendly bragging, and gives a feeling of accomplishment.

The trappers completed the questionnaire at the end of the season, rating each outcome on the extent to which it was caused by the continuous or variable schedule. They also rated the importance of each outcome. A five-point Likert-type scale was used for both ratings.

The results of the study show that the number of beavers caught increased significantly after the reinforcement program began. The performance for the continuous schedule was 50 percent greater than before the study, and for the variable-ratio schedule the increase was 108 percent, a significant difference.

As for the questionnaire, the total of the 33-item outcome ratings and their importance ratings were significantly higher for the variable-ratio schedule than for the continuous schedule. The questionnaire appeared to describe job-enrichment motivators. To test this position, the authors added 47 random items that were not job motivators (working conditions, pay, company policy, and job security) to the instrument and asked two company personnel representatives to evaluate the 80 items. There was significant agreement between the two personnel representatives that the original 33 items were job-enrichment motivators and the newly added 47 items were not.

Summary Review of Research Study 12-2-B   The study found variables considered by the trappers that differentiated the variable-ratio schedule from the continuous schedule. These distinguishing variables appear to be job-enrichment motivators and may explain why performance was higher on the variable-ratio schedule. The authors suggest that job-enrichment variables may improve behavior as well as money if they are administered on a variable-ratio schedule.

Research Study 12-2-C(A)

What takes place within an employee's value system when the employee receives a more responsible position with a higher-status title? What happens to the employee's performance if the position change and title were not really earned?

Greenberg and Ornstein[3] point out that equity theory interprets changes in behavior as one attempts to adjust inputs (one's level of contributions to the job) to match the ratio of outcomes (the rewards or pay level). However, an ambiguity may exist, in that an outcome may be considered by the employee to be an input. So when an employee receives more responsibility and a status title, these may be regarded not as a reward (outcome) but rather as an input requiring more work on the part of the employee.

The study investigated the effects on work performance of granting an earned high-status job title and an unearned one. Two experiments were made. In the first one, using a laboratory situation, a requirement for increased inputs was accompanied by either an earned or an unearned high-status job title with no added monetary compensation. The subjects were 40 male and 44 female undergraduate volunteers who agreed to work as proofreaders for up to two hours for $3.85 per hour. The experimenter explained and demonstrated the proofreading task. The subjects worked individually, and after twelve minutes, the end of the first session was announced. The subjects then completed a questionnaire booklet indicating via a seven-point scale their liking for the experimenter, liking for the task, perceived performance level, and perceived fairness of payment. Then the experimenter escorted each subject to an office. In the earned-title condition, after carefully examining the corrected proof, the experimenter told the subject it was among the best and then awarded the subject the title of senior proofreader. The subject was also told he or she was needed for the second hour but would not receive the $3.85 for that second hour. In the unearned-title condition, the subject was immediately given the title of senior proofreader (with no careful examination of the work) and also told of working the second hour for no money. For the no-title condition, the experimenter did not make the subjects senior proofreaders but merely told them of working for nothing in the second hour. There was also a control group that received none of these experiences. The work session began again, and when it ended, the questionnaire was administered again. The whole session lasted one hour and was divided into pre-title, posttitle, and final work sessions.

The results showed that performance error was low, with no significant difference among the groups, and that there were no significant sex effects. Those subjects in the earned-title condition demonstrated no significant change in performance across the pretitle, posttitle, and final work sessions. The control group performed as well as the earned-title group; there were no significant differences between them across the three work sessions. The no-title group exhibited significantly lower levels of performance across the posttitle and final work sessions than did the earned-title group—the underpayment inequity. The unearned-title group reacted unexpectedly by achieving the highest level of performance for all groups at the posttitle work session but then decreased to a level significantly below the base rate at the final work session. Subjects in the no-title group lowered their performance when they learned of the additional uncompensated work.

In regard to the questionnaire responses, the no-title group had a significant tendency to feel underpaid in the posttitle and final work sessions. This occurred after the unexpected uncompensated work was announced. The unearned-title group felt overpaid at the posttitle and underpaid at the final work session. All other groups felt equitably paid. During the posttitle and final work sessions, subjects in the earned-title group expressed high liking for the experimenter; the no-title group expressed high dislike; the unearned-title group liked the experimenter at the posttitle but disliked him at the final work session; and the control group demonstrated rather neutral levels of liking.

As for liking the task, the no-title group reported relative dislike for it in the posttitle and final work sessions. The unearned-title group expressed a high liking for the task at posttitle and then changed to disliking at the final work session. Other groups were relatively neutral. In regard to the perceived level of performance, the members of the earned-title group believed their performance was higher relative to the other groups in the posttitle and final work sessions. This suggests that the earned-title subjects believed they received the title because of their superior performance.

Summary Review of Research Study 12-2-C(A)   In the first experiment, an earned high-status job title was apparently a valued job outcome that compensated for an expected workload increase. Those subjects who believed they had earned their titles maintained their performance with the prospect of increased responsibilities. The earned-title subjects felt equitably paid, whereas the no-title subjects felt underpaid. The no-title subjects expressed their feeling of inequity by disliking both the experimenter and the task. However, receiving an unearned title caused the subjects to lower their performance, feel underpaid, and express dislike for both the experimenter and the task in the final work session. This response was the opposite to what the unearned-title group expressed at the pretitle, when their performance increased dramatically, they reported feeling overpaid, and they expressed high liking for both the experimenter and the task.

Research Study 12-2-C(B)

The second experiment investigated the unexpected findings of the unearned-title group described above; it was an attempt to replicate or duplicate those results. In this follow-up study, the questionnaire was expanded to include items to determine the subjects' perceptions of the experimenter's liking for them, a measure of the outcomes received and the necessary inputs needed, and a self-report of their mood state.

The second experiment consisted of a sample of 32 male and 28 female undergraduate volunteers from the same population as the first experiment. The work sessions were increased to four: pretitle, immediately posttitle, later posttitle, and final. The procedure was the same as in experiment 1 except that there were four 12-minute work sessions. Also, a version of the Mood Adjective Check List was used to obtain affective reactions. The checklist contained 30 adjectives describing mood states on a four-point scale (from "not at all" to "very much"), to measure elation, activation, social affection, aggression, anxiety, depression, and an overall comfort/discomfort index.

The results of the second experiment were consistent with those of the first. The error rate was low and not significantly different over the four work sessions. Again, there were no significant sex interactions. The results obtained for the measure of performance in experiment 2 replicated those of experiment 1. The results were also replicated in the fairness of payment, liking for the experimenter, liking for the task, and perceived performance level.

For the added measures in experiment 2, subjects in the unearned-title group expressed a moderate level of liking toward them by the experimenter at the pretitle session, increased experimenter liking at the immediately posttitle session, and then a decrease at the later posttitle and final work sessions. The level of perceived liking by the experimenter remained at a moderate level in all three posttitle work sessions for the other groups.

With respect to the perceived extent of contributions, the control group and those groups not yet given any added responsibilities felt their contributions were significantly lower than those of the groups expecting to perform more work. This suggests that the title manipulation worked, since subjects were aware of the increased demands on them.

As to the perceived extent of outcomes measure, the subjects in the earned-title group recognized increased rewards following receipt of title. However, the unearned-title group recognized the increased rewards on receipt of title but then deemphasized them in the later posttitle and final work sessions. Those subjects in the control and no-title groups did not perceive any increased rewards. The Mood Adjective Check List responses and the composite mood index failed to indicate any significant group differences. An additional analysis of the overall mood state of subjects reporting being overpaid, underpaid, and equitably paid also produced no significant differences.

Summary Review of Research Study 12-2-C(B)   The results of the second experiment replicated the findings of the first. However, the second experiment found that the immediate reaction by the subjects to the receipt of the unearned title was that it represented the experimenter's liking for them. Further, those subjects who felt they had earned the title demonstrated no difference in their perceived liking for the experimenter. Perhaps the unearned aspect of the title caused those subjects to search for a reason and thereby settle upon the experimenter's liking for them. The mood list and overall index failed to measure any significant affective reactions. The authors caution that the results for both experiments were the product of short-term laboratory studies.

REFERENCES

[1]Korman, A.K., A.S. Glickman, and R.L. Frey, Jr., "More Is Not Better: Two Failures of Incentive Theory," *Journal of Applied Psychology*, 66 (1981), 255–59.

[2]Saari, L.M., and G.P. Latham, "Employee Reactions to Continuous and Variable Ratio-Reinforcement Schedules Involving a Monetary Incentive," *Journal of Applied Psychology*, 67 (1982), 506–8.

[3]Greenberg, J., and S. Ornstein, "High Status Job Title as Compensation for Underpayment: A Test of Equity Theory," *Journal of Applied Psychology*, 68 (1983), 285–97.

QUESTIONS

1. What is the significance of the size of a reward to an employee? How would you approach this problem?
2. What effect does the scheduling of wages or salaries—payment by week or by month—have upon employees? Explain.
3. What is the value of a prestige title versus money? Should one or both be earned to be effective? Explain.

Research Incident 12-3:
Tom Crabtree Wants More

- What are the variables that sales representatives base their evaluations on?
- How do pay satisfaction and pay expectation relate to leaving one's job?
- What effect does pay as a motivator have upon the older, tenured employee?

Tom Crabtree had been at it again. The refrain was all too familiar—the company wasn't paying top sales producers what they were worth. However, this time Tom had added a new verse that suggested, none too subtly, that he was considering some better deals from the company's competitors. The bad thing this time around was that Tom's lament was made in earshot of all the sales staff.

Of course, Tom had a point (he usually did) about being underpaid. The company had a reputation of paying well but not high. This was supposed to be offset by the fact that the company had the best in-house sales training program in the industry. That meant a lot to young college graduates long on ambition but short on experience. However, Tom was no youngster, having been with the company for eight years. Yet there were other good sales reps, older than Tom, who had elected to make a long-term commitment to the company. Of course, they were not numero uno like Tom, nor the company's prima donna either.

There was no point in presenting his case to the company president, or to the human resource manager. Her hands were tied. Besides, it was a well-worn path that had never produced any results for other departed sales reps. Another well-known aspect of the company was the president's adamant position that no one need ask for a raise, since those who deserved it would already have it. Tom knew that the president expected superior sales figures; the company assumed the cost of a credit department, advertising department, and freight department, all designed to give the sales staff more time to sell, sell, sell.

So, as everyone knew, the ball was in Tom's court, and the question around the sales office was, "Will he drop the other shoe?"

RELEVANT EMPIRICAL
RESEARCH STUDIES

Research Study 12-3-A

How do high performers view their compensation as contrasted with that of average performers? What is the effect of external variables upon one's self-perceived performance?

Motowidlo[1] studied the relation between what people perceive as their contributions to work and their pay satisfaction. The author cites other studies showing that the amount of pay does not usually explain more than half the variance of pay satisfaction, and suggesting that there are other important factors to consider.

The present study investigated sales turnover through a self-report questionnaire that was mailed to 101 sales representatives of a large industrial cleaning manufacturer. All but one of the representatives were male.

Their compensation was part salary and the remainder based on commissions figured on a sales quota. Also, two sets of performance ratings were obtained from the supervisors of the sales representatives. The first set was obtained in August 1977 and the second in December 1977. The first set represented twelve graphic scales of personal qualities, such as work energy, sales acuity, and planning and organizing. The second set was seven graphic scales measuring parts of the sales job, such as identifying prospects, closing sales, and keeping records. These two sets of performance ratings were significantly correlated with total sales volume. Single items on the self-report questionnaire measured age, tenure, and education. A measure of self-evaluated performance was composed of 47 items. The sales representatives rated their overall effectiveness on a single item, their perceived amount of pay received was measured by one item, and pay satisfaction was measured by a scale of seven items.

The study found that in the relation between pay amount and pay satisfaction, the pay amount alone represented about 28 percent of the variance in pay satisfaction. The correlation between self-rated performance and pay satisfaction was not significant. However, with the amount of pay controlled, self-rated performance was negatively correlated with pay satisfacton. This indicates that when the amount of pay was controlled, those sales representatives who had high evaluations of their own job performance tended to be less satisfied with their pay. Their self-rated performance did not appear strongly related to age, tenure, or education. When age, tenure, education, sales volume, and the first set of supervisory ratings were combined, they explained only 19.5 percent of the variance in self-perceived performance. If the second set of supervisory ratings replaced the first set, the variables still only accounted for 23.3 percent of the total variance. So although sales volume, supervisory ratings, age, tenure, and education may partly determine self-perceived job performance, they do not appear important, since most of the variance remains unexplained.

Summary Review of Research Study 12-3-A   When the amount of pay was held constant, the sales representatives who believed they were high performers were less satisfied with their pay. The study found only a small amount of the total variance to be in common with the evaluations of the sales representatives' performance. This suggests that they based their own evaluations on other measures than sales volume and supervisory evaluations.

Research Study 12-3-B

How does one's confidence in finding a better-paying job affect quitting? Does the expectation of finding more job satisfaction in another job exert more influence on quitting than level of pay does?

A study by Motowidlo[2] looked at the relationships of amount of pay, pay satisfaction, other-job pay expectations, withdrawing, and quitting. The subjects were sales respresentatives of a company manufacturing industrial cleaning products. After a one-year sales training program during which the sales representatives had received a salary, in the second year their compensation was part salary and part sales commission. The sales reps were mailed self-report questionnaires, which were completed in December 1977, and by 19 months later, the sample size had been reduced from 101 people to 68. The measures used in the study included one item to determine the amount of pay received, a seven-item scale measuring satisfaction with pay, general nonpay satisfaction measured by the short form of the Minnesota Satisfaction Questionnaire, a five-item pay expectation scale, two items measuring withdrawal, and single items measuring age and tenure.

The results indicate the complex relationship between pay and turnover. One finding was that the best single predictor of termination was withdrawal cognition. This was measured by the two items on the questionnaire that asked the frequency with which the person thought of quitting and whether the person expected to quit voluntarily during the next two years. The only other variable that was found to correlate significantly with termination was pay satisfaction. Although the withdrawal cognition was strongly correlated with pay satisfaction, it was also significantly correlated with general satisfaction and pay expectation. The correlation between amount of pay and withdrawal cognition did not meet the significance test, although $P = .053$.

The data were analyzed to determine if the main effect of pay satisfaction would explain the variance beyond that explained by other variables that were believed to influence withdrawal cognition and turnover. It was found that after allowing for the effects of age, tenure, general nonpay satisfaction, amount of pay, and pay expectation, pay satisfaction still accounted for a significant 15.9 percent of the variance in the withdrawal cognition. Separating the effects of age and tenure, general satisfaction, amount of pay, and pay expectation, the partial correlation between pay satisfaction and withdrawal cognition was significant.

Yet pay satisfaction alone did not explain a significant amount of variance in actual termination compared to that explained by withdrawal cognition, age and tenure, general satisfaction, amount of pay, and pay expectation. Only the variable of withdrawal cognition explained a significant 9 percent of the terminal variance; none of the other variables explained a significant amount of additional variance. It appears that the withdrawal cognition was the significant event preceding voluntary turnover. The other variables influenced turnover mainly through their effects on withdrawal cognition.

If general satisfaction was added to the regression equation after age and tenure, pay expectation, and pay satisfaction, it explained only an additional insignificant 1.7 percent of the variance in withdrawal cognition. This suggests, at least in this study, that pay satisfaction may be a more important determinant of withdrawal cognition than is general satisfaction.

When pay expectation was added to the equation after age and tenure, general satisfaction, amount of pay, and pay satisfaction, it explained less than an insignificant 1 percent of the variance in withdrawal cognition and termination. Even when the only other variable in the equation was pay satisfaction, pay expectation still did not contribute more than 1 percent of the explained variance. It appears that pay expectation failed to contribute any explanatory variance after the effects of pay satisfaction had been determined.

The interaction effects of pay satisfaction and expectation score were multiplied by the pay-satisfaction score. When this interaction product was added to the regression equation after age and tenure, general satisfaction, amount of pay, pay satisfaction, and pay expectation, it accounted for less than 1 percent of the variance in the withdrawal cognition and termination. It appears that there is no basis for the conclusion that pay expectation moderates the effects of pay satisfaction on turnover decisions.

The effects of pay on turnover appeared to be influenced by pay satisfaction and withdrawal cognition. When the withdrawal cognition was added to the equation after pay amount and satisfaction, it explained an additional 4.8 percent of the variance in terminations. However, pay amount and satisfaction did not explain significantly more variance in termination after withdrawal cognition. When pay satisfaction was added to pay amount, it explained an additional 18.8 percent of the variance in the withdrawal cognition. However, pay amount did not explain any more variance in withdrawal cognition beyond that already explained by pay satisfaction. It appears that amount of pay affects turnover only through its effects on pay satisfaction. Further, pay satisfaction affects turnover only through its effects on turnover intentions.

Summary Review of Research Study 12-3-B Those sales representatives who were dissatisfied with their pay were more likely to have had frequent thoughts about quitting and to intend to quit. This relationship continued even after the effects of general satisfaction and amount of pay were taken into account. Both pay satisfaction and pay expectation were correlated with the withdrawal cognition. However, after pay satisfaction, pay expectation failed to contribute any explanatory variance. Pay satisfaction did explain variance in the withdrawal cognition beyond that explained by age or tenure, general nonpay satisfaction, amount of pay received, and pay expectation. The only significant variables correlated with actual turnover were withdrawal cognition and pay satisfaction. After withdrawal cognition, there were no other variables that could explain additional turnover variance. The study found no evidence of an interaction effect of pay satisfaction and pay expectation on withdrawal cognition or turnover. The effects of pay on turnover were moderated primarily by pay satisfactions and intentions to quit. The amount of pay variable explained about 26 percent of the variance in pay satisfaction, and pay satisfaction explained about 23 percent of the variance in turnover. Thus, although amount of pay has little direct relationship with turnover, it is associated with pay satisfaction, which, in turn, is related to turnover. As the study indicates, the relationship between pay and turnover is complex.

Research Study 12-3-C

How does the desirability of a compensation plan affect an employee's motivation? Does the attainability of the compensation affect motivation?

Oliver[3] studied these questions in a sample of 92 male life insurance agents, using a job-attitudes questionnaire. Thirty-eight of the agents were experienced and received a commission; the rest were new and were on a salary. Their mean age was 39 years, length of service with the company averaged 8.5 years, and the mean level of education was two years of college.

The questionnaire included one item to measure the valence or desirability of pay, one item measured the attainability of a necessary performance required to achieve a certain outcome, one item measured pay satisfaction, and age, tenure, job level, and compensation plan were obtained directly from the questionnaire.

The results of the study were that age, income, and pay satisfaction were correlated with valence, and job level and pay plan were not. Those agents who were on commission did not perceive higher probabilities of the attainability of a necessary performance required to achieve a certain outcome. Pay satisfaction was related to age, tenure, and income, but not to job level and pay plan. Also, the managers and commissioned agents were neither more nor less satisfied with their pay. The data suggested that income affects valence (desirability) through pay satisfaction. The younger agents and those more desirous of increasing their income were more likely to set higher probabilities for attaining the necessary performance for pay. However, the nature of the pay plan was unrelated to attaining the necessary performance required to achieve a certain outcome.

It appears that in this study, compensation plans had little effect on subsequent perceptions of pay. Further, there was a relationship between pay satisfaction and pay plan. The higher-level employees were less satisfied with their pay than were lower-level workers at the same pay level. Age was related to pay satisfaction, but tenure was not. It appears that the older agents were more satisfied with their pay regardless of the other variables.

Summary Review of Research Study 12-3-C   Valence or desirability is a negative function of age and pay satisfaction; that is, age reduces the importance one attaches to pay. Those agents with a higher valence for pay considered that there was a greater likelihood of receiving the pay through performance. The more tenured agents believed that there was a decreased opportunity for receiving more money, perhaps because of some perceived inequity in the compensation plan. The compensation plans generally failed to contribute to the variance in the pay perceptions.

The study suggests that older and more tenured workers have lower perceptions of pay as a motivator. Since pay satisfaction is associated with a decrease in the valence or desirability of pay, this has an unfavorable influence on the attainability of pay. Because age appears to adversely affect desirability and attainability of pay, the motivation of older agents becomes a problem. Tenure may allow the agent to more accurately perceive the unequal distribution of reward versus effort in a commission pay plan. The suggestion is that the higher the income resulting from favorable performance, the lower one's desire becomes for more pay and the resultant decreasing motivational effect of pay.

REFERENCES

[1]Motowidlo, S.J., "Relationship between Self-Rated Performance and Pay Satisfaction among Sales Representatives," *Journal of Applied Psychology*, 67 (1982), 209–13.

[2]Motowidlo, S.J., "Predicting Sales Turnover from Pay Satisfaction and Expectation," *Journal of Applied Psychology*, 68 (1983), 484–89.

[3]Oliver, R.L., "Antecedents of Salesmen's Compensation Perceptions: A Path Analysis Interpretation," *Journal of Applied Psychology*, 62 (1977), 20–28.

QUESTIONS

1. How do sales representatives with high personal evaluations of their performance tend to regard their monetary compensation? Explain.
2. What is the importance of withdrawal cognition to voluntary turnover?
3. What is the relation of a person's valence, or desirability of pay, to performance? Explain.

NON-EMPIRICAL RESEARCH ARTICLE ABSTRACTS

Abstract 12-1

- What is the recent trend in executive compensation plans—single or multiple plans?
- Where does the executive go to learn about prerequisites?

- What are some rules for achieving clear communication about compensation plans?

These questions are answered in a 1983 article by Lawrence Wangler,[1] a consultant.

The author says that executive compensation alternatives have become highly sophisticated and are further complicated by government agencies. An examination of the top 100 industrials indicates that single compensation approaches have given way to multiple plans. These multiple executive compensation plans have become so sophisticated that specialized disciplines have been developed to plan and administer them. Although such plans are often well designed, they may not be well communicated—for example, in making known the criteria for awarding stock options. Further, these plans have become so complex that no one can understand them. Employee benefits are usually explained in a pamphlet, but few such communications are available to executives. This is done to keep the plans totally discretionary, but management should be aware that ERISA requires that employees be told of their benefits in writing and in a language understood by the average participant.

To support the ERISA requirement, the author presents three excerpts from executive compensation plans and then translates the very complex and difficult language that is used into a more comprehensible form. In a fourth example, the author notes that executive prerequisites seldom appear in formal documents and are most often communicated by word of mouth. This procedure permits misconceptions to occur rather easily.

The author suggests several rules for achieving clear communication. First, management should determine the intended audience and decide what information they want and how they will use the information. Then the plan should indicate its significant parts, such as eligibility, award criteria, option price, termination effects, and tax consequences. Also, unnecessary and incomprehensible jargon should be avoided. Use only the necessary words to convey meaning, and use plain words, such as *deny* instead of *repudiate*. Another rule is that management must not evade responsibility but should indicate who announces the rewards and by what date. The final communication rule is to use not passive verbs, such as, "Record profits have been earned," but active verbs, as in, "We earned record profits."

Following these rules, the author believes, will make it easier to communicate the executive compensation plan to the participants.

REFERENCE

[1]Wangler, Lawrence, "Simplicity Improves Understanding of Executive Compensation." From the June 1983 issue of *Personnel Administrator,* copyright 1983, The American Society for Personnel Administration, 606 North Washington Street, Alexandria, VA 22314.

QUESTIONS

1. What appears to be the trend in executive compensation plans among the top 100 industrials?
2. While explanations of executive compensation plans are usually not available in pamphlet form, companies should be aware of ERISA requirements. Why?
3. One of the several rules the author suggests to achieve clear communication involves using active verbs, not passive verbs. Give an example.

Abstract 12-2

- What is happening to the cost of compensation benefits as a percentage of the total compensation cost?
- When would conjoint analysis be useful in a compensation benefit review?
- Why were the personnel executives in this study satisfied with conjoint analysis?

A 1983 article by Professors Kienast, MacLachlan, and McAlister and bank vice-president Sampson[1] deals with these questions.

The authors point out modern management's concern with cost effectiveness and the effect of compensation decisions upon bottom-line considerations. Fortunately, there are state-of-the-art analytical methods to redesign compensation packages to become more cost-effective.

Compensation benefits alone as a percentage of the total compensation-package cost have increased over the years from 24.4 to 41.2 percent. This is largely the result of a growing variety of benefits, such as prepaid legal services, college loans, and employee transportation. The authors present a method for the optimal design of compensation benefits that they say represents a quantum jump in technology analysis.

The method represents more than determining the importance employees place upon different benefit options. This is usually found through surveys that do not measure the utility that is gained or lost through adding or deleting certain benefits from a compensation package. The selection of one benefit over another requires comparing the degree of satisfaction that would result from the change with the cost. The optimal change would result in the highest employee benefit compared to the unit cost. In the opposite case, when the company is considering a benefit reduction, the consideration should be the lowest reduction in employee satisfaction per unit cost.

Recent developments in consumer research have achieved a large measure of success in measuring consumer reactions to different products. This is accomplished by measuring consumers' reactions to product choices, thereby obtaining a measure of consumer utility. If a number of people make an adequate number of rank-order judgments of products, methods are available to infer interval-scale numbers representing changes in customer satisfaction. This method has been used for automobiles, to determine customer utility of such factors as gas mileage, warranty, price, manufacturing country, car roominess, length of car, and maximum car speed. Customers indicated their preference for combinations of these factors, and then, using a process called *conjoint analysis,* levels of utility were obtained.

These authors believe that conjoint analysis can also be used for compensation benefits, as demonstrated by a study of employees of the Seattle First National Bank.

The first step required identifying every benefit by a single variable. For instance, the more central aspects for medical insurance were listed— the premium paid, the amount of the deductible, and the percentage paid by the insurance once the deductible was met. The next step was to take the variables for the whole compensation benefit package, 15 in all, and to specify the level of each. For instance, the medical-dental-vision insurance paid 80 percent after a $100 deductible was met.

The third step proposed realistic near-term options that would improve the 15 benefit variables, such as increasing coverage from 80 to 100 percent for medical-dental-vision. The fourth step indicated the costs resulting from these proposed benefits. For instance, the cost for the increased coverage of the medical-dental-vision was estimated at $800,000.

The fifth step measured employee utility for the various proposals. To obtain these measurements, a random sample of employees rank-ordered their preferences using 105 benefit cards representing benefit-level pairs. For instance, one card paired sick-leave improvement with medical-dental-vision insurance. The employee then compared that card with another card of paired benefits. The result was ranking data on 1,183 comparisons. Net satisfaction was the proportion of employees preferring benefit A to benefit B minus the proportion preferring B to A. A multiple regression analysis then provided a single utility measure for each benefit improvement.

In the final step, the utility measure was divided by the projected increment costs of providing that benefit. The result was a benefit/cost index that allowed the bank to compare the effectiveness of any particular benefit package. For example, the utility for improving medical from 80 percent to 100 percent was .35, and that for adding another half-day of paid sick leave per month was .60. These figures were divided by their cost, $1 million for the medical and $800,000 for the sick leave, resulting in utility costs for sick leave at .35 and for medical at .75. This indicated that the bank could double the employee satisfaction per amount spent by increasing the medical-dental-vision from 80 to 100 percent covered.

The authors believe this method is very useful in guiding management by distinguishing between benefit features. In budget-cutting situations, the least benefit/cost features can be cut or eliminated first. Also, as new compensation features are developed, they can be analyzed for preference.

Interviews with Seattle First National's top personnel executives indicated that this approach was useful in developing a long-range strategy for benefit changes. Further, personnel executives felt that their image was enhanced with top management, which was impressed with this sophisticated decision-analysis approach.

REFERENCE

[1]Kienast, Philip, Douglas MacLachlan, Leigh McAlister, and David Sampson, "The Modern Way to Redesign Compensation Packages." From the June 1983 issue of *Personnel Administrator,* copyright 1983. The American Society for Personnel Administration, 606 North Washington Street, Alexandria, VA 22314.

QUESTIONS

1. Compensation benefits alone as a percentage of the total compensation package costs have increased over the years from 24.4 to 41.2 percent. Why?
2. What is the relationship between recent developments in consumer research and compensation benefits?
3. The conjoint analysis suggested by the authors was useful in a study at Seattle First National Bank in developing a long-range strategy for benefit changes. What was another result of this analysis?

GLOSSARY

Additive scale   A scale whose unit measurements can be summated because the units are equal at all the points on the scale.

Affect   Name given to specific emotions or feelings.

Affiliation   A person's need to be near or to cooperate with another, to please important others.

Alternate hypothesis   The hypothesis the experimenter expects to be true.

Analysis of Variance   A statistical technique designed to divide the total variation in a set of data into parts that can then be allocated to particular sources.

Analytical statistics   Statistical techniques that permit rational decisions to be made under uncertainty.

Androgynous   Describing the presence of both male and female characteristics in one person.

Anova table   A table that sets out a general format for the Analysis of Variance statistical technique. The table includes SSTR, the between-treatment sum of squares; SSE, within-treatment sum of squares; and SSTO, the total sum of squares.

Arbitrator   One who hears both sides of a disagreement and then decides in favor of one of the parties. The decision may or may not be binding.

Assessment center   A simulated work environment in which the subject responds to work situations such as setting action priorities on the contents of an in-basket. Usually used for middle-management promotion decisions.

Association   The connection between variables. A strong association between two variables means that information about one of the variables assists in making predictions about the other. A weak association between two variables indicates that information about one is of little value in making predictions about the other.

Authoritarianism Characteristic of a person who depends upon clear authority hierarchies.

Autonomy The mastery of one's environment by imposing one's wishes and designs on it.

Baseline Usually, data collected at the start of a study that are used to measure any change in new data collected at a later date.

Behaviorially anchored scale (BARS) An evaluation tool that identifies job behaviors that are related to a certain characteristic. These behaviors are ranked and assigned values.

Benchmark A standard or measurement against which other standards or measurements are compared.

Biographical data Background information on a person, such as age, sex, education, etc.

Bona fide occupational qualification (BFOQ) A characteristic that allows discrimination on the basis of sex, religion, or national origin (but not race or color) if the characteristic is a genuine occupational qualification essential to a company's operations.

Causality The relation between a cause and an effect. In the matter of whether the variable causes the effect, there is a difference between the variable's being associated with the effect and being the cause of it.

Cause-and-effect phenomenon A difference among population means of which an effect is the indication. The problem is to determine what caused the effect.

Chi-Square statistic A statistic based on the Chi-Square distribution of data. It is widely used in goodness-of-fit tests to determine the relation of observed frequencies to expected frequencies.

Cognitive Of or related to ideas and thoughts. Cognition is the process by which one knows and is aware.

Compensation survey A survey that provides data identifying the competitive pay rates set by those organizations included in the survey.

Confidence coefficient The probability that the confidence intervals constructed for all differences among the population means will include the differences among the population means.

Confidence interval An interval or range arrived at as follows: Under the normal distribution, we know that, for example, 95% of the random sample means will fall within ± 1.96 standard deviations of the population mean at a 95% confidence level. So we multiply the standard error of the mean by (in this case) the 1.96 standard deviations. The answer is added to and subtracted from the sample mean, providing the confidence interval.

Confounded Characteristic of the entanglement of the effect of one variable with the effect of some other variable. More than one variable may be responsible for a particular experimental result.

Construct validity The clear definition of a concept or idea. The procedure used to select data must actually measure the concept or idea.

Contamination An outwardly similar but actually dissimilar relationship between variables caused by the influence on each other of independent and dependent variables.

Contrast effect The effect of one variable upon another when one is perceived either simultaneously or immediately with the other.

Control group A group similar in every respect to the experimental group receiving the training or stimulus, with the exception that the control group does not receive the training or stimulus.

Correlation analysis A description of the strength of the relationship between two variables, such as output and cost. In *positive correlation*, as one variable increases, the other increases. In *negative correlation*, as one variable increases, the other decreases. In *zero correlation*, the action of one variable has no relation to that of the other.

Correlation coefficient A measure that looks at the relationship of variables as they cluster around a line and measures the association. A *perfect correlation* is one in which all the points lie exactly on the line.

Criterion A standard by which to compare the results of other items.

Cross-validation The determination of validity by administering a test to a second group and seeing if the results coincide with the original results.

Decision rule A statistical rule that specifies for each sample outcome the alternative that should be selected, as an attempt to control the risks of incorrect decisions.

Descriptive statistics Statistics that summarize and describe a particular group of data items.

Directive leadership style The style of the leader who directs without counsel toward a specific goal.

Empirical research journals Journals publishing research articles that are the result of an experimental scientific method based on exposing samples to "treatments" and then analyzing the results. Such articles are the opposite of theoretical and observation articles.

Error sum of squares A part of the Analysis-of-Variance statistical test representing the within-group variation that is generally the result of an error in the experiment or in the experimental design. See **Within-group sum of squares.**

Exempt personnel Management personnel and others who are exempt from provisions of the union contract.

Experimental design (research design) A blueprint established to determine what is to be studied, the techniques to be used, and the anticipated results. In an experimental design, randomized units are treated differently from other units, and any difference that is obtained is then compared to measurable characteristics of the units.

Experimentation method A method in which subjects are treated differently, and any differences are measured and then analyzed. This method contrasts with merely observing data and writing one's impressions and/or theorizing about possible implications.

Extraneous variables Variables that do not belong or are not relevant to the particular circumstance or phenomenon being studied.

Extrinsic motivation Motivation that results from either positive or negative reinforcement. Such motivations are themselves external to the behavior itself rather than part of the behavior.

F distribution A statistical test based on the assumptions that the populations being compared are normally distributed, the variances of the populations are equal, and the observations are statistically independent. With these assumptions, the F distribution can be used to test the variance of one normal population with the variance of another. This test determines whether one variable is more variable than another.

Field experiment An experiment in which the data are collected from the same environment in which they originate, such as an office or a factory.

Forced choice A format to evaluate personnel by indicating certain percentage quotas ranging from high to low. Also, a method to determine individual attitudes by requiring a choice between two undesirable or two desirable alternatives.

Generalization   A statement or position having common qualities of a class that also applies to members of that class.

Global   Distinguished as a whole and not recognized by its parts.

Goodness-of-fit tests   Tests that determine whether or not a particular probability distribution is a suitable model for the population sampled, and whether or not the probability distribution suggested by the null hypothesis will be a good fit for the sample data.

Hawthorne effect   The fact that productivity is affected by emotional factors, not just by effective work-station design and other rational methods. From a series of experiments at the Hawthorne plant of Western Electric Company in the late 1920s.

Homogeneous   Similar or identical, having the same kind and terms of similar dimensions.

Hypotheses   Theories, assumptions. The *null hypothesis* is the hypothesis that is tested for possible rejection. It usually represents the absence of the effect being investigated. If the test statistic falls in the acceptance region, the null hypothesis is accepted; if the value falls in the rejection region, the null hypothesis is rejected. The *alternate hypothesis* is accepted when the null hypothesis is rejected. The alternate hypothesis is what the researcher expects to discover. In *hypothesis testing,* we test the hypothesis that the mean of a particular sample equals the population mean if the null hypothesis is true.

In-basket test   A test used in the selection process that requires placing in priority the contents of an in-basket.

Inferential statistics   A method to reach conclusions that extend beyond the range of the immediate data.

Interaction   The unique differences in or effects of combinations of treatments; used in comparing experimental groups of data.

Internal validity   The quality that exists when a change in the experimental group is due to the treatment itself and is not the result of any other factors.

Intervention phase   Techniques designed to alter the environment in which a person functions.

Intrinsic motivation   The incentive that exists within the behavior itself, rather than external to the behavior.

Invalid test   A test that does not measure what it was designed to measure.

Inverse relationship   A relation between two variables in which one increases as the other decreases. An example is the minus coefficient between two variables.

Job analysis   A study of the tasks performed by a person on a particular job that results in both a job description and a job evaluation.

Job description   A written description of the tasks, duties, and behaviors required of all applicants for a particular job.

Job evaluation   A rating of jobs for payment purposes, using the information obtained from the job analysis.

Job specification   A written description of the personal qualifications required of all applicants for a particular job.

Laboratory experiment   A research study conducted in an artificial setting, such as simulating a business environment in a classroom or in a business game.

Leadership Opinion Questionnaire   An instrument used in testing for structure in the workplace and consideration for subordinates. Structure is maintaining quality control over the process and over group behavior at every step. Consideration is having good interpersonal relations, resulting in self-confidence and self-respect.

Least-preferred co-worker (Fleishman's Leadership Opinion Questionnaire) A questionnaire item asking the respondent's attitudes toward the person with whom the respondent can work least well; these attitudes result in the person's management style.

Least-squares regression line A regression line used to show the relationship between two values, such as job satisfaction and output. The question to be answered is what is the best combination of these values. The answer is obtained by taking the deviation of each value in the sample from the regression line and summing the squared deviations. The minimum sum represents the best relationship.

Level of confidence The degree of probability of acceptance of the hypothesis. For example, if the level of confidence is .05 or .01, all hypothetical means within the appropriate confidence interval of the sample mean are accepted with only 5 chances in 100 of being wrong in accepting, or 1 chance in 100 of being wrong in accepting, respectively.

Level of significance The probability of rejecting the null hypothesis when it is true. It is usually set at .05 or .01 and represents the probability of a Type I error. If a Type I error would be costly, then a very low level of significance would be set. In a fixed sample size, a Type 1 error cannot be reduced without increasing the probability of a Type II error.

Likert Scale An attitude scale containing a number of steps, on which the subject indicates a degree of agreement or disagreement.

Linear regression An equation developing a line that is approximately straight to best fit the mean of the rows or columns in a correlation table.

Locus of control The location of the control over the events in a person's life—internal to the person or external.

Mean or **average** The sum of numbers representing a particular set of data, divided by the number of such numbers.

Median The middle value of a data set that divides the data in half, with 50% of the data above or equal to it and 50% below or equal to it.

Mode The most frequently observed value of measurements in a particular set of data. In a frequency distribution, it would be the interval containing the largest number of measurements. *Bimodal* means having two modes.

Non-empirical journal articles Journal articles based on observation, opinions, and theorizing. Sometimes statistical techniques are used, but not the experimental method of research design and treatment.

Normal curve (normal distribution) A normal probability density distribution. As more and more data are collected concerning a continuous random variable, the "density" of the data forms this smooth curve. The most important continuous normal probability density distribution is the normal distribution.

Normal distribution (normal curve) A continuous probability distribution that is symmetrical and bell-shaped. That is, the height of the normal curve at a certain value below the mean is equal to the height of the normal curve at the same certain value above the mean. Owing to this symmetry, the mean of a normal random variable equals both its median and mode. We also know, regardless of its mean or standard deviation, that the probability that the value of a normal random variable will be within one standard deviation of its mean is 68.3%, the probability that it will lie within two standard deviations of its mean is 95.4%, and the probability that it will lie within three standard deviations of its mean is 99.7%.

One-tail test A test used when the decision maker is concerned about detecting differences from the null hypothesis in one direction. For example, one would not reject a null hypothesis that the mean light life of a light bulb is 2,000 hours if the population mean is greater than 2,000 hours.

Parameters   Summary measures that can be calculated for a population if we have all the measurements in that population; for example, the average stock price calculated from all the stock prices in a relevant population.

Partial correlation   The net correlation between two variables when the influence of other variables has been removed.

Peer pressure   The pressure to conform to the behavior of one's equals, such as fellow students.

Pilot interview   Preliminary interview carried out as preparation for a more involved interview; used to test the appropriateness of the techniques and questions used.

Population   The total and complete collection of observations or measurements of a particular situation that will be of interest to the statistician or decision maker.

Posttest   A measurement used in the experimental method that is closely related to what the treatment is expected to accomplish. It is given after the treatment, and the score is compared to the score of the pretest to determine any change that may have resulted from the treatment.

Pretest   A measurement used in the experimental method that is closely related to what the treatment is expected to accomplish. It is given before the treatment so as to have a baseline from which to measure any change.

Primary   Occurring first in a sequence of events. The primary event will be remembered first compared to an event that occurred later.

Probability distribution   The assignment of probabilities to each basic outcome in a sample of data.

Questionnaire or survey method   A method of gathering data through questions directed to the sample subject. Such questions may be asked by the person doing the survey directly or mailed to the subject for completion.

Randomization   The selection of sample data purely by the result of chance and not by design. A *discrete random variable* can have only a definite number of values, such as the numbers on dice. A *continuous random variable* can have any value on a continuous scale.

Rating errors   Types of miscalculations in making evaluations. *Halo error* is generalizing one's overall opinion of a person to reflect the scoring of all factors in the evaluation. In *central-tendency error,* the ratings tend to cluster around one area of the rating scale. In *leniency error,* ratings tend to be higher than they should be.

Reactance   Freedom to make selection decisions felt to be unreasonably restricted.

Recency   Closeness to the present time. The occurrence of a recent event will be remembered before that of an event that occurred later.

Referent power   Charismatic power that is based on the interpersonal attraction of one person to another.

Referred journals   Journals containing articles that are reviewed prior to publication, usually by three scholars in the subject area, for accuracy and thoroughness. Some referred journals reject up to 90% of the articles submitted for review.

Regression analysis   A statistical technique that describes the way one variable is related to another variable. Regression analysis can accept more than two variables. This technique can be used to estimate the unknown value of one variable based on the known value of another. For example, it can be used to estimate the value of unknown costs on the basis of the known value of output.

Reliability The degree to which results are consistent with a repetition (replication) of the original study.

Replication Duplication of the original study or experiment to determine whether similar or dissimilar results are obtained.

Reversal phase A return to the original condition to determine how well the change condition that was learned continues to affect behavior.

Role conflict The struggle that occurs when a person attempts to fulfill the behavior expected of two differing roles.

Role playing A technique in which a person assumes the behavior pattern that is characteristic of a person occupying a particular role, such as the company president.

Sample A part of the population representing a subset of measurements or observations.

Sampling error A variation of samples from the population. Two random samples will not provide identical averages; some difference between samples is expected, since samples do not exactly match populations.

Self-actualization The striving towards one's completeness, the fulfillment of one's potential.

Semantics The study of the meanings of symbols, such as words.

Sensitivity training, or T-groups A method of developing self-awareness, in which the focus is on personal and interpersonal interactions. Group members are taught to observe their interaction with others and the nature of group interaction.

Significant others People who are important or who hold particular significance to an individual.

Sociability The desire to be with other people and to enjoy their company.

Social distance The degree of intimacy one is willing to extend to a member of a particular social group.

Standard deviation A figure that estimates the variability of the population from which the sample came. It indicates the degree of dispersion, so that the larger the dispersion, the bigger the standard deviation.

Standard error of a mean In random sampling, the variation of the sample mean from the population mean.

Standard error of estimate A figure that summarizes the squared discrepancies of actual measurements from the predicted measurements.

Statistical independence The situation when events have nothing to do with each other, when the occurrence of one does not affect the probability of the other.

Statistically significant Probably caused by something other than mere chance. Because of sampling variation, we do not expect the sample mean to equal the population mean. So if the sample mean is different from a specific value (one that equals the population mean if the null hypothesis is true), we cannot conclude that the population mean does not equal the specific value. The importance is the probability that the size of the difference between the sample mean and the specific value could have occurred by chance. If the probability is low enough, the null hypothesis is rejected, and this difference between the sample mean and the specific value is determined to be statistically significant.

Stereotype A biased perception of certain group members because of their racial, national, or social status.

Stimulus items Objects or items that cause action, either internal or external.

Structured Consisting of distinct, interrelated parts.

Student t distribution A randomly selected sample of at least 30 cases from a sampling distribution of means that, when plotted, produce a normal distribution. However, when the number of randomly selected sample cases is less, perhaps 20, the curve of the normal distribution changes. The area in the tails becomes larger as the area in the bell-shaped portion of the curve becomes smaller and more pointed. This is the student t distribution, and with knowledge of its characteristics, problems can be solved similar to those applied to normal distributions.

Subjective   Depending upon the person's own prejudices and experiences.

T statistic   A figure that changes the raw-measurement data to a type of a standard score that permits comparisons.

Thematic Apperception Technique   A test based on describing pictures that can be used to determine a person's achievement motive or other motives.

Treatments sum of squares (between-group sum of squares)   Part of the Analysis of Variance technique that reflects differences between the populations in the sample means resulting from the net effects of different treatments.

True experimental design   A design that allows the researcher much greater control over the exposure to the experimental treatment or independent variable than quasi-experimental research does.

Two-tail test   A test to detect changes in either direction in an investigation to determine whether a particular population parameter has changed or differs from a particular value. The two-tail test would determine whether the mean is too large or too small, too high or too short.

Type A   Designation of a person characterized by impatience, restlessness, aggressiveness, competitiveness, and time pressure.

Type B   Designation of a person characterized as having no pressing deadlines or conflicts and relatively free of hostility or time urgency.

Type I error   The error that occurs if the null hypothesis is rejected when it is true.

Type II erorr   The error that occurs if the null hypothesis is accepted when it is not true.

Valence   Value. Objects that attract a person have a positive valence or value, and objects that repel a person have negative valence or value.

Validity   The quality of a conclusion correctly derived. *Content validity* requires a study of the subject to establish the knowledge, skills, and behaviors that are appropriate. *Differential validity* occurs where different groups, such as by race or sex, score differently from each other on the same measuring instruments. *External validity* relates the findings of experimental research to what exists in the real world. *Face validity* requires that the task being completed appear to be appropriate to the subject being studied. *Synthetic validity* involves including a number of related elements that have something in common so as to obtain a large enough sample size to study.

Variable   Describing a characteristic that can take on possible outcomes, such as an age characteristic that changes from person to person. *Qualitative variables* are characteristics that are nonnumerical. *Quantitative variables* are characteristics that can be expressed numerically. A *discrete variable* differs in values only in fixed amounts. A *continuous variable* differs in varying amounts that may be arbitrarily large or small. The *independent variable* is thought to influence or have an effect upon the dependent variable rather than vice versa. The *dependent variable* is the outcome condition being investigated. A *dummy variable* is a qualitative variable that is assigned a value of zero or 1 so that it can be included in a formula.

Variance   A measure that considers all the values contained in a group of items. It is the square of the individual item differences from the mean of the group of items.

Within-group sum of squares (error sum of squares)   A part of the Analysis of Variance statistical technique measuring the variation within the populations.

It is sometimes called the *error sum of squares*, since the within-group variation is often interpreted as being due to experimental error.

Weighted application blank   A series of correlated and weighted questions concerning the job applicant's background to determine future success in a new job.

Z value   A statistic used for comparison. In correlation, we use a statistic (rxy) to represent the portion of variance in X that is associated with Y. However, as this statistic gets larger, the variance in X associated with Y gets disproportionately greater. This requires transforming the statistic into a Z value for comparison purposes.